T0261039

Web-Based Management of IP Networks and Systems

WILEY SERIES IN COMMUNICATIONS NETWORKING & DISTRIBUTED SYSTEMS

Series Editor: David Hutchison, *Lancaster University, UK*

Series Advisers: Harmen van As, *TU Vienna*
                  Serge Fdida, *University of Paris*
                  Joe Sventek, *Agilent Laboratories, Edinburgh*

The 'Wiley Series in Communications Networking & Distributed Systems' is a series
of expert-level, technically detailed books covering cutting-edge research and brand new
developments in networking, middleware and software technologies for communications
and distributed systems.
The books will provide timely, accurate and reliable information about the state-of-the-art
to researchers and development engineers in the Telecommunications and Computing sectors.

Other titles in the series:

Wright: *Voice over Packet Networks* 0-471-49516-6 (February 2001)

Jepsen: *Java in Telecommunications* 0-471-49826-2 (July 2001)

Sutton: *Secure Communications* 0-471-49904-8 (December 2001)

Stajano: *Security for Ubiquitous Computing* 0-470-84493-0 (January 2002)

Web-Based Management of IP Networks and Systems

Jean-Philippe Martin-Flatin

JOHN WILEY & SONS, LTD

Other Wiley Editorial Offices

John Wiley & Sons, Inc., 111 River Street, Hoboken, NJ 07030, USA

Jossey-Bass, 989 Market Street, San Francisco, CA 94103-1741, USA

Wiley-VCH Verlag GmbH, Boschstr. 12, D-69469 Weinheim, Germany

John Wiley & Sons Australia Ltd, 33 Park Road, Milton, Queensland 4064, Australia

John Wiley & Sons (Asia) Pte Ltd, 2 Clementi Loop #02-01, Jin Xing Distripark, Singapore 129809

John Wiley & Sons (Canada) Ltd, 22 Worcester Road, Etobicoke, Ontario, Canada M9W 1L1

British Library Cataloguing in Publication Data

A catalogue record for this book is available from the British Library

ISBN 0-471-48702-3

Produced from LaTeX files supplied by the author.
Printed and bound in Great Britain by T. J. International Ltd, Padstow, Cornwall.
This book is printed on acid-free paper responsibly manufactured from sustainable forestry
in which at least two trees are planted for each one used for paper production.

To Béatrice

To the memory of Louise and Henri

Γηράσκω δ'ἀιεὶ διδασκόμενος

The older I get, the more I learn

Solon

CONTENTS

LIST OF FIGURES

LIST OF TABLES

FOREWORD

Management is about monitoring the current state of network and system components, receiving event reports and controlling the components in order to provide the required service expected by users. Network management has concentrated on management of comparatively simple hardware devices such as routers and hubs. Telecommunications management has been concerned with managing more complex switches and intelligent network services. Systems management is concerned with managing resources such a disk store or memory and setting scheduling or security policies. However there is now a trend towards management of end-to-end services and applications rather than individual network and system components. These services may make use of many different network and system components, so a common standards based approach to management is essential.

Standards for management of networks and systems have been an elusive goal pursued by many in the Management Community over the past 10 years. In the early '90s we saw the war of words between protagonists for the Simple Network Management Protocol (SNMP), being developed for the Internet, and the various International Organization for Standardization (ISO) management standards being pushed by Telecommunications organisations. In spite of the so-called convergence between networking and telecommunications, SNMP was not widely used in telecommunications and the ISO standards were not used by the Internet community. Systems management was all vendor specific. The Distributed Management Environment (DME) from the Open Software Foundation was going to the be the saviour of all the world's management problems in the mid '90s but it quickly disappeared without trace. SNMP-based management is currently the dominant approach for network management and is being proposed as being suitable for systems and service management as well.

In this book, Jean-Philippe Martin-Flatin gives some interesting insights into the problems of SNMP-based management and evaluates many of the alternatives such as Java, mobile code and Web-based approaches. He proposes a Web-based Integrated Management Architecture (WIMA) which has the advantage that it makes use of widely used web standards such as the HTTP protocol and XML for data representation, rather than inventing something specific for management. The prototype implementations described in the book indicate the practicality of the work and that it can make use of distributed processing concepts which will be essential for management of large-scale systems. Although it is very difficult for an individual to influence the many large organisations developing management solutions, I hope that the simplicity of the approach described in this book does make some impact.

Professor Morris Sloman

Imperial College, London, UK

PREFACE

The management of most IP networks is currently based on an open management architecture named after its communication protocol: the Simple Network Management Protocol (SNMP). We analyze a number of problems with this approach. Some are related to the efficiency, scalability, latency, and expressiveness of SNMP; others are due to the way the management-platform market evolved in the 1990s.

Although IP systems can also be managed with SNMP, in practice, their management usually relies on proprietary mechanisms. This defeats the purpose of open management and does not facilitate the integration of network management with systems management.

After reviewing the numerous alternatives that are currently investigated by the management community (e.g., mobile code and intelligent agents), we propose to base the next generation of management applications on a new management architecture: WIMA, the Web-based Integrated Management Architecture. WIMA is based on standard Web technologies. It relies on a push-based organizational model for regular management (i.e., data collection for offline processing, and monitoring over a long period of time) and notification/event delivery, and a pull-based organizational model for *ad hoc* management (data retrieval over a very short time period).

Its communication model is characterized by (i) the use of a standard communication protocol (HTTP) instead of a domain-specific protocol (SNMP); (ii) the use of persistent connections between agents and managers (and between mid- and top-level managers in distributed hierarchical management); (iii) the independence of the information model (SNMP MIB, CIM schema, etc.) and the communication model; and (iv) a reversed client-server architecture that facilitates crossing firewalls.

In WIMA, the preferred method for representing management data in transit is XML. It is well suited to distributed hierarchical management, and unifies the communication model across the range of disciplines covered by enterprise management (i.e., network, systems, application, service, and policy-based management). This facilitates the integration of management and offers high-level semantics to management-application designers.

All the major problems that we identified in SNMP are solved in WIMA. Our architecture is validated by a research prototype, JAMAP, which is described in Chapter 10.

Audience of this book

This book presents rather advanced material. It is not a primer. We assume that the reader already knows the basics of network management and object-oriented analysis & design, and introductory textbooks are referenced. Great care was taken to make this material readable to a vast audience, from practitioners in industry to students, from programmers to designers, and from administrators to managers.

The terminology defined in Chapter 2 clarifies frequent misunderstandings and should be valuable to all. Chapters 3, 4, and 6 can be used by academics for teaching B.S. and M.S. courses in distributed network and systems management, or by consultants for training administrators. They can also be instructive to MIS directors who wish to update their knowledge of enterprise management. Chapter 3 should benefit engineers in charge of designing and developing SNMP-based management applications. In Chapter 5, our analysis of the solution space should be interesting to managers and administrators investigating the current market. It explains why Web-based management is not only trendy, but also makes technical sense. Chapters 7, 8, and 10 should be very useful to start-ups and corporate organizations developing management applications, and to M.S. and Ph.D. students embarking on a Web-based management project. They contain a wealth of technical hints and tips that could save software designers and developers months of work. Finally, by explaining the advantages of using XML for representing management data, Chapter 9 should enlighten those professionals and students who still believe that Web-based management is only about adding a Web browser to an existing management application.

Index Keys

IEEE Web Thesaurus
<http://www.ieee.org/web/developers/webthes/>

- Communication System Operations and Management
- Web and Internet Services
- Management Information Systems
- Computer Networks

Computing Research Repository (CoRR)
<http://www.acm.org/pubs/corr/>

Area: Computer Science
Subject Classes: Networking and Internet Architecture; Distributed Computing

Copyright Notices

This book is derived from the author's Ph.D. dissertation, which was published by the Swiss Federal Institute of Technology, Lausanne (EPFL) in October 2000 [163]. Some parts are copied *verbatim*, but many sections have been updated or rewritten.

A fraction of the material presented in Section 3.3.1 was published in March 1999 in *The Simple Times*, the online magazine of the SNMP community [243]. This article was co-authored by Ron Sprenkels, who contributed several ideas explained there. This section also benefited from discussions that took place during the first meeting of the IRTF Network Management Research Group.

Early versions of the material presented in Chapter 4 were presented by the author in two articles: one published by Plenum Press (now part of Kluwer Academic) in the *Journal of Network and Systems Management* [160], and another published jointly by the University of Technology, Sydney, Australia and the University of Western Sydney, Nepean, Australia in the proceedings of the DSOM'97 workshop [158].

In Chapter 4, Fig. 5 is adapted from Weinshall and Raveh [285, pp. 56–57], published by Wiley.

Early versions of the figures in Chapter 7 and Chapter 8 appeared in a paper by the author published by the IEEE in the proceedings of the IM'99 symposium [161].

An early version of the material presented in Chapter 10 appeared in an article by the author published by Springer Verlag in the proceedings of the DSOM'99 workshop [162].

In Appendix A, we give the IETF's definition of the Interfaces Group in RFC 1213 [173, pp. 16–23]. This material is reproduced with the permission of the Internet Society.

In Appendix C, we include an example of CIM-to-XML metamodel-level mapping given by the DMTF [73]. This material is reproduced with the permission of the DMTF.

In Appendix D, we include an example of remote method invocation of a CIM object given by the DMTF [77, Section A.10]. This material is reproduced with the permission of the DMTF.

Finally, JAMAP, the software described in Chapter 10, was released by the author under the GNU General Public License of the Free Software Foundation [97].

Acknowledgments

I would like to thank my editors at Wiley UK, Sally Mortimore and Birgit Gruber, for patiently explaining to me all the steps involved in the publication of this book.

I am grateful to the Swiss Federal Institute of Technology, Lausanne (EPFL) and the Swiss National Science Foundation (FNRS) for funding the research work that led to this book. Thanks also to AT&T Labs Research for funding extra developments on the research prototype described in Chapter 10 and for allowing release 0.4 of this software to be freely available under the GNU General Public License.

I thank my former Ph.D. supervisor, Jean-Pierre Hubaux, for welcoming me on his team at EPFL, for offering me exceptional working conditions, and for giving me a lot of freedom and independence while conducting my research. Thanks also to the members of my Ph.D. committee (Roland Balter, Subrata Mazumdar, André Schiper, and Morris Sloman) for the time they spent reviewing my dissertation and their valuable feedback.

I gratefully acknowledge that most of the implementation of JAMAP, the research prototype described in Chapter 10, was performed by Laurent Bovet [31] and Claire Ledrich [147] in the course of their M.S. theses, under my supervision. Laurent's work was funded by EPFL, Claire's by AT&T Labs Research.

I had the chance to work or discuss with many great people over the years and cannot name them all. I would particularly like to thank Simon Znaty, who taught me how to do research; Andrea Westerinen, who thoroughly reviewed this book and suggested useful changes and corrections; Jürgen Schönwälder, who reviewed several chapters and with whom I love to argue about the future of network management; Werner Almesberger, who helped me quantify the memory footprint of TCP connections in the Linux kernel and reviewed Chapter 8; Luca Deri, George Pavlou, and Gian Pietro Picco, who sent me precious comments on early versions of the material presented herein; Ditlef Martens, Otto Pesonen, and Baudouin Raoult, who taught me so much about the Unix internals; Tony Bakker and Dick Dixon, who taught me the basics of networking; Walter Zwieflhofer and Claus Hilberg, who taught me rigor when "selling" a technical solution to management; Holly Cogliati, who patiently improved my English, taught me the differences between American and British English, and proofread this book; and Patrick Lachaize, who encouraged me to move into IP networking back in 1989.

I express my deepest gratitude to Gilles Maignaud, Alain Martinez, and François Martin for teaching me, when I was 16–18, that mathematics, physics, and science at large can be great fun. Even in difficult times, I have always strived to take some pleasure in doing my job. Their advice has served me throughout my career.

Finally, I am very grateful to my family and friends for their unwavering support and positive feedback over the years. Most of all, I am indebted to my wife, Béatrice, who put up with the long nights and weekends that I spent writing this book. I knew that I had married a rare pearl...

Jean-Philippe Martin-Flatin, Lausanne, Switzerland, July 7, 2002

Chapter 1

INTRODUCTION

A peculiar property of Network and Systems Management (NSM) is that it looks pretty simple at first sight, at least in the IP world (that is, the realm of the Internet Protocol). But as soon as you set about implementing or using a management application, you unveil problem after problem and gradually unfold the *Big Book of Management Hassles*. After spending several years on this topic, most reasonable people decide to turn to other problems, perhaps more technically difficult, but also less multifaceted and, in the end, less complex and less challenging. The author decided to do otherwise and spent several years of his life looking for a better solution to manage IP networks and systems. Whether any conclusions can be drawn about his sanity is left for the reader to decide... Anyhow, what will now unfold before your eyes are the technical details of his proposed solution, a new management architecture for the decade that just began, and an attempt to convince you of its relevance to NSM in the IP world.

1.1 Background

In the past twelve years, the management of IP networks has relied almost exclusively on a single protocol, the Simple Network Management Protocol (SNMP), and a single management architecture, confusingly also called SNMP. The primary achievements of SNMP were its simplicity and interoperability. SNMP-based agents were easy to develop and integrate into network devices. As a result, proprietary network management solutions gradually gave way to open solutions. Whatever the equipment vendor, whatever the type of equipment, we could manage it with a single third-party management platform such as HP OpenView, Cabletron Spectrum, IBM/Tivoli Netview, or Sun Microsystems Solstice.

From 1990 to 1995, the IP-networks management market went through a period of great development, during which SNMP became ubiquitous. In 1990, the Requests For Comments (RFCs) specifying what is now called SNMPv1 were issued by the IETF[1]. In 1993, only three years later, it was commercially mandatory for a vendor to support SNMP on its entire range of network equipment, from the top-of-the-range backbone IP router to the bottom-of-the-range print server: Many customers made the support for SNMP a requirement in their requests for bids for network equipment.

The situation changed in the mid–1990s. SNMPv2 raised high hopes, but later proved to be a technical and marketing failure [168; 201; 249, p. 334]. By the time SNMPv3 was issued, in 1998, the market no longer believed in the capacity of SNMP to evolve and meet its needs. The relevance of traditional SNMP-based management was questioned by new management-platform vendors, who wanted to enter this lucrative market and were looking for ways to undermine the dominance of HP Openview (which reportedly peaked at 70% of market share at some point). They began to offer new platforms based on new technologies that were appealing to the market (e.g., AdventNet with Web technologies).

Customers also had issues with SNMP-based management. First, they were scared by the soaring costs associated with it. Second, they wanted to integrate network management with systems management, that is, manage IP networks and IP systems from the same management platform, and correlate events coming from both worlds. But while most IP networks were managed with open management platforms, the vast majority of IP systems were managed with proprietary, non-SNMP platforms (e.g., Novell NetWare and IBM/ Tivoli TME for Windows-based PCs, or RPC-based management platforms for Unix workstations), which made open integrated management wishful thinking.

The suitability of SNMP-based management was also questioned by equipment vendors, because their device-specific management GUIs (Graphical User Interfaces) had to be ported to an ever-growing number of management platforms and operating systems, which made their development costs sky-rocket.

Most of all, the relevance of SNMP-based management was undermined because the problem at stake was becoming more and more different from the problem solved by the fathers of SNMPv1. In the late 1990s (and still today), virtually all devices were networked; most of them embedded a reasonable amount of processing power; a growing proportion of devices were wireless; data and telephone networks were merging; customers demanded security for both Local-Area Networks (LANs) and Wide-Area Networks (WANs); customers not only wanted to manage networks and systems, but also services, Quality of Service (QoS), policies, etc.; the TCP/IP stack was everywhere, in every system and every network device; and Web technologies were ubiquitous. None of these assertions were true when SNMPv1 was devised! No wonder the solution selected in the late 1980s for slow and small networks, with mostly low-profile agents, no longer appeared adequate to the market a decade later!

---

1. For the sake of readability, many acronyms used in this introductory chapter will be expanded and explained in the next chapters.

In the second half of the 1990s, the main change in NSM was that many newcomers looked at it with software-engineering eyes, with no background (hence no habits) in NSM. Some of them came from the object-oriented world; others had a background in artificial intelligence or databases. And when these people analyzed how IP networks are typically managed with SNMP (that is, how management platforms are designed, how efficient SNMP is as an access protocol, whether the principle of data polling is efficient, etc.), they soon realized that most SNMP-based management applications do not withstand the comparison with modern distributed applications.

Why not use object-oriented analysis, design, and implementation, which are widely adopted by the software industry today? Why be limited to trivial protocol primitives (get and set) when a manager interacts with an agent? Why incur the network overhead of having the manager repeatedly tell every agent what set of Management Information Base (MIB) variables it is interested in, when this selection remains constant over time? Why not compress management data when it is transferred in bulk between agents and managers? Why use an unreliable transport protocol to send critically important notifications from agents to managers (e.g., when an interface goes down on a backbone router)? Why make it so difficult to manage remote offices across firewalls? Why concentrate all the management-application processing at the manager and let the agents do almost nothing?

The software-engineering community had many alternatives to offer: Web technologies, mobile agents, active networks, CORBA, intelligent agents, and so on. This resulted in a plethora of new proposals that often departed completely from the design decisions made in the late 1980s. This also utterly confused the market. Customers like simple messages such as "Buy SNMP because everyone does" or "Choose between CORBA and DCOM": They make their investments strategically safe and easy to justify to top management. But the market was telling them: "You can use mobile agents written in Java, Tcl/Tk, or Telescript; they are not totally secure yet, but they could be soon and they are technically attractive. You can also use CORBA, and DCOM, and Enterprise JavaBeans (EJBs), and intelligent agents speaking KQML or ACL, and cooperative object-oriented distributed platforms, and...". As expected, customers were (and still are) very reluctant to go from a very homogeneous and strategically safe market to such a hectic and hazardous one.

Since then, choosing a management solution in the IP world has become a strategic decision. It involves large investments (much larger than in the early 1990s) and the return on investment is very difficult to assess. Decision makers are thus exposed to hindsight analysis and retrospective criticism. In view of the risks incurred, some customers decided to go for the most powerful vendors; they became Microsoft-only shops for systems, Cisco-only shops for networks, and adopted whatever management solutions these large and resilient vendors had on offer. Others preferred to put their eggs in several baskets; they kept several brands of equipment, they used open management systems wherever possible, and they put up with the inconvenience of supporting multiple management systems: one for network devices, one for Windows PCs, one for Unix systems, one for databases, etc. But many customers decided to postpone heavy investments to better days, when the future of enterprise management is clearer to read and integrated management becomes a reality. Today, the situation has not changed: Investing in an NSM solution is still a risky business.

In the author's opinion, NSM goes through cycles like many technology-driven markets. Periods when the market is easy to read, standards are stable, and most customers make similar decisions to solve a given problem, alternate with periods when the market is difficult to read, many new standards are in the making, and neither vendors nor customers know what will succeed in the next management cycle. The 1980s was the era of proprietary management solutions. The 1990s proved to be the days of SNMP for network management, and proprietary solutions for systems management. What will be the basis for the NSM solutions of this decade in the IP world?

1.2 Context of This Work

The transition period between the management cycle of the 1990s, dominated by SNMP, and the new management cycle we are supposed to have entered, presents a rare characteristic: it goes on and on and on! The market has remained confused for over five years already, longer than we ever experienced in NSM, and there are no signs that this confusion will stop in the near future! In this context, the author decided to pull out from the industry, went back to academia, and took the opportunity of a Ph.D. thesis to try and identify what the next management cycle could be. This book presents the outcome of this work.

Having managed networks in a highly available, 24*7 environment for six years, and managed systems for a total of eight years, the author was familiar with the SNMP market and the strengths and weaknesses of SNMP-based management. The methodology adopted in this work was to (i) study the management architectures and technologies that could be used for the next cycle; (ii) propose a new technical solution; (iii) demonstrate its feasibility and simplicity by developing a prototype; and (iv) give a vision of how this solution could evolve during this decade—that is, propose a migration path from current management solutions to more visionary ones.

To achieve this, we studied NSM with both a network-management hat and a software-engineering hat. Due to market pressure, most project managers in industry are forced to jump on the bandwagon of the latest technology and develop as quickly as possible a fast-designed solution, only to be the first on the market to support that technology. The rule of the market these days does not seem to be "Do it right", but rather "Be there first and trumpet loud". Being outside the industry and immune to particular commercial interests, we took a different approach. We took the time to investigate most (hopefully all) management paradigms proposed to date, we critically analyzed them and thought about potential improvements. We compared different software-engineering approaches in the specific context of NSM, selected one (Web-based management), improved it significantly, and proposed what we believe is a good technical candidate for the management cycle of this decade.

To a software engineer discovering NSM, IP networks and systems appear to be fairly easy to manage because they impose no stringent requirements on the management application. If we ignore extreme cases such as embedded systems in spatial or military equipment, we usually have no real-time constraints, fault-tolerant systems are not required, and we can even afford to lose some management data (not too much). Therefore, from a software-engineering perspective, a management application is a fairly simple case of distributed application: We have one or several managers and many agents; most data goes from agents to managers; and we can process management data (e.g., compute usage statistics or correlate alarms) either in an agent, in a mid-level manager, or in a top-level manager. Similar tasks are routinely performed in other application domains, typically by relying on a Distributed Processing Environment (DPE, also called *middleware*) such as CORBA, EJBs, or DCOM, and by purchasing Commercial Off-The-Shelf (COTS) component software.

To this software engineer, the complexity of NSM only appears at a later stage of analysis. In the IP world, it mainly stems from its tight constraints *vis-à-vis* scalability, hetero-geneity, and resource usage:

- The number of nodes to manage can grow large and span multiple management domains, e.g. in a geographically dispersed corporate organization.
- The amount of management-related configuration data stored in a single device can be important. Consider, for instance, the access-control lists of an IP router in a filtering firewall.
- We want to manage a wide range of heterogeneous equipment. A $150,000 backbone router is vastly different from a $50 print server. The relative cost of management software is very different, compared with the overall cost of hardware and software. So are the CPU and memory resources available.
- We want to do many things (reactive management, proactive management, security, accounting, billing, etc.) which, taken individually, are reasonably simple to implement and manage, but become complex when put together.
- All resources allocated to management (memory, CPU, network bandwidth, manpower, etc.) are considered overhead, and should therefore be kept to a strict minimum. This requirement makes management applications very different from so-called *user applications*, which are often resource hungry by design. For instance, think of the layered software architectures used throughout the industry for writing even the simplest applications.
- Changing the habits of a market takes time. In the early 1990s, once SNMP-compliant products were commercially available, it took another two to three years to deploy a new generation of devices, with new hardware and new software.
- Changing the habits of a market costs a fortune, so you do not want to make a mistake when you decide to invest in a new management solution. As an equipment vendor, if you embed the wrong management software in all your devices (that is, the market decides to adopt a different standard after tens of thousands of your devices have been sold), the cost is enormous for you to migrate, and you cannot possibly charge your customers for it. But the situation is even worse for your customers, as they will have to install new software in equipment already deployed in real networks—the last thing you want to ask your customers to do. In other words, vendors and customers rarely embark on a new technology before they are certain that the market is heading in that direction—which leads to a chicken-and-egg situation.

Once we combine all of these problems, it becomes obvious that NSM is more complex and challenging than it first appears.

As mentioned before, there are many candidates to succeed SNMP in enterprise management. In this book, we explain why, in our view, Web-based management is the best candidate for the next management cycle. Our argument is sixfold. First, Web technologies allow us to solve most of the problems that we identified in SNMP-based management. Second, the solution proposed in this book is simple. It could be engineered and widely deployed in less than a year. Mobile agents, conversely, require environments that are both secure and fast (especially for WAN links), which no one can presently provide. Similarly, simple, yet efficient, multi-agent systems still remain to be seen in NSM. Third, Web technologies can have a very limited footprint on resource-constrained network devices, unlike CORBA. Fourth, Web technologies offer a smooth migration path toward the future currently envisioned by the industry, that is, dynamic service provisioning with mobile code. Fifth, Web-based management does not revolutionize NSM. It can cope with legacy SNMP-based systems, and can also smoothly integrate new information models such as CIM. Sixth and last, the Web has encountered a tremendous success in the enterprise world. Its simplicity, combined with the portability of Java, has made it ubiquitous. It is difficult today to find a software-engineering field that is not leveraging it. Web expertise is rapidly developing worldwide, and it makes sense to capitalize on this wealth in NSM.

The idea of using Web technologies in NSM is not ours. It is not even new: We will report on experiments made as early as 1993–94. The novelty of our proposal lies in our management architecture: WIMA (Web-based Integrated Management Architecture). Its main contributions are the following:

- an organizational model based on push technologies, which unifies the transfer of notifications and regular management data from agents to managers (or between managers in distributed management);
- a communication model that is totally independent of the information model; and
- the use of XML to represent management data, distribute the management application across a hierarchy of managers, and facilitate the integration of management.

1.3 *Caveat*

During the numerous seminars that the author had the opportunity to give in recent years, there was a standard misunderstanding about the types of network and system that this work addresses. In order to avoid a similar misinterpretation of this book, the reader is invited to pay attention to the following *caveat*:

> This work deals with the management of IP networks and systems typically used today in computer networks, as opposed to OSI-based telecommunication networks typically used in classic telephony. Our conclusions apply equally well to standard IP data networks, IP multimedia networks, and IP telephony networks. Due to time constraints, we did not fully investigate

wireless networks and therefore do not consider them here; but early work suggests that most of our conclusions apply to them, especially our push-based organizational model (permanent HTTP connections are inappropriate, however). In this book, when we refer to network and systems management, or NSM for short, we mean the management of IP systems and fixed IP networks interconnecting IP network devices.

1.4 Organization

The remainder of this book is organized as follows. In Chapter 2, we define our terminology and clarify frequent misunderstandings. In Chapter 3, we analyze SNMP-based management and state the problem that we are striving to solve. In Chapter 4, we present an overview of the solution space in the form of two taxonomies of NSM paradigms. In Chapter 5, we analyze this solution space and select Web-based management with weakly distributed hierarchical management. In Chapter 6, we summarize the state of the art in Web-based management. In Chapter 7, we describe WIMA, our management architecture, with its push-based organizational model for regular management data. In Chapter 8, we detail WIMA-CM, the communication model of WIMA. This very technical chapter is aimed at developers of management applications. In Chapter 9, we highlight the relevance of XML for representing management data and show that it can simplify the distribution and integration of management. In Chapter 10, we present JAMAP, a research prototype that was developed to demonstrate the feasibility and simplicity of the core ideas behind WIMA. In Chapter 11, we compare our solution with others. Finally, we conclude and give directions for future work in Chapter 12.

Chapter 2

TERMINOLOGY

Before we describe the problem at stake, let us first define the terminology used in this book. The need for it is primarily due to inconsistencies in the terminology used by the enterprise-management market. What is a manager: a person or a program? What is an NMS: a program, a machine, or a group of machines? The situation is even worse when you build interdisciplinary teams and bring together engineers with different backgrounds. What is an agent for people coming from the Internet, telecommunications, software engineering, or Distributed Artificial Intelligence (DAI) worlds?

In addition to clarifying frequent misunderstandings, this terminology also introduces a few new definitions, which we hope will be adopted by the NSM community (e.g., the useful distinction between regular management and *ad hoc* management).

We assume that the reader is reasonably familiar with network and systems management, SNMP, the way SNMP-based management platforms work in the IP world, how they are typically structured, and the management tasks they perform. We therefore do not redefine here all the well-established concepts, but only those whose definitions are not consensual and those that are specific to this work.

For a primer on SNMP, we recommend Rose and McCloghrie [218], Stallings [249], and Perkins and McGinnis [202]. For an introduction to network and systems management, see Hegering *et al.* [118] and Sloman [236].

2.1 IP World vs. Telecommunications World

In Section 1.3, we implicitly defined two separate worlds for networking:

- The *IP world*[1], where all pieces of equipment support the TCP/IP stack[2] for communication. A typical example is a data network sustaining an intranet.
- The *telecommunications world*, where all pieces of equipment support part or all of the Open Systems Interconnection (OSI) stack for communication. A typical example is a traditional telephone network (fixed telephony).

This book deals exclusively with the IP world, as highlighted by its title.

2.2 Different Types of Enterprise Management

In the IP world, *network management* primarily deals with network devices, that is, equipment whose sole purpose is to make the network operate properly. Typical examples include IP routers, bridges, Asynchronous Transfer Mode (ATM) switches, level-3 switches, level-4 switches, intelligent hubs, and plain hubs. Some people also include in this category the network-accessed peripherals that are shared by a group of people (e.g., printers), on the basis that they are accessed via the network. We do not, as a peripheral can usually be directly attached to a host and is useful *per se*: Its usefulness does not depend on the network. In contrast, an IP router in itself is totally useless for end users.

In the OSI world, there is a fundamental distinction between *element management*, which is the management of individual pieces of equipment, and *network management*, which is the management of an entire network abstracted as an entity of its own. For years, the IP world has been interested exclusively in the former. With the advent of concerns related to the Quality of Service (QoS) delivered by IP networks, the IP world has become increasingly interested in managing end-to-end networks as well. As a result, network management in the IP world now encompasses both element management and network management (in OSI parlance). In this book, we consider both when we refer to network management. The agent-manager interactions described in the next chapters are typically about element management, whereas manager-manager interactions are generally about network management.

In its simplest sense, *systems management* is concerned with hosts, that is, machines that can operate and fulfill useful tasks for users without a network. The main objective of systems management is to make sure that the hosts run smoothly. Typical areas of interest to systems management include the monitoring of the Central Processing Unit (CPU),

---

1. Some people call it the *Internet world*. This name is confusing because, for certain people, it only refers to the Internet backbones controlled by the telecommunication operators.
2. The so-called *TCP/IP stack* not only includes the Internet Protocol (IP) and the Transmission Control Protocol (TCP), but also the User Datagram Protocol (UDP), the Internet Control Message Protocol (ICMP), the Simple Network Management Protocol (SNMP), etc.

memory, and disk usage; the management of processes, file systems, and access-control lists (see the Host Resources MIB [281]); and the detection of hardware faults. We include shared peripherals in this category.

Any piece of equipment can be classified either as a network device or a system. The former is dealt with by network management, the latter by systems management. *Application management*, conversely, deals with software. It is about managing programs that interact with users or other programs. These programs run on top of an operating system. The management of the programs belongs in the application-management realm, whereas the management of the underlying operating system belongs in the systems-management realm. Examples of applications that must be carefully managed are relational databases and object-oriented databases. Application management commonly deals with access control, performance monitoring, fine-grained buffer allocation, etc. The objective here is to ensure that the application performs correctly, and to detect and repair a problem before users complain. Systems management is generic to a certain extent, whereas application management is inherently site specific.

Unfortunately, these nice, clear-cut definitions are no longer valid when we consider distribution aspects. Initially, a *distributed system* was a group of hosts that collectively offered a service and appeared as a single virtual machine to that service. A typical example of distributed system is a *cluster*, that is, a group of machines sharing multiaccess storage devices[1]; a cluster allows for transparent load balancing and automatic recovery (*failover*); it provides applications with some kind of fault tolerance, hence increased robustness. Another example is a massively parallel system with hundreds of microprocessors; to the program running on it, the entire system appears to be a single machine[2].

Initially, a *distributed application* was an application running on several hosts, possibly on a distributed system. A distributed application consisted of several application modules, each of them running on a different machine on top of an operating system, itself running on top of the hardware. An example of such a distributed application is NIS (Network Information Service), a popular network lookup service developed by Sun Microsystems in the 1980s and now supported by most Unix flavors. NIS relies on different programs that run on different machines, but it is used by administrators as a single global program.

But then came a major advance in product technology, probably the main outcome to date of years of research in distributed operating systems: *Distributed Processing Environments* (DPEs), also called *middleware*. Middleware sits between the operating system and the application. It can be viewed as a distributed application because it fulfills the above definition: It consists of several modules running on top of the operating system of different machines. But it can also be viewed as a distributed system, because it offers a pseudo operating system to the application running on top of it: This application need not be aware

---

1. The concept of *cluster* was popularized by Digital Equipment in the late 1970s and early 1980s, and later adopted by many vendors of PCs, workstations, and servers in the Windows and Unix worlds.
2. Actually, there are some cases when we do not want to conceal all the details of the distributed system from the application. For instance, the programmer may want to know the number of processors available on the system to optimize the run-time efficiency of the code.

whether the operating system underneath is distributed or not. A well-known example is the Common Object Request Broker Architecture (CORBA). Another example is a distributed relational database: It is not an operating system, but it is not a real application that an end-user can interact with; it is a building block, on top of which real applications may run.

Another source of misunderstandings is the frequent confusion, in the literature, between *distributed systems management* (where the management application is distributed, and the systems may be stand-alone or distributed) and *distributed-systems management* (where the management application may be centralized or distributed, and the systems are distributed). This confusion is sometimes (but rarely) created on purpose, when people want to encompass both (e.g., in conferences).

Today, the expression *systems management* covers the management of stand-alone hosts, the management of tightly coupled groups of machines, the management of middleware, and the distributed way of managing systems. As a result, there is a large overlap between distributed systems and distributed applications—so much so that many people now include application management in systems management. Kramer, for instance, uses these two expressions interchangeably [143]. The distinction between the two is not an important issue in our view, because systems and application management are very similar in terms of management architecture and communication protocol.

Service management[1] is not far from application management either, because most services are implemented by applications. However, there is an important nuance between the two. The term *service* implicitly refers to a contract between a provider and a customer. Thus, service management is mostly concerned with what the customers see: the Application Programming Interfaces (APIs) they interact with, the type of service they purchased, and the monitoring of the service actually delivered to ensure that the contract defined by the Service-Level Agreement (SLA) is fulfilled. Two important aspects of service management are thus QoS management and SLA monitoring. Conversely, tuning the internals of the service (e.g., increasing the number of large memory buffers and decreasing the number of small memory buffers in a memory pool used by a database) belongs in application management. For service providers, application management deals with the nuts and bolts that make up services and are hidden to end-users.

To put it simply, service management is high level, application management is low level. Service providers keep application management internal, and hide it from customers and competitors. Customers do not see the nitty-gritty of the databases and infrastructure that underpin the provision of the service. But service providers do disclose data relevant to service management. Some of it is destined for their customers, to prove that the contracts have been honored (provider-side SLA monitoring). Some management data is also exchanged between service providers (e.g., when the provision of one service requires the availability of others, provided by other companies).

---

1. The expression *service management* originated from the telecommunications world and spread to the IP world in the mid-1990s.

Policy-based management is concerned with the definition and enforcement of high-level management decisions called *policies* [235]. An example of policy is the following. In the case of network congestion, the traffic of customers paying for a gold service gets the highest priority; if there is some bandwidth left, customers paying for a silver service get up to 90% of the remaining bandwidth, while customers paying for an economy service get the remainder. This policy has repercussions on service management (SLAs) and network management (configuration of queues in IP routers). More generally, policy-based management interacts with network, systems, application, and service management. A detailed terminology for policy-based management is defined in RFC 3198 [288].

The boundaries between *enterprise management* and *integrated management* are somewhat fuzzy and need clarification. Until the mid-1990s, enterprise management was generally considered to be part of business administration. The integration of network and systems management was then referred to as *integrated management*, as reflected by the name of the main international conference in this field: Integrated Management (IM). But since then, *enterprise management* has been used more and more often to encompass all the *types* of management relevant to an enterprise: network management, systems management, application management, service management, policy-based management, etc. This new fashion was cast in iron in 1996 by Web-Based Enterprise Management (WBEM), an important industry effort that will be studied in the next chapters. Most of the management community now follows suit.

In large and geographically dispersed corporations, the problem is not so much managing networks, systems, and so on *per se*: It is managing networks, systems, applications, services, and policies that are deeply intertwined. The objective of *integrated enterprise management*, or *integrated management* for short, is thus to integrate all *types* of enterprise management within a single, distributed management platform, as opposed to having one management platform per enterprise-management type. In this book, we are concerned with the integration of network and systems management. But in some places, we also make some observations relevant to application, service, and policy-based management. A large part of Chapter 9 is dedicated to integrated management.

The reader may be surprised to see that some important management activities have not been mentioned thus far, e.g. user management and inventory management. We "forgot" them on purpose! As explained by Hegering *et al.* [118], it is customary to group management tasks into five functional areas: Fault, Configuration, Accounting, Performance, and Security management [52, 53]. They are called FCAPS and form the *functional model* of a management architecture. FCAPS is orthogonal to the types of enterprise management listed above. User management, which spans configuration management (database of users) and security management (access rights), is found in all types of enterprise management: network management, systems management, application management, etc. Inventory management, which is part of configuration management, is also used by all management types. In consequence, standardization activities in enterprise management are organized into a matrix structure. Some Working Groups at the Internet Engineering Task Force (IETF) and Distributed Management Task Force (DMTF) work on different management types, while others address transverse issues that are part of FCAPS.

2.3 Manager, Agent, Management Application, Management Platform, and Management System

In network management, the management software is called the *Network Management Application*. In reality, several independent applications may be run to manage an entire network; in this case, we consider them collectively as a single distributed application. A Network Management Application is composed of *managers* running in *Network Management Stations*, and *agents* running in network devices (also known as managed devices). The terms *manager* and *agent* come from the manager-agent paradigm followed by the OSI management model and the SNMP management architecture—i.e., the piece of software is named after the management role played by the machine it runs on.

Likewise, in systems management, a *Systems Management Application* is composed of managers running in *Systems Management Stations*, and agents running in managed systems. These systems may be related (e.g., components of a distributed system) or independent (e.g., hosts in an intranet). The Network Management Application and the Systems Management Application can be integrated. To keep the text fluid and remain generic, we will refer to the *management application* when we actually mean the Network Management Application, the Systems Management Application, or both. Similarly, a *management station* can be a Network Management Station, a Systems Management Station, or both.

By extension, the *managers* often refer to the management stations, and the *agents* refer to the managed devices or systems. These are clearly misnomers, for they confuse the management application running on a machine with the machine itself. But these terms are seldom ambiguous once placed in context.

Note that managers and agents need not necessarily run on different machines. If a network device (or a system) is self managed, the manager and the agent are two applications running on the same device (or system). This case is typically encountered in embedded systems.

A *management platform* is the manager side of a management application. It is characterized by the version numbers of the manager, the operating system of the management station, the middleware (if need be), and the hardware of the management station (especially the CPU). A management platform may be specialized for network management (*Network Management Platform*), systems management (*Systems Management Platform*), or may integrate both.

In the early days of SNMPv1, the acronym *NMS* used to stand for *Network Management System*. Its precise definition was unimportant because management was centralized and limited to network devices, so we had only one manager, one management station, one platform, hence one NMS. But what exactly is a Network Management System in the days of distributed management? Does it perform only network management, as opposed to systems management? Or is it synonymous with management station, in which case the management of a large network requires many NMSes? Does it refer to the management platform? Does it encompass all the management stations and the (possibly distributed) management application? There is no consensus in the market. Some authors even use different definitions in different contexts. To avoid these ambiguities, we refrain from using the acronym *NMS* and the expression *Network Management System* in this book.

2.4 Manager vs. Administrator

To avoid any confusion between programs and people when we use the term *managers*, the people in charge of managing networks or systems are called *administrators*. This convention is widely adopted within the IETF, but, unfortunately, magazines in the networking industry still use the term *manager* with both meanings.

2.5 Agent, Mobile Agent, and Intelligent Agent

The meaning that we have retained for the word *agent* is standard for the NSM community. It is inherited from the manager-agent paradigm, one of the building blocks of the OSI and SNMP management architectures. But we experienced that it is misleading to people coming from software engineering or Distributed Artificial Intelligence (DAI), because they routinely use it in a different sense. To avoid any confusion, an agent in the software-engineering sense is called a *mobile agent*, which is essentially a technique to dispatch and execute code on a remote entity. Likewise, we speak of an *intelligent agent* when we mean an agent in the DAI sense, that is, a paradigm enabling elaborate (and sometimes complex) forms of cooperation between remote entities that "think" independently of each other. We will come back to mobile agents and intelligent agents in Chapter 4.

2.6 Proxy vs. Gateway

To cope with legacy systems whose internal agent does not support the capabilities expected by the manager, we assume hereafter that legacy systems make use of *management gateways* if necessary (see Fig. 1). A management gateway is generally dedicated to a certain legacy system, and external to it. It is located between the manager and the agent, and is transparent to the management application. It can, for instance, translate a CORBA request into SNMP protocol primitives, and *vice versa*. When a management gateway is used, the agent embedded in the legacy system is called a *legacy agent*. Throughout this book, when we refer to an *agent*, we actually mean either the pair {legacy agent, management gateway} or a single agent.

A management gateway is called a *proxy agent* by some authors [117, 145]. The problem with this designation is that the concept of proxy is confusing and ill-defined. This was acknowledged by the IETF: "The term 'proxy' has historically been used very loosely, with multiple different meanings" [149, p. 4]. The definitions of a proxy proposed in RFC 2573 [149] and RFC 2616 [88] are very specific and different from our definition of a management gateway. Our choice of the term *gateway* was based on the definition given in

RFC 2616 [88, p. 10]: "[A gateway is] a server which acts as an intermediary for some other server. Unlike a proxy, a gateway receives requests as if it were the origin server for the requested resource; the requesting client may not be aware that it is communicating with a gateway". Therefore, we do not use the expression *proxy agent*.

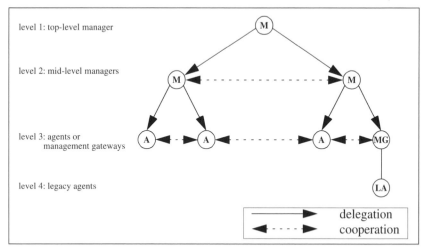

Fig. 1. Delegation and cooperation

For the sake of completeness, we should also mention that a management gateway is sometimes called a *delegated agent* [300]. This phrase is ambiguous, as some authors give this name to programs remotely transferred to an agent [105]; so we avoid it, too.

2.7 Delegation

Decentralized management is to the enterprise world what distributed management is to NSM: a paradigm based on the delegation of tasks to other entities. These entities are people in the enterprise world; they are machines or programs in computer science. *Delegation* is used in both contexts as a generic word to describe the process of transferring power, authority, accountability, and responsibility [83, 186] for a specific task to another entity.

Distributed NSM can follow a hierarchical paradigm, a cooperative paradigm, or a combination thereof. Any paradigm that is not centralized belongs in the realm of distributed NSM. We will study management paradigms in detail in Chapter 4.

When management is hierarchically distributed in NSM, delegation always goes *down* the management hierarchy: A manager at level (N) delegates a task (i.e., a management processing unit) to a subordinate at level (N+1). This is known as *downward delegation*. In the enterprise world, we can also find *upward delegation*. For example, an employee implicitly delegates his tasks to his manager when he is out due to illness [186]. Downward delegation and upward delegation are two kinds of *vertical delegation*, typical of hierarchical paradigms.

In most enterprises, organization charts follow a hierarchical paradigm. They are characterized by a multi-layer pyramid comprising a *chief executive*—called a *Chief Executive Officer*, *President*, *Managing Director*, or *Director* depending on the type of enterprise—at the top (level 1 on Fig. 1), several layers of *mid-level managers* (levels 2, 3...), and *workers* at the lowest level [83]. In NSM, the chief executive is called a *top-level manager*, mid-level managers keep the same, and workers are called *agents*. The top- and mid-level managers are globally called *managers* in NSM.

Orthogonal to vertical delegation, we have *horizontal delegation* between two peers at the same level of hierarchy. Horizontal delegation is typical of the *cooperative paradigms* used in DAI. It is rarely used in the enterprise world; we find it in small start-ups, for instance.

Delegation is normally a *one-to-one relationship*, between a manager and an agent in a hierarchical management paradigm, or between two peers (be they managers or agents) in a cooperative management paradigm. Arguably, delegation may also be considered, in some cases, as a *one-to-many relationship*, where a task is delegated to a group of entities collectively responsible for the completion of the task. One-to-many delegation is forbidden by many authors in business administration [13, 83, 186, 285]. It can be considered in DAI however, notably because the concept of accountability applies differently to people and pieces of software. In NSM, we classify one-to-many delegation as a form of cooperation, by coupling hierarchical and cooperative paradigms: A manager delegates a task to an agent, and this agent in turn cooperates with a group of agents to achieve this task. In the case of a *many-to-many relationship*, we are clearly in the realm of cooperation rather than delegation.

2.8 Paradigm vs. Technology

Many people confuse management paradigms with management technologies, although the concepts are very different. A typical example is CORBA: In the literature, we find it referred to indistinctly as a paradigm, a technology, or even a framework. In the tradition of software engineering, and especially object-oriented analysis and design, we consider that technologies implement paradigms [99]. At the analysis phase, the designers of a management application select a *management paradigm* (e.g, object-oriented middleware). At the design phase, they select a *management technology* (e.g., CORBA). At the implementation phase, they use a certain instance of that technology (e.g., versions X.Y of the Orbix Object Request Broker (ORB) and CORBA Services) to program the management application in a certain language (e.g., a specific version of Java [107]).

2.9 Architecture vs. Framework

The definitions of the terms *architecture* and *framework* are still not consensual in computer science. At the IETF, these two terms are often used interchangeably. But to the object-oriented community, frameworks and architectures are very different concepts [81]. An *architecture* refers to the collection of models devised at the analysis and high-level design phases of an application; an architecture is therefore abstract in nature. A *framework*, conversely, refers to both an architecture and a set of template classes that implement this architecture. A framework provides hooks for site-specific extensions. It gives a common basis for different sites to build similar applications. It provides code that implements a specific model. A framework is related to a specific implementation and is language specific; an architecture is not.

In this book, we adopt the definitions of the object-oriented community. The three SNMP frameworks are therefore called the *SNMPv1, v2c, and v3 management architectures*, and the OSI management framework is called the *OSI management architecture*.

2.10 Firewalls and Trust Domains

Years ago, when SNMPv1 was devised, IP networks were modeled as self-contained connex networks[1], where the division between "us" and "them" was very simple. By "us", administrators meant the machines inside their network, under their control, machines that could be physically accessed only by their colleagues—in short, machines they trusted. By "them", they meant the machines out there, possibly compromised by hordes of security breakers (*attackers*), machines that could be physically accessed by people they did not know—machines they did not trust. In terms of security administration, the entire world was split into two *trust domains*: IP networks and systems "inside" were trusted by administrators, while IP networks and systems "outside" were not.

Every day that goes by, real-life networks depart farther away from this simple model. Today's small enterprises often have remote offices, and need to remotely manage at least the IP routers connecting these offices to the WAN (see Fig. 2). Midsize enterprises are geographically dispersed, and when a remote branch cannot afford a management platform, it is usually managed remotely, from the main office. Large corporations manage large networks, sometimes several of them[2], and their headquarters are interconnected to many subsidiaries. Whatever the size of the enterprise, the traffic between its remote offices and its main office goes over WAN links. Rich companies with static networking needs use private lines, which are rather secure because access to their constituents is not easy for attackers. But few companies have static networking needs: Most of them want to add or suppress WAN links fairly frequently, which rules out the use of private lines (installing a

---

1. By analogy with mathematics, a connex network is a network with no "holes". In such a network, all the nodes, and all of the network links between any two nodes, belong to the same administration domain. When a packet is routed from your node A to your node B, it needs not go through a node C managed by a third party.
2. It is often easier for one to buy and sell a company than to merge one's network with another's!

new private line is expensive and takes months). One solution for dynamically provisioning WAN links is to use leased lines; but they are expensive, and most network operators do not let their customers provision leased lines themselves. To do so, companies use Virtual Private Networks (VPNs), which are overlaid on top of public networks controlled by network operators, and also happen to be a lot less expensive than leased lines.

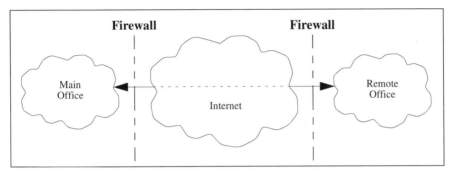

Fig. 2. Management across firewalls: the real picture

In these WAN settings, the distinction between the "inside" and the "outside" of an enterprise is blurred, and the definition of trust domains can be complex. While the machines at the main office remain physically secure and still form a natural trust domain, those located at remote offices can be tampered with. Even though they belong to the same company, they are no longer "inside". Worse, if one of the routers or switches that make up the VPN (see Internet cloud in Fig. 2) is controlled by an attacker, or is poorly set up and does not filter attacks as it should, traffic coming into the main office might impersonate machines from the remote offices (that is, the source IP address indicated in the IP packet header is fake). Even though service providers and network operators do their best to secure their networks and services, machines in remote offices clearly do not belong in the same trust domain as those in the main office. And if administrators place different levels of trust in different service providers, different remote offices may even belong to different trust domains.

When a network is not connex, the data communication between different "islands" of the network is usually protected by *firewalls* [58, 59]. With respect to security, each "island" of the network corresponds to a trust domain. To perform a management task, a manager at the main office accesses an agent at a remote office via one or two firewall(s). The firewall of the main office is mandatory (see Fig. 2); it is likely to be a full-blown, feature-rich, and expensive piece of software. The firewalls of the remote offices are optional; in small enterprises, they can be minimalist (e.g., a filtering router).

As far as manager-agent interactions are concerned in NSM, the scenario depicted in Fig. 2 can be abstracted as shown in Fig. 3. We use this simplified representation throughout the book, especially in Chapter 7 and Chapter 8, for the sake of readability. But it is important to keep in mind the more complex reality of firewalls and WAN links. Firewalls are studied in more detail in Section 8.2.

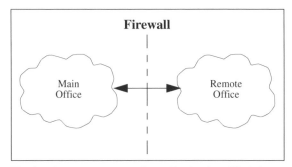

Fig. 3. Management across firewalls: the simplified picture

2.11 Regular Management vs. *Ad Hoc* Management

If we focus on the flow of management data, the tasks achieved by a management application can be classified into four categories:

- regular management
- *ad hoc* management
- configuration management
- background analysis

Regular management consists of management tasks that run continuously, almost permanently. It encompasses monitoring, data collection, and event handling. It requires that a manager be always up and running. To improve robustness, it is recommended that this manager be dedicated to the management application. Otherwise, another application running on the same machine could cause havoc—e.g., freeze the machine while the network is unstable.

In large networks, or in enterprises where the network is critical to the smooth running of the business, regular management is typically supervised by staff dedicated to monitoring (*operators*). Some small and midsize enterprises cannot afford this and therefore do not perform regular management at all. Others rely on fully automated management, without people (*unattended mode*). For instance, when a critical fault is detected by a monitoring application, the administrator is automatically paged; but when a minor fault is detected, he/she is simply sent an e-mail message.

The data received by the manager for the purpose of *monitoring* is processed immediately, in pseudo real-time, and then discarded. The data received for the purpose of *data collection* goes directly to the data repository; it is not directly processed by the manager and serves for background analysis (see next). On the manager, the event correlator processes two types of events: some originating from the agents (*notifications*) and some originating from the manager itself (especially from its rule-based system).

In regular management, the management-data flow goes from the agent to the manager (see Fig. 4).

Ad hoc management consists of management tasks that run from time to time, if need be, for a short time. It comprises troubleshooting and short-term monitoring. Troubleshooting is reactive; e.g., a network problem just showed up and an operator tries to identify and correct it by looking at per-interface error rates. Short-term monitoring is proactive; e.g., an administrator may randomly check, once in a while, how the percentage of CPU usage evolves over a two-minute time window on all the backbone routers—just in case something weird shows up.

In essence, *ad hoc* management cannot be automated. It is always manual (*attended mode*) and requires a user (administrator or operator) to interact with the management application. *Ad hoc* management takes place in virtually all companies. It complements regular management in large enterprises that can afford operators, or in small and midsize enterprises that rely entirely on automated regular management. In small organizations, *ad hoc* management generally replaces regular management. There is no operator, no dedicated manager, and the part-time administrator works in purely reactive mode, on an *ad hoc* basis.

In *ad hoc* management, the management-data flow goes from the agent to the manager (see Fig. 4).

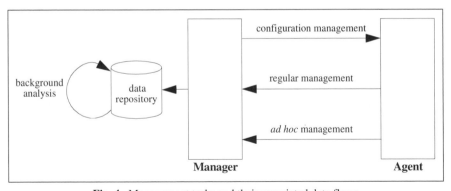

Fig. 4. Management tasks and their associated data flows

Configuration management is about actively changing the state of an agent to make it operate differently. Regular and *ad hoc* management, conversely, are both passive in the sense that they simply retrieve data from an agent and do not alter its state. We distinguish two modes in configuration management: manual (e.g., with GUIs) and automated (e.g., with scripts). Under normal circumstances, manual configuration management takes place on an *ad hoc* basis, when the need arises. (When it occurs on a regular basis, manual config-uration management ought to be automated.) Automated configuration management is usually regular. For instance, the routing of transoceanic traffic over multiple links may be automatically altered every morning and every evening to benefit from slack-hour discounts. But automated configuration management can also occur on an *ad hoc* basis. For instance, the real-time enforcement of policies may trigger, whenever necessary, the automated update of the configuration of a group of network devices. Another example is when a new customer signs in for a new service: The type of service he/she pays for often results in new settings at an access router controlled by the service provider. Note that, unlike regular and *ad hoc* management, the management-data flow goes from the manager to the agent in the case of configuration management (see Fig. 4). This is why we do not split configuration management into regular and *ad hoc* management.

Background analysis includes report generation (usually on a daily, weekly, and monthly basis), billing, security analysis, data mining, and more generally any application that leverages and makes sense out of the wealth of data gathered by regular management. These applications run offline, in the background, on a machine which is often not the manager. This prevents number-crunching background tasks from slowing down monitoring and event correlation, which are supposed to operate in pseudo real-time. For background analysis, there is no management-data flow between the agent and the manager (see Fig. 4).

In this book, we concentrate on agent-manager and manager-manager interactions, that is, on the organizational and communication models (see Section 7.1). We take *ad hoc* management into account, but we focus on regular management, which accounts for most of the network overhead, manager's processing overhead, and agent's processing overhead.

2.12 Ontologies, Schemas, and Models

Different communities often use different terminologies. The jargon related to information modeling is no exception. In artificial intelligence and knowledge engineering, people typically model application domains with *ontologies*. In the database world, they define data models with *schemas*. In software engineering, particularly in the object-oriented world, they use *models*. In enterprise management, people refer to *information models*, rather than object models or data models. Are all these terms equivalent in practice? To some degree, the answer is *yes*. But because different communities focus on different aspects, there are some differences, too.

The definitions that we propose to adopt are inspired by previous work by Meersman [174] and Fensel [87], who compare ontologies with schemas.

Ontologies, schemas, and models all share two goals:

- provide a shared and common understanding of an application domain;
- facilitate the exchange of information, with well-accepted semantics, between people and/or heterogeneous distributed systems.

The main differences between ontologies, schemas, and models are the following:

- The information described by an ontology is expressed in structured text (usually predicates), using either a formal language or a semi-structured natural language.
- Schemas typically describe tabular information for relational databases [87]. With the advent of object-oriented databases and eXtensible Markup Language (XML) repositories, new forms of schemas have recently appeared.

- Models are usually expressed in the Unified Modeling Language (UML [219]), i.e. in the form of graphical diagrams: class diagrams, interaction diagrams, etc.
- "An ontology provides a domain theory and not the structure of a data container [87]".
- Many authors consider that ontologies should be machine readable (some people even make it mandatory, e.g. Gruber [109]). Conversely, models are often graphical and do not require machine readability[1].

So, there are two dividing lines. First, the schemas defined by the database community are directly linked to the data repository and its internal structure, whereas ontologies and models are independent of the data container. Second, the ontologies defined in artificial intelligence and knowledge engineering map onto the *domain models* used by the software-engineering community. An ontology is thus a special case of a model. For each domain, we have a single ontology but several models (at least three: the conceptual, specification, and implementation models [94, p. 51]).

A third dividing line, which is not agreed upon by all authors, is that ontologies ought to be expressed in a formal language (in the form of predicates) and should thus be readable by machines, whereas this is not a requirement for models.

---

1. Some models support both a graphical format and a textual, machine-readable format (see Chapter 6).

Chapter 3

PROBLEM STATEMENT

Now that we have a clear terminology, we can substantiate our claim that SNMP-based management is not appropriate for the next management cycle, and justify why a new management architecture is needed.

This chapter is organized as follows. In Section 3.1, we characterize implicit and explicit design decisions that were made in the SNMP management architecture. In Section 3.2, we acknowledge the main strengths of SNMP. In Section 3.3, we review the main problems that we identified in SNMP-based management. In Section 3.4, we show that the problem solved by SNMPv1 has changed; what we need today, more than a decade later, is a new solution to a new problem. Finally, we summarize this chapter in Section 3.5.

3.1 Characteristics of SNMP-Based Management

To begin with, let us summarize the main characteristics of SNMP-based management. This section is mostly meant for people who have had little exposure to SNMP, but even SNMP experts should find some paragraphs interesting.

Partial specification

Many characteristics of SNMP-based management appear explicitly in the specifications (IETF RFCs). But some are transmitted more informally via textbooks, research articles, magazines, SNMP-related mailing lists, or open-source software. For instance, the change in the recommended use for the `inform` Packet Data Unit (PDU), from a manager-to-manager notification in SNMPv2 to a general-purpose acknowledged notification in

SNMPv3, does not explicitly appear in any RFC[1]; it gradually imposed itself in the mailing list of the IETF SNMPv3 Working Group, and was formally documented by Perkins in *The Simple Times*, the online magazine of the SNMP community [203]. Another example will be encountered in the next chapter, when we study the issue of the maximum size of an SNMP message; one value (1,472 octets) is considered well-known only because it appears in a famous textbook on SNMP and was used in some open-source implementations of SNMP in the early 1990s.

Other characteristics of SNMP-based management have no technical roots at all and are solely due to the way the SNMP market developed over time.

Interoperability

SNMPv1 was designed in the late 1980s, in the days of proprietary management. Just like its main competitor in those days, the OSI management architecture, the main goal of the SNMP management architecture was to achieve interoperability between multiple vendors, to pave the way from proprietary to open management. Interoperability was undeniably the main merit of SNMPv1.

In the SNMP management architecture, interoperability is guaranteed by:

- SNMP agents and managers complying with the IETF specifications;
- generic MIBs that rarely change;
- vendor-specific MIBs whose internals are advertised;
- a single metamodel for all MIBs;
- a *lingua franca* (SNMPv1 PDUs) used by most sites, and a small variation of it (SNMPv2 PDUs) used by a few others;
- management platforms developed by third-party vendors with supposedly no interest in favoring one equipment vendor over another.

Simplicity

OSI management encountered very little success in the IP world because it was overly complex. It tried to do everything right—and failed. SNMP, conversely, focused on the bare minimum, the bottom line, and postponed everything else *sine die*: security, distribution, etc. As a result, SNMP was simple and inexpensive to implement for equipment vendors. Open-source code for SNMP agents was freely available on the Internet (the Carnegie Mellon University and Massachusetts Institute of Technology distributions were probably the most popular in the early 1990s, when the SNMP market exploded), so it was very easy for a vendor to take this code, customize it, and integrate it in a piece of equipment. SNMP was simple to learn for customers, too, and it took little time for administrators and operators to get accustomed to it. Simplicity was the second most important achievement of SNMP after interoperability and, in our view, the main reason for its commercial success.

---

1. We are not saying here that the `inform` PDU is not *specified* in SNMPv3.

Generic vs. vendor-specific MIBs

Agents support two types of virtual management-data repositories, called MIBs in the SNMP world. *Generic MIBs* are usually defined by the IETF[1] and supported by multiple vendors. The most famous is RFC 1213 [173], better known as *MIB-II* for historical reasons (strictly speaking, MIB-II is a superset of RFC 1213). It is *the* standard MIB in the IP world, and is supported by virtually all SNMP-compliant network devices and systems on the market. *Vendor-specific MIBs*, on the other hand, are controlled by the vendors but their definitions are available to all (e.g., the Cisco MIB, initially unique and now broken down into separate entities, is available from `<ftp://ftp.cisco.com/pub/mibs/>`). MIBs constitute the main element of the SNMP information model.

A stable metamodel: SMI

Another characteristic (and strength) of SNMP is that its information metamodel[2], the Structure of Management Information (SMI), has been very stable over time. There have been only two versions of it in more than a decade. SMIv1 [216] is still used by MIB-II[3]. Most other MIBs now use SMIv2 [48].

For completeness, we should also mention that a third version of SMI, called SMIng, was proposed in 1999 by Schönwälder and Strauss [224]. This led to the creation of the IETF SMING Working Group. This is ongoing work, and there is no evidence as yet that SMIng will be standardized by the IETF, let alone adopted by the SNMP market. We therefore do not consider it in this book when we refer to SNMP-based management.

Not one but several SNMPs

When we say *SNMP-based management*, we are actually ambiguous. There are currently three SNMP management architectures (SNMPv1, SNMPv2c, and SNMPv3), three SNMP protocols (SNMPv1, SNMPv2, and SNMPv3), two metamodels (SMIv1 and SMIv2), and two sets of Protocol Data Units (PDUs): PDUs for SNMPv1 protocol operations (`get`, `get-next`, `set`, and `trap`) and PDUs for SNMPv2 protocol operations (a new `get`, a new `get-next`, `get-bulk`, a new `set`, `SNMPv2-trap`, and `inform`) [203, 249].

The SNMPv1 management architecture uses the SNMPv1 protocol, SMIv1, and PDUs for SNMPv1 protocol operations. The SNMPv2c management architecture uses the SNMPv2 protocol, SMIv2, and PDUs for SNMPv2 protocol operations. The SNMPv3 management

---

1. Some MIBs are defined by other consortia; e.g., the SNMP M4 Network Element View MIB is defined by the ATM Forum [15].

2. *Stricto sensu*, SMI is not the SNMP information metamodel, but rather the language used for defining the SNMP information model (i.e., SNMP MIBs). The IETF did not specify a metamodel *per se*, if we refer to Atkinson's definition [14]. But the vocabulary of the SMI language relies on an implicit metamodel that we also call SMI in this book.

3. Back in 1996, MIB-II (RFC 1213) was translated into SMIv2 and split into three RFCs [169, 170, 171], but not all vendors support this new version.

architecture uses the SNMPv3 protocol, SMIv2, and PDUs for SNMPv2 protocol operations.

Got it? Do you want to read the last two paragraphs another time? Believe it or not, to simplify the picture, we omitted the response PDUs. All of this is all the more confusing because the clear separation between the versioning schemes of PDUs, protocols, and management architectures (*frameworks* in SNMP jargon, see Section 2.9) was only made in 1998, when SNMPv3 was released—that is, eight years after SNMPv1 was released, four years after SNMPv2p was released, and two years after SNMPv2c was released. Just imagine the state of confusion in customers' minds... We will come back to this variety of SNMPs in Section 4.1.

Manager-agent paradigm, client-server architecture

As OSI management, SNMP-based management relies on the manager-agent paradigm [197]. This paradigm is based on the client-server architecture for communication. For data collection and monitoring, the manager is the client and the agent is the server. For notifications, the roles are reversed. In NSM, the same machine can play the manager and agent roles; in this case, it runs a client and a server.

All agents are created equal... and "dumb"

In the organizational model[1] of the SNMP management architecture, there is an implicit assumption that all agents should be managed alike. As a result, we use the same type of interaction between a manager and an agent, whatever the agent, be it powerful or not. In such situations, the weakest link of the chain rules: All agents must be managed alike, and some agents can be "dumb"[2], so all agents are managed as if they were "dumb". The manager does not have to cope with "dumb" agents and "smart" agents in parallel: there is no differentiation. SNMP leverages the least common denominator between bottom-of-the-range and top-of-the-range equipment.

The suitability of this implicit assumption was destroyed in the mid-1990s by Wellens and Auerbach, when they exposed the *Myth of the Dumb Agent* [286], and by Goldszmidt, when he justified the suitability of his new organizational model: Management by Delegation [105]. The IETF became aware of this in the late 1990s. The Script MIB [150, 225] is its first achievement to provide management *à la carte*, with a differentiation by the manager between "smart" and "dumb" agents. But for security reasons, the Script MIB requires SNMPv3, which is hardly used anywhere at the time we write these lines.

---

1. The organizational model [118] explains who does what, how managers and agents are organized, etc.
2. This term is often used in NSM: We have "dumb" network devices or systems just as we have "dumb" terminals. "Dumb" agents do not really participate in the management application; they only passively collect data on behalf of the manager. Note that some SNMP agents do not deserve to be called "dumb", e.g. those that can process an atomic set of several MIB variables (which is not a trivial task).

Small footprint on agents

Because agents are supposedly "dumb" and short of resources, the footprint of SNMP on agents is small—as opposed to the OSI management stack used in fixed telephony, for instance. Apart from the MIBs they support, all the network devices and systems of a given vendor can therefore run the same generic SNMP code, from bottom- to top-of-the-range equipment. Note that on top-of-the-range pieces of equipment, which usually support dozens of MIBs, the footprint of SNMP MIBs is not negligible at all.

Monitoring is not notification driven

In the telecommunications world, most of the problems with the agents are detected by the agents themselves. When it detects a problem, an agent generates a notification and sends it to the manager. Parallel to this, the manager's rule-based system routinely checks a number of things (e.g., that an aggregate value remains below a certain threshold), and generates an event when a problem is detected (e.g., this threshold is exceeded). The main task of the manager, with respect to monitoring, is to correlate all these types of events: those generated by the agents and those generated by the manager. Because most events originate from the agents, we say that *monitoring is notification driven in the telecommunications world.*

In the IP world, conversely, most of the problems with the agents are detected by the manager. This is a direct consequence of the assumption that agents are "dumb" and short of resources: They are not sufficiently instrumented to detect what goes wrong, let alone to take corrective action by themselves. Most agents in the IP world are able to send only a few different notifications to a manager. The author even came across some pieces of equipment that could not send any notifications at all! Because few events originate from the agents, we say that *monitoring is not notification driven in the IP world.* This mode of operation explains why notifications are not very important in the IP world—and also, indirectly, why so many NSM engineers with a telecommunications background are confused when they move to the IP world.

Note that nothing inherent in the SNMP specifications prevents vendors from basing monitoring on notifications issued by agents. For instance, in recent years, Cisco increased very significantly the number of SNMPv1 traps and SNMPv2 notifications that can be generated by agents. Management applications could thus more systematically leverage notifications for Cisco devices—and in a few enterprises, they already do. But to date, in SNMP-based management, managers typically rely on polling instead of notifications for detecting problems.

Polling for regular management

In SNMP, monitoring and data collection are based on *polling*. The manager patiently asks the same things to the agents, at each poll cycle, and the agents return the values of the requested MIB variables. On the manager, the *polled-data analyzer* is in charge of detecting whether anything goes wrong with the agents. It does so by analyzing the data pulled off the agents, e.g. by checking whether the value of a given MIB variable remains between the minimum and maximum thresholds.

In the early days of SNMP, its designers promoted a concept known as *trap-directed polling* [215, p. 20; 249, pp. 79–81]. Upon receipt of a notification from an agent, a manager was expected to poll a number of MIB variables on this agent to work out the cause of the reported problem. This vision was abandoned in practice because, as we just saw, agents are typically not instrumented to generate many different notifications. To learn that an agent experiences a problem, a manager must actively poll this agent; it cannot remain passive, waiting for incoming notifications.

Vendor-specific management GUIs

Management platforms generally come with a few generic management GUIs, but many customers complement them with vendor-specific management GUIs. The latter are dedicated to one specific vendor, and sometimes even limited to one line of products of a vendor (e.g., IP routers or ATM switches); they offer user-friendly GUIs, customized for a specific piece of equipment. For instance, to report that a port has gone down on a network device, a vendor-specific GUI typically displays a picture of the connectors at the back of the device (the image looks exactly like the real device), and turns the corresponding port red; this makes it easy for an operator to check that the corresponding connector is not loose. A generic GUI, conversely, simply represents a generic device with ports randomly placed; this view does not look like the real device, and finding the actual location of the corresponding port on the device can be time consuming for a novice operator.

Vendor-specific management GUIs are common today in Network Operations Centers (NOCs), because they make the operators' life a lot easier. They have an important drawback, however: They defeat the purpose of open management. The ultimate for open management is to create a commodity market of network devices and systems. If vendor A is less expensive than vendor B, we buy equipment from vendor A; a few months later, if vendor B is less expensive, we purchase from vendor B, irrespective of the equipment we already own: all systems, all devices are interchangeable. But once NOCs use vendor-specific GUIs, accepting new suppliers implies retraining operators—something companies legitimately want to avoid. Differences between Command-Line Interfaces (CLIs) from different vendors make this issue of retraining even worse. With these discrepancies, equipment vendors have managed to segment a large commodity market into a collection of captive markets, which are obviously more lucrative [159].

No distribution between managers

The organizational model of the SNMPv1, v2c, and v3 management architectures is centralized. There is currently no standard and open way of distributing management across a hierarchy of managers in SNMP-based management, especially when the managers are written by different vendors. This issue will be studied in Section 4.1. To work around this limitation, some vendors support distributed management through proprietary extensions.

One consequence of this lack of support for open distributed management is that problems that occur on management-domain boundaries are generally difficult to analyze, and are often dealt with by people on an *ad hoc* basis. Another problem is that it is *very* difficult to merge two administrative domains when the managers are developed by different vendors—so much so that some companies simply give up, and continue to manage two separate networks with two different management platforms. The need for such a merge arises when a large corporation buys a company and looks for "synergies" to cut costs.

Most management platforms support only a fraction of FCAPS

In the telecommunications world, management platforms generally support most (if not all) of the OSI functional areas (FCAPS [52, 53]). It is not the case in the IP world, where most platforms support only a fraction of FCAPS. Management platforms are usually much simpler (hence less expensive) in the IP world than their counterparts in the telecommunications world. We distinguish two types of management tasks in the IP world: mandatory tasks and optional tasks.

Mandatory tasks are performed by the vast majority of the management platforms found on the market. They are the following:

- Monitoring for the purpose of reactive fault management, reactive performance management, and reactive provisioning.
- Data collection for the purpose of proactive fault management, proactive performance management, and proactive provisioning.
- Data analysis (because agents cannot work out the origin of problems by themselves).
- Event correlation. Events can be SNMPv1 traps (`trap` PDU), SNMPv2 notifications (`SNMPv2-trap` PDU), SNMPv3 informs (`inform` PDU), or events generated by the manager's monitoring engine.

Management tasks that are supported by only some management platforms are called *optional tasks*. They include configuration management, inventory management, user management, accounting, billing, and log analysis.

MIBs offer instrumentation APIs

Due to the way the SNMP market developed over time, SNMP MIBs offer only low-level APIs, often called *instrumentation MIBs*. These MIBs deal only with the nuts and bolts of NSM. Unfortunately, as we will see in Section 4.2.2.1, administrators would rather use high-level MIBs, which are better suited to the way humans think. This limitation is not inherent in the SNMP management architecture itself, or its information model: it is simply historical.

Note that the current work of the IETF Policy Framework Working Group could eventually bring an end to this lack of high-level MIBs in the SNMP world.

New MIBs appear at a slow pace

In the IETF Working Groups, MIBs are created and modified by consensus. This is at the heart of the IETF's business model. Reaching consensus takes time, so new MIBs appear at a slow pace. As time goes by, the commercial interests behind any technical decision become increasingly important, and more and more vendors get involved in the IETF Working Groups with both technical and commercial agendas. As a result, decisions take even more time to be made. This phenomenon is illustrated by the slow pace at which the standardization of policy-based management has progressed since it is reasonably well understood (that is, since the mid-1990s [181, 235, 289, 5]).

Tightly coupled data repository

For commercial rather than technical reasons, customers in the IP world depend on peer-to-peer agreements between SNMP-based management-platform vendors and third-party database vendors. This is due to the tight coupling of the data repository and the management platform in this market.

If a customer already owns and masters a Relational DataBase Management System (RDBMS), and then purchases a management platform[1], he/she cannot necessarily use this RDBMS to store management data: This database must be already supported by the management platform of his/her choice. Since only a fraction of the databases on the market are supported by each management platform, he/she has to be lucky... Alternatively, customers can ask vendors to port their management platforms to a given RDBMS, but the price is prohibitive for most companies. This uncomfortable situation is caused by the way management-platform developers usually write their code and interface with data repositories in the SNMP world: They use the proprietary APIs provided by RDBMS vendors to get the best performance out of the databases. While this renders database accesses efficient, it also makes it costly to support multiple RDBMSes.

No integrated management

The last important characteristic of SNMP-based management is its lack of support for integrated management. This is not due to intrinsic limitations in the SNMP management architecture, but rather to the lack of interest (or, at least, the lack of deliverables) in integrated management within the IETF Working Groups. As a result, enterprises run different management platforms from different vendors in parallel and independently. Today, there is no standard and open way of integrating all types of enterprise management in the IP world. The few management platforms that currently integrate management to a certain extent (e.g., HP OpenView and CA Unicenter TNG) do so by using proprietary mechanisms.

---

1. This situation was frequent in 1990–95, as RDBMSes spread earlier than SNMP-based management platforms.

3.2 Strengths of SNMP-Based Management

Before we set about criticizing the SNMP management architecture, the SNMP protocol, and SNMP-based management platforms, let us first acknowledge the tremendous success experienced by SNMP, especially SNMPv1. At the turn of the millennium, most IP networks in the world were managed with SNMP. SNMP-based management is one of the great successes of open systems to date, together with Linux and a few others.

As we were reviewing the main characteristics of SNMP-based management in the previous section, we came across the following strengths of SNMP-based management:

• interoperability
• simplicity
• wide support by IP-equipment vendors
• small footprint on agents
• low extra cost of adding management to a network device or system
• same minimal middleware everywhere

In light of the technologies widely used today, many design decisions in SNMP-based management appear inefficient or outdated, as we mentioned in the introduction. But they did not in the late 1980s, when SNMPv1 was devised. Moreover, if we place ourselves in a historical perspective and take into account how the management market evolved [159], many deficiencies in today's commercial management platforms can be analyzed and understood. The success of SNMP-based management, especially in network management, is due to a large extent to its simplicity, so it would be unfair to criticize this simplicity afterward. In short, the designers of SNMP deserve to be congratulated rather than booed! They did a great job in the context of proprietary management that characterized the late 1980s. Turning a closed, proprietary market into an open, standard-based market within a few years is a remarkable accomplishment.

3.3 Problems with SNMP-Based Management

During more than a decade of operational use in the IP world, SNMP-based management has exposed a number of problems. Some of them are minor, but others are serious and require drastic changes in the management architecture, communication protocol, or management platforms. In this section, we describe the main problems that we have identified. We distinguish scalability issues, missing features, and non-technical issues. For each of them, we briefly summarize the solution offered by WIMA

3.3.1 Scalability and efficiency issues

Throughout the 1990s, several independent evolutions gradually exposed a major weakness in the SNMP management architecture: scalability. It is mainly affected by four factors.

The first factor is network overhead. In NSM, *network overhead* is the proportion of a link capacity used to transfer management data, and thus unavailable for user data. The purpose of a network is to transfer user data, not management data, so the lower the network overhead the better. In general, network overhead should not account for more than a small percentage of the network capacity—except for the manager's local segment, as we will see. The upper bound for management-related network overhead varies from site to site; typical values are 1% for fast LANs and 5% for slow WANs. The traffic associated with NSM is considered *entirely* as network overhead, so an important goal in NSM is to keep network overhead low. For a given capacity, network overhead increases almost linearly[1] with the amount of management data that is transferred.

The second factor is latency. For polling, *latency* is the time elapsed between the moment the manager requests the value of a MIB variable and the time it receives it from the agent. It is important to keep latency reasonably low. If it is too high, the manager can reach a point where it does not fulfill its mission: It detects operational problems too slowly and corrects them too late, thereby possibly causing new problems. Latency can be split into two components. *End-host latency* includes marshaling and unmarshaling of data, compression and decompression, security-key computation, etc. It mostly depends on the effectiveness of the communication protocol, and we will see that the SNMP protocol leaves a lot to be desired in this respect. Keeping end-host latency low on the manager frees up some resources that can be allocated to the actual management application. Keeping it low on the agent prevents the management processing overhead from hampering the operation of the agent[2]. *Network latency* includes the time spent in the network links (propagation delay) and network equipment. It depends on the capacity and error rates of the links, on the speed of the IP routers traversed between the agent and the manager (software- or hardware-based routing, busy or empty input-output queues), on the speed of the switching fabric, etc. The main effect of the management application on network latency is the amount of data to move about. This impact varies with the network overhead. The main effect of the communication protocol on network latency is the number of messages that are exchanged (see Section 3.3.1.2).

The third factor with a direct impact on scalability is the manager's processing capacity. The manager's hardware resources (CPU, memory, etc.) that are dedicated to the management application cannot be indefinitely increased, due to cost and hardware constraints; so there is only so much that the manager can process per time unit. In Section 4.1.1, we will explain that the three SNMP management architectures (v1, v2c, and v3) follow a centralized paradigm. This exacerbates the need to relieve the manager from performing any superfluous processing.

The fourth factor is the capacity of the manager's local segment[3]. This is a direct consequence of the centralization of management. The management data sent by all the agents converges toward a single point: the network segment to which the manager is connected. By design, this creates a bottleneck. It is therefore important to reduce the

---

1. In fact, it is a non-continuous piecewise linear function due to the IP-, transport-, and application-layer headers.
2. After all, the purpose of an agent is to fulfill its mission, not to be managed!

network overhead as much as possible, in order to postpone the threshold at which the manager's local segment saturates and cannot cope anymore with all the incoming data. One way to achieve this is to improve the efficiency of the communication protocol. Note that for large or busy networks, the manager's local segment is usually *dedicated* to management: Network overhead is not limited to just a small percentage on this segment, but solely by the segment capacity.

The SNMP protocol and the SNMP management architecture exhibit problems with respect to all of these scalability factors. Eight problems are described in this section.

3.3.1.1 No mechanism to cope with ever more management data

Since the inception of SNMP, the total amount of management data that must be transferred over the network, and processed by the manager, has augmented relentlessly. Despite the increase in the installed network capacity (by one or two orders of magnitude for LANs, between one and three for WANs), the network overhead caused by management data is larger today than in 1990, and is expected to continue to grow. We identified three core reasons for this need to transfer and process ever more management data.

First, the number of agents to manage has soared, because:

- The installed base of IP network devices and systems has increased dramatically throughout the 1990s. Most of the growth was fueled by PCs until the late 1990s. Since then, wireless, Web-enabled handheld devices are spreading fast.
- The proportion of equipment supporting TCP/IP has grown very rapidly. Today, the TCP/IP stack is almost ubiquitous. In contrast, most PCs did not have a TCP/IP stack when SNMPv1 was released.
- The proportion of networked equipment has grown asymptotically toward 100% in the 1990s, whereas many machines (especially PCs) were stand-alone in the late 1980s.

Second, the total amount of management data that needs to be retrieved per agent has accrued significantly, because:

- Agents support more MIBs today than in the early 1990s. The days are over when an IP router supported only MIB-II and a vendor-specific MIB.
- The size of many SNMP tables has increased with the size of the networks (e.g., IP routing tables, TCP connection tables, and accounting tables).
- The number of ports per interconnection device has increased by an order of magnitude between the typical equipment of the early 1990s (routers, bridges, and repeaters) and the typical equipment of the early 2000s (level-3 switches, level-2 switches, switching hubs, and intelligent hubs).

---

3. A *segment* is a section of a network that is bounded by switches, routers, or bridges. In the past, it referred to a piece of wire, e.g. an Ethernet segment. Today, in the days of switched LANs, the technology has changed but the old term is still used. The *local segment* of a machine is the segment to which its network interface is connected; singlehomed machines have one local segment, multihomed machines have several. When a machine is singlehomed, its local segment is traversed by *all* the traffic to and from this machine.

- A growing proportion of enterprises critically depend on their networks for the smooth running of their business. As a result, they follow more closely than ever the health of their networking equipment (smart proactive management with management platforms, as opposed to simple reactive management performed manually).
- One of the golden rules of network architects is over-provisioning; but it is costing more and more as networks grow in size. Usage monitoring (see Section 6.1) helps reduce the over-provisioning ratio and allows for substantial savings.

Third, the amount of management data to move about and process is expected to continue to increase in the future, because:

- The installed base of IP network devices and systems keeps growing, year after year.
- The advent of multimedia networks and pseudo real-time services (e.g., streaming video) calls for QoS management, and thus more transfers of management data.
- Service management, which only recently appeared in the IP world, generates extra management data.
- If SNMPv3 is used in the future, some of its most useful new features (authentication and access control) require large configuration tables to be transferred over the network, especially View-based Access Control Model (VACM) tables [291].

SNMP-based management cannot cope indefinitely with this increase in the amount of data transferred over the network and processed by the manager. To keep network overhead low on each network link, there is a limit to the amount of management data that each agent can send. To keep the manager's latency low, there is an upper bound on the total amount of data that the manager can receive from all the agents. To ensure that the manager keeps up with the workload of the management application without falling behind, there is a maximum amount of data that can be processed per time unit. And finally, to keep the load on the manager's local segment below its saturation point, there is a limit to the total amount of data that can be sent by the agents to the manager. As the amount of management data grows indefinitely, sooner or later we must reach one of these limits: It is not possible, due to cost and hardware constraints, to increase indefinitely the capacity of all the network links and the manager's processing capacity. SNMP-based management has no built-in mechanisms to avoid these four threshold effects.

In WIMA, we face the same increase in the amount of management data to transfer and process; this is a given for all management architectures. We deal with it in two ways. First, we improve the efficiency of data transfers by changing the communication and organizational models. Second, if we reach one of the limits mentioned above, we split the management domain and distribute management across several managers.

3.3.1.2 Bulk transfers require too many SNMP messages

As the amount of data to transfer grows, it makes sense to send the data in bulk, that is, many MIB variables at a time (typically, between 10 kbytes and 1 Mbyte of data). The problem is that the SNMP protocol is not tuned to do this. In SNMPv1, v2c, and v3, the retrieval of several MIB variables at a time requires the exchange of many request-response PDUs over the network. We have identified three basic problems: the design of get-next, the get-bulk overshoot effect, and the maximum size of an SNMP message.

Design of get-next

With SNMPv1, we have only one practical option to retrieve a table: the get-next protocol operation. The problem with bulk transfers is that, by design, get-next cannot fill up SNMP messages efficiently. If the table has many rows, the manager must perform at least one get-next per row. If a table row does not fit entirely into a single SNMP message, the agent must return an error message; then, the manager issues a new get-next with a new varbind list[1] consisting of only some of the OIDs in the table row. This guess-work by the manager ("How much space will the agent require to answer my request?") is inefficient. It unnecessarily increases the number of computations by the manager and therefore augments end-host latency. Also, because the manager fills up the messages by trial and error, the filling ratio can be poor. By putting in too little data, the manager unduly increases the number of round trips, which augments the network latency, the network overhead, and the end-host latency. By putting in too much data, the manager causes an error at the agent, which unnecessarily increases network overhead, network latency, and end-host latency at the manager and the agent.

Sprenkels's get-bulk overshoot effect

With SNMPv2c and SNMPv3, we can also use the get-bulk protocol operation to retrieve a table. With get-bulk, we can retrieve more than one table row at a time. If a table row does not fill up an entire SNMP message, get-bulk is more efficient than get-next because we can transfer more data per SNMP message. This reduces the network overhead, the network latency, and the end-host latency. But the manager still has to perform some guess-work because of the maximum size of an SNMP message; Sprenkels calls this problem the *get-bulk overshoot effect* [243].

Because the manager does not know in advance the length of the table it wants to retrieve, it has to guess a value to use for the max-repetitions parameter. Using a low value causes more PDU exchanges than necessary. Using a high value, however, can result in an *overshoot* effect: The agent can return data that does not belong to the table of interest to the manager. For instance, let us suppose that max-repetitions is equal to 50 and the table only contains 10 additional rows. The agent will first receive the request, unmarshal it, and identify the input varbind list. Then, 50 times in a row, it will retrieve object values from the SNMP instrumentation, encode them with Basic Encoding Rules (BER), and store them in a large buffer in memory. Finally, it will send the SNMP message to the manager. The manager will have to decode the 50 objects in the varbind list returned by the agent, but will keep 10 and discard 40. This is a waste of network resources and a waste of

---

1. A *varbind list* is a vector of MIB variables in SNMP (*varbind* stands for *variable binding*). An OID (Object IDentifier) identifies a MIB variable in a unique way.

processing resources at both the manager and the agent: Many OIDs are BER-encoded, marshaled, transferred, unmarshaled, and BER-decoded only to be disposed of by the management application.

Scotty [228] is one of the network management applications that implement a slow-start adaptive mechanism to find out empirically a good value for `max-repetitions`. This mechanism only partially addresses the issue, however. First, if the initial seed for `max-repetitions` is too large, we still experience an overshoot effect. In the previous example, if the seed is set to 20 instead of 50 due to slow start, we process 10 useless objects instead of 40, which is better but still not very good. Second, if the initial seed for `max-repetitions` is too small, this mechanism only partially fills the first SNMP messages and more messages are sent than really necessary—again, not optimal.

Maximum size of an SNMP message

The third problem is the maximum size of an SNMP message: it is too low for bulk transfers. This size is always constrained by the following factors:

- We must have exactly one PDU per SNMP message [49].
- An SNMP message cannot expand over multiple UDP datagrams, by design of UDP (packetization is performed by a layer on top of the transport protocol).
- UDP datagrams cannot be longer than 64 kbytes [206].
- All SNMP agents must accept SNMP messages that are up to 484 octets in length, but may legally refuse longer messages [50, 283].
- Some TCP/IP stacks (especially old ones) limit the maximum size of a UDP datagram to 8 kbytes. This is a carry-over from the days when memory was a scarce and expensive resource on agents[1].
- SNMPv2c defines the concept of a *maximum message size* [49], which allows the manager to further constrain the maximum size of an SNMP message generated by the agent. The problem is that SNMPv2c does not convey this information from the manager to the agent, so it is unusable in practice. SNMPv3 solved this problem by clearly specifying how to transfer the maximum message size.

The maximum size of an SNMP message can also be constrained by the following optional factors:

- The size of a UDP datagram is limited to the Maximum Transfer Unit (MTU) if we must not fragment at the IP layer. This usually occurs on busy backbone routers, which are generally configured not to fragment IP packets so as to conserve resources for routing. This MTU is typically equal to 1,472 bytes for a LAN (1,500 bytes of Ethernet payload, less 20 bytes of IP header and 8 bytes of UDP header) and 548 bytes for a

---

1. We find a trace of this limitation in the Network File System (NFS), another application-layer protocol based on UDP. In 1989, when NFS version 2 was specified, the maximum size for data transfers was set to 8 kbytes [257, p. 21]. This limit was relaxed only in 1995, when NFS version 3 was released [44, pp. 11–12].

WAN (576-byte MTU for non-local destination network [32], less 20 bytes of IP header and 8 bytes of UDP header).

- In his famous textbook [215], Rose specifies minimum guaranteed sizes for SNMP messages for each transport domain. These values are: 1,472 octets for UDP [215, p. 171], 1,472 octets for the OSI ConnectionLess Network Service (CLNS) and Connection-Oriented Network Service (CONS) [215, p. 172], 484 octets for Appletalk's DDP [215, p. 173], and 576 octets for Novell's IPX [215, p. 174]. Although these values are not specified in any RFC, they reflect habits in the SNMP market. Note that the recommended value of 1,472 octets for UDP is identical to the LAN MTU in the previous bullet.
- A get-next request cannot retrieve more than one table row at a time.

In short, the maximum size of an SNMP message is always between 484 bytes and 64 kbytes. Typically, it is equal to 1,472 bytes for a LAN and 548 bytes for a WAN. Old SNMP agents have a maximum size of only 484 bytes.

Let us translate this in terms of SNMP messages exchanged over the network. When the manager retrieves several MIB variables or tables in one bulk, the agent must split the data into many SNMP messages: 10 kbytes divided by 1,472 yields only 7 SNMP messages, but 1 Mbyte divided by 484 requires more than 2,000 SNMP messages! If the table has many rows and each individual row is not particularly large, the SNMP messages are only partially filled, so their number is even greater when get-next is used. (This is commonly the case in networks today, because they use SNMPv1 in their majority).

This multiplication of SNMP messages is highly undesirable because the overall latency of a data transfer increases with the number of PDU exchanges. The reasons for this are fourfold. First, end-host latency increases because both the agent and the manager have to process more packets, generate or parse more headers, marshal or unmarshal more data, etc. Second, network latency augments because more SNMP messages induce more round trips and increase the overall transmission delay[1]. Third, a larger number of SNMP messages has a slightly adverse effect on network overhead because the higher the number of packets, the higher the number of headers to move about and the higher the network overhead. Last but not least, this multiplication has an impact on routers along the path between the agent and the manager, because what takes time in a router is the header parsing and analysis; once the router knows which interface to send the packet to, what the Type Of Service (TOS) field is, and what the IP options are, the length of the packet has comparatively little impact on the latency. Therefore, the more packets the larger processing overhead for all traversed IP routers. By unnecessarily increasing the number of packets, we unnecessarily fill up the buffers used by the IP routers for input and output queues, and therefore increase the risks of having buffer overflows.

---

1. Note that in networks where collisions are frequent, e.g. Ethernet-based LANs, many small packets actually have a better chance to go through without retransmissions than fewer large packets. Network latency may not be badly affected in such networks.

In WIMA, we address the issue of bulk transfers by allowing for indefinitely large messages to be exchanged between the agent and the manager (or between the mid- and top-level managers in distributed hierarchical management).

3.3.1.3 Table Retrievals

In the previous section, we described how cumbersome it is to retrieve SNMP tables with `get-next` and `get-bulk`. Two problems make this situation even worse in SNMPv1, v2c, and v3: the possible presence of holes in tables and the consistency of large tables.

Holes in sparse tables

Retrieving SNMP tables is more complicated than retrieving simple MIB variables (managed objects), because the SNMP information model does not define tables in the common sense of the term: it defines *conceptual tables*. In a conceptual table, none of the columnar objects is mandatory in a table row; in other words, conceptual tables allow their rows to have missing cells that we call *holes*. In the presence of holes, tables are called *sparse tables*. Let us illustrate this problem with an example.

With SNMPv1, a common practice for retrieving a table from an agent is to perform repeated `get-next` protocol operations at the manager. The retrieval process starts off with a varbind list initialized with the OIDs of the first row of the table. Afterward, the varbind list of each `get-next` operation holds the last retrieved OID in each column. If a hole is encountered in table row N (that is, the corresponding cell of the table is not defined by the vendor for that device), the `get-next` operation returns the next object that does have a value in that column. The row of that object is *a priori* unknown: it could be row (N+1), (N+2), etc. The manager detects a hole by comparing, column by column, the expected next OID with the OID returned by `get-next`. If they differ, the next expected OID is a hole. All this processing increases the end-host latency at the manager when the table is large, be the table sparse or not.

If none of the remaining table rows has a value in that column, then the next OID in the MIB is returned (the rule for MIBs traversal is to use a depth-first tree search). The retrieval ends when all OIDs in the returned varbind list start with a sequence that is different from that of the table; e.g., for the IP routing table of MIB-II, when none of the OIDs start with 1.3.6.1.2.1.4.21. Thus, the overshoot effect described earlier for `get-bulk` is integrated *by design* in the retrieval of conceptual tables, which is remarkably inefficient.

In retrospect, one wonders why a clean concept of table was not introduced from the outset in SNMP. Would it not be more intuitive to return the error code `noSuchInstance` when an empty cell is retrieved from a table? Four reasons may justify what appears to be, today, a weird engineering decision.

First, this scheme was devised by the designers of SNMPv1 in the late 1980s, when memory was a scarce and expensive resource in agents. The holes in sparse tables allowed vendors to save memory in the agents. Later, while agents were fitted with more memory, conceptual tables remained unchanged in SNMPv2c and SNMPv3 for backward compatibility. Probably all agents put on the market today have enough memory to store an error code in memory when a cell is empty, hence the argument of the scarcity of memory does not hold anymore.

Second, in those days, it seemed a good idea to keep network transfers as slim as possible; every single byte that could be saved had to be saved. By explicitly allowing the agent to skip holes in a table [217, pp. 3–4], the designers of SNMPv1 helped keep the network overhead low and redeemed the verbosity of BER-encoded data (see Section 3.3.1.4). Today, the speed of development of an application generally prevails over the network efficiency of the solution (there are some exceptions). Layered approaches such as CORBA or Distributed Component Object Model (DCOM) are routinely used to develop software, despite the fact that they induce a large network overhead and do little to reduce it. Therefore, it no longer makes sense to save every single byte in SNMP when most of the user traffic is grossly inefficient *vis-à-vis* network overhead.

Third, when SNMPv1 was designed, the managers were supposed to have plenty of resources (as opposed to the agents), so the extra processing induced by this convoluted encoding of tables was not deemed to be a problem. Today, networks are much larger than in the early 1980s and managers often get close to (or even reach) the limits of their resources. Putting the unnecessary burden of reconstructing oddly structured tables on the shoulders of managers is no longer considered a good idea.

Fourth, there was no `noSuchInstance` error code in SNMPv1: This code was only introduced in SNMPv2p, the precursor of SNMPv2c, and later maintained in SNMPv3.

In summary, holes in tables were not a problem when SNMPv1 was designed; but they are today, because SNMP-based management relies heavily on OIDs stored in tables and the decoding of these OIDs by the manager is inefficient and increases the latency. We need a better mechanism for table retrievals.

Consistency of large tables

A serious, yet often forgotten, problem encountered with SNMP tables is their potential inconsistency. With all existing SNMP protocols (v1, v2, and v3), the manager has no way of retrieving an entire table in a consistent state! There is no guarantee of data consistency; in the SNMP world, table retrievals are performed on a best-effort basis. If the agent updates the table in the middle of a retrieval, the manager ends up with an inconsistent view of this table. This issue is particularly critical for large tables, whose retrievals demand the exchange of many messages over the network, and for which the elapsed time between the first request and the last response can exceed the mean time between two consecutive changes of the table.

The retrieval of an entire MIB in a consistent state can reasonably be considered unrealistic: This may require that the agent halt its operation for several seconds, which, in many cases, is neither possible nor desirable. But retrieving an entire table in an atomic operation is a very reasonable expectation from administrators.

The issue of SNMP-table retrievals is not specifically addressed by WIMA because it requires a change in the SNMP information model. In WIMA, we do not define our own information model; instead, we make it possible to use just any information model. Note that the support for the `noSuchInstance` error code can easily be added to a management gateway.

3.3.1.4 Poor efficiency of BER encoding

The three SNMP protocols (v1, v2, and v3) use Basic Encoding Rules (BER) [128] to encode management data prior to sending it over the network. BER encoding can be implemented with very compact code and has a small footprint on agents. It causes a reasonable overhead on agents and managers for both encoding and decoding. But BER-encoded data is verbose: The amount of administrative data (*identifier* and *length*) is large compared to the payload (*content*). This makes the network overhead unnecessarily large. It also increases the end-host latency, because more data takes more time to marshal and unmarshal. Mitra [180] and Neufeld and Vuong [188] describe in detail the performance issues with BER.

BER encoding was not designed with a view to reducing latency or network overhead: it was just simple to implement. This simplicity was the very reason why it was selected for SNMPv1. Later, it was kept in SNMPv2 and SNMPv3 for backward compatibility. But the price to pay for this simplicity is its poor track record regarding network overhead and, to a lesser extent, latency.

The ISO has standardized three alternatives to BER. These are studied and compared by Mitra [180]. To summarize, Packed Encoding Rules (PER [129]) generate data that is approximately 30% more compact than BER-encoded data, at the expense of a significant increase in the encoding time. Distinguished Encoding Rules (DER [128]) slightly improve the encoding time over BER, and have a low impact on network overhead compared to BER; but the gain offered by DER over BER remains marginal. Canonical Encoding Rules (CER [128]) are less demanding than PER in terms of encoding time, but encoded data is more verbose. CER is better than DER if the value to encode is so large that it does not entirely fit into the available memory. Note that LightWeight Encoding Rules (LWER [124]) have been investigated but not standardized by the ISO. They decrease latency by ensuring quick encoding and decoding. But LWER-encoded data can be much larger than BER-encoded data, which has a negative effect on network overhead.

As we can see, none of these encodings are clearly superior to BER. On a case-by-case basis, some are better than others; but none are ever superior. As far as ISO encodings are concerned, there is always a trade-off between end-host latency and network overhead: we cannot win on both sides. If we gain on end-host latency, we lose on network overhead, and *vice versa*. A quick but simple encoding results in a smaller end-host latency but a larger network overhead, whereas a slow but smart encoding increases end-host latency while decreasing network overhead.

In WIMA, we solve this problem by allowing for any representation scheme and any encoding scheme in the communication model, instead of imposing BER. By compressing data, we significantly reduce network overhead while keeping latency almost unchanged.

3.3.1.5 Verbose OID naming

Another problem with SNMP-based management lies in the OID naming scheme used by the information model (that is, the naming conventions for MIB variables). When we take a close look at the OIDs that are transferred in SNMP messages, we observe a high degree of redundancy. For instance, all objects stored in MIB-II are prefixed with 1.3.6.1.2.1. If this prefix could be omitted, 20% to 50% of the OID name would be saved. More significantly, if we consider the objects stored in a table (these account for a large proportion of MIB variables), the prefixes of the OIDs are all identical up to the column number, and the index postfixes of all the entries of a single row are the same. In this case, more than 90% of the OID name is redundant. This naming scheme is really inefficient!

If we compare the OID naming scheme of SNMP with that of the Unix file system, we see that there are no concepts similar to the cd command (*change directory*) or relative paths: All OIDs are specified as absolute paths from the root iso(1). The use of relative paths within a varbind list would make OIDs shorter, especially for tables, thereby decreasing the network overhead.

The second problem associated with OID naming is that each number composing the OID (each *sub-identifier* in SNMP jargon) is BER-encoded separately—except the first two sub-identifiers, which are coded on a single byte. This is inefficient. For instance, the 9-byte OID of sysDescr in MIB-II (1.3.6.1.2.1.1.1.0) is BER-encoded as 06:08:2B:06:01:02:01:01:01:00 (10 bytes). This leaves us with a compression ratio of about one: The encoded data takes as much space as the initial data. By comparison, the compression ratios obtained with gzip on large files of textual data typically range from two to five: The compressed data is two to five times smaller than the initial data.

For these two reasons, there is ample room for decreasing network overhead by simply changing the OID naming scheme of SNMP. Note that latency is also affected: If the OID naming scheme of SNMP were more efficient, the agent would not have to encode so many integers and the manager would not have to decode them all.

In WIMA, we do not define a new naming scheme. It would require the specification of a new information model, and we want to be able to use any information model. Instead, we compress all the data, which reduces network overhead without affecting too much the latency.

3.3.1.6 No compression of management data

Strangely enough, the designers of SNMPv1 worked hard to conserve resources with conceptual tables, but they did not allow for the transparent compression of management data in transit. This unnecessarily increases network overhead and, as a result, network latency. One reason for this may be the *Myth of the Dumb Agent* [286] that we already mentioned: If the agent is "dumb" and short of resources, it does not have the CPU and memory resources to compress data dynamically.

As of SNMPv3, it is theoretically possible to compress management data by adding encryption envelopes to SNMP messages [243]. Although this feature was initially intended for encrypting data in transit, it also allows for data compression. By adding an encryption algorithm that compresses the message, the size of the messages that are transmitted over the network can be decreased substantially. Preliminary tests by Schönwälder showed that BER-encoded SNMPv3 PDUs can be compressed by 90%[1] when using the DEFLATE format [71] and get-bulk operations. By defining compression as an encryption algorithm, we can add compression to SNMPv3 without making any changes to the protocol. However, since there is no noAuthPriv security level in SNMPv3, one has to use authentication in order to take advantage of compression. This is a major limitation of this scheme, which was discussed at length by the IRTF Network Management Research Group. We came to the conclusion that it made this scheme unusable in practice.

In WIMA, management data can be easily compressed, e.g. with gzip, which significantly decreases network overhead. It increases end-host latency (the agent and the manager have to do more work), but significantly decreases network latency because there is less data to move about. Preliminary tests with our research prototype showed that the overall effect of compression on latency is almost negligible.

3.3.1.7 Polling

In the SNMPv1, v2c, and v3 management architectures, monitoring and data collection are based on polling, that is, on the pull model. This scheme is inefficient with respect to:

- *network overhead*: the manager repeatedly sends the same requests to the agents, which unnecessarily loads the network;
- *end-host latency at the manager*: the manager keeps putting together, encoding, and marshaling the same requests for sending them to the agents, which unnecessarily loads the manager;
- *end-host latency at the agent*: the agent unmarshals and decodes the same SNMP messages time and again, which unnecessarily clutters the agent's CPU and memory resources;
- *network latency*: the pull model requires a round trip whereas the push model requires a one-way transfer.

This problem is discussed in detail in Section 7.1.4.2. In WIMA, we solve it by going from a pull to a push model, which involves changing the organizational and communication models of the management architecture. This is one of the most drastic changes that we propose.

---

1. This value is only indicative. Schönwälder stresses that more tests should be performed to confirm it in general. But it already indicates that significant savings can be achieved.

3.3.1.8 Unreliable transport protocol

Another serious problem in SNMP-based management is the transport protocol used underneath the SNMP communication protocol. Why use UDP to send critical or fatal notifications to the manager? By using an unreliable transport protocol, we run the risk of losing important notifications for silly reasons such as buffer overflows in IP routers[1]. Why be exposed to the small-message-size problem described in Section 3.3.1.2, partially due to the use of UDP, when we could use TCP and large-size, application-level messages?

When the SNMPv1 protocol was devised, the underlying transport protocol was not mandated. In the IP world, it could be either UDP or TCP. In practice, virtually all commercial offerings opted for UDP from day one, sometimes on technical grounds, but generally because everyone else did (snowball effect). The technical grounds for the superiority of UDP over TCP were that TCP-based SNMP traffic makes a bad situation worse when a network is severely congested, because of TCP's three-way handshake and automatic retransmissions (both increase network overhead). This rationale was defended for years by Rose, one of the fathers of SNMP and a fervent opponent to using SNMP over TCP [215, pp. 20–22]. The relevance of this argument was destroyed by Wellens and Auerbach when they denounced the *Myth of the Collapsing Backbone* [286]. In short, most real-life networks are over-provisioned, and SNMP is of no use whatsoever for trouble-shooting serious congestions in such networks. Instead, operators typically resort to tools such as `ping`, `traceroute`, etc. This counterargument is fully endorsed by the author, as it corroborates his experience in managing real-life networks.

We identified three good reasons for choosing TCP to transport management data. First, it significantly reduces data losses (although we still have no guarantee of delivery). Two facts are often overlooked by administrators: Buffer overflows do occur in real life, and some management data is lost. The frequency of these losses is site specific, even network-link specific, and it varies considerably over time. Some administrators are unaware of the proportion of management data that never reaches the manager, including some critically important notifications. With TCP, notifications are less often lost *en route* due to buffer overflows in IP routers.

Second, TCP allows for very large application-level messages. This makes bulk transfers more efficient and diminishes network and end-host latency, as the number of messages exchanged over the network is significantly reduced (provided that the TCP window size does not change too often). TCP's window mechanism allows several chunks of data to be in transit in parallel. This suppresses the latency caused by additional round trips when a table row does not fit into a single UDP message, or when the requested `max-repetitions` parameter for a `get-bulk` request does not fit into a single UDP packet. Not only does latency decrease, but SNMP-table consistency also improves, as we shorten

---

1. Buffer overflows are a normal way to deal with bursts of traffic in the IP world. When an IP router experiences buffer overflows in its input or output queues, it silently drops packets. The origin hosts of the packets are not notified that these packets were dropped.

the time window during which the agent might update a table while the manager is recursively retrieving it.

A third reason for using a reliable transport protocol to transfer management data is to relieve the management application from managing all the timers and performing all the retries currently necessary to recover from network losses in the case of SNMP polling. In our view, this task does not belong in the application layer, but rather in the transport layer.

For the sake of completeness, we should mention that the IRTF Network Management Research Group proposed an SNMP-over-TCP transport mapping [227] as an alternative to the standard SNMP-over-UDP transport mapping [50]. To date, this work is still confined to the research community, and it is too early to tell whether this SNMP-over-TCP mapping will be adopted by the SNMP industry.

In WIMA, we solve these problems by using TCP instead of UDP. We will revisit this issue in Section 8.2.2 and present two other reasons for using TCP instead of UDP.

3.3.2 Missing features

Now that we have investigated what hampers scalability in SNMP-based management, let us identify the features that are missing altogether. Some of them pertain to security; others are related to the low level of semantics of the SNMP information model.

3.3.2.1 Security

In the security arena, the three SNMP management architectures lack the support for simple, transparent security and for going across firewalls easily.

No simple, transparent security

SNMPv1 and v2c support no security at all. Identification based on a *community string* is so simplistic that it cannot be counted as a security scheme. There is no authentication, and the community string is even transmitted in clear text over the network!

Security is the main novelty brought by SNMPv3. SNMPv3 notably supports identification, authentication, encryption, integrity, and access control [249]. This requires significant configuration (keys management, VACM tables, etc.) and is anything but transparent to the end user. SNMPv3 does not support strong security, because the keys can be stolen by a smart attacker [223]. In cryptography, SNMPv3's security scheme is considered weak because there are known ways to break it. For the purpose of NSM, we classify it as *medium security* because it offers sufficient security for most customers to date.

SNMP-based management gives us the choice between two levels of security:

- no security (SNMPv1 and SNMPv2c);
- medium security (SNMPv3).

In our view, there are actually four levels of security in NSM:

- *no security*;
- *simple security*: transparent, *à la* SSL;
- *medium security*: reasonable protection against casual attackers; suitable for people who are not paranoid about security;
- *strong security*: reasonable protection against smart attackers; appropriate for people who are paranoid about security (e.g., banks and the military).

If we compare our risk levels in NSM with those defined by Smith in a general context [238, pp. 60–61], our *simple security* roughly corresponds to his *low risk*, our *medium security* to his *medium risk*, and our *strong security* to his *high risk*. Smith defines yet another risk level, called *critical*, when the loss of life or a major disaster is at stake. In NSM, we include this last category in *strong security*. Note that total security does not exist, neither in enterprise management nor elsewhere.

In NSM, people are mostly interested in our second and third levels of security: *simple security* and *medium security*. For most sites, these levels offer enough security, but no more than needed. In SNMP-based management, we have the first and third levels of security, but we miss the second and fourth levels. In Section 3.4, "Security and firewalls", we will see that a management architecture should not rely on strong security; so it is not a problem if we miss it in SNMP-based management. But the absence of support for simple security causes a real problem.

In NSM, we need the support for simple, transparent security because this is what many small and midsize enterprises want to use. They do not want passwords to be transmitted in clear text, as in SNMPv1 and v2c: They simply want transparent identification and authentication *à la* SSL. Some enterprises also demand layer 7, layer 3, or layer 2 encryption [238] so that attackers cannot easily access their sensitive data. But to date, many companies do not really mind whether the confidentiality of management data is *always* guaranteed, because most of this data is not really confidential. In NSM, strong security comes at a price (hiring experts, buying hardware, etc.) that many enterprises are not yet willing to pay[1].

In WIMA, security is decoupled from our own communication model. We rely entirely on standard security techniques such as data-link encryption hardware [238], IP Security (IPSec [251]), HyperText Transfer Protocol (HTTP) authentication [96, 144], and Secure Sockets Layer (SSL [247]). We will elaborate on the security aspects in WIMA in Section 8.2.4.

Firewalls are difficult to cross

Firewalls were never really taken into account by the designers of SNMPv1, v2c, and v3. Each time the author discussed this issue with members of SNMP-related Working Groups

---

1. Having said that, we expect the market to become increasingly aware of security issues and to demand ever more security in NSM. As usual with technology markets, it is a question of money, maturity, and mimicry.

at the IETF, he received answers that all boiled down to this: "Why would you want to go across a firewall with SNMP?". In Section 7.2.4, we will present several scenarios justifying the need for management data to go across one or several firewall(s).

In WIMA, the communication model was changed to facilitate the crossing of firewalls.

3.3.2.2 Information model: low level of semantics

The second important feature that is missing in SNMP-based management is the support for high-level semantics in the information model. Since it will be described in great detail in Section 4.2, we just briefly summarize it here. As far as semantic richness is concerned, the main shortcomings in SNMP are the absence of high-level MIBs, the limited set of SNMP protocol primitives, and the data-oriented nature of the SNMP information model. Because of these limitations, writing smart management applications is difficult; so people often write very basic applications, which requires a great familiarity with low-level instrumentation. This partly explains why management applications are often limited to little more than monitoring in the IP world.

No high-level MIBs

In Section 3.1, "MIBs offer instrumentation APIs", we pointed out the lack of high-level MIBs in SNMP-based management. This is a major problem for management-application designers. We will elaborate on this important issue in Section 4.2.2.1.

Too few SNMP protocol primitives

Because of the *Myth of the Dumb Agent*, all SNMP protocols (v1, v2, and v3) support only three basic protocol primitives, if we aggregate them by similar semantics: get, set, and notify. This is extremely limiting. It is typical of what software engineers call a *data-oriented model*, that is, an information model devised by programmers who focus on the definition of data structures. In object-oriented software engineering, this is considered to be a mistake, known as the *Blob* antipattern [37] or the *God Class* problem [212]. Object-oriented models, on the contrary, should be devised by designers who focus on the definition of objects and relationships. Information models for NSM are no exceptions to this rule.

SNMP information model: not object oriented

Object-oriented models are widely used in industry today. Objects are certainly not the panacea; we all know that, one day, they will be replaced or complemented by another technique, maybe aspects [82]). Still, they have proved time and again their superiority over good old data-oriented modeling, and it is a shame for SNMP information modelers to be forced to use ancient modeling techniques. Strangely enough, object-oriented modeling was already in the air in the late 1980s, but the fathers of SNMPv1 did not adopt it.

The absence of an object-oriented information model in SNMP is regarded by many as one of the main shortcomings of SNMP. When the Distributed Management Task Force (DMTF) endeavored to define a new management architecture in the second half of the 1990s, it came as no surprise that its first delivery was a new object-oriented information model: the Common Information Model (CIM). CIM will be presented in Section 6.6.1.

Programming by side effect

If we combine the limited number of SNMP protocol primitives with the data-oriented nature of the SNMP information model, we see that SNMP information modelers have a lot of difficulty implementing an equivalent to *methods* in object-oriented software engineering. Because management-application designers need methods anyway, information modelers (that is, MIB designers) resort to an ugly technique known as *programming by side effect*.

To trigger an action on a remote agent, the manager sets an integer MIB variable (let us call it `doIt`) to a certain value. Different values trigger different actions. If we set `doIt` to say 39, we reboot the machine; if we set `doIt` to 57, we reset an interface; and the list goes on. This very poor design often leads to "spaghetti code" in management applications: Programmers do not use wrapper libraries offering a higher-level API, but hard-code the different values (39, 57, etc.) all over the code. This makes it impossible to maintain management applications in the long run. In software engineering, it is well known that a poor design of the API often leads to a poor design of the applications using it. It is unfortunate that SNMP does not provide management-application designers with a smarter metamodel supporting object-oriented methods.

In WIMA, we propose several ways of alleviating or correcting this problem. One of them uses CIM and XML.

3.3.3 Non-technical problems in SNMP-based management

In this section, we study the last category of problems that we identified in SNMP-based management: non-technical problems. They have to do with the multiple meanings of the term *SNMP*, SNMP-based management platforms, the need for domain-specific expertise, and SNMP's slow evolution pace.

3.3.3.1 One word, two meanings

For SNMPv1, v2c, and v3, the IETF uses the same name for the management architecture and its underlying communication protocol—unlike the International Organization for Standardization (ISO), which distinguishes the OSI management architecture from the communication protocol (CMIP—Common Management Information Protocol) and the protocol primitives (CMIS—Common Management Information Service). This has confused many people, especially when solutions were proposed to replace the SNMP communication protocol while preserving the rest of the SNMP management architecture.

This problem was acknowledged by the IETF in 1999, nine years (!) after SNMPv1 was specified, and an RFC [113] now recommends to refer explicitly to an *SNMP protocol* or an *SNMP framework* (what we call an *SNMP management architecture* in this book, see Section 2.9). But updating all the SNMP-related literature takes some time, and changing deeply rooted habits is not easy...

In WIMA, this confusion is avoided by using different names for the communication protocol, the protocol primitives, and the management architecture.

3.3.3.2 Problems with management platforms

The problems related to SNMP-based management platforms are not technical in nature; they are due to the way the management-platform market evolved over time. These problems are not inherent in the SNMP management architecture or the SNMP protocol. But as we have already had to deal with them for more than a decade, there is little hope of seeing them disappear from the SNMP market.

Customers' grievances

For customers, SNMP-based management platforms present four shortcomings. First, they are too expensive in terms of hardware and software. Small enterprises, in particular, resent being obliged to dedicate a machine to manage their small networks. Second, customers do not like to be told what database they should use to store management data. If they already own a database, they want to use it! They do not want to be constrained by preexisting peer-to-peer agreements between management-platform and database vendors (see Section 3.1, "Tightly coupled data repository"). Third, they want to be able to move the manager easily from one machine to another, e.g. from a Windows PC to a Linux PC, without having to pay for a new software package (manager). Fourth, current management platforms offer insufficient integration of management (see Section 3.4).

In WIMA, the second and fourth problems are solved. The first and third problems are only partially addressed.

Vendors' grievances

Equipment vendors are primarily dissatisfied with the huge costs they have to bear to port their device-specific management GUIs (one for IP routers, one for level-3 switches, one for ATM switches, one for intelligent hubs, one for plain hubs, etc.) to all existing management platforms, that is:

- to all existing processors: Intel X_1, X_2, X_3; Motorola Y_1, Y_2, Y_3; etc.
- to all existing operating systems: Linux X_1, X_2, X_3; Windows Y_1, Y_2, Y_3; Solaris Z_1, Z_2, Z_3; etc.
- to all existing managers: HP OpenView X_1, X_2, X_3; Cabletron Spectrum Y_1, Y_2, Y_3; etc.

This explosion of the number of different platforms to support (and test before each release of a new management GUI) leads to an exponential growth in the development and testing costs incurred by equipment vendors. Over time, developers of vendor-specific management GUIs have learned to live with this heterogeneity, and wrapper code generally hides system-specific idiosyncrasies from the rest of the management application. This reduces the development costs, but definitely not the testing costs.

This problem is solved in WIMA by embedding Java management applets into network and systems equipment, and by relying on the portability of Java code.

Customers and vendors' common grievances

Some grievances are shared by customers and equipment vendors alike. First, they all want to reduce the time-to-market of vendor-specific management GUIs. In SNMP-based management, there is often a time lag of several months between the time a new piece of hardware appears on the market and the time a customer can purchase a vendor-specific management GUI for his/her favorite management platform. Ideally, customers and vendors would like any IP network device and any IP system to be manageable via a nice management GUI (not a mere MIB browser) as soon as it is launched on the market.

Second, in order to attract more customers, start-up companies want to have access to the major management platforms. So do their customers, because this enables them to drive their costs down by increasing competition. Too often, start-ups cannot afford the peer-to-peer agreements that give equipment vendors (i) access to the APIs of the major management platforms of the market, and (ii) an entry in the catalogs of the major management-platform vendors. Neither can they afford the development costs for porting their management GUI to myriads of management platforms. Ideally, a start-up would like its customers to be able to download their vendor-specific management GUIs into any management platform, without the start-up having to pay royalties to any management-platform vendor. Instead, in SNMP-based management, customers typically use a separate, dedicated management platform when they buy a piece of equipment from a start-up. This defeats the purpose of open management. While the author was working in industry, this problem proved to be a major restriction when purchasing new equipment.

Third, both vendors and customers need a solution to the problem of MIB versioning. From time to time, equipment vendors release a new version of their proprietary MIB and management GUIs. As it is not possible to upgrade all the agents and the manager simultaneously, and as old pieces of equipment may not support the latest vendor-specific MIB, customers have to live with several versions of a MIB coexisting in the same network, either temporarily or permanently. Unfortunately, there is no MIB-discovery protocol in SNMP[1]. Thus, it is not easy to maintain the manager's knowledge of an agent's MIB

---

1. Agent capabilities (e.g., MIBs) can be documented in sysORTable [51]. In theory, this feature could be used to implement a MIB-discovery protocol. In practice, administrators cannot rely on it because it appeared only in 1996, with the second SNMPv2 generation, and most sites still use SNMPv1. Moreover, among SNMPv2c- and SNMPv3-compliant agents, some do not maintain the sysORTable table up to date.

version synchronized with the actual version of this MIB in that agent. Some management platforms require that the manager be updated manually; others demand that it be updated externally via scripts; yet others do not allow several versions of a MIB to coexist in a manager.

In WIMA, all of these problems are solved by embedding management applets into network and systems equipment.

3.3.3.3 Domain-specific expertise

SNMP expertise is domain specific, hence rare and expensive. In particular, new SNMP programmers need specific training. This may seem absurd to a newcomer in SNMP-based management. If we compare the technical merits of SNMP (especially the SNMP protocol) with those of other existing technologies, they hardly compete because the design of SNMP is, by and large, outdated. Is SNMP another incarnation of the *Reinvent the Wheel* antipattern [37]?

It is not, because it came first in the IP world. When SNMPv1 was devised, none of the technologies that we use in WIMA existed. Therefore, it made sense in the late 1980s to define a new protocol and a new management architecture: the existing ones were inappropriate. But now that the *corpus* of Internet technologies has grown enormously, and many of these technologies are routinely reused in different domains, it no longer makes sense to use a domain-specific technology for management, especially for the communication protocol. Transferring management data is not vastly different from transferring user data!

In WIMA, we solve this problem by using standard and ubiquitous Web technologies.

3.3.3.4 SNMP evolves too slowly

The last problem that we identified in SNMP-based management is its inability to evolve quickly enough to meet the market's demands in a timely manner. Despite the growing expectations and needs of the market (see Section 3.4), the IETF Working Groups in charge of SNMP progressed too slowly in the 1990s. Two of the reasons for the initial success of SNMPv1 were that it was lightweight compared to OSI management, and it did not have to go through the four-year standardization cycles of the International Telecommunication Union—Telecommunication standardization sector (ITU-T). But experience has shown that SNMP sometimes evolves at an even slower pace. SNMPv1 was released in 1990. In 1994, SNMPv2p proved to be a failure [168; 201; 249, p. 334]. In 1996, SNMPv2c added very little to SNMPv1 and hardly justified the headaches of a massive upgrade. In the end, it took eight years before the IETF delivered a substantial new release, SNMPv3, and another two years before major companies began supporting it[1]. By this time, the market had lost confidence in the ability of SNMP to meet its needs. The SNMP brand was *passé*.

---

1. For instance, Cisco officially supports it since March 2000, when IOS 12.1 was released [61].

Despite all the good work that was done by the SNMPv3 and DIStributed MANagement (DISMAN) Working Groups at the IETF, many customers reportedly do not even contemplate the prospect of using SNMPv3 in the future. In the next management cycle, we expect SNMPv1 to survive unchanged as a simple solution for monitoring network equipment, while alternatives to SNMP will be used to perform more advanced management tasks.

Only time will tell whether the WIMA management architecture is able to evolve and meet the changing needs of the market. But our clear separation between management-specific and generic components gives us confidence in its resilience, for it allows us to leverage the latest technologies standardized by the W3C, IETF, DMTF, OMG, etc. without changing the management architecture itself.

3.4 We Need a New Solution to a New Problem

In view of all the problems reviewed in Section 3.3, one could be tempted to criticize the designers of SNMPv1 for overlooking or poorly engineering so many things. However, this would be grossly unfair. First, we recalled in Section 3.2 the strengths and achievements of SNMP. SNMP has been a tremendous success story in network management. Today, most IP network devices deployed in the world are managed with SNMP-based management platforms. Second, we should keep in mind that retrospective analysis is an easy art. With hindsight, it is simple to analyze how things should have been designed in the first place. It is considerably more difficult to make the same analysis beforehand. Third, the requirements for managing IP networks and systems have changed considerably since the inception of SNMP, more than a decade ago. The problem that we are trying to solve today is different from the problem that was successfully solved in the late 1980s. No wonder SNMP is not appropriate for NSM today!

In this section, we substantiate this third argument by summing up the requirements that we identified for tomorrow's network and systems management. In the remainder of this book, we will see how WIMA fulfills these requirements.

Scalability

The main requirement for tomorrow's NSM is that we *must* improve the scalability of the management architecture for the next management cycle. SNMP-based management is centralized, and there is no way it can cope forever with the continuous increase in the amount of management data to move about and process (see Section 3.3.1.1). There are many agents deployed worldwide that are not "dumb" at all and have plenty of memory and CPU cycles to offer.

In WIMA, scalability was the first issue that we addressed. Our push model requires agents to do more than in SNMP-based management while not imposing on them the footprint of full-blown, object-oriented middleware like CORBA.

Cost

In its early days, SNMP-based management was reasonably inexpensive. The extra cost of adding an SNMP agent to a network device was small for equipment vendors, and the support for SNMP was a selling argument, so vendors did not charge a lot for SNMP. The first management platforms on the market were perhaps minimalist and concentrated on monitoring, but they were inexpensive.

Over time, the initial vision of a commodity market allowing for open management evolved toward a mosaic of secure, niche markets where competition is seriously hampered by peer-to-peer agreements between vendors [159]. With this new business model, the management-platform market has become unfavorable to customers. The marketing concept of a *preferred business partner* basically means that sheer competition does not work and prices remain artificially[1] high.

In the next management cycle, the business model of the management-platform market should be changed to reduce the costs for both equipment vendors and customers, and to place start-up companies on a par with larger equipment vendors. Some customers want to pay less for the same service, that is, only integrate NSM in a single management platform. Other customers want to pay the same amount of money, or marginally more, for a better service: They want full-blown integrated management (see p. 55, section "Integrated management"). To meet these demands, vendors must find a way to reduce the amount of money that they charge per management task. To do so while preserving their margins, they must significantly cut the design, development, testing, and maintenance costs of their vendor-specific management GUIs.

In WIMA, embedded management applets and component-based management platforms allow precisely for that.

Higher level of semantics

The third requirement for the next management cycle is to improve the user-friendliness of NSM in the IP world. When analyzed by a software engineer of the 2000s, the SNMP protocol and the SNMP management architecture seem outdated in many respects. Designers and programmers in industry are used to manipulating higher levels of semantics, and to working at a higher level of abstraction than what management-platform APIs typically offer them today in SNMP-based management. People should be offered the same kind of user-friendly environments, whether they design and develop a distributed application for integrated management, aeronautics, or banking. Nothing inherent in enterprise management forces application designers and programmers to work at an instrumentation level. This habit in SNMP-based management only has historical reasons.

In WIMA, we either use CIM, the object-oriented information model devised by the DMTF during the late 1990s, or wrap low-level information models like SNMP's with XML.

---

1. As opposed to the *natural equilibrium* that competitive markets are supposed to reach, according to some economists.

Security and firewalls

When SNMPv1 was devised, most enterprises did not care about network and systems security because the Internet was not what it is today. Security concerns have grown enormously during the 1990s, especially after attacks on well-known Web sites and e-mail-based virus infections were largely advertised by the press. As a result, firewalls are now very common, and customers have become much more demanding in terms of security. They want management platforms that offer them secure management and management of security.

Another requirement imposed by many customers is that the management architecture for the next management cycle must not require strong security. Strong security can be implemented at different levels. Data-link encryption hardware is the most secure way of simultaneously guaranteeing access control, authentication, confidentiality, integrity, non-repudiation, etc. It works by making the traffic incomprehensible to an eavesdropper. But to date, apart from banks and the military, most enterprises cannot afford this type of hardware; it is very expensive and thus cannot be mandated in general.

Alternatively, strong security can be based on strong cryptography. Cryptographic protocols work with keys, some public, others private [238, 250]. These keys pose two problems. The first problem is technical. Although the complex mathematics of cryptography are now reasonably well understood, the more mundane engineering issue of key management in a geographically dispersed enterprise is still considered an unsolved problem. The main issues at stake are key certification, key infrastructure, and trust models [175]. The second problem is commercial. How can we have all NSM vendors agree to abide by the same interoperable security standards in management when they have been selling proprietary security solutions for years? Consider how long it takes major credit-card organizations to convince the industry to adopt and widely deploy a single standard (Secure Electronic Transaction) for secure e-commerce, in a business that depends *entirely* on interoperability to live. We can guess how difficult it would be in the management industry, which can live happily without security interoperability... In short, it would be very unwise to make strong security mandatory in NSM.

In the next management cycle, management applications must be able to communicate across firewalls, and should support different levels of security. In Section 3.3.2.1, "No simple, transparent security", we proposed three levels: no security, simple security, and medium security. Support for strong security should only be optional.

In WIMA, we took into account the importance of firewalls and changed our communication model to facilitate their traversal for management purposes.

Integrated management

The final requirement for managing tomorrow's IP networks and systems is to integrate enterprise management. We propose a three-phase integration path for the next management cycle.

First, we should integrate systems management across all markets: network devices, Windows PCs, Linux PCs, Unix workstations, Web-enabled handheld devices, distributed systems, etc. Today, systems management is, to a great extent, proprietary—especially for Windows PCs. Now that network management has successfully shown the way, systems management ought to move to open management technologies and architectures. No technical reasons can justify why customers should currently use separate platforms for managing different types of system.

Second, network management should be integrated with systems management. Not only would this integration reduce the running costs of NOCs, it would also allow for a more accurate event correlation. When systems management is decoupled from network management, we leave it to a human to correlate network problems (e.g., the crash of a router) with systems problems (e.g., the lack of responsiveness of a server). Rule-based systems can automate this task provided that NSM is integrated.

Third, for several years, customers have been requesting the full-scale integration of all types of enterprise management. In particular, they want management platforms to swiftly integrate service management and policy-based management. The rationale is that by integrating all the management tasks, administrators will be able to better automate management, to routinely support what is currently exceptionally offered (e.g., QoS management and dynamic service provisioning). By migrating from a largely reactive management paradigm to a more proactive paradigm, they will reduce the sources of potential problems.

In WIMA, we address the first two levels: integration of systems management in a hetero-geneous environment, and integration of network and systems management. We decided to leave the third level of integration for future work, although preliminary investigations suggest that WIMA can be extended to application, service, and policy-based management.

3.5 Summary

This concludes our problem statement. In Section 3.1, we reviewed the main characteristics of SNMP-based management and described the concepts of "dumb" agent, polling, and vendor-specific management GUIs. We saw that in the IP world, monitoring is not notifi-cation driven. In Section 3.2, we summarized the main strengths of SNMP-based management. Even though the aim of this book is primarily to replace SNMP with a new management architecture, better suited to today's requirements, it is important to keep in mind that SNMP-based network management was very successful in the 1990s. In Section 3.3, we identified the main problems in SNMP-based management. Some of them are due to the scalability of the management architecture and the efficiency of the communication protocol. Others result from the lack of support for certain important features. Yet other problems are related to management platforms, domain-specific expertise, and the capacity of SNMP to evolve in a timely manner. Finally, in Section 3.4, we explained why we need a new solution to a new problem, and summarized the main requirements for the next management cycle.

Chapter 4

OVERVIEW OF THE SOLUTION SPACE

Our goal in this chapter is to answer the question: "How *could* we manage IP networks and systems tomorrow?". In Chapter 5, we will analyze the solutions presented here and try to answer the question: "How *should* we manage IP networks and systems tomorrow?".

To achieve this, we endeavor to classify most, and hopefully all, open[1] NSM technologies known to date into a limited set of paradigms, and give criteria to assess and weigh the relative merits of different paradigms and technologies. We propose two ways of categorizing NSM paradigms; we call them the *simple taxonomy*[2] and the *enhanced taxonomy*.

The main contribution of this chapter is to provide administrators with sound technical grounds to choose management paradigms and technologies, and to take an evolutionary rather than a revolutionary approach to NSM. Many vendors like to sell "revolutionary" solutions because they bring in more revenue in the short term, and because they enable them to sell hype based on thin air rather than real features implemented through hard work. The goal of administrators, conversely, is to find an evolutionary path in the midst of these revolutionary approaches, and to save money in the short and long run.

Another contribution is to show that there is no win-win solution: Different technologies are good at managing different enterprises. Evolving IP networks and systems and evolving needs and requirements call for evolving NSM solutions.

---

1. In this book, we ignore proprietary solutions such as Microsoft's DCOM.
2. In organization theory, people generally refer to a *typology* when they mean a *classification by types* [115]; so did the author initially [157, 158]. But several people pointed out that usage has opted for the word *taxonomy* in computer science, so we now use this term. In their meanings of interest to us, these two words are synonymous.

57

The remainder of this chapter is organized as follows. In Section 4.1, we present our simple taxonomy, based on a single criterion: the organizational model. In this taxonomy, NSM paradigms are grouped into four broad types: centralized, weakly distributed hierarchical, strongly distributed hierarchical, and strongly distributed cooperative paradigms. We then expose the strengths and weaknesses of this simple taxonomy, and explain why we need to enhance it. In Section 4.2.1, we draw a parallel between the ways in which enterprises and networks are organized; we delineate a common trend and identify the delegation granularity as a criterion for our enhanced taxonomy. We then introduce the concepts of microtask and macrotask. In Section 4.2.2, we study three other criteria retained for our enhanced taxonomy: the semantic richness of the information model, the degree of automation of management, and the degree of specification of a task. This leads us to our enhanced taxonomy, depicted in Section 4.2.3.

4.1 Simple Taxonomy of Network and Systems Management Paradigms

Let us begin with our simple taxonomy of NSM paradigms. When we built it, we tried to meet seven objectives:

- provide an intuitive categorization of NSM paradigms;
- identify a small number of types;
- clearly separate centralized paradigms from distributed paradigms;
- highlight the differences between traditional and new paradigms;
- distinguish paradigms relying on vertical and horizontal delegation;
- enable administrators and management-application designers to find out easily what paradigm is implemented by a given technology;
- help administrators and management-application designers classify quickly a new NSM technology.

To keep this taxonomy simple and thereby meet the first two objectives, we decided to base it on a single criterion: the organizational model. This choice is rather intuitive and was already made by other authors [117, 148], although their classifications are not as complete as ours. To meet the third objective, we began with two types: the centralized paradigm and distributed paradigms. The *centralized paradigm* concentrates all the management-application processing into a single node, the manager, and reduces all the agents to the role of "dumb" data collectors. *Distributed paradigms*, conversely, spread the management application across several machines.

To meet the fourth objective, we further divided the *distributed paradigms* type. By studying the different technologies that implement distributed management, we realized that regardless of their idiosyncrasies, they could all be classified into two categories, according to the role played by the agents in the management application. We called them *weakly* and *strongly* distributed technologies; they implement weakly and strongly distributed paradigms.

Weakly distributed paradigms are characterized by the fact that the management-application processing is concentrated in only a few nodes. For example, the network is split into different management domains, with one manager per domain, while all the agents remain limited to the role of "dumb" data collectors. Another example is to keep a single manager but to make a few agents smarter than the others. In both cases, we have one or two orders of magnitude between the number of smart machines and the number of "dumb" machines. Only a small proportion of the network devices and systems are involved in the actual management-application processing.

Strongly distributed paradigms decentralize management processing down to every agent. Management tasks are no longer confined to a happy few: All agents and managers are involved. Many strongly distributed technologies have been suggested in the past years. As we will explain in Section 4.1.3, we found it natural to group them into three sets of paradigms: mobile code, distributed objects, and intelligent agents. The first two implement vertical delegation; we call them the *strongly distributed hierarchical paradigms*. The third implements horizontal delegation; we call this family the *strongly distributed cooperative paradigms*. This distinction allows us to meet our fifth objective.

Our simple taxonomy thus consists of four types:

- centralized paradigm
- weakly distributed hierarchical paradigms
- strongly distributed hierarchical paradigms
- strongly distributed cooperative paradigms

We refer to the first two as the *traditional paradigms*, and to the last two as the *new paradigms*. The strong distribution of the management application is a characteristic of new paradigms. The fourth type is also called *cooperative paradigms* for short, because the cooperative paradigms that we consider in NSM are always strongly distributed[1].

Our first five objectives have now been met. Let us delve into the details of these management paradigms and review the main technologies that implement them. We assume that the reader is familiar with the traditional management paradigms and protocols, that is, the different variants of SNMP, OSI management, Telecommunications Management Network (TMN), and Remote MONitoring (RMON). These are presented by many authors [3, 117, 148, 151, 201, 202, 215, 218, 236, 246, 249, 296]. New paradigms and new protocols will be presented in more detail. At the end of this section, we will summarize our simple taxonomy in a synthetic diagram that will allow us to meet our sixth and seventh objectives.

---

1. This is not necessarily true in other fields; e.g., in DAI, some forms of cooperation rely on a central entity.

4.1.1 Centralized paradigm

The centralized paradigm is characterized by a single manager concentrating all the management-application processing, and a collection of agents limited to the role of "dumb" data collectors (see Section 3.1, "All agents are created equal... and "dumb""). Both SNMP- and HTTP-based management follow a centralized paradigm.

4.1.1.1 SNMP-based management

To date, in the IP world, most networks and systems are managed with centralized platforms based on SNMPv1 [46]. As we saw in Section 3.2, the success of this management architecture has been phenomenal. But exposure to real-life networks and systems showed a major weakness in it, and more generally in the centralized paradigm: scalability (see Section 3.3.1). SNMPv1 is good at managing relatively small networks, but it does not scale to large networks (e.g., geographically dispersed enterprises) and cannot cope with ever more management data.

Soon, people realized that a new SNMP-based management paradigm was needed to address scalability. The telecommunications world had already shown how to solve this problem: by distributing the management application across a hierarchy of managers (see Section 4.1.2.1). But strangely enough, this type of distribution of management was never a priority at the IETF. Since SNMPv1, four management architectures have been specified: SNMPv2p, SNMPv2u, SNMPv2c, and SNMPv3. We will see in Section 4.1.2.2 that SNMPv2p is now obsolete. SNMPv2u "saw no significant commercial offering" [201, p. 14] and is no longer used. SNMPv2c is useful to manage busy backbone routers, because it supports 64-bit counters and offers better error handling than SNMPv1; but it brings nothing new regarding distribution. As for SNMPv3, its main focus is on security, not scalability [248]. In short, the three SNMP management architectures used to date (SNMPv1, SNMPv2c, and SNMPv3) still do not support the distribution of NSM across a hierarchy of managers. In Section 4.1.2.2 and Section 4.1.3.1, we will show that they can support the delegation of tasks to some agents (with RMON and the Script MIB). However, SNMP-based management generally follows a centralized paradigm.

4.1.1.2 HTTP-based management

Since the mid-1990s, with the Web becoming ubiquitous, inexpensive, and so easy to use, many people have argued that Web technologies were the way to go for NSM in the IP world [120]. New vendors, most notably start-ups, saw an opportunity to enter the lucrative market of management platforms. This led to a large family of approaches known as *Web-based management*, which supports different management paradigms. In this section, we describe the approaches implementing a centralized paradigm. In Section 4.1.3, we will present those implementing strongly distributed hierarchical paradigms. Web-based management will be revisited in great detail in Chapter 6, so we remain concise here.

HTTP-based management consists in using HTTP (either HTTP/1.0 [23] or HTTP/1.1 [88, 144]) instead of one of the three SNMP protocols to transfer management data between agents and managers. For this to work, all agents must have an HTTP server embedded.

The simplest form of HTTP-based management relies on simple Web pages written in HyperText Markup Language (HTML) [209]. The manager retrieves HTML pages from the agent and displays them in a Web browser, without processing them any further. Agents can send two types of document: static and dynamic HTML pages. Static pages do not change over time and are stored in the agent (e.g., in Erasable Programmable Read-Only Memory, or EPROM for short). A typical example is a Web page for configuration management. Dynamic pages are generated on-the-fly by the agent in reply to a request received from the manager. They reflect the state of the agent at a certain time. An example is a Web page for performance management.

A second form of HTTP-based management consists in running a Java applet in a Web browser, or a Java application, on the manager side, and using HTTP to communicate between the manager and the agent [19, 161, 286]. Management data can be pushed by the agent or pulled by the manager. Within HTTP messages, the data can be encoded in XML, HTML, strings, etc.

Compared with SNMP-based management, there is no change whatsoever in all these scenarios with respect to the management paradigm. We only change the communication protocol between the manager and the agent. In Chapter 6, we will describe more types of Web-based management that can follow a centralized paradigm.

4.1.2 Weakly distributed hierarchical paradigms

Weakly distributed hierarchical paradigms spread the management application across several machines. The telecommunications world has followed this management paradigm for many years with TMN. In the IP world, we saw one failed attempt with SNMPv2p and one successful, but partial, attempt with RMON.

4.1.2.1 In the telecommunications world

Unlike the SNMP management architecture, which proved to be successful in many sectors of activity, the OSI management architecture [53, 54, 296] encountered little success outside the telecommunications world. In 1992, the ITU-T adopted it as the basis for its TMN model [127, 231, 3] and for the specification of some of the TMN interfaces that mandate the use of CMIP [56] and CMIS [55]. Since then, OSI management has flourished in the niche markets of fixed and mobile[1] telephony, where it is used to manage both networks and systems.

TMN/OSI is based on a weakly distributed management paradigm that distributes management along a hierarchical tree of managers. Each manager is in charge of a

---

1. Also known as *cellular telephony*.

management domain. If the contact is lost between a mid-level manager and the top-level manager, independent corrective actions can be undertaken by the mid-level manager. If the contact is lost between a mid-level manager and an agent, the agent is left on its own.

One of the management services offered by CMIS is M_ACTION. It allows for the delegation of simple tasks from a manager to an agent. In practice, this service is rarely used by network operators in the telecommunications industry. But it is conceptually rich: Any agent can execute a static, pre-defined task when requested by the manager. This gives us a taste for what strongly distributed management is about.

4.1.2.2 In the IP world

At the time we write these lines, the IP world is still waiting for a viable solution for distributing management across a hierarchy of managers. The first attempt was made in April 1993, when a new management architecture now called SNMPv2p was issued [100]. It relied on a new protocol and three new MIBs. Distributed management was supposedly made possible by a new protocol primitive, inform, and the Manager-to-Manager (M2M) MIB [47]. We call it the *SNMPv2p + M2M MIB management architecture*. This architecture was primarily targeted at geographically dispersed enterprises. But the SNMPv2p security model (based on the concept of *party* [172]) and the M2M MIB were flawed and proved to be "unworkable in deployment" [168]. In 1996, SNMPv2p was superseded by SNMPv2c and SNMPv2u [201], both of which only support a centralized management paradigm.

In 2000, the IETF set the stage for distributing policies across a hierarchy of managers. RFC 2753 [295] defines the concepts of a *Policy Decision Point (PDP)*, which makes decisions and runs in a policy server, and a *Policy Enforcement Point (PEP)*, which enforces these decisions and lives in a network device or system. A policy server may embed both a PDP and a PEP, which makes it possible to organize policy managers into a hierarchy. Although this scheme does not cater to full-fledged NSM, it does support policy-based management and has already encountered a certain success in industry. As we mentioned in Section 2.2, policy-based management is outside the scope of this book and covered in detail by other authors [142, 273].

Despite the failure of SNMPv2p, the IETF managed to successfully define a weakly distributed management technology. But instead of assigning different management domains to different managers organized hierarchically, it kept a single manager and made some agents smarter than others. RMON probes were the first and simplest form of delegation added to the SNMPv1 architecture. They supported the RMON1 MIB, issued in 1991 [278] and updated in 1995 [279]. RMON2 was released in 1997 [280] and is now widely supported by intelligent hubs and switching hubs. By gathering usage statistics in RMON-capable equipment, administrators can delegate simple network-management tasks to these specialized network devices. This relieves the manager of the burden of the corresponding processing and decreases the amount of management data to move about. Tasks achieved by RMON are rather static, in the sense that only the gauges and traps hard-wired in the RMON MIB are available, together with all kinds of combinations thereof (via the *filter* mechanism). If the contact is lost between the RMON-capable agent and the manager, statistics are still gathered, but no independent corrective action can be undertaken by the agent. RMON is well suited to manage busy LANs and is widely used today in the IP world.

4.1.3 Strongly distributed hierarchical paradigms

Weakly distributed hierarchical paradigms address the main shortcoming of centralized models: scalability. But they also exhibit some limitations. We identified three. First, they lack robustness. If the contact is lost between the agent and the manager (e.g., due to a network link going down), the agent has no means to take corrective action in case of emergency. Second, they lack flexibility. Once a task has been defined in an agent (e.g., via RMON or M_ACTION), there is no way to modify it dynamically in pseudo real-time: It remains rather static and can only be updated infrequently. Third, they can be expensive in large networks. By concentrating most of the management-application processing in managers, they require powerful (hence expensive) management stations.

To address this, a new breed of technologies, based on strongly distributed hierarchical paradigms, emerged in the mid-1990s. The full potential of large-scale distribution over all managers and agents was first demonstrated in NSM by Goldszmidt with his Management by Delegation (MbD) architecture [105], which set a milestone in this research field. The novelty of his work stems on the simple, yet insightful, idea that with the constant increase in the processing power of every system and network device, NSM no longer ought to be limited to a small set of powerful managers: All agents could participate actively in the management application. For the first time with MbD, network devices were promoted from "dumb" data collectors to the rank of full-fledged managing entities.

MbD triggered a lot of research in NSM. The impact of the novel concepts it brought to this community was taken advantage of by many promising technologies that emerged, at about the same time, in other research communities. Most of these technologies came from software engineering, especially from the object-oriented and distributed-application communities. Let us present the paradigms underlying these technologies. They are grouped in two broad types: mobile code and distributed objects.

4.1.3.1 Mobile code

Mobile-code paradigms encompass a vast collection of very different technologies, all sharing a single idea: To provide flexibility, one can dynamically transfer programs into agents and have these programs executed by the agent. The program transfer and the program execution can be triggered by the agent itself, or by an entity external to the agent (e.g., a manager or another agent).

Remote evaluation, code on demand, and mobile agents

Fuggetta *et al.* [99] define *strong mobility* as the ability of a mobile-code system to allow an execution unit (e.g., a Unix process or a thread) to move both its code and its execution state to a different host. The execution is suspended, transferred to the destination host, and resumed there. *Weak mobility*, on the other hand, is the ability of a mobile-code system to allow an execution unit on a host to dynamically bind code coming from another host. The code is mobile, but the execution state is not preserved automatically[1] by the mobile-code system. Clearly, strong mobility is more difficult to implement than weak mobility.

By analyzing many mobile-code systems, Fuggetta *et al.* identified three different types of mobile-code paradigm[2]:

- *Remote EValuation* (REV [252]): When a client invokes a service on a server, it not only sends the name of the service and the input parameters, but also the code. So the client owns the code needed to perform the service, while the server owns the resources. This is a form of *push*.
- *Code On Demand* (COD): A client, when it has to perform a given task, contacts a code server, downloads the code needed from that server, links it in dynamically (dynamic code binding), and executes it. Thus the client owns the resources and the server owns the code. This is a form of *pull*.
- *Mobile Agent*: It is an execution unit able to autonomously migrate to another host and resume execution seamlessly. So the client owns the code, while the servers own the resources and provide an environment to execute the code sent either by the client or another server.

A number of technologies can be used to implement these paradigms. Some of them are just languages; others are complete systems that possibly include a virtual machine, a secure execution environment, etc. Agent Tcl, Ara, Emerald, Sumatra, Telescript, and Tycoon are examples of strong mobile-code systems. Aglets, Facile, Java, M0, Mole, Obliq, and Tacoma are examples of weak mobile-code systems (see references in [99]). Some technologies can be used to implement several paradigms [99].

Management by delegation and variants

Mobile-code paradigms were first used in NSM by Goldszmidt and Yemini, in 1991, when they devised Manager-Agent Delegation [297]. This management architecture was later enhanced and renamed Management by Delegation (MbD); it was fully specified in 1995 [105]. MbD is a mixture of the REV paradigm (to send delegated agents to elastic servers) and the client-server paradigm (to remotely control the scheduling and execution of delegated agents).

---

1. Of course, it is still possible to program this preservation explicitly.
2. As opposed to the client-server paradigm, where the client invokes a service on a server, while the server owns both the code and the resources (that is, it provides the environment to execute the code).

In 1996, Burns and Quinn [42] were among the first to describe the use of mobile agents in NSM. Since then, mobile-code systems have triggered a lot of research in this field [16, 26, 27, 36, 222]. The ISO integrated mobile code in its OSI management architecture by specifying a new management function: the Command Sequencer [131]. In 1998, Baldi and Picco [17] studied the network traffic generated by mobile-code systems implementing REV, COD, and mobile-agent paradigms; they made a quantitative theoretical evaluation of the effectiveness and suitability of these paradigms in network management.

In 1999, the IETF defined the Script MIB [150, 225], which allows a manager to delegate management tasks to an agent in the form of scripts. To operate in a secure manner, the Script MIB requires SNMPv3[1]. We thus call it the *SNMPv3 + Script MIB management architecture*. We saw in Section 3.3.3.4 that major vendors only recently began supporting SNMPv3, and the market is still hesitant to adopt this new technology. The use of the Script MIB is therefore expected to remain marginal in the near future.

Active networks

One area where mobile-code paradigms have encountered a large success is known as *active networks*. There are two approaches to active networks. The evolutionary approach, called *programmable switches*, *active nodes*, or *programmable networks*, provides a mechanism for injecting programs into network nodes [4, 298]. These programs can dynamically perform customized computations on the packets flowing through them (e.g., encrypt and decrypt data at the edges of the network). They can also alter the payload of these packets (e.g., when streaming-video images are encoded in multiple layers, these programs can discard fine-grained layers and transmit only coarse-grained layers, so as to conserve bandwidth). Clearly, this breaks the principle that transport networks should opaquely carry user data. The revolutionary approach, also known as *capsules* or *smart packets*, considers packets as miniature programs that are encapsulated in transmission frames and executed at each node along their path [266].

The concept of active networks was first proposed in 1995 by Tennenhouse and Wetherall [266]. It was first applied to NSM by Yemini and da Silva in 1996 [298]. Research is now extremely active in this field [39, 45, 138, 194, 207, 211, 229, 239]. In NSM, active networks are of great interest because they bring in flexibility and robustness. Network monitoring and event filtering [84, 265] are especially good candidates, as monitoring programs can easily be dispatched through the network. These programs are high-level filters that watch and instrument packet streams in real time. They maintain counters and report results back to the manager. Active networks can also be useful for performing active congestion control [84].

The main problems associated with active networks are security, performance, and interoperability [194]. A lot of work is under way to solve them, including coupling active software with active hardware in the area of Field-Programmable Gate Arrays (FPGAs) [119].

---

1. But the specification of the Script MIB does not mandate the use of SNMPv3 [150].

4.1.3.2 Distributed objects

Parallel to mobile code, a second type of strongly distributed hierarchical paradigm has emerged, based on distributed object technologies. We describe the four main approaches in this section: the Common Object Request Broker Architecture (CORBA), Java Remote Method Invocation (RMI), Web-Based Enterprise Management (WBEM), and the Open Distributed Management Architecture (ODMA).

CORBA

Faced with the issue of interoperability in the object-oriented world, the Object Management Group (OMG) standardized the Object Management Architecture, now commonly referred to by its main component: CORBA [232]. CORBA 2.0 [192] was released in 1995. Unlike its predecessors, this release proved very successful in the software-engineering community, particularly for large corporations with huge investments in legacy systems. Because OSI is object oriented and SNMP managed objects can be mapped onto objects, it took little time for NSM researchers to begin working on the integration of CORBA with existing management architectures. Pavlou was among the first when he proposed to use CORBA as the base technology for TMN [196, 198].

The Joint Inter-Domain Management (JIDM) group, jointly sponsored by The Open Group and the Network Management Forum (NMF)[1], was created to provide tools that enable management systems based on CMIP, SNMP, and CORBA to work together. The SNMP/ CMIP interoperability was previously addressed by the ISO-Internet Management Coexistence (IIMC) group of the NMF, which specified the translation between the SNMP and CMIP/CMIS services, protocols, and information. Both CMIP/CORBA and SNMP/ CORBA [165] interworking were solved by JIDM, who addressed specification translation and interaction translation. Algorithms were defined for the mapping between GDMO/ ASN.1 (Guidelines for the Definition of Managed Objects / Abstract Syntax Notation 1) and CORBA IDL (Interface Definition Language) [166], and between SNMP SMI and CORBA IDL [167]. The JIDM mappings allow CORBA programmers to write OSI or SNMP managers and agents, without any knowledge of GDMO, ASN.1, or CMIP. Inversely, these mappings also allow GDMO, CMIS or SNMP programmers to access IDL-based resources, services or applications, without knowing IDL.

CORBA has also been integrated with Web technologies. One example from industry is IONA's OrbixWeb, a Java Object Request Broker (ORB) coded as a Java applet. Once loaded into a Web browser, it runs as a CORBA server communicating via the Internet Inter-ORB Protocol (IIOP). Another example is CorbaWeb [176], from academia.

CORBA has been well accepted in the telecommunications world, where it is becoming a *de facto* standard—a rarity in this industry traditionally based on *de jure* standards. One of the achievements of the Telecommunications Information Networking Architecture (TINA [20, 22]) was to convince network operators and service providers to add a Distributed

---

1. Since then, the NMF has become the TeleManagement Forum (TMF).

Processing Environment (DPE) to TMN. CORBA proved to be a natural choice for this DPE [199, 200]. Several major equipment vendors now support CORBA for managing their telephone switches and networks.

Java RMI

Java RMI makes it possible to program a management application as a distributed object-oriented application. Everything is an object, and all objects can interact, even if they are distant (that is, if they are running on different machines). When combined with Object Serialization, Java RMI allows the state of an object (*properties* in Java jargon) to be transferred from host to host. This powerful combination allows management-application designers to mix mobile-code and distributed-objects paradigms.

Distributed Java objects can be mapped directly onto SNMP or OSI managed objects. In this case, they are low-level. They can also be high-level; e.g., the set up of a Virtual Path (VP) across multiple ATM switches can be defined by a single method call on a remote object living in the source switch. This high-level object will take care of all subsequent method invocations on all switches along the path to the destination. We will discuss this important concept in Section 4.2.

To date, Sun Microsystems and the Java Community have released three specifications leveraging Java RMI in NSM: the Java Management Application Programming Interface (JMAPI [263]), the Java Management eXtensions (JMX [260]), and the Federated Management Architecture (FMA [262]). These three approaches will be described in Section 6.7. JMAPI is now obsolete, but it was a successful proof of concept. JMX concentrates on the agent side while FMA focuses on the manager side of the management application.

JMAPI, JMX, and FMA have demonstrated that distributed Java-based management allows for a powerful way of building a strongly distributed management application. But it mandates that all managers and agents support Java, or that all agents be accessed via a Java-capable management gateway, which is a strong requirement. And the fact that Java is now split into the J2EE, J2SE, and J2ME frameworks causes interoperability problems (see Section 11.3). In addition, FMA relies on Jini[1], which is even more demanding.

WBEM

In the IP world, open standards have virtually wiped out proprietary network-management solutions. But apart from network management, proprietary management platforms are still the rule and open platforms are the exception. A few years ago, the Distributed Management Task Force (DMTF) issued the Desktop Management Interface (DMI [72]) specification and tried to promote open management for desktops. But this effort encountered little success [41, p. 2]. To date, most networked desktops are either managed with proprietary solutions or not managed at all.

---

1. Jini [258] is a plug-and-play technology promoted by Sun Microsystems (see Section 6.7.2).

The situation could soon change, however. Many enterprises are now bearing the costs of two parallel management platforms: one to manage their IP-based network equipment, and another to manage their desktop and laptop PCs. Some support even more platforms for managing servers, workstations, etc. These companies, who did not give much importance to open management a few years ago, are now paying a high price for this lack of interoperability; and they are pushing the industry to integrate the management of all kinds of network and systems equipment: PCs, routers, printers, switches, etc.

To address this need, a new management architecture called Web-Based Enterprise Management (WBEM) was defined by the DMTF [78]. WBEM will be presented in detail in Section 6.6.1, so we briefly summarize it here. WBEM has evolved a lot since its inception in 1996. So far, the main outcome of this effort has been the specification of a new information model: the Common Information Model (CIM [41]). Its main strength is that it is object oriented, unlike the SNMP information model. Its main drawback is its terminology, which departs radically from the SNMP and OSI-management terminologies and mixes the concepts of *schema* and *model*. WBEM's communication model relies on two standard technologies: HTTP for the communication protocol, and XML for representing management data in HTTP messages. Unlike CORBA and Java RMI, the communication between distant objects does not rely on distributed object-oriented middleware, but rather on XML-based serialization via HTTP. WBEM is backed by most vendors in the NSM industry; it is likely to emerge as one of the main management architectures of this decade.

ODMA

The purpose of the Open Distributed Management Architecture (ODMA) [125] is to extend the OSI management architecture (thus the TMN architecture) with the Reference Model of the ISO Open Distributed Processing (RM-ODP) architecture, which provides for the specification of large-scale, heterogeneous distributed systems. This joint effort of the ISO and the ITU-T led to a specialized reference model for the management of distributed resources, systems, and applications. It is based on an object-oriented distributed management architecture composed of *computational objects*. These objects offer several interfaces, some of which are for the purpose of management.

In ODMA, there are no longer managers and agents with fixed roles, like in the OSI management architecture. Instead, computational objects may offer some interfaces to manage other computational objects (manager role), and other interfaces to be managed (agent role). Moreover, by adopting the computational viewpoint of ODP, ODMA also renders the location of computational objects transparent to the management application. As far as the management application is concerned, computational objects may live anywhere, not necessarily inside a specific agent or manager. Consequently, agents may execute advanced management tasks, like managers. In short, the ISO and the ITU-T have gone from a weakly distributed management paradigm, with the OSI management architecture, to a strongly distributed management paradigm, with ODMA.

4.1.4 Strongly distributed cooperative paradigms

Unlike centralized and hierarchical paradigms, cooperative paradigms are *goal oriented*. What does this mean? For example, in REV-based mobile-code technologies, agents receive programs from a manager and execute them without knowing what goal is pursued by the manager. Managers send agents the "how", with a step-by-step *modus operandi* (coded in the program), and keep the "why" for themselves. Agents execute the program without knowing what it is about: they are "dumb". Conversely, with intelligent agents, managers just send the "why", and expect agents to know how to devise the "how". In this sense, agents used in cooperative paradigms are "intelligent".

Obviously, there is a price to pay for this. First, cooperative technologies are considerably more complex to design and implement than their centralized or hierarchical counterparts. Second, they use more CPU and memory resources. Third, they usually (but not always[1]) consume much more network bandwidth.

Cooperative technologies are still fairly new to the distributed NSM community. Until the mid-1990s, NSM authors simply ignored them [105, 117, 148, 179, 236, 246]. They originate from DAI, and more specifically from Multi-Agent Systems (MASes), where people model complex systems with large groups of intelligent agents. This research field is fairly recent, so its terminology is still vague. Specifically, there is no consensus on the definition of an intelligent agent. Many authors have strong and different opinions about this (Franklin and Graesser [95] listed 11 definitions!), which does not help. In 1994, Wooldridge and Jennings took a new approach. Instead of imposing on others what an intelligent agent should or should not be, they defined a core of properties shared by all intelligent agents, and allowed any other property to be application specific. This approach has encountered a great deal of success, and contributed significantly to the dissemination of MASes outside the realm of DAI. For these authors, intelligent agents (or, to be precise, what they call *weak agents*) must exhibit four properties [293]:

- *autonomy*: An intelligent agent operates without direct human intervention, and has some kind of control over its actions and internal state.
- *social ability*: Intelligent agents cooperate with other intelligent agents (and possibly people) to achieve their goals, via some kind of agent-communication language.

---

1. In hierarchical management, network overhead is mostly due to the traffic induced by polling, that is, the management data sent from agents to managers, or from mid-level managers to the top-level manager. Notifications also cause a bit of extra network overhead. In cooperative management, network overhead is partly due to the exchanges of knowledge between intelligent agents, and partly due to peer-to-peer interactions between agents. Knowledge exchanges can cause significant network overhead because the same data is often sent to multiple agents. Interactions between peer agents are caused by the distribution of the management application over many agents. Management tasks are no longer executed within a process, or within a host, but over the network. The communication overhead is thus no longer located in the backplane of a network device or in the bus of a host, but rather in the network. The resulting network overhead, added to that caused by the exchange of knowledge data, usually exceeds the network overhead of hierarchical management. Sometimes it does not, e.g. when the management task is trivial but requires a very large amount of management data.

- *reactivity*: An intelligent agent perceives its environment, and responds in a timely fashion to changes that occur in it.
- *proactiveness*: An intelligent agent is able to take the initiative to achieve its goals, as opposed to solely reacting to external events.

Proactiveness is a very discriminating property. While many implementations of intelligent agents are reactive, few qualify for proactiveness, particularly outside the AI community. We believe that this is the main difference between mobile agents from the software engineering community, and intelligent agents from the DAI community.

For Wooldridge and Jennings, optional properties of weak agents include mobility, veracity (intelligent agents do not knowingly communicate false information), and rationality (intelligent agents are not chaotic, they act so as to achieve their goals). In addition, they define *strong agents* as weak agents modeled with human-like characters, e.g. by using Rao and Georgeff's Belief, Desire, Intention (BDI) model [210]. Strong agents are the type of intelligent agents generally used by the DAI community, whereas weak agents are the type often used by other research communities.

In 1996, Franklin and Graesser [95] compared the approaches taken by many authors and, as Wooldridge and Jennings, distinguished between mandatory and optional properties. For them, intelligent agents must be reactive, autonomous, goal-oriented (proactive, purposeful), and temporally continuous (an intelligent agent is a continuously running process). Optionally, they can also be communicative (that is, able to communicate, coordinate, and cooperate with other agents,), learn (they improve their skills over time, storing information in knowledge bases), be mobile, and have a human-like character. In our view, the fact that intelligent agents should be continuously running processes is an important property. It also distinguishes intelligent agents from mobile agents.

Because we consider intelligent agents in the context of cooperative paradigms in distributed NSM, their ability to communicate, coordinate, and cooperate should be, in our view, a mandatory property. The ability to learn is often expected from intelligent agents in NSM; but like many authors, we do not consider this property to be mandatory. We therefore propose that, in NSM, intelligent agents should always be:

- goal oriented (proactive)
- autonomous
- reactive
- cooperative (communicative, coordinating)
- temporally continuous

When intelligent agents are cooperative, they are exposed to heterogeneity problems, and therefore need standards for agent management, agent communication languages, etc. Two consortia are currently working on such standards: the Foundation for Intelligent Physical Agents (FIPA [90]) and the Agent Society [2]. Among all the agent communication languages that have emerged in DAI [293], two have encountered a certain success in the

NSM research community: the Knowledge Query and Manipulation Language (KQML [89]) and the Agent Communication Language (ACL [91]).

More and more researchers are now trying to use intelligent agents to manage networks and systems [183, 205, 241, 299]. But we should remember that the limits between mobile agents (following a mobile-code paradigm) and intelligent agents (following a cooperative paradigm) are sometimes fuzzy. And when Knapik and Johnson [141] advocate the use of object-oriented agents, to combine the advantages of both worlds, the classification becomes even trickier. In fact, object-oriented agents implement two paradigms simultaneously, distributed objects and intelligent agents, and can even implement a third: mobile code.

4.1.5 Synthetic diagram

	centralized paradigm	hierarchical paradigms	cooperative paradigms
not distributed	SNMPv1, SNMPv2c, SNMPv2u, SNMPv3, HTTP		
weakly distributed		RMON, SNMPv2p + M2M MIB, OSI/TMN, PDP/PEP	
strongly distributed		SNMPv3 + Script MIB, mobile code, distributed objects	intelligent agents

Table 1. Simple taxonomy of NSM paradigms

All the management paradigms of our simple taxonomy are summarized in Table 1. The chief contribution of this simple taxonomy is that it highlights some similarities between apparently very diverse approaches. Despite the fact that new technologies appear at a fast pace, administrators are no longer overwhelmed by the variety of approaches offered to them: They have a simple way to analyze them and group them, which reduces the scope of their investigation.

The main disadvantage of this simple taxonomy is that it is primarily of academic interest. By only considering the organizational model, it remains theoretical and does not give many clues as to what paradigm or technology should be used in the context of a given enterprise. In industry, administrators and designers of management applications need more pragmatic criteria. They have difficult software-engineering decisions to make at the analysis and design levels. They need to think twice before investing in expensive technologies such as CORBA, or before embarking for uncharted territories inhabited by roaming intelligent agents! Administrators would rather base their choices on sound technical grounds. Ideally, they would like case-based studies or "cookbook recipes". The purpose of our enhanced taxonomy is to fulfill this need, although we are still a long way from having "cookbook recipes" in NSM!

4.2 Enhanced Taxonomy of Network and Systems Management Paradigms

We identified the first criterion of our enhanced taxonomy, delegation granularity, by comparing the organizational models used in NSM with enterprise organizational structures considered in business administration. The three other criteria were chosen by comparing the technologies introduced in the previous section.

4.2.1 A stroll through organization theory

Empirical evidence shows that the topology of an enterprise's computer network tends to be modeled after its organization chart. In NSM, this chart is also reflected in the way administrative domains, trust domains, and even Lightweight Directory Access Protocol (LDAP) directories are divided. The main reason for this is that the people accountable for the smooth operation of this network belong to this chart, and it makes their life a lot easier if different people have a hold on different computers and network devices. In addition, such a network topology is often justified in terms of budget: Different departments pay for their own equipment. Sometimes, it also makes technical sense, for instance when different departments are located on different floors or in separate buildings. In short, NSM is not orthogonal to an enterprise's organizational structure.

In this section, we show that the first criterion of our enhanced taxonomy was derived by comparing the NSM organizational models identified in Section 4.1 with enterprise organizational structures. To do so, we study how delegation works in enterprises, how it maps onto organization structures, and how the two fundamental paradigms that we identified in NSM (delegation and cooperation) map onto the enterprise world.

4.2.1.1 Enterprise organizational structures

Mullins [186] distinguishes eight ways of dividing work in an enterprise:

- by function (one department per function: whether in production, R&D, marketing, finance, or sales, all staff share a common expertise within a department);
- by product (autonomous units, all functions are present in each unit);
- by location (geographically dispersed companies, subsidiaries abroad);
- by nature of the work to be performed (e.g., by security clearance level);
- by common time scales (e.g., shift work vs. office-hours work);
- by common processes (e.g., share a production facility in the manufacturing industry);
- by the staff employed (e.g., surgeons, doctors, and nurses in a hospital);

• by type of customer or people to be served (e.g., home vs. export sales).

For Mullins, delegation can take place at two levels: enterprise or individual. At the enterprise level, it is (or is supposed to be) depicted in the organization chart and relies on either federal or functional decentralization. *Federal decentralization* is defined as "the establishment of autonomous units operating in their own market with self-control and with the main responsibility of contributing profit to the parent body" [186, p. 276]. *Functional decentralization* is "based on individual processes or products" [186, p. 276]. At the individual level, delegation is "the process of entrusting authority and responsibility to others" [186, p. 276] for a specific task.

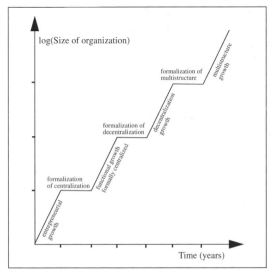

Fig. 5. The effect of size on the enterprise structure
(adapted from Weinshall and Raveh [285, pp. 56–57])

Weinshall and Raveh [285] identify three basic managerial structures: entrepreneurial, functional, and decentralized (see Fig. 5). The *entrepreneurial structure* is typical of an organization recently created, fairly small, and growing fast. It must be managed in an informal and centralized fashion in order to survive. Everything is centered on one person: the entrepreneur who created the enterprise. When organizations grow beyond a certain size, they must go through a major transformation. An entire set of rules by which the work is managed and carried out needs to be formalized, "in order to cope with the growing quantities of product and services, their variety, and the complexity of the organization" [285, p. 55]. In this new setting, the enterprise is said to have a *functional structure*. The chief executive directly controls the various functional heads, such as the Production Manager, the Marketing Manager, the Sales Manager, etc. Next, the formalized and centralized nature of any functional structure evolves toward a *decentralized structure*. As a result of expansion, the number of managers (people, not programs, this time) grows far beyond the number that can efficiently report to a single person. At this stage, the organization must slow down its growth and introduce a new formal and decentralized structure, organized by product/service line or by geographical area.

These three structures are uniform, in the sense that "all subordinates of the chief executive are structured either in an entrepreneurial, or a functional, or a product line or area structure" [285, p.188]. Beyond a certain size, this uniformity cannot be maintained: The decentralized structure needs to change into a *multistructure*, i.e. a federated managerial structure where "different building blocks may be combined into different kinds of structures" [285, p. 189]. The Japanese, according to Weinshall and Raveh, were the first to operate their large organizations in multistructures, in a type of organization known as *zaibatsu*. The multistructure is inherently flexible, in that it enables changes in the composition of the federated basic structures. This natural evolution as enterprises grow from an entrepreneurial structure to a multistructure is depicted in Fig. 5. The actual values of the time on the x axis and the logarithm of the size of the organization on the y axis depend on the sector of activity of the enterprise, and change dramatically from one type of industry to another.

Before we conclude with enterprise organizational structures, let us take a look at the *evolutions and revolutions cycle*, an evolution trend identified by Greiner in 1972 [108]. According to him, as an organization grows in size and maturity, it goes through five phases of development known as *evolution stages*:

- growth through creativity
- growth through direction
- growth through delegation
- growth through coordination
- growth through collaboration

Two consecutive evolution stages are separated by a *revolution stage*:

- crisis of leadership
- crisis of autonomy
- crisis of control
- crisis of red tape

In retrospect, it is amazing to see how this cycle, devised for business administration, suits NSM well. While the first three phases look similar to those identified by Weinshall and Raveh, the last two, coordination and collaboration, are incredibly visionary and predicted three decades ago what distributed artificial intelligence in general, and intelligent agents in particular, are now striving to achieve in NSM with cooperative management! It is also interesting to notice that the last crisis (after *growth through collaboration*) is left as unknown. Would the combination of hierarchical and cooperative paradigms be the ultimate solution? Or was the idea of collaboration so new to business administration in the early 1970s that Greiner, lacking hard evidence, did not want to speculate on what could make it fall into disfavor or what could come next?

4.2.1.2 Delegation granularity

What do Mullins, Greiner, and Weinshall & Raveh tell us that could apply to NSM? First, all the management paradigms they consider are hierarchical—except for the last two phases described by Greiner, which are characterized by a mix of hierarchical and cooperative paradigms. Likewise, most distributed NSM paradigms to date are hierarchical, and cooperative paradigms have only just begun to appear in hybrid structures similar to Weinshall and Raveh's multistructures.

The second lesson to be learned is that delegation schemes should evolve as enterprises grow in size, otherwise they become inefficient. Similarly, distributed NSM should rely on different distributed NSM paradigms as networks grow in size and complexity. In this respect, the recent explosion of distributed paradigms seems justified, because networks have grown considerably in terms of size and complexity since the SNMPv1 and OSI management architectures were devised.

Third, although there are many ways of dividing up enterprise organizational structures, depending on the granularity of the analysis, most authors agree with Weinshall and Raveh that they all coalesce in three broad types: by function, by product/service, and by geographical area. Once again, we can see some similarities here between organization theory and NSM. The division of management domains by geographical area, for example, makes sense in both worlds. But there are clear discrepancies too, since the basic entities are people in one case, machines or programs in the other. The division by function only makes sense in the enterprise world. For instance, it takes many years for a person to become an expert in accounting or electrical engineering, and an accountant cannot be turned into an engineer overnight; but a computer can be equipped with new competencies in a matter of minutes, by simply transferring a few programs. We will explain next that Mullins's federal decentralization and Weinshall and Raveh's decentralized structure map onto our *delegation by domain* scheme in distributed NSM, while Mullins's functional decentralization and Weinshall and Raveh's functional structure map onto our *delegation by task* scheme.

The fourth and most important lesson we can learn from organization theory is this common evolution trend, of which Greiner and Weinshall & Raveh give two different, but compatible, versions. There is a natural evolution of enterprises from centralized structures to decentralized ones, and from lightly decentralized structures (organized by function) to more decentralized ones with independent units (organized by product/service or by geographical area), to even more decentralized structures based on federation or cooperation. In NSM terms, these four stages map easily onto the different types presented in our simple taxonomy. The evolution which occurred in enterprise organizational structures over the 20th century suggests that the same evolution may take place in NSM in the years to come. The time scale may be different, but the evolutionary trend toward more distributed and cooperative management is the same.

Delegation by domain vs. delegation by task

How do the eight types of delegation identified by Mullins translate into NSM terms? We saw that delegation by geographical domain applies equally well to both worlds, but what about the other types? In the early 1990s, several European ESPRIT projects investigated the concept of *management domains*, or *domains* for short; a number of criteria were thus selected to define domains in NSM [271]. Resources can be grouped into domains when they share a common feature. This may be the organizational structure (same department, same team), the geographical location, access permissions (resources accessible to a user, a group of users, or everybody), the type of resource (same vendor, same management protocol), the functionality of the resource (printer, mail system), or the systems management functional area [52]. Some items in this list resemble Mullins's types, although they were identified in very different contexts. But both of these lists are far too detailed for our taxonomy. In NSM, we propose to group all possible types of delegation into just two: delegation by domain and delegation by task.

Delegation by domain relies on static tasks. A manager at level (N) assumes that every manager at level (N+1) knows all of the management tasks to be completed within its domain (N=1 for the top-level manager, N=2,3,4... for the mid-level managers; see Fig. 1, p. 16). In today's networks, delegation by domain typically translates into delegation by geographical domain, to manage geographically dispersed enterprises. For instance, let us suppose that the headquarters of a multinational organization are located in Sydney, Australia. This enterprise cannot afford to manage its large subsidiaries in the USA, Asia, or Europe over expensive and relatively slow transoceanic WAN links. Let us consider its European subsidiary located in Geneva, Switzerland. The manager (i.e., the management application) in Sydney delegates the entire management of the Swiss subsidiary to the manager located in Geneva, and expects it not to report that a local printer goes down, but to report that the number of errors per minute exceeds a given threshold on the Switzerland-Australia WAN link. The point here is that the Australian manager does not tell the Swiss manager what to report; instead, the Swiss manager is expected to make this decision by itself. In practice, this translates into a human being, the administrator, hard-coding in the Swiss manager what to report back to Sydney and how to manage the rest of the network. There is no mechanism for the Australian manager to alter the way the Swiss manager manages its domain. It is a *carte blanche* type of delegation, whereby the Geneva-based manager has total control over its own network. NSM is not automated, and the headquarters' manager cannot enforce a management policy over all the subsidiaries.

Delegation by task, conversely, offers a finer-grained vision at level (N) of the management processing occurring at level (N+1). As a result, the manager at level (N) can see the different tasks at level (N+1), as well as other tasks of its peers at level (N). Tasks need not be static and hard-coded in every manager; they can also be modified dynamically. This idea was first applied to NSM with Management by Delegation, as we already saw in Section 4.1.3.1. Goldszmidt departed from the notion of static tasks, which was well established then, and introduced the notion of dynamic tasks, transferable from the manager to its subordinate agents. This paradigm was later generalized by others to transfer dynamic tasks from a manager at level (N) to a manager at level (N+1).

Microtasks vs. macrotasks

Now that we have defined two broad types of delegation in NSM, let us refine the concept of *delegation by task* and clarify what kind of task can be delegated. A manager at level (N) has several ways of driving a subordinate at level (N+1). With traditional paradigms, the basic unit in the manager-agent dialog is the protocol primitive. With SNMPv1, the manager issues a series of `get` and `set` requests to the agent. The data manipulated are MIB variables, which are statically defined when the MIB is designed. With large MIBs or large networks, this leads to the micro-management syndrome [105], which entails significant network overhead and a poor use of the resources of the managers, managed devices, and managed systems.

Recent approaches avoid this syndrome by splitting the management application into many different units, or *tasks*, and by distributing these tasks over a large number of managers and agents, while still letting the manager at level (N) be in control of what subordinates at level (N+1) do. The underlying mechanism of this distribution is independent of the tasks being delegated. It can rely on program transfer, message passing, Remote Procedure Calls (RPCs), etc. The focal point for the management application is the granularity of the delegation, that is, the way the work is divided. In practice, there is a wide spectrum of task complexities, ranging from the mere addition of two MIB variables to the entire management of a backbone router. We propose to distinguish only two levels in our enhanced taxonomy: microtasks and macrotasks.

A *microtask* simply performs preprocessing on static MIB variables, typically to compute statistics. It is the simplest way of managing site-specific, customized variables. There is no value in these data *per se*, which still need to be aggregated by the manager one level up. If contact with the manager is lost, statistics are still gathered, but there is no way for the subordinate to take corrective action on its own. In the case of a *macrotask*, the entire control over an entity is delegated. A macrotask can automatically reset a network device, or build an entire daily report, etc. If contact is lost with the manager one level up, corrective actions can be automatically undertaken.

With these definitions in mind, let us now classify the management architectures reviewed in Section 4.1 according to their delegation granularities. SNMPv1-, SNMPv2c-, SNMPv2u-, SNMPv3-, and HTTP-based management support no delegation (see Fig. 6). The SNMPv2p+M2M MIB management architecture supports the delegation by domain. OSI/TMN supports the delegation by domain and microtask. RMON supports the delegation by microtask. The SNMPv3+Script MIB management architecture supports the delegation by microtask and macrotask; so do mobile code, distributed objects, and the PDP/PEP architecture (i.e., policy-based management *à la* IETF). Intelligent agents support the delegation by macrotask. As for WBEM, it currently supports no delegation, delegation by domain, and delegation by microtask; in the future, it may also support delegation by macrotask, as nothing prevents it in the management architecture itself.

4.2.2 Other criteria for our enhanced taxonomy

In previous work [157], we identified a dozen selection criteria that influence designers and users of management applications when they choose a management paradigm. We showed that in addition to interoperability, which is a given in open management, and scalability, which is addressed by all distributed management paradigms, the most important criteria are the semantic richness of the information model, the degree of specification of a task, and the degree of automation of management.

4.2.2.1 Semantic richness of the information model

The *semantics* of a management application designates the kind of entities and actions that can be defined in the information model and constitute the building blocks of a management application. The *semantic richness* of the information model is an indication of the expressive power of the abstractions used in this model. It measures two things: the facility for designers of management applications to specify a task to be executed by a manager or an agent, and the usefulness of these tasks to administrators and operators.

The higher the level of abstraction used to model a management application, the higher the semantic richness of the information model, and the easier it is for someone to build and design a management application. This is due to the way the human brain works, as we know from cognitive sciences. Computers can easily be programmed to deal with many low-level abstractions, which are precisely defined; but it is difficult to make them manipulate higher-level concepts, which are often under-specified. People, conversely, are used to thinking at a high level of abstraction, but they are easily overwhelmed by too many low-level concepts.

The same is true in NSM, when people design or use large and complex management applications. Consider, for instance, how people and computers have different aptitudes for enforcing the task "improve the service delivered to customer X". Unfortunately, people have traditionally used fairly poor APIs in NSM. These APIs constrain designers to model management applications with low-level abstractions, which forces administrators and operators to work at a level of abstraction that is not suited to the way they think.

In this section, we show that some of the new management paradigms attempt to address this issue. Designers of management applications now have the choice among three types of abstractions to build an information model:

  • managed objects, offering low-level abstractions;
  • computational objects, offering high-level abstractions;
  • goals, offering very high-level abstractions.

Managed objects

In the SNMP and OSI worlds, people use *protocol APIs*. For instance, with SNMPv1, v2c, and v3, administrators have to think in terms of get and set when they write a management application in Perl [282], Tcl [195], Java [107], C++ [256], C [140], etc. Many people still use the very simple SNMPv1 API developed by Carnegie Mellon University in the early 1990s (which includes the snmpget and snmpset C programs [64]).

This is due to the tight coupling between the communication and information models, in ISO/ITU-T parlance [54]. The semantics offered to the designer of a management application are constrained by the primitives of the communication protocol used underneath. The communication protocol is not transparent to the application, which breaks a well-established rule in software engineering.

We call it the *managed-object* approach, as both the IETF and ISO use this term to describe a unit of the information model in their respective management architectures. All technologies based on centralized or weakly distributed hierarchical paradigms share this approach. When a management application is designed with managed objects, a protocol is automatically imposed; the managed objects must live in full-blown agents (in the case of TMN, these agents need to implement a large part of the OSI stack, including CMIP and CMIS); and the manager-agent style of communication is imposed. These are very strong constraints imposed on management-application designers.

In principle, nothing prevents people from building richer APIs on top of snmpget and snmpset and using them to develop better management applications. For instance, Znaty and Cherkaoui proposed an API [300] based on the Structured Query Language (SQL) to leverage the natural mapping between SNMP tables and tables found in relational databases. One advantage of issuing SQL queries from the management application, rather than SNMP get's, is that handling SQL tables is less tricky than working with SNMP conceptual tables (see Section 3.3.1.3, "Holes in sparse tables"). But SQL-based APIs have not encountered much success so far, probably because relational databases are too slow and consume too many resources to be viable in agents. In practice, most people still use very low-level APIs.

Computational objects

Protocol APIs are based on ideas that began to be criticized by researchers in the late 1970s and early 1980s, particularly when the concept of *objects* gradually emerged in the software-engineering community. Since the mid-1980s, this community has been advocating the use of *programmatic APIs* instead, which have been one of the selling points of the object-oriented paradigm for distributed systems. With such APIs, any object belonging to a distributed system is defined by the interface it offers to other objects. The distributed object model is independent of the communication protocol. It only defines a programmatic interface between the invoker and the operations (methods) supported by the invoked object. This programmatic API relies on a protocol at the engineering level, but this protocol is completely transparent to the management-application designer.

We call it the *computational-object* approach, with reference to the terminology used by the ISO for ODP and ODMA. In this approach, designers of management applications can use class libraries that offer high-level views of network devices and systems. Few constraints are imposed on the design: Objects may be distributed anywhere, and need not live in specific agents that implement specific protocol stacks. The only mandatory stack is the one that implements the distributed processing environment. No specific organizational model is imposed or assumed. The management application relies solely on object-to-object communication. The administrator may define site-specific classes and use them in conjunction with libraries of classes that implement standard MIBs.

The computational-object approach was adopted by many recent management technologies, notably distributed object technologies. In NSM, it accounts to a large extent for the success of Java in the IP world. Strangely enough, it is not responsible for the even greater success of CORBA in the telecommunications world: So far, CORBA has mostly relied on a managed-object approach. Telephone switches are very complex to manage, considerably more than IP routers. The fact that, with CORBA, the millions of lines of code necessary to manage a switch can be written in parallel by many independent programmers, from different companies, in different languages, is a blessing and justifies in itself the use of CORBA. Moreover, dealing only with well-known managed objects is often perceived as a guarantee of interoperability. Even though CORBA objects could convey higher levels of abstraction than OSI managed objects, the telecommunications industry has been happy so far to simply translate managed objects into CORBA objects. The success of Java-based management in the IP world may suggest new ways of using CORBA in NSM in the future.

Goals

The third type of abstraction that may be used in information models is the *goal*. In Section 4.1.4, we saw that cooperative paradigms are goal oriented. The management application is split into tasks, which are modeled with very high-level abstractions and partially specified with goals. Once these goals have been sent by the manager to the agent, it is up to the agent to work out how to achieve these goals.

This approach is fundamentally different from the one taken by weakly and strongly distributed hierarchical paradigms, whereby the management application is broken down into fully specified tasks. Whether the implementation of the task relies on communication-protocol primitives or object-method calls, the agent is given by the manager a step-by-step *modus operandi* to achieve its task. With strongly distributed cooperative paradigms, it is not.

Goals may be specified via a great variety of APIs, including programmatic APIs, protocol APIs, and artificial-intelligence APIs (e.g., using predicates of first-order logics). They do not require an object-oriented distributed system to be used underneath. But the coupling of agents and objects looks promising in NSM. Knapik and Johnson [141] describe different styles of communication between intelligent agents: Object-oriented agents rely on remote method calls, whereas plain agents rely on communication languages such as KQML [89]. The primitives (*performatives*) of KQML are considerably richer than those of SNMP and CMIP/CMIS, hence goals are less limited by protocol APIs than managed objects.

To date, goals represent the highest level of abstraction available to designers and users of management applications. They rely on complex technologies known as *intelligent agents* (see Section 4.1.4), which often support some kind of inference engine and pattern learning, and are generally not yet available on IP systems and network devices (we need to go through management gateways). There is still a large market for simpler technologies that support computational objects, or even simpler technologies that support only managed objects. But goals are a type of abstraction that makes it possible to manage very complex networks, systems, and services to which simpler abstractions are not suited. They are particularly useful to SLA negotiation, resource-usage optimization, and load balancing.

As depicted in Fig. 6, most management architectures support only managed objects; the semantic richness of their information models is low. WBEM, mobile code, and distributed objects support both managed objects and computational objects; their semantic richness ranges from low to high. Cooperative management (i.e., intelligent agents) supports goals and offers a high level of semantic richness to designers and users of management applications; but, unfortunately, it is still confined to research. This situation may evolve in the future.

4.2.2.2 Degree of specification of a task

Managed objects and computational objects rely on fully specified tasks, whereas goals rely on partially specified tasks (see Table 2). In other words, the semantic richness of the information model and the degree of specification of a task are closely linked. We decided to retain the latter as a criterion for our enhanced taxonomy, because it shows two very different ways of specifying tasks in a management application. But we must keep in mind that these two criteria are not independent.

management-application unit (= information model abstraction)	managed object	computational object	goal
abstraction level	low	high	very high
where does it live?	MIB	object	intelligent agent
how do we access it from the management-application code?	management protocol primitives (SNMP, CMIP, HTTP)	method call	1) agent communication language primitive (KQML) 2) method call
degree of specification	full	full	partial

Table 2. Semantic richness of the information model

In Fig. 6, only intelligent agents can cope with the partial specification of a management task. All other management paradigms require the full specification of all tasks.

4.2.2.3 Degree of automation of management

In the early days of SNMP-based management, very few management tasks were automated. The main drive behind the automation of management was to relieve the staff who were monitoring IP networks (operators) from the burden of doing mundane, repetitive tasks manually. In the 2000s, administrators have even more reasons to be eager to automate enterprise management, especially NSM.

Why should NSM be automated?

The first and foremost reason for automating management today is scalability. If we translate this into economic terms, the (same) objective is to keep operating costs under control while IP networks and systems continue to grow in size (see Section 3.3.1.1). Because enterprises cannot afford to hire ever more monitoring staff, they must somehow automate management. Large corporations have two financial incentives for doing so. First, as most NOCs have already realized, certain management tasks are simple to automate and have a very short Return On Investment (ROI)—less than a year. Second, once you have monitoring staff and management platforms in place in your organization, the marginal cost of managing an extra network device or system is *usually* lower with management software than with operators, because duplicating a program is simpler than training new people. There are exceptions to this rule of thumb.

Not only do IP networks and systems grow in size, but they also become increasingly complex, hence difficult to manage. Their increased complexity requires smarter operators and administrators. But it is difficult to find skilled people on the job market: expertise is rare and expensive. It is equally difficult to retain qualified staff within your company: They are courted by many other companies, even outside your business domain. There is thus a growing tendency in NSM to rely on a limited number[1] of talented people for solving unknown and unanticipated problems, and to rely on software for management tasks that can be automated. We see this trend not only in NSM, but also in enterprise management at large, especially service management. Sooner or later, anything that is well understood and somewhat repetitive can be automated.

By replacing some of the staff with software, two issues that most NOCs are faced with can be addressed: human errors and panic. People make mistakes, it is a fact of life. *Errare humanum est!* Machines are not as smart as humans, but they are more systematic. They follow procedures to the letter, because they are programmed to do so. They rarely make errors, even when the network topology is very complex, even when thousands of events occur simultaneously, even when the chief executive is watching over their shoulders! Most errors are due to design flaws or bugs in the management application, and these can be ironed out by administrators over time. Human errors cannot. In addition, machines still

---

1. This number depends on the size of the enterprise. Typically, once NSM is reasonably automated, small enterprises require one smart administrator working part-time, midsize enterprises need one or two administrator(s) working full-time, and large corporations need dozens of them. Large network operators usually need hundreds of them, because NSM is part of their core business.

have no feelings and do not panic, despite all the efforts of the robotics research community! Experience shows that panicking operators can make all sorts of decisions leading to all sorts of disasters. Software programs do not panic: They stubbornly keep doing the same things. By reducing the sources of errors, automated management can help administrators better manage their networks and systems, thereby increasing the robustness and reliability of the services and applications that end-users interact with.

Under certain circumstances, automating management makes it possible to reduce the Total Cost of Ownership (TCO)[1]. There is a trade-off between high-quality management software and highly skilled support staff: Both are expensive, and different enterprises make different trade-offs. Machines can only do what they have been programmed to do, but they make very few mistakes. People make mistakes, but they can also improvise. Some enterprises want their monitoring staff to be able to cope with unforeseen situations, which cannot be automated. Others want them to play by the book and strictly follow the procedures, only the procedures, which can be automated. A frequent problem in this context is that, under the excuse of reducing the TCO, some IT (Information Technology) and networking executives really want to lay off people so as to improve a few *per capita* ratios—some people consider that these ratios are indicative of an enterprise's productivity. In the author's experience, it is often a mistake to automate management *solely* for cutting staff costs. The main objectives behind the automation of management should always be to better manage networks and systems, and to guarantee the scalability of the management application.

In summary, the larger and the more complex the IP networks and systems, the more automated the management application should be. The following statement, made by Yemini back in 1993, is as topical as ever: "Management should pursue flexible decentralization of responsibilities to devices and maximal automation of management functions through application software" [296, p. 28].

Note that despite all the technical and economic reasons we have just mentioned for automating NSM, there are also psychological reasons for *not* doing so, including:

- *cost of automation*: Some IT and networking executives do not hesitate to invest in hardware, or in software destined for end-users, but find it difficult to invest in NSM software;
- *return on investment*: Companies who only care about the next quarter's results tend to postpone investments indefinitely when the ROI exceeds three months.

But enterprises who accept ROIs of up to 18 months can, in general, reasonably automate the management of their IP networks and systems.

---

1. The TCO of a network device or system includes the purchase price, training costs, upgrade costs, the cost to include the new equipment in the current environment, the possible purchase of a new vendor-specific management GUI, the possible purchase of a new disk for the management platform, the possible upgrade of the management platform, etc.

Why should service management be automated?

Another area where automation has proved to be of critical importance is service management. Thanks to automation, dynamic service provisioning allows administrators to offer better services faster. Faster, because service provisioning is performed considerably faster by programs than by people; manual service provisioning is inherently slow. Better, because dynamic service provisioning significantly improves the service offered to end-users. To illustrate this, let us consider a simple example of service provisioning.

In several European countries, until the telecommunications industry was deregulated in the mid-1990s, time slots for videoconferences used to be reserved by fax. A typical scenario was the following. An end-user would contact support staff several days in advance. Support staff would fax the single provider for their country (i.e., their local network operator) to make a reservation. They would receive a confirmation of their reservation by fax or phone, several hours later, and an invoice the next day. International videoconferences had to be scheduled even more in advance. Finally, support staff would inform the initial end-user that the reservation had been made. This process was time consuming, very inefficient, and error prone. Today, monopolies (or near monopolies) have given way to a plethora of competing network operators, service providers, service traders, content providers, etc. This fierce competition has encouraged service providers to offer new services or improve existing ones. In the above-mentioned example, some of them now automate the provisioning of videoconferences so as to enable their customers to reserve a videoconference via user-friendly GUIs. Tomorrow, end-users would like to deal with their favorite service trader instead of contacting several service providers. Via user-friendly GUIs, they would receive several offers issued by different service providers, and choose the best deal for a videoconference scheduled at most an hour in advance. In the future, thanks to automation, videoconferences would not even have to be scheduled in advance: They could be provisioned immediately, with a click of a mouse.

Note that in order for services (e.g., video on demand, videoconferencing, teleteaching, or telemedicine) to be provisioned dynamically, NSM must also be automated to a certain extent. For instance, for video-on-demand, network management needs to handle resource reservations in a transparent way, while systems management must provide for automatic failover (*hot stand-by*) of video-on-demand servers.

High, medium, and low degrees of automation of management

The degree of automation of management is directly linked to the delegation granularity. As depicted in Fig. 6, NSM has a low degree of automation with paradigms that support the delegation by domain or no delegation at all. We also see that management applications based on new paradigms can be more automated than those based on traditional paradigms. NSM can be better automated with macrotasks (high degree) than with microtasks (medium degree), because macrotasks enable remote agents to take corrective actions independently from the manager. The highest degree of automation is provided by intelligent agents, distributed objects, mobile code, PDP/PEP, and SNMPv3+Script MIB.

4.2.3 Synthetic diagram

Our enhanced taxonomy is now complete. It consists of four criteria: delegation granularity, semantic richness of the information model, degree of automation of management, and degree of specification of a task. As we have stressed already, these criteria are not independent. The semantic richness of the information model is closely related to the degree of specification of a task; so is the delegation granularity to the degree of automation.

Note that in Fig. 6, the axes take discrete values, not continuous values. In other words, the relative placement of different paradigms in the same quadrant is meaningless.

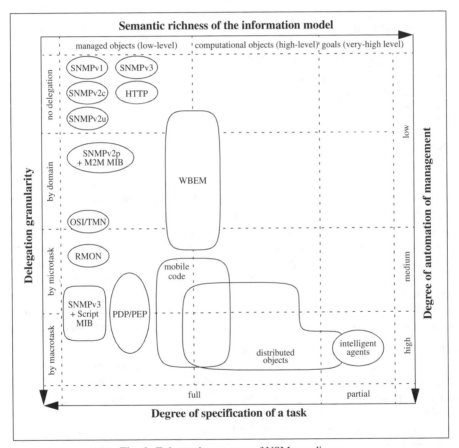

Fig. 6. Enhanced taxonomy of NSM paradigms

We do not list all existing technologies in our enhanced taxonomy. For strongly distributed management, for instance, only paradigms are depicted. The reason for this choice is threefold. First, we want to keep this taxonomy readable. Second, technologies evolve so quickly, and this market is currently so active, that such information would be obsolete as soon as it is published. Java, for instance, blurred the boundaries between mobile code and distributed objects only a few years ago. Third, we believe that the criteria we selected and presented are easy to understand, and that potential users of such technologies should be able to decide where to locate a given release of a given technology in Fig. 6, based on a short technical description of it.

By counting the quadrants that are populated in Fig. 6, we see that our enhanced taxonomy consists of nine types:

- no delegation with low-level semantics;
- no delegation with high-level semantics;
- delegation by domain with low-level semantics;
- delegation by domain with high-level semantics;
- delegation by microtask with low-level semantics;
- delegation by microtask with high-level semantics;
- delegation by macrotask with low-level semantics;
- delegation by macrotask with high-level semantics;
- delegation by macrotask with very high-level semantics.

4.3 Summary

In this chapter, we proposed two taxonomies to classify all major management paradigms and technologies available to date for managing IP networks and systems. In our *simple taxonomy*, all NSM technologies were classified according to their underlying organizational model. We grouped them into four different types of NSM paradigms: (i) centralized paradigm, (ii) weakly distributed hierarchical paradigms, (iii) strongly distributed hierarchical paradigms, and (iv) strongly distributed cooperative paradigms. Faced with dozens of commercial or prototype NSM technologies on the market today, with new ones appearing every month, designers of management applications run the risk of being overwhelmed by the abundance of choice. With this simple taxonomy, they now have a simple tool to find out quickly which management paradigm underpins a given technology.

The purpose of our *enhanced taxonomy* was to go beyond the sole understanding of the management paradigm by providing criteria to actually select a paradigm first, and then a technology. To this end, we identified four criteria: (i) the granularity at which the delegation process takes place (by domain, by microtask, or by macrotask); (ii) the semantics of the information model (managed object, computational object, or goal); (iii) the degree of specification of a task (full or partial); and (iv) the degree of automation of management (high, medium, or low). This enhanced taxonomy complements the previous one and is more practical. It gives some arguments for designers and users of management applications to select one paradigm rather than another.

Chapter 5

ANALYSIS OF THE SOLUTION SPACE

Our objective in this chapter is to analyze the solution space described in Chapter 4 and draw some high-level conclusions for our management architecture. In particular, we explain why we selected Web technologies and weakly distributed hierarchical management in WIMA.

This chapter is organized as follows. In Section 5.1, we show that there is no single winner and that different solutions are best suited to different management tasks. In Section 5.2, we highlight the importance for administrators not to focus immediately on selecting a technology. In Section 5.3, we perform a reality check on the different technologies and paradigms investigated in Chapter 4. The issues of support and technical maturity lead us to eliminate cooperative management. In Section 5.4, we explain why the *my-middleware-is-better-than-yours* syndrome leads us to rule out all the solutions based on distributed object-oriented middleware. In Section 5.5, we investigate why mobile code is not ready yet, and why we need to prepare for its future integration. In Section 5.6, we come to the conclusion that the distribution of NSM should rely on a weakly distributed hierarchical management paradigm. In Section 5.7, we decide to adopt Web-based management for the next management cycle. Finally, we summarize this chapter in Section 5.8.

5.1 No Win-Win Solution

The first conclusion that can be drawn from our taxonomies is that there is no win-win solution for the next management cycle. Some paradigms are more appropriate than others, depending on the size and complexity of the network and depending on the nature and complexity of the system, application, service, etc. to manage. This diversity gives us flexibility. Certain paradigms, e.g. mobile code, encompass a large number of technologies and can be further subdivided into several paradigms. This yields a wide variety of fine-grained designs. Designers should thus no longer feel constrained when they model management applications. Among all available paradigms, they should select the one that allows them to model the problem at hand in the most natural way. The days of protocol APIs, when the focus was on the nuts and bolts of NSM, are over. Management applications can now rely on programmatic APIs, where the focus is on software development and user friendliness.

To illustrate that different solutions are best suited to different tasks, let us study a simple scenario that illustrates the growing management needs of an enterprise over time. In this example, we are concerned only with the design qualities of the management paradigms. Their practicality will be investigated in subsequent sections.

In a small company, to manage a small LAN or a distributed system comprising a dozen machines or so, there is no need for an expensive technology offering a high level of automation with computational objects, or even goals. A less expensive solution based on managed objects and microtasks is sufficient. Centralized management is suitable in this case.

Over time, this enterprise develops and opens branches abroad. It then becomes a geographically dispersed midsize enterprise, but still has fairly simple needs (data network, no multimedia services). A weakly distributed hierarchical technology is well suited. The required degree of automation is medium, and managed objects are sufficient to deal with simple needs. RMON is a good candidate for monitoring and performance management. When the bandwidth of the WAN links connecting the main office to the remote offices (or, at a larger scale, the headquarters to the subsidiaries) becomes too expensive, it is time to migrate from centralized to weakly distributed hierarchical management: Each subsidiary is equipped with a local management platform.

As people in this enterprise begin using multimedia services on a more regular basis, there comes a time when the semi-automated handling of reservations and bandwidth allocations is no longer an option: A higher degree of automation is required. Inexpensive, distributed object technologies usually suffice. But some cases can be better handled by intelligent agents. Typically, when confronted by a new service, an intelligent agent can make a decision automatically, without any human intervention, based on what it learned in the past with other services. For instance, it can make a trade-off between the (usually too high) requirements set by a new end-user and the cost that the user's department is willing to pay for reserving network bandwidth. Manual intervention by an administrator is performed afterward, only when the trade-off turns out to be poor.

As this enterprise develops, the number of entities to manage grows so large that the management application becomes too complex and cumbersome. It becomes difficult to use, awkward to modify, and any change may cause a new problem due to unforeseen side-effects. The semantics of the information model are too poor: managed objects have become inadequate. Even for simple day-to-day management tasks, the time has come to use computational objects instead. As new services are adopted by users, new intelligent agents are added on an *ad hoc* basis.

The midsize company then becomes a large enterprise. Intelligent agents are no longer restricted to dealing with novel services. They can be used for complex tasks such as distributed pattern learning or data mining. For example, they can dynamically learn the peak and slack hours of a VPN overlaying an ATM network, and can automatically readjust the bandwidth rented from the service provider in order to reduce the running costs for the enterprise. Intelligent agents can also learn dynamically at what time of the day voice-over-IP and data traffic must be routed over different WAN links to guarantee the required QoS, and when it becomes possible to route them through the same WAN links (slack hours); this allows the enterprise to temporarily rent less bandwidth and thus reduce its costs.

Later, this enterprise is bought by a large multinational with tens or hundreds of thousands of managed systems and devices. The degree of automation of management then becomes critical. This time, day-to-day NSM should entirely rely on distributed objects, and managed objects should be banned from interactive APIs. There is no way the operators can find the time to go down to instrumentation types of abstraction to understand or correct a problem: They must have only high-level decisions to make. Clearly, if day-to-day NSM is already based on distributed objects prior to the merger, the integration of a smaller management application with a larger one is considerably easier.

Finally, in the large multinational, the number of requests for advanced services (e.g., multimedia services requiring bandwidth reservation) gradually increases. So does the diversity of the services that are used on a daily basis. The number of specialized intelligent agents then becomes high, and it no longer makes sense to segment this knowledge. This calls for elaborate multi-agent systems, whereby a large number of intelligent agents cooperate in order to optimize network-bandwidth usage and reduce the number of reservations that could have been, but were not, granted. To the best of our knowledge, no one has already tested such systems on a large scale in NSM.

We hope to have highlighted one important point in this example: The relative weights given by the administrator to the different selection criteria of our enhanced taxonomy give a clear indication of the best management paradigm in a given context.

5.2 Do Not Focus on Technology Immediately

The second conclusion that can be derived from our enhanced taxonomy is that there is not a unique relationship between a quadrant (see Fig. 6, p. 85), a management paradigm, and a technology. Several paradigms span multiple quadrants and therefore offer different degrees of automation, or different levels of semantic richness of the information model. Similarly, a single technology can support different paradigms, and can thus offer different degrees of automation, different delegation granularities, different degrees of specification of a task, or different levels of semantic richness.

The practical consequence of this remark is that selecting a technology solves only a fraction of the problem—although many administrators today focus mostly on this step. Initially, one should determine the criteria of our enhanced taxonomy that are the most relevant to one's enterprise. Once this has been done, the management paradigm can easily be derived from our enhanced taxonomy. After these two steps have been made, it is time to select a technology with our simple taxonomy.

This is illustrated by the following example. Convinced by an advertising campaign, an administrator decides that mobile code is the solution to manage his/her network. Before delving into the design of a new, powerful management application, he/she decides to investigate the market of mobile-code technologies. All vendors claim to sell the best product, so what technology should he/she choose? With our enhanced taxonomy, our administrator can see at a glance that under the same name, he/she can actually purchase four very different types of technology, because mobile code spans four quadrants. Some technologies offer low-level semantics, others high-level semantics; some offer a high degree of automation of management, others a medium degree; some support delegation by microtask, others by macrotask. The administrator can also see immediately that mobile code encompasses three finer-grained paradigms: remote evaluation, code on demand, and mobile agents. In the end, our taxonomies allowed this administrator to realize that mobile code is multifaceted, and to choose the technology offering the best value-for-money according to the relative weights that he/she gave to the four selection criteria of our enhanced taxonomy.

5.3 Reality Check: Support and Technical Maturity

In our two taxonomies, we classify and compare many different technologies and paradigms that can be used in NSM. The fact that these potential solutions are presented side by side does not imply that they are equally ready to be used in industry, let alone appropriate for such a large market as NSM. We structured the solution space in technical terms, based on the elegance and promises of the designs rather than the feasibility of the solutions. But in order to select an appropriate solution for the next management cycle, it is important to put candidate solutions through a reality check. Among the technologies we described in the solution space, many lack proper support and are confined to the research community. Some do not even go beyond the proof of concept... To deploy a solution in a production environment, as opposed to prototyping in a test environment, it does not suffice that the design be technically appealing: The technology itself must be well tested and well supported. In addition to its technical qualities, the solution retained for the next management cycle should therefore exhibit two important qualities: support and maturity.

Support includes commercial and technical support. *Commercial support* is necessary in almost all production environments. If a management application does not work, the only guarantee of the customer is that the supplier of the application be legally bound to delivering quality software. Many solutions presented in Chapter 4 are not commercially supported because they are research prototypes simply demonstrating a good idea.

Technical support is equally important; it is primarily about maintenance. In case a major problem occurs, the customer must be able to receive technical support by the supplier's support team. This, too, is mandatory in a production environment. As far as the management architecture is concerned, we should thus select a solution for which commercial and technical support are available.

To put it simply, *technical maturity* means that a solution is not appropriate until it has been sufficiently debugged by others. If the provider has not yet acquired enough experience by working with other customers, the management platform is not really a commercial software; it is rather a prototype for beta-test sites. And many enterprises do not have the skills, manpower, and organization to enroll as a beta-test site. An important aspect of technical maturity is that it takes time for a technical support team to become efficient: The staff needs to be trained through a variety of problems at many sites and a lot of trial-and-error stumbling. Consequently, the market for the paradigm that we select for the next management cycle should be a commodity market: It would be too hazardous to select a technology that is still confined to a niche market.

These two criteria, support and technical maturity, lead us to eliminate all the technologies that pertain to cooperative management. The DAI community is still at an early stage of research with respect to intelligent agents and multi-agent systems. Many technological problems are still unsolved. For instance, it is not clear what language should be used to communicate between agents (KQML [89], ACL [91], etc.), or what format should be used by the agents to exchange "knowledge" (Knowledge Interchange Format [102], etc.). In the specific case of NSM, it is not clear at all what ontologies should be used for managing IP networks and systems. Worse, it is not even clear what properties should be exhibited by a "good" agent-communication language, a "good" ontology, etc. All of these problems are very exciting to study, but it will take years before the DAI community builds the *corpus* of knowledge necessary for the cooperative-management paradigm to be usable in application domains. We are still very far from a commodity market. Until this level of maturity is reached, it remains unrealistic to base the management architecture of the next management cycle on intelligent agents, multi-agent systems, or more generally on the cooperative management paradigm. The slow pace at which the FIPA consortium is progressing in the telecommunications application domain is an indication that these problems are not yet well understood and not easy to solve.

In short, WIMA should be based on a management paradigm for which there are commodity technologies that are both technically mature and well supported.

5.4 The *My-Middleware-Is-Better-Than-Yours* Syndrome

There is a fundamental problem with using object-oriented middleware in NSM. It is pictured by the following analogy with viruses.

The *my-middleware-is-better-than-yours* syndrome is a disease that has spread in the software industry since the mid-1990s. It is known to have already infected most middleware platforms on the market, be they based on open standards such as CORBA and Java, or on proprietary solutions such as Microsoft's DCOM. The symptoms of this syndrome are common to all well-known forms of infection:

- Only consenting individuals can be infected.
- Once infected by middleware, an individual is obliged to use it to communicate with all other individuals because it immediately loses all its previous communication skills.
- Once infected, an individual takes time to learn to live with middleware.
- Unlike what happens with most diseases, an individual is free to replace its middleware framework with another one at any time. But because of the previous point, this should be avoided.
- Once an individual is infected, its middleware platform quickly takes up most of its CPU, memory, and disk resources. Middleware likes to have a large footprint on individuals.
- Middleware is very exclusive: To communicate with an infected individual, you must have already caught the same disease. This trait is the sheer result of adaptation through darwinian selection: The disease spreads by consent, so there must be an incentive for individuals to voluntarily get infected!
- Middleware loves gambling: You must be infected *before* you know what middleware will be supported by the majority of the population in the future.
- Middleware is antisocial: It prevents individuals from communicating with a large proportion of the population (that is, the individuals infected by another middleware framework).
- Middleware is merciful: If an individual cannot get infected but really needs to communicate with an infected individual, it can use a translation service called *gateway*. This service is slow, cumbersome to use, and loses some semantics. But how could you possibly argue once you have been pardoned...

In other words, object-oriented middleware packages have largely diverged from their initial objective: to allow all machines to interoperate in an open way, with a high level of semantics, via standard interfaces, with a standard protocol, through an object-oriented DPE. Due to diverging commercial interests, the object-oriented middleware market has been segmented, with different vendors or consortia trying to justify why their middleware is better than the others. Today, it is anything but a commodity market. When we select a middleware platform, we must choose our camp: CORBA, EJBs, DCOM, etc. And of course, we can make the "wrong" choice—that is, the market can coalesce around another middleware framework two years after we have invested a fortune in the "wrong" framework. In the author's opinion, this situation will last a long time: There will be no winner in the middleware battle, at least for many years. As a result, a management architecture cannot reasonably rely on a specific object-oriented middleware framework to be available on all network devices and systems worldwide.

Another issue with object-oriented middleware is interoperability within a given framework. CORBA products developed by different vendors rarely interoperate smoothly, so much so that many enterprises prefer to standardize internally[1] on a single CORBA platform such as Orbix or Visibroker. One well-known interoperability problem is the Basic Object Adapter (BOA [192]), an API used by the server side of CORBA applications (*implementations* in CORBA parlance) to interact with the ORB. For years, the BOA was so under-specified that developers were forced to use vendor-specific extensions [208]. Only in 1998 did the OMG release the Portable Object Adapter (POA [193]), which enables CORBA developers to write portable code. The BOA has now been deprecated by the OMG, but in the meantime, millions of lines of non-interoperable CORBA code have been written... Other examples of interoperability problems include CORBA Services, which are often implemented by vendors before they are standardized by the OMG. Porting the code written in the meantime is expensive, so not all enterprises do this—and relying on the interoperability of pre-standard code is... risky, to put it mildly!

Note that CORBA is not the only object-oriented middleware framework exposed to interoperability problems. The multitude of versions of Java released by Sun Microsystems in recent years are renowned to pose such problems. In Section 11.3, we will mention another example: RMI.

A third problem exhibited by most object-oriented middleware platforms is their large footprint on agents. In the telecommunications world, the CPU, memory, and disk overhead induced by CORBA is not critical because, in this market, agents are rarely resource bounded. The cost of adding more memory or processing power to a $1,000,000 telephone switch is negligible[2]. But in the IP world, the footprint of CORBA or J2EE (Java 2 Enterprise Edition, based on EJBs) on agents is a no-no. Even lighter-weight middleware such as J2SE (Java 2 Standard Edition, based on standard Java) or a Java Virtual Machine (JVM) are not always an option. In the IP world, a number of agents have limited resources available to management because cost is more of an issue: The average cost of an IP system or network device is much lower than that of a telephone switch.

A fourth problem is the license fee of object-oriented middleware. When a simple network device costs less than $100, who is willing to pay another $50 to $100 to run an Object Request Broker (ORB) and a handful of CORBA services on it? Because bottom-of-the-range equipment cannot be expected to support middleware for the sole purpose of NSM, our management architecture cannot rely on distributed object-oriented middleware.

---

1. Note that even this safety measure causes problems, e.g. when two organizations merge.
2. In Section 4.1.3.2, we mentioned the growing acceptance of CORBA as the standard object-oriented middleware in the telecommunications world. In fixed telephony, agents can even afford to support several DPEs simultaneously (although they are not always easy to integrate).

In summary, the two main messages that we try to capture in the catchphrase *my-middleware-is-better-than-yours* are the fight among vendors who think they know better, and the risk factor for customers who must choose their camp before the market is mature.

For WIMA, high-profile, object-oriented middleware frameworks such as CORBA or EJBs are not an option, even though they allow for neatly designed management applications. We must limit ourselves to a lower-profile solution, with a reasonably small footprint and a low cost per agent.

5.5 Mobile Code and Security

Mobile code has received a lot of attention lately, as we explained in Section 4.1.3.1. However, so far, we have not really seen a good reason for using mobile code in NSM instead of more standard technologies. On a case-by-case basis, remote evaluation, code on demand, or mobile agents can perform better than the client-server model that underlies most other solutions. But we still have not found a management task that is *always* performed better by mobile code.

The situation is different in service management, where mobile code has proved to be very useful for dynamic service provisioning, especially in the area of *active services* [39]. It is currently considered *the* way to go by the people who believe that we cannot possibly have interoperable middleware on all machines worldwide.

The main problem with mobile code is security. This is the main obstacle to its wide deployment. Actually, there are two different problems: We must secure the host—i.e., the machine executing the mobile code—from a malicious code [220] and the code from a malicious host [136]. In enterprise management, the first problem has attracted more attention from researchers than the second. But both need to be solved before we can use mobile code in a new, general-purpose management architecture. Note that these security problems have proved harder to solve than many people initially expected. For a good introduction to the range of issues at stake, see Vigna [274].

Because these security issues are still unsolved, it is too risky, in our view, to base the next management cycle on this new paradigm. Software engineers first need to understand how to secure mobile code in general. Then, NSM specialists will be in a position to leverage it in management. But since it is likely that people will soon use mobile code for service management in real life, it seems appropriate to devise a management architecture that can easily integrate mobile-code technologies as soon as they have been secured.

In WIMA, we did precisely that. Our organizational and communication models do not require mobile code, but we offer a simple means of integrating it with XML.

5.6 Distribution

As we saw in Chapter 4, the way to address the scalability issue in SNMP-based management is to distribute management. In Section 5.3, we ruled out cooperative management. So we are left with two alternatives: weakly and strongly distributed hierarchical management.

In Section 4.1.3, we grouped strongly distributed hierarchical paradigms into two categories: mobile code and distributed objects. We explained in Section 5.4 that because of the *my-middleware-is-better-than-yours* syndrome, we must eliminate distributed objects. We cannot expect all agents worldwide to support interoperable object-oriented middleware. In Section 5.5, we concluded that mobile code is a promising paradigm, but it cannot be used as the basis for the next management cycle until security issues are completely understood and solved—and many researchers expect this to take some time. Neither distributed objects nor mobile code are viable options; we therefore have to eliminate strongly distributed hierarchical management, despite all its qualities.

In conclusion, WIMA should be based on weakly distributed hierarchical management. At first, this might appear to be a setback, if we compare this solution with the more advanced solutions that were investigated in Chapter 4. But as we describe, chapter after chapter, all the features supported and all the SNMP problems that are solved by our management architecture, it is hoped that the reader will become convinced of the relevance of this decision.

5.7 Web-Based Management

Our simple taxonomy gives three examples of weakly distributed hierarchical management paradigms: TMN, RMON, and PDP/PEP. We ignore the PDP/PEP architecture here because it is not a general-purpose management architecture: It is only valid for policies and is too limited for what we want to do. Similarly, RMON is only useful to manage network devices; in addition, it can perform just a few management tasks. As for TMN, we already saw that it is not appropriate for the IP world. We therefore have to rule out all of these solutions.

In the end, we decided to devise a new weakly distributed management paradigm that does not appear in our taxonomies. WIMA is a form of *Web-based management*. This expression groups together different types of management paradigms, centralized or distributed, which all share the same characteristic: they use standard Web technologies. This explains why Web-based management does not explicitly appear in our simple taxonomy: It does not qualify for the criterion retained to build this taxonomy. It does not constitute a type *per se*, but overlaps several types.

The scope of Web-based management will be precisely defined in Chapter 6. This will allow the reader to grasp the innovations of WIMA that are detailed in the subsequent chapters. The distribution aspects of WIMA will be covered in Chapter 7.

5.8 Summary

In this chapter, we analyzed the solution space presented in Chapter 4. In Section 5.1, we saw that there is no win-win solution: Different solutions are best suited to different management tasks. We studied a series of examples where different management paradigms are considered solely with respect to their design elegance, without taking into account any deployment constraints. In Section 5.2, we highlighted an important problem in NSM: All to often, administrators focus on the selection of a technology rather than a management paradigm. Our two taxonomies can help solve this problem. In Section 5.3, we explained that cooperative management technologies do not survive the reality check of support and technical maturity. In Section 5.4, we described the *my-middleware-is-better-than-yours* syndrome and explained that it prevents us from using solutions based on object-oriented middleware, especially CORBA and Java. In Section 5.5, we investigated the case of mobile code and concluded that security issues are not yet understood well enough. It is thus too risky to base a new management architecture on this paradigm. But mobile code is expected to be used in service management in the near future, e.g. for dynamic service provisioning, so it is a good idea to pave the way for it in NSM. In Section 5.6, we investigated the distribution aspects of the new management architecture and selected weakly distributed hierarchical management. Finally, we concluded in Section 5.7 that the best candidate for the next management cycle is Web-based management.

Chapter 6

STATE OF THE ART IN WEB-BASED MANAGEMENT

Web-based management is an ill-defined concept, because it has greatly evolved over the years. Many people confuse it with the use of a Web browser to perform a management task—a very simple approach that we call *browser-based management*. The extent of this confusion is such that Harler entitled his book "Web-Based Network Management: Beyond the Browser" [112], to stress that there is more to Web-based management than a mere Web browser. Other people confuse Web-based management with Web-Based Enterprise Management (WBEM), notably because of the considerable marketing hype that plagued WBEM in its early days, before its takeover by the DMTF.

The state of the art presented in this chapter highlights the multiple facets of Web-based management and the increasing richness of the solutions that are based on it. In its full meaning, Web-based management is about leveraging *any* Web technology in *any* area covered by enterprise management. In this book, we restrict our scope to NSM. The Web technologies considered here are Web browsers, HTTP (HyperText Transfer Protocol), HTML (HyperText Markup Language), XML (eXtensible Markup Language), CGI (Common Gateway Interface) programs[1], Java applications, Java applets, Java servlets, and Java RMI. Proprietary technologies such as Microsoft's ActiveX and Active Server Pages (ASPs) are not investigated here. Compared to their standard counterparts, they add no general-purpose features but simply make it easier to work in a specific proprietary environment. For the sake of completeness, we include Java RMI (i.e., distributed Java) in

---

1. CGI programs can be coded in the form of Perl scripts, Korn shell scripts, binary C programs (compiled and linked), etc. More details on Web technologies can be found in Krishnamurthy and Rexford [144].

this review of Web-based management, although we already ruled out this solution for the next management cycle in Section 5.4.

This chapter is organized as a taxonomy based primarily on the type of Web technologies supported by the manager and the agent. These types are sorted by increasing order of sophistication and complexity of the manager and the agent. Initially, we present them almost in chronological order, as the first uses of Web technologies in NSM were also the simplest. Later, we depart from history because some advanced solutions were proposed several years before less elaborate solutions were adopted by the market.

In Section 6.1 through Section 6.4, we describe browser-based usage monitoring, browser-based metamanagement, browser-based management, and three-tier management. These four types work with plain SNMP agents and are characterized by a growing sophistication of the manager. In Section 6.5 through Section 6.7, we detail HTTP-based management, XML-based management, and distributed Java-based management. These three types correspond to an increasing sophistication of the agent, and thus of the agent-manager interactions. In Section 6.8, we give references to the ever-growing number of commercial products in this active field. Finally, we summarize this chapter in Section 6.9.

6.1 Browser-Based Usage Monitoring

In our view, Web-based management was born in 1993, when NCSA Mosaic began spreading all over the planet [292, pp. 12–14]. That year is often considered the outset of the Web, when it left a closed circle of initiated researchers and reached out for the world. Early Web technologies (that is, Web browsers, HTTP, HTML, and CGI programs) were used in NSM almost from day one. For instance, the author used them in a test environment in early 1994 and in a production environment from mid-1994. Discussions in Web-related mailing lists and Usenet newsgroups showed that many people were doing similar experiments at the same time.

Initially, administrators learned by trial and error how to leverage early Web technologies in NSM. Most notably, they developed Web-based GUIs and simple CGI programs and made it possible to perform simple management tasks via any browser on any machine. This led to different types of *browser-based management*. The first two are equally simple but address different issues, so we present them separately in Section 6.1 and Section 6.2. The third type is more advanced and will be described in Section 6.3.

Network and systems usage is often monitored with daily, weekly, monthly, and yearly reports providing coarse-grained usage statistics in graphical format. Regularly checking these automatically generated reports is called *usage monitoring*; it is part of everyday life for most administrators in the world. Monitoring network usage is called *aggregate traffic analysis* by Metzler and DeNoia [177].

When these statistics are displayed in the form of bar charts, one bar typically represents 15 minutes, one hour, or one day. These reports enable administrators to perform capacity planning. By detecting in advance that a resource is used close to full capacity, they can take action before problems arise—e.g., increase this capacity or reduce the need for it. This is a simple form of proactive management. Note that usage monitoring is not only useful for capacity planning, but also for detecting certain faults that show up on bar charts or line graphs. In the latter case, we are in the realm of reactive management.

In NSM, *browser-based usage monitoring* is characterized by the interactive use of a Web browser for visualizing usage reports for network links, network devices, and systems. These reports can be generated by an external, Web-independent process, or by CGI programs extracting data directly from a data repository. With Web technologies, instead of printing usage reports on paper, administrators can put them online[1] on an open or restricted-access internal Web server and make them accessible via simple HTML forms (with option menus, multiple-choice boxes, etc.). Once in electronic format, usage reports can automatically be archived on tape or Compact Disk (CD): It is no longer necessary to store print-outs in binders, which saves a lot of time and space. Browser-based usage monitoring proved immediately successful in NSM. It was the first large-scale use of Web-based management by the market.

Graphical usage reports could already be viewed in the past with expensive, proprietary solutions. But Web technologies enabled administrators to do it themselves, simply, quickly, at a low cost; and they allowed people to access the same data from a Windows PC, a Mac, a Unix workstation, etc. Even better, since many administrators were developing similar tools to view network and systems usage reports via a Web browser, a number of software packages, with different degrees of maturity, were made available to the NSM community. To date, many people still use them, thereby avoiding the expense of a commercial management platform. Some packages are freely available to academics and researchers; others are open source and available to all. Two packages are currently used all over the world: Multi-Router Traffic Grapher (MRTG [190]) and ntop [70]. Both of them have become fairly sophisticated over time while remaining simple to use. WebTrafMon [121] is another example of freely available software supporting browser-based usage monitoring.

6.2 Browser-Based Metamanagement

In parallel to usage monitoring, early Web technologies were swiftly leveraged in NSM for performing collateral management tasks such as reporting problems to helpdesks, trouble-ticketing, managing procedures and technical documentation, etc. We group them under a single generic name: *browser-based metamanagement.*

Although the sophistication of the manager and the agent is similar, in this type of management, to that found in browser-based usage monitoring, we distinguish two separate types in our taxonomy because the management tasks are very different: Almost all sites perform usage monitoring, whereas metamanagement is ignored by many, at least to a

---

1. Typical graphics formats include Portable Network Graphics (PNG), Graphics Interchange Format (GIF), and Postscript.

certain extent. Also, in retrospect, we can see that the markets corresponding to these two types have followed different tracks. A number of good-quality software packages are freely available for browser-based usage monitoring, and many organizations (especially small and midsize companies) use them. This is not the case with browser-based metamanagement. To date, administrators usually rely on commercial packages for metamanagement; otherwise, they often ignore it.

6.2.1 Online problem reporting

Administrators discovered by trial and error that, by writing a dozen HTML forms and interfacing them with the troubleticket database via a few CGI programs, they could easily standardize and automate problem reporting and troubleticketing. Users were delighted by this new tool, because it suppressed a major source of inconvenience: misunderstandings! Anyone who has reported, over the phone, an IT or networking problem to another person knows how challenging and error prone this apparently simple task can be. The situation is even worse when the helpdesk is outsourced, because the person you speak to is not familiar with your own environment.

Another source of problems disappeared: the management of log numbers—what we call troubleticket numbers in modern systems. When problems were reported over the phone or via e-mail, users were informed of their log numbers by helpdesk staff, that is, people. And when you have people, you have errors (see Section 4.2.2.3). Sometimes they would forget to give users their log numbers; sometimes they would give a wrong number by reading the wrong field on their screen; and even more frequently, the user would lose the piece of paper on which the magic log number had been hastily noted! With Web-based interfaces, the opening of troubletickets and the assignment of log numbers were automated. Troubletickets and their associated log numbers were displayed by the browser in a systematic way, in a form that could easily be saved in electronic format.

Web-based problem reporting eliminated potential sources of human errors, and simplified and decreased the work of helpdesks, sometimes very significantly [185]. Today, few people would consider purchasing a problem-reporting system without a Web interface.

6.2.2 Online management procedures, online documentation

In production environments operating 24*7 (24 hours a day, 7 days a week), monitoring staff in charge of NSM typically follow well-defined management procedures to identify the root cause of a problem and correct it. This is mandatory in heterogeneous environments, where no single person can know by heart how to troubleshoot thousands of problems on different types of equipment from different vendors.

Web technologies gave administrators the opportunity to transfer online all the management procedures that used to be printed on paper and kept in binders, filling up entire shelves. This required the transcription of thousands of files (the originals of the procedures) into HTML pages, but it did not involve writing elaborate applications. The indexing system used by the operators to work their way through the procedures remained the same. But instead of flipping through many binders of procedures, the operators had online access to all the procedures from their own machine. Their navigation through the procedures could be facilitated by using hypertext navigation or search engines. Once the procedures had been converted to HTML, a search engine allowed operators to identify and retrieve a procedure by typing in a few keywords—and this could be implemented in only a few hours with Wide-Area Information Servers (WAIS [245, 204]).

At about the same time, equipment vendors began distributing their documentations in electronic format instead of paper, e.g. on CD-ROM (Compact Disk - Read-Only Memory). By putting these documentations online, administrators made them easier to access. They also made it possible to embed hyperlinks to the relevant manual pages within the HTML procedures.

6.2.3 Online troubleshooting assistance

Administrators also helped operators identify the cause of frequent problems with online troubleshooting assistance. This involved writing more elaborate applications with numerous HTML forms and CGI programs. Symptom-driven navigation through HTML forms helped operators narrow down the origin of a network or systems problem to only a few possibilities. Operators were asked simple questions such as the type of equipment, the type of fault, the error message displayed on the console, the severity of the notification received by the management platform, etc. With a few clicks, an operator could save a lot of browsing through entire catalogs of procedures.

The integration of online management procedures, online vendor documentations, and online troubleshooting assistance proved to be an important step forward in NOCs. Interactive Web interfaces were more user-friendly than the thick binders full of procedures that operators were used to, and online procedures were simpler to update for administrators and operational staff.

6.3 Browser-Based Management

Chronologically, the next step for administrators (and operators) was to directly interact with agents via a Web browser—what we call *browser-based management*. They not only executed ancillary management tasks via a browser, or access usage reports generated from data retrieved externally via regular polling, but they also interactively managed equipment. At that time, in the IP world, agents had only two embedded servers: one for SNMP and another for telnet. Thus, in browser-based management, manager-agent interactions are either based on SNMP or telnet.

6.3.1 Troubleshooting scripts executed via a Web browser

Certain management procedures can be automated because they consist only of commands to execute. They do not require that the operator be physically present in front of the faulty equipment to handle hardware. Some of the troubleshooting operations can easily be coded as scripts. For instance, an operator can use the `snmpset` command [64] to reset an interface via SNMP, or the `ping` command to test the reachability of a host. But other troubleshooting operations are not straightforward to automate, because some client-server programs can only work in interactive mode (e.g., the connection to a remote device via `telnet`). A well-known problem with SNMP is that, for many pieces of equipment, not all the commands supported by the Command-Line Interface (CLI) have an equivalent in an SNMP MIB. In other words, some commands can only be performed from the console or, and this is generally the case for NOCs, via `telnet`. For years, such commands could not be coded in scripts. This problem was solved in 1994[1] by `expect`, a Tcl-based toolkit for automating interactive programs [152]. By wrapping interactive commands with `expect`, administrators could code them as scripts and execute them automatically, in unattended mode (we will come back to `expect` in Section 6.5.1). Since then, all the management procedures that did not require hardware handling could be automated.

By sheer coincidence, 1994 was also the year when Web technologies spread out in NSM. A useful feature of CGI is that troubleshooting scripts can easily be turned into CGI programs, or invoked by CGI programs. Coupling HTML pages with troubleshooting CGI programs allowed administrators to automate management procedures one step further. Instead of simply displaying the management procedure to follow, they could make operators run it via their Web browser, in case the procedure could be automated. This was typically achieved by using an HTML form: A proposed action would be displayed to the operator, and by clicking on a push button, he/she would trigger the execution of the adequate script—with no chance of mistyping commands in a `telnet` session. This possibility to interactively launch the execution of a troubleshooting procedure was a useful complement to symptom-driven HTML pages. Web technologies enabled operators to perform online troubleshooting, as opposed to simply getting online assistance.

6.3.2 Configuration management

Browser-based management also allows for a simple form of configuration management that leverages the ability of some agents to download their configuration file from a remote server upon reboot; e.g., Cisco IP routers can use the Trivial File Transfer Protocol (TFTP [240]) for that purpose. By interacting with HTML forms specific to the agent, the administrator generates a new configuration file on the Web server where the CGI program is executed. Then, this file is moved to the server where all of the agents' configuration files are stored. Finally, when the agent is rebooted by the operator (locally or remotely), it

---

1. Note that some sites solved this problem before, on an *ad hoc* basis, by modifying the source code of the `telnet` client. But there was no general solution to this problem, and many NOCs relied on operators to `telnet` into a device and type in some commands in interactive mode— still a common practice today.

automatically loads its new configuration file. The advantage of this solution is that it works with legacy SNMP agents: Web technologies are only used to generate new configuration files. In Section 6.5.2, we will describe a more elaborate type of configuration management.

6.3.3 Java applet with an SNMP stack

Another type of browser-based management appeared several years later with Java. In 1997–98, we saw a number of start-ups (AdventNet, Metrix, etc.) come up with new management applications developed partially or entirely in Java. In this scenario, the new Java-based management application is independent of the traditional SNMP-based management platform. It complements it and runs in parallel. The Java-based management application provides operators with more user-friendly GUIs than HTML forms, which are somewhat limited in terms of graphics. The interaction with the agent still relies on well-known technologies—typically SNMP, or possibly others such as expect or ping—but the front-end that operators interact with is now highly graphical. The management application can be implemented as a Java applet running in the operator's browser, or as a standalone Java application[1]—the difference in the code is limited.

Bruins was among the first to describe this way of using SNMP to communicate between the manager (Java applet or application) and the agent. He calls it *Java-based SNMP* [38]. In this approach, the agent cannot tell whether it is communicating with a traditional SNMP-based management platform, a management application written in Java, or a Java applet running in a Web browser.

This type of browser-based management is well suited to the sites who need simple online performance monitoring. Via a Web browser, it is possible to configure an SNMP agent (e.g., an intelligent hub supporting RMON) via a Java applet, then retrieve management data via SNMP for several minutes, process it within the applet, and finally display it with elaborate graphics.

The commercial market of Web-based management has thrived on this concept, with a slight nuance: The Java-based management application did not run parallel to, but instead of, the SNMP-based management application. Most of the start-ups in this market jumped on the bandwagon because it allowed them to take a share of a lucrative market that was then dominated by just a few SNMP-based management-platform vendors.

6.4 Three-Tier Management

The last step before using HTTP end-to-end between the manager and the agent is to go via an external management gateway, typically an HTTP-SNMP gateway. We call it *three-tier management* because it relies on a three-tier architecture. In this scenario, the communi-

---

1. In the case of a Java application, the expression *browser-based management* is stretching it a bit, but the principle remains exactly the same.

cation between the Web browser and the gateway can be tightly or loosely coupled with the communication between the gateway and the agent. When it is tightly coupled, each request from the Web browser triggers a request from the gateway to the agent. When it is loosely coupled, the gateway independently retrieves and processes data from the agents, and requests from the Web browser are directly served from this aggregated data.

6.4.1 Deri *et al.*: SNMP-to-URL mapping

In 1996–97, the IBM Zurich Research Laboratory ran a project called Webbin'. This project leveraged Web technologies to hide the idiosyncrasies of the SNMP and CMIP communication protocols to the management-application developer [19]. The core element of this project is the Liaison architecture. One facet of this work is a precursor of HTTP-based management: Deri's mapping [67, 68] between SNMP and Uniform Resource Locators (URLs [24]). In Liaison, an external management gateway[1] performs the translation between HTTP and SNMP. For instance, to retrieve the MIB variable sysDescr (description of the agent) in MIB-II, a manager can request the following URL from the management gateway:

```
<http://kis.zurich.ibm.com/SNMP/GET/sysDescr.0?Host=
bal.zurich.ibm.com&Community=public>
```

In this example, `kis.zurich.ibm.com` is the management gateway and `bal.zurich.ibm.com` is the agent. A CGI program called GET processes the input on the gateway. It receives the OID `sysDescr.0` in input with two attributes: Host (the agent) and Community (the community string in SNMPv1 and v2c). The communication between the three tiers is tightly coupled here: The manager sends an HTTP request to the gateway, which translates it into SNMP, sends an SNMP request to the agent, receives an SNMP response from the agent, translates it into HTTP, and sends it to the manager.

6.4.2 Kasteleijn: HTTP and SNMP

Another type of three-tier management was described by Kasteleijn in 1997 [137]. At that time, a new high-speed ATM backbone was deployed in The Netherlands. Kasteleijn developed a prototype called the Web-based ATM-Switch Management tool (WbASM) to allow organizations connected to the backbone to have access to management information related to it. SNMP data was prefetched by the WbASM server via SNMP, and stored in files. Users could later access the WbASM server from their Web browser and, after authenticating themselves, access various usage statistics (e.g., average link utilization) and instantaneous measurements (e.g., uptime per link). In this scenario, communication between the browsers and the WbASM server relied on HTTP, while communication between the WbASM server and the agents relied on SNMP. Both communications were loosely coupled.

---

1. In Liaison, this is called a *proxy*. But we use the term *management gateway* to comply with the terminology defined in Section 2.6.

6.4.3 Integration of a Web browser in the SNMP-based management platform

A more common type of three-tier management is the integration of the Web browser into the SNMP-based management platform. Instead of using proprietary graphical interfaces, management-platform vendors can recode their GUIs as Java applets. For instance, by using the Java Native Interface (JNI), they can easily interface the Java servlets, which interact with the applets for the graphical part of the management application, with the rest of the application, which does the real work and is usually written in another language (e.g., C or C++) for a question of efficiency. In this scenario, operators use their Web browser as a single interface to all management tasks, and the SNMP-based management platform becomes an external HTTP-SNMP gateway that can operate in loosely and tightly coupled modes.

6.4.4 Deri: Java RMI and SNMP

In 1998, Deri described a three-tier approach to locate mobile equipment for asset management: JLocator [69]. This is the most sophisticated of all the approaches considered here in three-tier management, because it uses distributed object-oriented middleware (Java RMI) to communicate between the Java applets (JLocator clients) loaded in the Web browser and the external management gateway (JLocator server). In other words, the JLocator server is an external RMI-SNMP gateway, as opposed to the external HTTP-SNMP gateways presented in the previous examples. For instance, once he/she is authenticated, the administrator can access detailed information about a roaming PC from the Web browser: The Java applet displays information retrieved by the JLocator server from a database accessed via Java DataBase Connectivity (JDBC). Different JLocator servers can communicate via Java RMI, which allows management to be distributed. As in all the approaches presented in this section, the external management gateway communicates via SNMP with the agents. Note that JLocator is not simply a prototype: It has been deployed in production networks by Finsiel in Italy to locate thousands of assets in different sites.

6.5 HTTP-Based Management

The agents that we have considered so far did not support any Web technology; only the managers did. A milestone in Web-based management was the advent of embedded HTTP servers in network devices and systems. This led to *HTTP-based management*, whereby the manager and the agent communicate via the HTTP protocol instead of SNMP or `telnet`. This type of Web-based management comprises three variants.

The first is depicted in Fig. 7. The user (either an administrator or an operator) manages the agent via a management GUI running in a Web browser. This GUI is coded as a Java applet. On the agent, we can have different kinds of internal gateways: an HTTP-SNMP gateway, an HTTP-CLI gateway, etc.

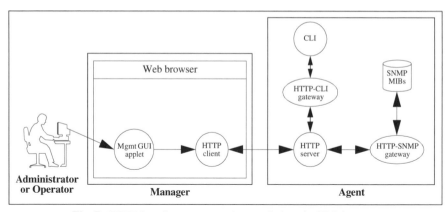

Fig. 7. HTTP-based management in attended mode: Web browser

The *SNMP MIBs* icon represents all the MIBs supported by the agent, be they generic or vendor specific. This icon is graphically represented as if the MIBs were stored on local storage, because a MIB is a virtual management-data repository. In practice, this data is very rarely stored persistently (e.g., on disk or in EPROM) because doing so would be grossly inefficient; instead, it stays in volatile memory. An SNMP MIB is often implemented by agents as a collection of C function pointers that retrieve proprietary data structures and convert them into MIB format. Depending on the degree of optimization of the code run by the agent, the HTTP-SNMP gateway can either access the in-memory data structures or do an explicit SNMP `get` or `set`.

The second variant is illustrated by Fig. 8. The agent side remains unchanged, but on the manager side, the management GUI is now integrated into the management application. The communication is still based on HTTP, but the user does not use a Web browser anymore. The application can be coded in Java, C++, C, Perl, Tcl/Tk, etc.

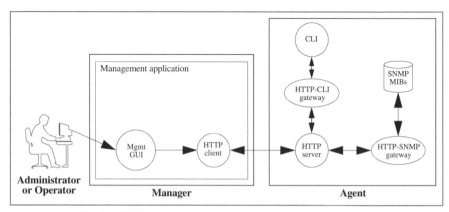

Fig. 8. HTTP-based management in attended mode: application

The third variant appears on Fig. 9. Unlike the previous two, this scenario operates in unattended (i.e., fully automated) mode. Different modules of the management application communicate with the agent via HTTP, without the intervention of a user.

In this book, most figures depict the first variant when we talk about manager-agent interactions, but we also implicitly consider the other two variants. The reader is thus invited to keep these three variants in mind.

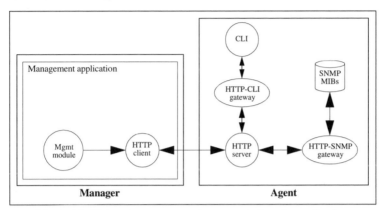

Fig. 9. HTTP-based management in unattended mode: application

An important characteristic of HTTP-based management is that it is not necessarily interactive. As far as the agent is concerned, it makes no difference whether the manager side is an applet or an application, and whether it is running in attended or unattended mode. The agent cannot tell whether it is used in the first, second, or third variant. It only sees an HTTP-based communication with the manager.

HTTP-based management is still rarely used to date, except for configuration management. But it is already a realistic option in NSM, and we have reasons to believe that its acceptance will grow in the future. In the IP networking market, since 1997–98, most large vendors have routinely embedded HTTP servers in all their devices, except sometimes for bottom-of-the-range ones. Moreover, since 1994–95, there have been freely available HTTP servers for almost all the systems on the market. If we consider that the average lifetime of an IP network device or system is about four years, we can state that a large proportion of the deployed equipment *could* rely on HTTP-based management today.

Let us now delve into the details and describe four types of HTTP-based management: CLI wrappings and mappings, embedded HTML pages and CGI programs, embedded management applications, and low-footprint embedded HTTP servers.

6.5.1 CLI wrappings and mappings

Despite all the past attempts to promote and standardize open management, many people working in NOCs still use `telnet` to connect directly to network devices and systems and debug problems via the CLI. Some of them do this because not all the commands available through the CLI have counterparts in SNMP MIBs, and not all MIB variables can easily be accessed or modified via user-friendly interfaces. For instance, a number of organizations forbid the use of SNMP `set` because SNMPv1 and v2c are insecure; in order to change the configuration of a device, operators connect to it interactively. Other people continue to use the CLI simply because they are used to it. It is their favorite tool since it is the only one they really know and feel comfortable with. However, for the majority of administrators and operators, the main reason for using the CLI via `telnet`, which will not disappear any time soon, is that it is incredibly flexible when we need to troubleshoot urgent problems, e.g. when the network appears to go berserk. Most NOCs staff spontaneously use `telnet` when thousands of users are experiencing a major problem and the "big boss" is frantically watching over their shoulder, falling prey to ever more despair as the clock ticks on... The CLI gives operators total control over a device or system, and management GUIs are no longer "getting in their way", as heard by the author.

So, CLIs will continue to be used in practice for a long time. But `telnet` need not be, as we will now demonstrate.

6.5.1.1 CLI wrappings

Although CLIs are designed for interactive use, they can also be used in unattended mode. In Section 6.3.1, we mentioned `expect` [152], a useful tool for automating management. By emulating `telnet` sessions, which normally operate in attended mode, `expect` enables operators to wrap interactive CLI commands into scripts and run them in unattended mode (as opposed to having people type in these interactive commands via `telnet`). This technique is known as *CLI wrapping*.

CLI wrapping into XML

```
POST /xml-cli-gateway.pl HTTP/1.0
Content-Length: 156

<?xml version="1.0" encoding="UTF-8"?>
<!DOCTYPE CLI-WRAPPING SYSTEM "cli-wrapping.dtd">
<document>
  <command>show interface ethernet0</command>
```

Fig. 10. Example of CLI wrapping into XML

CLI wrappings can also rely on Web technologies. In the simple example presented in Fig. 10, we wrap an interactive command into an XML document and send it via an HTTP POST request to the agent. The command is executed via an HTTP-CLI gateway coded as a Perl script (`xml-cli-gateway.pl`). The output is wrapped into a new XML document that is sent by the agent as an HTTP response to the manager's request. This response can be displayed by a Web browser (see Fig. 7), parsed and processed by a management application (see Fig. 9), etc. Although the output is wrapped into XML, it does not have a fine-grained XML structure; it is just one chunk of opaque textual data.

Another simple example of CLI wrapping into HTML is given in Fig. 11. It works as in the previous example, except that the Perl script (`html-cli-gateway.pl`) parses HTML input instead of XML.

```
POST /html-cli-gateway.pl HTTP/1.0
Content-Length: 68

<html><head></head>
<body>
show interface ethernet0
</body>
```

Fig. 11. Example of CLI wrapping into HTML

More complex examples of Web-based CLI wrappings rely on HTML metadata, HTTP PUT, etc. We do not describe them here because few embedded HTTP servers support such advanced features. In Section 6.5.1.2, we will see that HTML forms lead to CLI mappings rather than CLI wrappings.

Two ways of using CLI wrappings

Whether Web-based or not, CLI wrappings can be used in two ways:

- *Semi-automated management:* The execution of the command (i.e., the launch of an `expect` script or the sending of an XML/HTML document) is triggered interactively by an administrator or an operator (attended mode). In the case of statically defined commands (e.g., with the symptom-driven HTML pages described in Section 6.2.3), the user clicks on a pre-defined command, via a Web browser (see Fig. 7) or a management-application GUI (see Fig. 8). In the case of dynamically defined commands, the user types a command in a GUI. This command is wrapped in the background into an `expect` script or an XML/HTML document, which is sent via `telnet` or HTTP `POST` to the agent. The next steps are identical for static and dynamic commands. The command is executed by the CLI (for `expect`) or the HTTP-CLI gateway (for Web-based wrappings), without any user intervention (unattended mode). In the `expect` case, the output of the command is wrapped into `expect`. In the XML/HTML case, a new XML/HTML document is generated by the agent; the output of the command is inserted into it (e.g., between `<cli-output>` and `</cli-output>` tags for XML) and sent to the manager (unattended mode). On the manager, the command output is displayed to a person, e.g. in a Web browser (attended mode). Finally, the output is interpreted interactively by this person (attended mode). We call this approach *semi-automated management* because the execution of the command is triggered by a user, and the output of the command is not parsed automatically by a program.

• *Fully automated management:* This time, `expect` scripts are launched, or XML/ HTML documents are sent, automatically by the management application (see Fig. 9). The command is wrapped automatically. Its execution is triggered in unattended mode. The command is transferred via `telnet` or HTTP and executed by the CLI or the HTTP-CLI gateway in unattended mode. The output is wrapped as above. Finally, this output is parsed and interpreted in unattended mode. People are never involved here. We refer to this approach as *fully automated management.* It is the ultimate goal of management automation, as described in Section 4.2.2.3, "Why should NSM be automated?".

Using CLI wrappings interactively does not make much sense, except for debugging purposes. Entering interactive commands via a `telnet` session is much simpler, and less error prone, than typing in an `expect` script or an XML/HTML document that wraps the same commands.

6.5.1.2 CLI mappings

In addition to wrapping commands from the CLI, Web technologies enable operators to map commands onto URLs—what we call *CLI-to-URL mappings*, or *CLI mappings* for short. Let us study two examples of such mappings.

Bruins's CLI-to-URL mapping

Bruins [38] reports an experiment with CLI-to-URL mappings conducted by Cisco in 1995, whereby each whitespace in the command line is replaced with a slash in a URL. For instance, a manager requests the following URL:

```
<http://router_name/exec/show/interface/ethernet0/>
```

The destination router is identified by its fully qualified domain name `router_name` or by its IP address. It runs an HTTP-CLI gateway that translates this URL into the corresponding standard CLI command for a Cisco router:

```
show interface ethernet0
```

The gateway forwards this command to the command-line interpreter, which parses it and acts upon it as if it had been typed in interactively. The output of the command is sent to the HTTP-CLI gateway in return. The gateway translates it into an HTML page and sends it to the manager. The user can thus use his/her Web browser or management-application GUI as if it were the console of the managed device or system.

CLI-to-URL mapping with HTML forms

Another type of CLI-to-URL mapping consists in using an HTML form and sending a command as input parameter(s) to the CGI program that processes the form. Examples of mappings include the following:

```
<http://router_name/cli?arg1=show&arg2=interface&arg3=ethernet0
&arg4=&arg5=&arg6=&arg7=&arg8=&arg9=&arg10=>
```

```
<http://router_name/cli?command=show+interface+ethernet0>
```

One problem with such mappings is that special characters in the command line may clash with the syntax of URLs. There are ways to escape special characters, but different vendors may use different escaping techniques and this heterogeneity is not user friendly.

Three ways of using CLI mappings

Whether Web-based or not, all CLI mappings allow for:

- *Interactive management*: A URL is entered interactively by the user in a Web browser (or in a text browser such as lynx [156]) and sent to the agent via HTTP. This URL is processed by a CGI program, and the command is run in the background via an HTTP-CLI gateway. The output of the command is inserted into an HTML page (e.g., between <PRE> and </PRE> tags), then sent by the agent to the manager, and finally displayed by the Web browser.
- *Semi-automated management*: In the case of statically defined commands (e.g., with the symptom-driven HTML pages described in Section 6.2.3), the user clicks on a pre-defined command, via a Web browser (see Fig. 7) or a management-application GUI (see Fig. 8). With a Web browser, the hyperlink behind the command is the URL itself. With a management application, the selected command is mapped in the background onto a URL. In the case of dynamically defined commands, the user types a command in a text field displayed by a Web browser or a management-application GUI, and validates the HTML form by clicking on a Submit button. The next steps are identical for static and dynamic commands. A request for the URL is sent by the manager to the agent via HTTP. This URL is processed by a CGI program, and the command is run in the background via an HTTP-CLI gateway. The output of the command is inserted into an HTML page, then sent by the agent to the manager via HTTP. Last, the output of the command is displayed to the user by the Web browser or the management-application GUI.
- *Fully automated management*: Everything is automated, no user is involved (see Fig. 9). The URL is put together, and its output is parsed, by the management application alone. All the other steps (including the transit via the HTTP-CLI gateway) are similar to the previous case.

Straightforward CLI-to-URL mappings present two advantages. They are very simple for vendors to implement. They are also easy for operators to use, as they usually know by heart the CLIs of the different network devices and systems in their management domain and can thus create URLs interactively—they do not have to learn yet another language.

CLI-to-URL mappings are particularly appropriate for configuration management and symptom-driven HTML forms.

6.5.1.3 Using the CLI: `telnet` vs. wrappings vs. mappings

Let us analyze the different ways of using the CLI in NSM.

Comparison

The chief advantage of using CLI wrappings or mappings instead of `telnet` is that they give access to the entire CLI of a piece of equipment in unattended mode. In this respect, these techniques complement SNMP because, for most network devices and systems, SNMP MIBs give access to only a fraction of the CLI[1].

CLI wrappings and mappings present another important advantage over interactive `telnet`: identification and authentication can be automated. Administrators and operators need no longer know (or have easy access to) usernames and passwords for all the devices and systems in their management domain: Application gateways or scripts are in charge of all security credentials within a domain. This feature facilitates scalability, so it is important for large organizations who manage a plethora of network devices and systems.

One advantage of using Web-based CLI mappings or wrappings instead of `telnet` or `expect`, is that they are easier to secure than `telnet` when we need to go across a firewall. Almost all firewalls filter out `telnet` access to prevent well-known attacks, whereas most firewalls let some HTTP traffic go through under certain conditions. There are also standard ways of securing HTTP traffic [144].

One advantage of using `telnet` instead of CLI wrappings or mappings is that it is a relatively basic technology. It does not depend on a lot of software to work, which is good when we face a disastrous situation and services stop working one after the other. CLI wrappings and mappings, conversely, require more sophisticated software to function properly: the `expect` toolkit, HTTP servers, NFS-served XML parsers, etc. In the case of network meltdown, the more elaborate, the more vulnerable a piece of software.

With CLI wrappings and mappings, XML/HTML documents and `expect` scripts can be generated dynamically provided that the output requires no parsing—that is, if we simply run a command and do not want to extract data out of its output. This dynamic generation can be triggered by the management application in unattended mode (fully automated management), or by a user in attended mode (interactive or semi-automated management).

Finally, CLI mappings allow for interactive, semi-automated, and fully automated management. CLI wrappings, on the other hand, make no sense in interactive mode and should only be used in semi- or fully automated management. Based on this difference, some people claim that CLI mappings are more versatile than, and thus superior to, CLI wrappings. Others argue that parsing a command output wrapped into HTML or XML is more difficult than parsing the same output with `expect`. In our opinion, the differences between the two are not such that one technique clearly beats the other.

---

1. Symmetrically, not everything is available through the CLI. For instance, RMON statistics are usually only accessible via SNMP.

Problems

CLI wrappings and mappings are not the panacea, however, and are less flexible than they may appear at first sight. We have identified several problems with them.

A serious problem is robustness. Extracting data out of the output of a command is not robust because this output is not strongly structured. Humans are good at handling weakly structured data, but parsers are not: They get easily confused, because they are generally programmed to pay attention to the syntax rather than the semantics. (For instance, consider how people and programs react when a field is missing in the output of a command.) Programmers of `expect` scripts need to know in advance what the output will look like *exactly*, in order to parse it and act accordingly. Similarly, data can be successfully extracted from the HTML or XML document returned by the agent if, and only if, the parser knows *exactly* how the document is structured and what errors may look like. But three facts ruin the assumption that the output can be precisely known in advance:

- The output of a CLI command does not always depend on this command alone. Sometimes, it also depends on the commands that preceded it. For instance, depending on previous settings, a field may be blank or set to a character string, which changes the number of parameters to parse. In theory, this could be dealt with by storing the state of the managed device or system in a Finite State Machine (FSM). But in the IP world, such FSMs are rarely advertised by vendors (we do not know any who do), and finding them out empirically is difficult and error prone. Worse, when a managed device or system is concurrently updated by several sources (e.g., a user works interactively via `telnet` while an `expect` script updates the same device), script-specific FSMs are bound to be wrong because they capture only part of the picture. In practice, almost no one uses FSMs for increasing the robustness of command-output parsing.
- Some side-effects are hard to predict. For instance, if the length of a certain field (e.g., a character string) in the output of a CLI command exceeds the maximum value expected (but not advertised) by the programmer of that command, the output might wrap over two lines instead of fitting into one, or might no longer fit into a column when the output has a matrix structure. This can seriously confuse parsing programs whose implementers did not anticipate such a problem. Many similar formatting problems are not detected until we actually face them and discover their side-effects in real life.
- Although IT and networking vendors rarely admit it, experience shows that they do not always modify the CLIs of their managed equipment in an incremental, backward-compatible manner. Sometimes they slightly modify existing commands; sometimes they completely change an existing command; sometimes they alter the output of existing commands. Although a majority of these changes are minor, they suffice to break `expect` scripts and HTML/XML parsing code.

A second problem shows up when NSM is fully automated: The changes in the CLIs carried out by IT and networking vendors discourage NOCs from updating the management software of their equipment. Each time an administrator upgrades the CLI of a network device or system, all related `expect` scripts and HTML/XML parsing programs in his/her management domain must be taken out of production and checked again; some of them require an update or a complete rewrite; and all of them have to go through a full test cycle before they can be put back into production[1]. Needless to say, these small CLI changes are a major reason for NOCs to hold up management-software upgrades, particularly for network devices. As management software is often bundled with the operating system on network equipment, administrators rarely upgrade such operating systems and therefore cannot use the latest functionalities of a piece of equipment[2].

A third problem is that, for fully automated management, CLI wrappings and mappings are only a stopgap solution. This may sound odd, as these techniques were primarily designed for better automating management, but it is a direct consequence of the first problem. Customers demand the automation of management (see Section 4.2.2.3, "Why should NSM be automated?"). When we use CLI wrappings and mappings, fully automated management requires that data be extracted automatically out of the output of the CLI commands. But doing so is not robust, as we saw in the first problem, and it is not reasonable to automate management at the cost of robustness. As a consequence, administrators should use sparingly CLI wrappings and mappings in fully automated mode—only when no alternative tool is available. It is relatively easy to write an `expect` script, or a piece of code that parses the output of a command in an HTML or XML document. But it takes more time and skill to debug and test it enough to feel confident about putting it into production. In fully automated management, when we need to extract data out of the output, CLI wrappings and mappings should be limited to executing routinely the same, well-debugged programs. Only in interactive and semi-automated management can they be used as general-purpose gateways to the agent's entire CLI.

A fourth problem is overhead. Compared to SNMP and `telnet`, CLI wrappings and mappings can increase the agent's overhead. For instance, when people use `expect` in semi-automated management, they usually create one `telnet` session per command. When the number of commands to execute is small, the overhead is negligible; but when it is large, the aggregate overhead of all the session creations and teardowns can have a significant effect on the agent. Imagine the footprint that policy-based management would have on an access router subject to frequent policy updates if we were using `expect` and one `telnet` session per command! And then consider the network overhead... To reduce this overhead, we can run several commands through the same `telnet` session. But then we face robustness issues, because the execution of one command depends on the successful parsing of the output of the previous command. As usual in software engineering, there is a trade-off between robustness and overhead.

---

1. A weaker form of this problem shows up in interactive and semi-automated management: Some of the commands have to be updated. As a result, operators need training in order to update their knowledge of the CLI, and all the scripts and XML/HTML documents where the commands are hard-coded must be updated. Doing this, however, is generally less problematic than debugging and testing the extraction of data out of the output of a command—although the frequent training of operators can be an issue in some organizations.
2. Note that this is not the sole reason for cancelling upgrades. New releases of operating systems often come with new bugs, and the need for new functionalities does not always justify the loss of existing ones!

In summary, administrators and operators will continue to use CLIs for a long time, particularly to troubleshoot urgent problems under stressful conditions. Using CLIs does not require the interactive use of `telnet`. Alternatives include `expect` and a number of Web-based CLI wrappings and mappings. Their main advantage is to enable management tasks to be semi- or fully automated. Another advantage is the possibility to hide security credentials from administrators and operators. Their main drawback is that all the solutions that resort to the CLI for executing management tasks are exposed to a number of problems. In particular, the extraction of data out of the output of a command leaves a lot to be desired with respect to robustness.

6.5.2 Embedded HTML pages and CGI programs

The presence of embedded HTTP servers makes it possible for network devices and systems to embed HTML pages and CGI programs. These are locally stored on the agent, typically in EPROM. Embedded HTML pages are static, read-only documents. Some of them describe the characteristics of the system or network device. Others, coded as HTML forms, are used in conjunction with embedded CGI programs for configuration management. They enable administrators to set up network devices and systems in a more user-friendly way than what we saw in Section 6.3. By directly interacting with the agent via HTTP, administrators no longer have the inconvenience of first generating an external configuration file, then moving it to the right server, and finally loading it into the agent; instead, they directly configure the agent.

HTTP servers embedded in agents also allow CGI programs to generate dynamic HTML pages on demand. This feature is particularly useful for performing simple performance monitoring, by updating an image and refreshing the Web browser at regular time intervals[1]. This approach is a step toward Management by Delegation, which promotes the delegation of part of the management application to the agent itself. Clearly, a trade-off must be made between the agent's CPU cycles dedicated to management and the cycles devoted to the agent's operational tasks.

Static and dynamic embedded HTML pages, as well as embedded CGI programs, were all described in 1996 by Mullaney when he reported on a prototype developed by Cabletron [184]. Similar work at Cisco was reported in 1997 by Maston [164]. Over time, these features have gained a growing popularity in the market, especially for configuration management. A growing number of equipment vendors are now supporting embedded HTML pages and CGI programs. We expect that, in the near future, it will become the common way of configuring network devices and systems in interactive mode. Of course, interactive configuration is not always an option, especially in large networks. We will solve this problem in our own management architecture.

---

1. Netscape's Web browser supports a proprietary extension for refreshes: `<META HTTP-EQUIV="Refresh"` `CONTENT=XYZ>` where `XYZ` is the number of seconds that the browser must wait between two successive retrievals of the same URL [187].

6.5.3 Embedded management applications

The concept of *embedded management application* was described (and also criticized!) by Wellens and Auerbach in 1996 [286]. Because agents are typically managed via vendor-specific management GUIs integrated in a management platform, these two authors argue that GUIs could be stored and run inside the agents. This is basically a variant of Goldszmidt's Management by Delegation, with different technical implementation details. The embedded management application is coded as a collection of HTML pages and CGI programs, and the operator directly interacts with it from his/her Web browser.

As with the previous approaches, this one uses HTTP rather than SNMP to vehicle data between managers and agents. The main advantage is that the network device or system is directly sold with its management application. The main drawback is that a person must sit in front of a Web browser to manage the agent: management cannot easily be automated. Another problem, not mentioned by Wellens and Auerbach, is the cost of management. With standard SNMP-based management platforms, one piece of software (the vendor-specific management GUI) allows us to manage an infinite number of devices of the same type from the same platform. But if we have to purchase one embedded management application per managed device, the cost of management skyrockets when the number of devices becomes large. To avoid this, we need a new business model for management software. A third problem, still not mentioned by Wellens and Auerbach, but inherent in the concept of delegation, is that many CPU cycles are burned on the agent for mundane tasks such as generating graphics and formatting the output for the user. The primary task of an agent is to fulfill its operational role, not to perform management tasks; so the amount of management overhead must be limited. But embedded management applications enable operators, with just a few clicks, to clog up an agent with management overhead and thus, without realizing it, temporarily hinder the execution of its operational tasks.

6.5.4 Low-footprint embedded HTTP servers

Two research teams have focused on the minimization of the footprint of embedded HTTP servers on the agents: Reed *et al.* at IBM Almaden Research Center and Hong *et al.* at POSTECH.

In 1996–97, Reed *et al.* developed a minimal HTTP server that fits into a single C++ class. To achieve this, they had to remove several features from HTTP. HTML forms are not processed by external CGI programs but by the minimal HTTP server itself, which is multithreaded. Incoming HTTP requests specify what handler should process them (a handler is an HTTP server with a specific HTML-form parser). RPCs are used to perform the systems-management tasks requested via HTTP. This minimal server was used in a distributed management tool for PCs. The authors benchmarked their minimal HTTP server and showed that it uses less CPU than a conventional HTTP server that spawns a CGI program for each incoming HTTP request.

During 1999–2001, Hong *et al.* developed the POSTECH Embedded Web Server (POS-EWS) [60, 134]. Its design goals were to minimize the overhead of HTTP-based management on the agent and to maximize the efficiency of the HTTP server. POS-EWS is a very compact piece of C code (30 kbytes). Its average runtime memory footprint is only 64 kbytes, which is remarkably low. Instead of being multithreaded as most HTTP servers freely available today, it is singlethreaded and runs multiple finite state machines to handle concurrent connections (see Welsh [287] for a description of the advantages of event-driven servers over multithreaded servers). POS-EWS was integrated into a commercial IP router developed in Korea.

6.6 XML-Based Management

The next degree of sophistication in Web-based management is characterized by the use of XML to represent management data inside an HTTP pipe. We call it *XML-based management*. This type of Web-based management should *a priori* be included in HTTP-based management, because XML data is transferred by the HTTP protocol. We created a separate category for it to emphasize that, this time, XML data has a fine-grained structure. In Section 6.5.1.1, the CLI wrapping into XML did not have structured data like the solutions we will now describe.

The most famous example of XML-based management is WBEM, which is backed by an important industrial consortium and currently has a lot of momentum. We will also describe a hybrid solution devised by John *et al.*, which uses both SNMP and XML for manager-agent communication. In Chapter 7, we will see that our own proposal (WIMA) can also be classified as a type of XML-based management.

6.6.1 Web-Based Enterprise Management (WBEM)

So far, WBEM's past has been the opposite of SNMP's. After initially receiving a cold welcome from the NSM market and research community, it is now raising high hopes. We explain this bizarre situation by reviewing a bit of history. Next, we summarize the main technical aspects that have already been specified by the DMTF.

A bit of history

The Web-Based Enterprise Management (WBEM) initiative was launched in 1996 by an industrial consortium led by Microsoft [28]. Its precise technical objectives were blurred by sensational marketing announcements that it would integrate enterprise management by changing drastically everything the management market was used to.

WBEM initially consisted of high-level definitions of (i) a new information model called the HyperMedia Management Schema (HMMS), (ii) a new communication model limited to a new communication protocol called HyperMedia Management Protocol (HMMP), and (iii) a sketch of a new organizational model whereby clients accessed HyperMedia Object

Managers (HMOMs) [120]. All deployed systems and devices worldwide were considered legacy systems and had to be managed via management gateways—necessarily slow and awkward to use. By adopting this revolutionary approach and pretending to render obsolete all deployed management solutions, WBEM did not gain much credibility. To many people, it was yet another instance of the *Reinvent the Wheel* antipattern [37].

Over time, the supporters of WBEM became more realistic. In the communication model, the brand new, domain-specific technologies were replaced with existing, standard ones. HMMP, the protocol that was supposed to be layered on top of HTTP, was dropped in favor of the well-known and pervasive HTTP. XML was selected to represent management data inside HTTP messages [29]. In May 1996, HMMS was given to the DMTF, where it evolved and became the Common Information Model (CIM). In April 1997, CIM 1.0 was officially released by the DMTF [270]. CIM was enhanced very significantly in the following year, and most of the building blocks of what we call CIM today were present in CIM 2.0, released in March 1998. In parallel to these changes in the information model, HMOM was replaced by CIMOM (Common Information Model Object Manager) in the organizational model.

In June 1998, the WBEM Consortium formally handed over the entire WBEM initiative to the DMTF, who integrated it into a global work plan [40]. This gave the WBEM management architecture a much-awaited guarantee of independence *vis-à-vis* any particular vendor's interests. Since then, a lot of progress has been made, and the focus has clearly shifted from plain marketing to real technical work. WBEM, once considered vaporware, has now grown into a large-scale standardization process involving most of the major vendors on the market, especially in the areas of networking and systems. The DMTF's work on WBEM is split across several Working Groups (see section "CIM schemas" below). Their activities range from applications to events, from databases to networks, and from security to SLA.

In the entire 1990s decade, we have never had such a flavor of integrated enterprise management in the IETF realm. The DMTF has also learned from the IETF's mistakes; it not only works on instrumentation data models, but also on higher-level models. Reportedly, a number of large vendors now focus the bulk of their NSM engineering forces on WBEM/CIM and only do maintenance work on SNMP software.

Let us now go through WBEM's main contributions to date: CIM (metaschema, schemas, and operations), CIM-to-XML mapping (xmlCIM), and the CIM operations over HTTP.

CIM metaschema

In DMTF parlance, a schema is (i) a collection of class definitions that describe managed objects and (ii) a namespace for these classes. This is what we are used to calling a MIB in the SNMP world, or a model in object-oriented information modeling (e.g., in TMN). Similarly, a metaschema corresponds to a metamodel. The terms *schema* and *metaschema* come from the database world, from which originates the father of HMMS; his terminology survived in CIM. The terms *model* and *metamodel* are well established in the object-oriented community, especially at the OMG. The IETF, ITU-T, and ISO all use *models* rather than *schemas*.

This change in the terminology caused (and still causes) some confusion in the NSM world, which is traditionally tied to the object-oriented world (e.g., with CORBA) rather than the database world. To add to the discomfort of newcomers to CIM, a *model* initially referred to a set of schemas at the DMTF, but all CIM models were grouped into the so-called *CIM Schema* [41]! Over time, because many of the engineers who joined DMTF Working Groups had an object-oriented background, the terms *schema* and *model* have become synonymous in this standardization organization. Similarly, *metaschema* and *metamodel* are now used interchangeably. The nuances introduced in Section 2.12 (notably the independence *vis-à-vis* the data repository) are ignored by the DMTF.

The main characteristic (and strength) of CIM is that it is object oriented. The CIM metaschema is specified in a document known as the *CIM Specification*. The metaschema defines the entities that can be used to define CIM schemas: classes, properties (state), methods (behavior), qualifiers (metadata), etc. Version 2.2 of the CIM Specification [74] was released in June 1999 and has remained stable since then.

CIM schemas

CIM schemas are organized into three conceptual layers: the Core Model, the Common Models, and the Extension Models [41, 79].

The *Core Model* is the most abstract layer. It captures information that pertains to all management areas. It defines high-level classes such as `System`, `Service`, `ManagedElement`, `ManagedSystemElement`, `PhysicalElement`, `LogicalElement`, etc.

The *Common Models* are produced by different DMTF Working Groups. Each Working Group used to be responsible for one Common Model, but this is no longer true[1]. We currently have eleven schemas in CIM 2.6: the Application, Device, Events, Interop, Metrics, Network, Physical, Policy, Support, System, and User Schemas. The division between these schemas roughly corresponds to the different management types that we consider in enterprise management: networks, systems, applications, services, policies, etc. Each Common Model defines classes that are specific to a management area. For instance, the System Schema defines classes such as `Cluster`, `UnitaryComputerSystem`, `SystemPartition`, `ClusteringService`, etc. The top-level classes of the Common Models are all subclassed from classes defined in the Core Model.

The *Extension Models* are specific to a given technology or vendor and are not directly controlled by the DMTF. Classes defined in the Extension Schemas are subclassed from those defined in the Core and Common Models. No single organization controls all extension schemas. No one can say: These are all the extension schemas defined to date.

---

1. The number of DMTF Working Groups varies over time as Working Groups come and go, merge, subdivide, etc. For the latest information, readers are referred to <http://www.dmtf.org/about/committees.php>.

Finally, below these three conceptual layers, we find instrumentation and management applications (agents and managers in standard NSM parlance). Designers of CIM agents and managers can define their own schemas, but they are strongly encouraged to subclass from the Core, Common, and Extension Models.

Unlike the CIM Specification, most CIM schemas are still regularly updated and should thus be considered ongoing work. As we saw with SNMP MIBs several years ago at the IETF, CIM schemas should gradually become mature, hence stable, in the years to come. New versions of the Core and Common Models are released jointly by the DMTF as a set of documents collectively called the *CIM Schema*. The latest version, CIM Schema v2.6 [80], is currently under final review and is expected to come out by the time this book goes to print. A preliminary version is already available to the public.

CIM schemas can be expressed in two ways: with Managed Object Format (MOF) files or with UML diagrams. In the past, UML diagrams were often afterthoughts for DMTF Working Groups. Many of them were updated at the last minute, just before the release of a new CIM Schema. But since models have grown in complexity, more and more members of the DMTF Working Groups use UML diagrams as well as MOF files during modeling and standardization activities. Occasionally, the DMTF also publishes whitepapers that explain how to leverage specific models. These whitepapers are particularly useful to the people who do not closely follow the DMTF's standardization activities, and catch up with the latest features each time a CIM Schema is released (that is, once or twice a year).

The DMTF's reference documents are the MOF files. UML diagrams are currently produced separately; they are visual aids that help understand MOF files. By the time this book goes to print, it should be possible to convert MOF into XMI (XML Metadata Interchange) automatically. This would allow CIM schemas expressed in MOF to be translated into other languages without any loss of semantics, and UML diagrams to be generated automatically from the MOF files.

The grammar of the MOF syntax is formally defined in the CIM Specification [74]. It is derived from the Interface Definition Language (IDL) defined in the specification of RPCs in the Distributed Computing Environment (DCE) [268]. An example of MOF syntax is given in Appendix C. The DMTF conventions for drawing UML diagrams of CIM schemas are defined in the CIM Specification [74].

If we compare CIM with the SNMP information model, vendor-specific MIBs roughly map onto extension schemas, while generic MIBs map onto common and extension schemas. There is no equivalent to the Core Schema in the SNMP world.

CIM operations

CIM supports two types of methods (operations). *Extrinsic methods* are standard methods defined in a schema. *Intrinsic methods* are special methods directly invoked on a namespace. They provide a means to discover[1], define, delete, and manipulate classes,

---

1. See the mechanism known as *reflection* in object-oriented software engineering [178].

objects, properties, methods, and properties. Some of these methods are read-only, e.g., `EnumerateClasses`, `EnumerateInstances`, `GetProperty`, and `GetQualifier`. Others allow for modifications, e.g., `DeleteClass`, `DeleteInstance`, `CreateClass`, `CreateInstance`, `ModifyClass`, `ModifyInstance`, `SetProperty`, etc. Because all namespaces are instances of the class `__NameSpace`, or instances of a class subclassed from it, and because all CIM servers must support the `root` namespace, all standard operations on classes and instances also apply to namespaces. For historical reasons, CIM intrinsic methods are specified in Section 2.4 of the specification for CIM operations over HTTP [77], although they are totally independent of HTTP and ought to be defined in a separate document.

CIM-to-XML mapping (xmlCIM)

The representation of CIM in XML is known as *xmlCIM* in the DMTF realm. As this name is a bit bizarre, we call it *CIM-to-XML mapping,* which we find more self-explanatory. The latest specification is version 2.0, released in July 1999 as two separate documents: an XML Document Type Definition (DTD) [75] and a clear text explaining the conventions cast in iron in the DTD [76]. Version 2.1 is expected to come out very soon.

The CIM-to-XML mapping defines XML elements, entities, and attribute lists to represent the information stored in CIM schemas. For instance, these documents specify how to represent a class, a method, a property, etc. We will come back to the CIM-to-XML mapping in detail in Section 9.2. In particular, we will explain that the DMTF opted for a metamodel-level mapping.

CIM operations over HTTP

The specification for CIM operations over HTTP complements the previous document. Version 1.0 was released in August 1999 [77]. Version 1.1 should be finalized by the time this book is printed. Unlike the specification of the CIM-to-XML mapping, which is independent of the communication protocol used to transfer XML documents, this one is specific to HTTP.

The encapsulation of CIM operations in HTTP uses a number of standard HTTP header fields, and defines several error codes that are compliant with the HTTP/1.1 specification [88]. It also uses HTTP extension headers [189] to provide greater visibility into the contents of the HTTP messages for filtering by firewalls and handling by proxies.

HTTP extension headers are an add-on to HTTP/1.1. They allow HTTP clients and servers to add new, application-specific HTTP header fields to the standard HTTP/1.1 header fields. An HTTP server is warned that an incoming request uses extensions by the use of the prefix "`M-`" in front of the HTTP method. CIM operations over HTTP use the `M-POST` HTTP method. The prefix "`M-`" means that this HTTP `POST` request contains at least one mandatory extension header field. Upon receipt of such a request, and prior to processing it, the HTTP server must tell the HTTP client whether it understands all the extensions used in the HTTP header.

Six HTTP extension headers have been defined by the DMTF: `CIMOperation`, `CIMProtocolVersion`, `CIMMethod`, `CIMObject`, `CIMBatch`, and `CIMError`. HTTP extensions are currently published as an experimental RFC [189] and are far from being supported ubiquitously.

WBEMsource Initiative

Many implementations of WBEM are already available from commercial vendors. Listing all of them here would be futile, as we will see in Section 6.8. One of them, however, is worth mentioning: the WBEMsource initiative [269]. This is a joint effort by the DMTF, The Open Group, and several vendors to promote WBEM and CIM by making open-source software freely available to all: customers, vendors, researchers, etc. This can be a starting point for readers interested in implementation aspects of WBEM. It is also a way to become familiar with the details of this management architecture.

6.6.2 John *et al.*: XNAMI

Another, more research-oriented example of XML-based management was described by John *et al.* in 1999 [132]. In the XNAMI architecture, the agent maintains an explicit runtime representation of its MIBs (unlike most SNMP agents) and uses XML to represent managed objects internally. For each OID, the agent stores Java bytecode for the `get()` and `set()` methods. The agent's SNMP server is modified so as to execute the `get()` method of an OID upon receipt of an SNMPv3 `get` (ditto with `set`). This feature allows the agent to support dynamically extensible MIBs, as opposed to standard, statically defined SNMP MIBs.

OIDs can be added or removed at runtime by using the Document Object Model (DOM [275]) API. The agent supports a new MIB called the XNAMI MIB, which defines two new OIDs: `methods_proxy` and `mib_proxy`. By sending an SNMP `set` PDU containing the OID `methods_proxy`, the XNAMI manager can transfer compressed Java bytecode for the `get()` and `set()` methods of any OID (mobile code paradigm). By sending an SNMP `set` PDU containing the OID `mib_proxy`, the XNAMI manager can transfer an XML string specifying that a new OID should be created, an existing OID deleted, etc.

The compressed Java bytecode and the XML string are both transferred as BER-encoded SMIv2 strings. The XNAMI manager is implemented as a Java servlet, the XNAMI agent as a Java application.

The XNAMI manager and agent exchange management data via SNMPv3, while the Web browser and XNAMI manager communicate via HTTP. The two communications are tightly coupled. This approach is an example of hybrid Web-based management because XML data is transferred via SNMPv3 rather than HTTP.

6.7 Distributed Java-Based Management

The highest degree of sophistication in Web-based management is what we call *distributed Java-based management*. This approach is based on Java RMI for distribution aspects and is a variant of the distributed objects described in Section 4.1.3.2. We already ruled out this option for the next management cycle in Chapter 5, because of the *my-middleware-is-better-than-yours* syndrome. But it is a valid form of Web-based management, so we summarize it here for the sake of completeness. The main industrial supporters of this technology are Sun Microsystems and the Java Community; so far, they have proposed three solutions: JMAPI, JMX, and FMA. Anerousis has also developed an elegant solution based on Java RMI: Marvel.

6.7.1 Java Management Application Programming Interface (JMAPI)

Java RMI was officially released in early 1997 with JDK 1.1 (JDK stands for Java Development Kit). At the end of 1996, when RMI was still a beta release, Sun Microsystems leveraged it to specify a radically new way of managing networks and systems: the Java Management API (JMAPI [263]). This API is a set of tools and guidelines to build management applets supporting Java RMI. In this approach, everything is an object: Every managed object in every SNMP MIB is mapped onto a full-blown Java object[1], and the manager can interact directly with the JMAPI managed objects in the agent. On the manager side, a JMAPI object acts as an SNMP trap handler, receiving all incoming SNMP traps from non-JMAPI agents and converting them into JMAPI events. The Notification interface allows administrators to develop event-driven management applications. In the evaluation code that Sun Microsystems made freely available for about a year in 1997, MIB-II was entirely translated into JMAPI managed objects.

Strangely enough, one of the main reasons of JMAPI's success eventually became the main cause of its dismissal. In those days, the JDK was still lacking a proper library of graphical components. Swing did not exist, and programmers had to interact directly with the low-level AWT (Abstract Window Toolkit). JMAPI came with its own library of high-level graphical components, offering most of the widgets then available in Motif, and many people used it to build all sorts of applications, not necessarily related to management. Later, once Sun Microsystems had released JavaBeans and Swing, JMAPI was swiftly abandoned. But by then, it had already demonstrated the possibility of viewing management as a distributed object-oriented application.

---

1. Clearly, this approach does not scale when the number of Java objects grows large for a single agent. But JMAPI was a proof of concept more than anything else.

6.7.2 Java Management eXtensions (JMX)

In the Java world, Jini [258] promotes a vision similar to Microsoft's Universal Plug and Play in the Windows PC world: You buy a device, you connect it to your network; by itself, the device finds its IP address, registers with a naming service, describes what functionality it supports, gets its configuration data, etc. A real administrator's dream! Unfortunately, Jini's vision of management is simplistic and limited to automated registration and configuration. JMX [260] filled this void with a comprehensive management framework, in the object-oriented sense of the term.

Once known as JMAPI 2.0, JMX was officially released to the public in May 1999. It is a form of object-oriented and component-oriented Web-based management. Most of the work so far has concentrated on the agent side [261]. JMX does not define a new information model: it interfaces with existing ones. APIs have been specified for SNMP and WBEM/CIM. The agent and the manager can communicate via Java RMI, HTTP, or SNMP. As far as SNMP is concerned, JMX relies on a general-purpose SNMP-to-Java MIB compiler that translates the managed objects defined in any SNMP MIB into components called *MBeans* (short for *Management Beans*). It is not yet clear what technology should underpin the manager side; the JMX specification leaves its definition for a future phase [261, p. 21].

6.7.3 Federated Management Architecture (FMA)

Independent of JMX, the Federated Management Architecture (FMA [262]) was devised in 1999 by the industrial consortium in charge of developing Jiro, a Java technology for storage management. Initially begun as an effort to standardize management in the storage industry, FMA grew into a general-purpose management architecture. The initial concept of *FederatedBeans* was dropped in favor of standard JavaBeans and EJBs, thereby addressing the main problem with Jiro. With FMA, all agents must be Jini-enabled. FMA defines static management services (e.g., the event service, the log service, and the controller service), and dynamic services that extend Java RMI semantics to the management-application level. FMA also specifies management aspects related to security, transactions, persistence, etc. Manager-agent communication can rely on any protocol: SNMP, HTTP for WBEM, etc. The manager side of FMA is completely specified. To date, it is still unclear whether Sun Microsystems will eventually unify JMX and FMA into a single management architecture for Java-based management.

6.7.4 Anerousis's Marvel

Work on distributed Java-based management has not been confined to Sun Microsystems and the Java Community. In the research community, we have also seen several proposals and prototypes that use Java RMI. The most sophisticated and comprehensive solution published to date is probably Marvel by Anerousis [8, 10]. Marvel is a distributed, object-oriented management architecture, as well as an NSM platform. At the architectural level, it supports Java RMI, CORBA, SNMP, CMIP, and DMI for manager-agent communication; but in practice, object services are implemented with Java RMI. Marvel's information model supports the generation of computed views of management information [9], thereby increasing the level of semantics available to the management-application designer. Computed views consist of monitoring, control, and event views of management data collected from agents. This data is aggregated into Marvel objects (also known as *aggregated managed objects*) using spatial and temporal filters. Marvel objects can reside in the agents or in external repositories, depending on the amount of processing required (some aggregations can be very CPU intensive). This makes Marvel's management architecture very scalable. Note that this aggregation in external nodes applies to the IP world the TMN concepts of element-level MIBs and network-level MIBs: Marvel objects can serve as the building blocks to a full-fledged Network Information Model (NIM) in the IP world.

6.8 Commercial Products

The Web-based management market is currently booming. In addition to the software giants, many start-ups are very active in this lucrative market. Because new products appear at a fast pace, and because marketing people often take the opportunity of a major software release to change the name of a product, publishing an up-to-date list of commercial products in Web-based management is doomed to fail.

For instance, in 1999, Harler [112] published a book that includes a 141-page list and analysis of commercial software packages in the area of Web-based management. Terplan [267], the same year, published a similar list of 79 pages. In 2001, both of them were largely obsolete. For instance, AdventNet, Metrix, Rapid Logic, and SNMP Research all offer Web-based management packages today, but they are referenced neither by Harler, nor by Terplan.

In the author's view, people looking for the latest and greatest commercial products in Web-based management should attend a trade show (e.g., Networld+Interop) or search the Web. For instance, during several years, Lindsay maintained a compilation of commercial packages on Web-based management [153]; unfortunately, this list does not appear to be updated anymore. On the SimpleWeb site, the University of Twente lists many commercial network-management software packages [233]; some of them are based on Web technologies. This list was still maintained at the time these lines were written. Probably the easiest and most efficient solution is to search for the expression "Web-based management" with your favorite Internet search engine!

6.9 Summary

In this chapter, we presented the state of the art in Web-based management. In Section 6.2, we began with browser-based metamanagement, an entry-level approach that deals with collateral management tasks. In Section 6.3, we described browser-based management, a simple approach whereby the agent supports no Web technologies and the manager directly accesses the agent via a Web browser. In Section 6.4, we detailed three-tier management, whereby the manager and the agent communicate via an external management gateway. The manager can use advanced techniques to communicate with the gateway, whereas the agent is still a plain SNMP agent. In Section 6.5, we reviewed HTTP-based management, a more sophisticated approach that leverages an embedded HTTP server in the agent to communicate via HTTP between the manager and the agent. In Section 6.6, we studied XML-based management, an advanced approach that is epitomized by WBEM. This time, the agent supports not only HTTP, but also fine-grained XML data. In Section 6.7, we completed our taxonomy of Web-based management with distributed Java-based management, whereby the manager and the agent communicate via object-oriented middleware. Unfortunately, this very elaborate approach is exposed to the *my-middleware-is-better-than-yours* syndrome. Finally, we indicated how to find up-to-date information about commercial software packages in Web-based management.

This concludes the first part of this book. We have now defined the problem at stake, investigated the solution space, selected Web-based management, and reviewed in detail all the current approaches in Web-based management. In the second part of this book, we will present our new management architecture and a research prototype that implements it.

Chapter 7

A NEW MANAGEMENT ARCHITECTURE: WIMA

In this chapter, we propose a new management architecture for IP networks and systems in place of the SNMP management architecture used today. Our architecture is called WIMA (Web-based Integrated Management Architecture) and consists of two parts: a push-based architecture for regular management and notification delivery, and a pull-based architecture for *ad hoc* management. Our main innovations lie in the former, which combines Web and push technologies to communicate between agents and managers (or between managers in distributed hierarchical management). We claim that WIMA solves the problems identified in SNMP-based management in Section 3.3 and meets the new requirements set by the market. We also propose an elegant way of dealing with legacy agents which, at the same time, paves the way for future agents supporting yet-to-be-defined information models.

Although we used both top-down and bottom-up approaches to devise WIMA, this chapter is organized in a top-down manner for the sake of clarity. In Section 7.1, we draw the main lines of our management architecture (analysis phase) and outline its novel organizational and communication models. In Section 7.2, we present our main design decisions (design phase) and point out the most significant differences between the SNMP and WIMA management architectures. In Section 7.3, we describe our push-based architecture and its organizational model, WIMA-OM-push. We also propose a migration path to gradually implement them in real-life networks. In Section 7.4, we introduce our pull-based architecture and its organizational model, WIMA-OM-pull, and again describe a migration path. Finally, we summarize this chapter in Section 7.5. The communication model of our management architecture will be presented in Chapter 8, with XML complements in Chapter 9.

7.1 Main Architectural Decisions (Analysis Phase)

In this section, we analyze the main architectural decisions behind our proposed management architecture, and the main differences between the SNMP and WIMA management architectures. We also explain why we focused our attention on the organizational model (WIMA-OM) and communication model (WIMA-CM).

7.1.1 One management architecture, four models

In NSM, management architectures are traditionally broken down into four models[1]: an information model, a communication model, an organizational model, and a functional model [118, 54]. Which of these models should be changed to solve the problems listed in Section 3.3?

New functional model?

For many years, there has been a great consensus around the management tasks defined by the functional model. As we mentioned in Section 2.2, these tasks are traditionally grouped into five functional areas: Fault, Configuration, Accounting, Performance, and Security management (FCAPS [52, 53]). Even the OSI and SNMP research communities agree on this! As new techniques appear or are better understood, new functions are defined, such as the Command Sequencer [131] in the OSI world and the Script MIB [150, 225] in the IP world. But there is no fundamental questioning of the OSI/SNMP functional model itself. We therefore chose to keep it unchanged in WIMA.

Apart from the functional model, there is no consensus at all in the research community as to which model should be preserved and which should be changed to address SNMP issues.

New organization model?

Since the early 1990s, we have seen a number of proposals calling for a radical change in the organization model (see Chapter 4). The most relevant to us are the following:

- Management by Delegation [105] proposed a new organizational model, but it did not go as far as specifying a new communication model. Goldszmidt's prototype used a new communication protocol (the Remote Delegation Protocol), but it was a proof of concept to demonstrate the gains of his new organizational model rather than a plea to use a specific communication model.
- Along the same lines, the Script MIB proposed a change in the SNMP organizational model to delegate tasks to agents. It defined a new management task, thereby complementing the SNMP functional model, and a new MIB for storing related management data. But it kept the SNMP communication model unchanged.

---

1. Hegering *et al.* call them *submodels* [118].

- Many proposals based on mobile code were also made, some in the area of active networks, others in mobile agents, etc. (see Section 4.1.3.1). In NSM, we still have not seen any proposal mature enough to specify a new organizational model. The main problem with mobile code is security, and as long as this problem remains unsolved by software engineers, mobile-code technologies will remain confined to prototyping in NSM (see Chapter 5).
- Finally, the engineering problems in multi-agent systems, and DAI in general, are such that we are nowhere near seeing a detailed proposal for a new organizational model for NSM, let alone a new, comprehensive management architecture (see Chapter 5).

New information model?

During the same period of time, we have seen two attempts to replace the SNMP information model: one based on OSI management and another on CIM.

The OSI management metamodel, made up of GDMO [57] and the General Relationship Model (GRM [130]), is much richer than the SNMP metamodel (SMIv2 [48]). Said otherwise, the expressiveness and semantic richness of information modeling are much higher in OSI management. The OSI management metamodel is object oriented and supports named relationships, actions, etc. [103]. All of these are missing in SNMP, so programmers and modelers resort to ugly workarounds such as programming by side effect[1]. To address these deficiencies in SNMP, some people suggested using OSI information modeling in the IP world. This led to a "religious war" between the IP and telecommunications worlds [25]. Although the expressiveness of OSI information modeling was undoubtedly superior to SNMP's, the market did not adopt it because of the very design of OSI. The four models of the OSI management architecture are deeply intertwined; by snowball effect, the adoption of its information model requires the adoption of its communication model (CMIP and CMIS), its seven-layer OSI stack, its connection-oriented transport layer, etc. SNMP was created precisely to avoid this complexity, thus OSI information modeling never really made it to the IP world.

Several years after this "religious war" was over, the DMTF issued a new object-oriented information model for the IP world: CIM [41]. By being object oriented, CIM addresses the main shortcoming of the SNMP metamodel and increases the expressiveness and semantic richness of information modeling in NSM. Another advantage of using CIM is that it can be independent of the communication model: Adopting CIM does not mandate the adoption of an entire protocol stack.

New communication model?

Despite well-known problems in the SNMP protocol (see Chapter 3), little attention has been paid to the communication model in the past decade. Only the DMTF has made a proposal [77]. After erring for some time with a new transfer protocol (HMMP), the DMTF

---

1. By setting the same SNMP MIB variable to different values, we make the agent invoke different actions such as "reboot" or "shutdown" (see Section 3.3.2.2).

decided that agent-manager and manager-manager transfers should rely on HTTP. This proposal specifies the encapsulation of XML-encoded CIM operations in HTTP, and HTTP/1.1 extensions to facilitate the traversal of firewalls.

New management architecture?

The DMTF claims to have defined a complete management architecture: WBEM. It indeed includes a new information model. The CIM metamodel[1] is now fairly stable [74]. Many CIM schemas are under development, but few of them are already stable. WBEM also includes a communication model. Some details pertaining to agent-manager interactions still need clarification, but the issue of events was recently addressed, and the new specification for CIM operations over HTTP, due in 2002, is expected to complete the communication model.

But WBEM still lacks an organizational model. It does not specify how agents and managers should be organized (hierarchically, peer-to-peer, etc.), and does not specify the nature of agent-manager and manager-manager interactions (push, pull, etc.). As a result, Web-based management-platform vendors are implicitly encouraged to simply add support for a new information model to their existing SNMP-based platforms, and to tweak HTTP proxies and servers to support the DMTF's HTTP/1.1 extensions for going across firewalls—without changing anything to the way managers and agents interact.

So, as it stands today, WBEM can hardly be considered a full-blown management architecture. It will become a viable alternative to the SNMP management architecture only when it includes an organizational model, its communication model has stabilized, and the most common CIM schemas have reached maturity.

WIMA

In summary, many efforts have been devoted in the past to defining new organizational models, some efforts to defining new information models, and none to defining both a new organizational model and a new communication model. This might explain why none of them are widely adopted today, and why the SNMP management architecture is still the only reasonable alternative in the IP world.

We believe we have filled this void with WIMA, our new management architecture. We changed the way managers and agents interact and exchange management data, we studied how this change affects the four different models, and we specified new communication and organizational models. We also kept the information model orthogonal to the communication and organizational models, which allows us to deal with agents supporting any information model: SNMP MIBs, CIM schemas, etc. Let us investigate these different architectural decisions in more detail in Sections 7.1.2 through to 7.1.5.

---

1. Or *metaschema* in DMTF parlance, see Section 6.6.1.

7.1.2 No need to define yet another information model

The enterprise-management community has been plagued for many years by "religious wars". One of them is about informations models. Whenever a new problem (or idea) comes up, some people believe that it should be solved (or implemented) by inventing a new *ad hoc* information model. For instance, we saw this problem already with network-topology information management [191]. Saperia and Schönwälder also exposed it in policy-based management [221]. This rationale "forgets" that the success encountered by the SNMP management architecture in the 1990s owes a great deal to the facts that (i) we had a single information model to manage IP networks and (ii) the metamodel remained very stable (only two variants in 10 years: SMIv1 and SMIv2). The time it takes to educate a large market with new information-modeling techniques should not be underestimated, and the number of information models that need to be mastered by management-application designers, programmers, and administrators should be kept to a strict minimum.

In the late 1990s, the DMTF released a new information model: CIM. By replacing data-oriented SNMP MIBs with object-oriented CIM schemas, CIM addresses the main shortcoming of the SNMP information model. In view of the number of vendors now backing the DMTF, there is little doubt that CIM will get some share of the information-modeling market. Whether CIM schemas will eventually replace SNMP MIBs, or simply complement them, remains to be seen and will only partially be based on technical merits. But now that we have two information models at our disposal in the IP world (SNMP, very simple and widely deployed, and CIM, conceptually rich), we believe that we have enough information models to cover all our needs for the next management cycle in NSM, and even in integrated enterprise management at large. What is needed today is new SNMP MIBs or new CIM schemas, not a new metamodel, not a new way of modeling management information. In consequence, we do not specify another information model in WIMA.

7.1.3 Dissociation of the communication and information models

We actually went one step further and decided that our management architecture should be orthogonal to the information model(s) supported by the agents and managers. In other words, WIMA does not prescribe the use of a specific information model but copes with any information model. With a single communication model, we can transfer management data pertaining to different information models: SNMP MIBs or CIM schemas for IP networks and systems, OSI MIBs for hybrid networks (when we mix IP and telecommunication networks), etc. We made this possible by completely dissociating the information and communication models. Each bundle of management data sent by an agent to a manager is self-describing, with metadata indicating the type of management data being transferred (e.g., SMIv2-compliant MIB variable encoded in BER, or CIM 2.2 object encoded in XML). To make this possible, we dropped the SNMP communication protocol in favor of HTTP and proposed an original way of structuring data in persistent HTTP/TCP connections. The details of our solution will be presented in Chapter 8.

With this architectural change, new information models can be defined over time, if need be, without altering the communication model. If CIM were replaced tomorrow with a new, more efficient object-oriented information model, we could still use the same communication model in our management architecture. When a new information model comes up, we only have to define a way to encode management data and encapsulate it in HTTP. This characteristic is very important for dealing with legacy systems, especially already deployed SNMP MIBs (see Section 7.2.7). It is also important for the future because it does not mandate an information model that could prove to be too limiting in the future (as we experienced with SNMP, for instance).

Our architectural decision to completely dissociate the information and communication models represents a major breakaway from the SNMP and OSI management architectures. The close ties between these two models are, in our view, a conceptual mistake in the OSI and SNMP management architectures. The DMTF has not yet fully defined a communication model for its WBEM management architecture, but the definition of CIM-oriented HTTP extensions to facilitate the traversal of firewalls leads us to believe that the same mistake is about to be repeated (we will come back to this in Chapter 11).

7.1.4 A new organizational model: WIMA-OM

In our organizational model, we changed the way agents and managers interact and specified how management should be distributed. One of our main innovations is to use push technologies for transferring notifications *and* regular management data between agents and managers (or between managers in distributed hierarchical management), and not simply for delivering notifications as in SNMP- and OSI-based management. Let us first summarize the main differences between the push and pull approaches. We will then present the advantages of push over pull to transfer regular management data, and justify why the pull model should be preserved for *ad hoc* management. Finally, we will describe how to distribute management.

7.1.4.1 Push model vs. pull model: two organizational models

In software engineering, the pull and push models designate two well-known approaches for exchanging data between distant entities. The newspaper metaphor is a simple illustration of these models. If you want to read your favorite newspaper everyday, you can either go and buy it every morning, or subscribe to it once and then receive it regularly and automatically at home. The former is an example of pull, the latter of push.

In NSM, the pull model is based on the manager-agent paradigm, a variant of a standard paradigm in software engineering: the request-response paradigm, typically used in client-server architectures. The client sends a request to the server, then the server answers synchronously or asynchronously. In SNMP-based management, this is called *data polling,* or simply *polling*. It is functionally equivalent to the client "pulling" management data off the server. In this approach, the data transfer is always initiated by the client, i.e. the manager. This model is the basis for most management-data transfers in the SNMP and OSI management architectures.

The push model, conversely, is based on a variant of the publish-subscribe design pattern[1] [43]. In this model, the agent (or the mid-level manager in distributed hierarchical management) advertises what information model it supports (SNMP MIBs, CIM schemas, etc.), and what notifications it can send (SNMPv1 traps, SNMPv2 notifications, CIM events, etc.). Then, the administrator subscribes the manager (or the top-level manager in distributed hierarchical management) to the data he/she is interested in, specifies how often the manager should receive this data, and disconnects. Later on, each agent individually takes the initiative to push data to the manager, either on a regular basis via a scheduler (e.g., for network monitoring) or asynchronously (e.g., to send SNMP notifications). In the SNMP and OSI management architectures, only notification delivery follows the push model.

In WIMA, our organizational model uses both approaches. The push-based organizational model is called WIMA-OM-push; the pull-based organizational model is called WIMA-OM-pull.

7.1.4.2 WIMA-OM-push for regular management and notification delivery

For IP networks and systems, the pull model has been used for over a decade for regular management and *ad hoc* management, whereas the push model was used only for notification delivery. Yet we claim that the push model is better suited to regular management than the pull model. In WIMA, we use push technologies for both regular management (data collection and monitoring) and notification delivery. The advantages of using push technologies in NSM are fourfold: We save network bandwidth, we transfer some workload to the agents, we improve scalability, and we facilitate the support for redundant managers, thereby improving the robustness of the management application.

Save network bandwidth

Much of the network overhead caused by SNMP polling is due to the fact that data collection and monitoring are very repetitive: There is a lot of redundancy in what the manager keeps asking all the agents. For instance, in SNMP-based network monitoring, a common way to check if a machine is still up and running is to request the same MIB variable, typically its `sysObjectID` (MIB-II), every few minutes. This scheme works but is very inefficient, as the manager marshals and sends the same OID to all the agents, at every polling cycle, endlessly. Instead, with the push model, the manager contacts each agent once, subscribes to this OID once, and specifies at what frequency the agent should send the value of this MIB variable. Afterward, there is no more traffic going from the manager to the agent (see Fig. 12). All subsequent traffic goes from the agent to the manager (except in the rare cases when the administrator wishes to update the list of OIDs

---

1. The publish-subscribe design pattern is called the *Observer* pattern by Gamma *et al.* [101].

that the manager is interested in, or change a push frequency). So, by using push technologies instead of polling, we reduce the network overhead of management data, thereby saving network bandwidth.

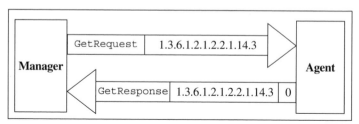

Fig. 12. Network overhead of an SNMP get

How much do we save? Is this difference significant or marginal? For instance, in SNMP, the error rate for inbound traffic through interface #3 is given by the OID 1.3.6.1.2.1.2.2.1.14.3 in MIB-II [173], as depicted in Fig. 12. The manager issues a get request to the agent. It consists of a small header specifying that this is a GetRequest PDU, and a long OID that indicates the MIB variable of interest to the manager. The agent sends a reply that consists of a small header (GetResponse PDU), a long OID, and a short value for that MIB variable. So, with an SNMP get, the same OID is sent twice over the network and accounts for most of the network overhead. With push technologies, the manager no longer sends a get request for each MIB variable for each agent. Once the subscription is performed, the network overhead is only due to the agents pushing {OID, value} pairs to the manager. As the value and header take little space compared to the OID, we roughly halve the traffic by choosing pull over push technologies.

Under certain circumstances, the network-bandwidth saving can be even greater. In SNMP, MIB traversals or table retrievals are usually achieved with get-next. In this case, three OIDs are transmitted instead of two: In its reply, the agent includes not only the OID described above, but also the next OID that the manager should request. By using push technologies instead of pull, we then divide by about three the network overhead caused by transfers of management data.

In short, compared with SNMP polling, push technologies significantly reduce the network overhead caused by management data.

Transfer some of the workload to the agents

The second advantage of using push technologies is to delegate some of the processing from the manager to the agents (or from the top-level manager to the mid-level managers in distributed hierarchical management). In the SNMP management architectures, the agent is supposedly dumb, so the manager does everything. This makes it easy to cope with bottom-of-the-range, as well as top-of-the-range, network equipment, but it also causes significant CPU overhead on the manager. SNMP was really designed to cope with small LANs, where the aggregated overhead is easily bearable for the manager. With large networks, or with small networks where the manager has to execute a large number of rules (e.g., LANs experiencing instability), the total processing overhead can be unbearable for the manager, which can become a bottleneck and slow down the entire management application. One way to solve this problem is to transfer some of the CPU burden from the manager to the agents, as advocated by Goldszmidt with Management by Delegation [105], or Wellens and Auerbach when they exposed the Myth of the Dumb Agent [286]. The main argument behind this transfer is that more and more agents have powerful microprocessors and significant memory, thereby rendering the vision of a "dumb" agent obsolete.

By transferring some of the workload to the agents, not only do we free the manager from some of its CPU load, but we also decrease the requirements put on the manager in terms of CPU and memory. In large networks, management platforms are often big servers that cost a fortune to purchase and maintain. Agents, on the other hand, are more powerful than they used to be, and most agents can reasonably do some processing locally.

Improve scalability

The third advantage of push technologies is that they improve the scalability of NSM. This is the direct result of saving network bandwidth and transferring some of the workload to the agents. By reducing the network overhead per transferred management data (e.g., per SNMP MIB variable), we make it possible to transfer more management data, that is, to manage more agents from a single manager or to transfer more management data per agent. And by transferring some of the CPU workload to the agents, we free up some resources on the manager, thereby allowing it to cope with more management tasks. As we expect the management-related traffic to increase in the future, we improve the scalability of NSM if we transfer data between agents and managers in a more efficient way.

Improve robustness through redundancy

A fourth advantage of the push model is that it makes it easy to support redundant managers, either through IP multicasting or duplicated push. Although most network devices and systems to date are managed by a single manager, some environments require several managers to run in parallel to improve the robustness of the management application. This allows for automatic failover (when a manager takes over another in case of failure) and quorum consensus (when several managers vote to make a decision).

Redundant managers are fairly simple to support with push technologies. When an administrator subscribes to some management data (see Section 7.3.3), he/she tells the agent what manager it should send the data to. Instead of specifying a single unicast IP address, the administrator can specify a multicast address or several unicast addresses. For an agent, sending data to a unicast or a multicast address is identical, and sending it to two or three unicast addresses is not immensely different. The only requirement in the first scenario is that it should support IP multicasting, which modern implementations of the TCP/IP stack generally do. Management data is thus sent to multiple managers in parallel, which makes the management application more robust. For example, one manager can crash while another takes over transparently ("hot standby"). Alternatively, standby managers can receive data passively until they are configured to replace the master manager ("cold standby").

With pull technologies, we can also have the agent send management data to several managers. But in this case, all of the managers have to request the same data independently, which increases significantly the network overhead (we multiply it by the number of managers) and consumes more CPU cycles (we multiply the overall CPU overhead by the number of managers). Moreover, the information retrieved from the same agent by different managers can be different, because the polls are not perfectly synchronized across all the managers. This lack of a consistent view of the network shared by all the managers can cause problems in the case of failover. It also makes fault tolerance based on quorum consensus [65] unusable (we need a consistent view of the network to do so).

Even if this improved robustness is still a long way from survivability and fault tolerance, it can be very attractive to organizations whose network is of critical importance to the smooth running of their business, but who cannot afford expensive, full-blown, fault-tolerant systems.

7.1.4.3 WIMA-OM-pull for *ad hoc* management

Push technologies beat polling in many respects, but there is a price to be paid: the overhead caused by the configuration of the agent during the subscription phase. Obviously, push is superior to pull if, and only if, this overhead is outweighed by the network-overhead gains described earlier. This is the case only when the same MIB variable is transferred many times from an agent to a manager.

For *ad hoc* management, by definition, we are in the opposite situation. We want to retrieve a MIB variable just once, or perhaps ten times in a row. In such cases, the overhead of configuring the agent is not offset by the gain of pushing management data from the agent to the manager. So we have a threshold effect. The value of this threshold can only be determined empirically. For troubleshooting, whenever we want to monitor a MIB variable over a short period of time (typically, up to 5 minutes), we are in the realm of *ad hoc* management and should use pull technologies; beyond that threshold, we are in the realm of regular management and should use push technologies. Note that there is an overlap zone where it does not really matter whether we use push or pull technologies, as the relative gains or losses are negligible.

7.1.4.4 Distributed hierarchical management

As we saw in Chapter 3, distribution was a late concern in SNMP. When the M2M MIB was rendered obsolete and the semantics of the `inform` PDU, initially destined for manager-manager interaction, were changed into an acknowledged notification, distribution in SNMPv2 was killed *de facto*. In SNMPv3, manager-to-agent delegation is based on the Script MIB, but manager-to-manager delegation still does not work because manager-manager interactions are not yet specified in any SNMP management architecture (v1, v2c, or v3). The few management-platform vendors that support distributed management in the IP world currently have to resort to proprietary mechanisms (e.g., HP OpenView). As a result, it is exceedingly complex to base a distributed management solution on management platforms developed by different vendors—a situation often encountered when two large enterprises merge.

To solve this problem and allow vendors to distribute management in an open and interoperable way, we decided to specify how management should be distributed in WIMA. In Chapter 4, we saw that we had two options: hierarchical and cooperative management. Which one should we choose in WIMA?

As we showed in Section 4.2.1, the topology and administration of an enterprise's IP networks often map directly onto the organization chart of this enterprise. The issue of distributed management arises when networks grow large, that is, when enterprises grow large. Large enterprises are generally organized in a hierarchical rather than cooperative way, so it makes sense to distribute hierarchically the management of large networks or distributed systems. Distributed hierarchical management is also easier to implement than distributed cooperative management, as we said in Chapter 5, because the technologies that support cooperative management (e.g., goal-based multi-agent systems) are still not mature enough to be used in NSM.

Therefore, in WIMA, management is distributed across a hierarchy of managers. To make the deployment of distributed management simple, we decided that manager-agent and manager-manager interactions should work similarly. As a result, in WIMA, everything we say about agent-manager interactions applies equally to manager-manager interactions. In particular, all the figures depicting an agent and a manager in the remainder of this book implicitly also depict a mid-level manager and a top-level manager. Another consequence is that in WIMA, we also have the choice between push-based and pull-based interactions to distribute management, depending on the number of times a management data is transferred from a mid-level to a top-level manager.

7.1.5 A new communication model: WIMA-CM

Our last architectural decision was to define a new communication model. This was required by the new push-based interactions between agents and managers (or between mid- and top-level managers in distributed hierarchical management) and by the dissociation between the communication and information models. Just as we had to split the organizational model into two parts, we also split the communication model into two components. One follows a push model (WIMA-CM-push) to transfer regular management data and notifications. The other follows a pull model (WIMA-CM-pull) for *ad hoc* management data. Both of them will be described in detail in Chapter 8.

7.2 Main Design Decisions (Design Phase)

In this section, we present the main design decisions behind our proposed management architecture: WIMA.

7.2.1 Web technologies

Our first design decision was to adopt Web technologies: HTTP, HTML, XML, Java applets, Java servlets, etc. The advantages of using them in NSM are numerous. We identified eight.

First, Web technologies are ubiquitous today: They are used throughout the software industry. They are standard as long as developers follow the specifications and do not use proprietary extensions (e.g., browser-specific extensions). By going from domain-specific technologies such as SNMPv1, SNMPv2c, SNMPv3, BER, SMIv2, etc. to standard Web technologies, we make it much easier and less expensive for enterprises to find and train programmers, and we decrease the development and maintenance costs of the management application.

Second, Web technologies increase the portability of code. By coding management GUIs as Java applets instead of binaries, we dramatically reduce the development costs faced by vendors. Management GUIs no longer need to be ported to many operating systems and many management platforms offering different APIs: The same code can run anywhere, as long as proprietary Java extensions are avoided. As management GUIs are less costly for vendors, they should be less expensive for customers, too.

Third, by embedding the vendor-specific management GUIs directly in the agent, we address the issue of MIB versioning. We can have different versions of a vendor-specific MIB in the same network, and we no longer require a MIB-discovery protocol. A MIB update on the agent simply requires an update of its embedded management GUI.

Fourth, by embedding the management GUIs directly in the agent, we also bring their time-to-market down to zero. We no longer have a time lag between the availability of a new, highly performing piece of hardware and the possibility to manage it with a full-blown management GUI ported to *the* management platform and *the* operating system owned by the customer. This factor is crucial in production environments.

Fifth, by embedding the management GUIs directly in the agent, we also suppress the need for separate management platforms for start-up companies. We properly integrate the management of equipment from different vendors, which puts small and large equipment vendors in fair competition. As a result, start-ups are no longer disadvantaged by their difficult or expensive access to the APIs of the major management platforms.

Sixth, by using HTTP over TCP instead of SNMP over UDP, we simplify the management of branch offices and subsidiaries across firewalls (we will explain this in detail in Section 8.2.2.2).

Seventh, by using HTTP instead of SNMP as a transfer protocol, we can easily compress management data and consequently reduce the network overhead caused by management data (see Section 8.4.4).

Eighth, XML and JDBC make it easy to store management data in any third-party database (see Section 7.2.5). This frees customers from the impediment of peer-to-peer agreements between management-platform and database vendors.

7.2.2 Three-tier architecture

Our second design decision was to adopt a three-tier architecture instead of the two-tier architecture typically used by SNMP-based management platforms. The advantages of adding an application server between the client and the server are well-known and presented by many software-engineering authors [6, 93, 146, 290]. In short, they increase reusability and flexibility by allowing implementers to modify the middle tier without changing the other two. These three tiers are often given different names by different authors. Larman [146, p. 273] calls them the presentation, application logic, and storage tiers. Fowler [93, Chapter 12] calls them the applications, domain, and database tiers. Wijegunaratne and Fernandez [290, pp. 41–78] call them the client, composite service, and data access server tiers. Ambler [6, pp. 144–148]) calls them the interface business system, business system, and business persistence system tiers, or simply client, application server, and server for short. We use Ambler's simplified terminology in this book.

To adopt a three-tier architecture in WIMA, we must split the manager (that is, the monolithic, SNMP-based management platform) into three entities (see Fig. 13):

- the management station (any machine running a Web browser)
- the management server (a fixed, dedicated machine)
- the data server (a fixed, dedicated machine)

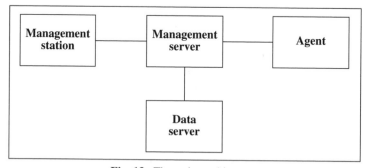

Fig. 13. Three-tier architecture

The management server and the data server should be dedicated machines for the reasons of robustness mentioned in Section 2.11. Our three-tier architecture operates with three types of interactions: between the management station and the agent, between the management station and the data server, and between the agent and the data server.

Interactions between the management station and the agent

In interactive mode, a typical interaction goes from the management station (client), through the management server (application server), to the agent (server) and back. Such interactions typically occur in *ad hoc* management, but also happen during the subscription phase in regular management.

Interactions between the management station and the data server

During the subscription phase, the configuration data also goes from the management station (client), through the management server (application server), to the data server (server) for persistent storage in the data repository.

Interactions between the agent and the data server

This type of interaction typically occurs during the distribution phase in regular management (data collection): Data goes from the agent (client), through the management server (application server), to the data server (server). It also takes place when an agent reboots; if the agent has no local persistent storage, it can retrieve its configuration data from the data server via the management server.

We will detail all of these interactions in Section 7.3.

7.2.3 Management server: COTS components and object-oriented frameworks

Our third design decision was to improve the design of the management server by using COTS components and object-oriented frameworks instead of an opaque, monolithic, proprietary piece of code. In the 1990s, the software-engineering research community particularly studied the issue of reusability of code and design, which many researchers regarded as the main failure of object-oriented programming. They proposed a new concept to facilitate reusability: component software [264]. One outcome of this work, the component-based programming of distributed applications [126], can be very useful in NSM.

By integrating COTS components and object-oriented frameworks, we increase the competition between software vendors by making this competition more fine-grained. Today, in SNMP-based management, once you have opted for a certain management platform, you are forced to buy an event correlator, an accounting system, a billing system, or an authentication system from your management-platform vendor's catalog. You are therefore dependent on the peer-to-peer agreements signed by this vendor with third-party vendors. If you want to use a certain technology, say smart cards from RSA, you have to pray that your management-platform vendor has signed an agreement with RSA. Clearly, for commercial rather than technical reasons, not all technologies can be used with all management platforms; and some are available at unreasonable prices. Said otherwise, the drawback of integrated management is that customers soon become captive. Once they have invested a lot of money in a management-platform-specific solution, they can no longer drive prices down by comparing offers from different competitors.

With a component-based management server, different parts of the management application are written by different vendors. By design, these components must be interoperable and offer open APIs[1]. In the component-software industry, we no longer see companies striving to keep their code opaque and proprietary in order to secure a niche market. COTS components and object-oriented frameworks make it possible for a customer to plug and play a new set of components to add new functionality to an existing management application, or to replace an old component by a new, smarter one. This new business model requires that existing NSM applications be restructured entirely. To follow up with the previous example, it is possible to write the security-related code in such a way that the actual security technology used by the customer is transparent to the rest of the application. Another example is the event correlator, often considered as the core of a management platform. Almost all management platforms on the market come with an event correlator. Smart event correlators are difficult to write. To make it easier for customers to work out and specify correlation rules, new languages keep appearing, either as commercial products or research prototypes. With a component-based architecture, we can plug and play a new event correlator as soon as a company releases a new smart piece of software; we no longer have to purchase *the* management platform that comes with it.

The advantages of using component software to implement the management server are numerous. First, the customer is freed of the peer-to-peer agreements between vendors, and is no longer enchained to a single vendor by previous large investments. This drives prices down by increasing competition. It also gives customers total freedom as to what technology they can use. Second, this makes manager-manager interactions more interoperable, as third-party component vendors depend on openness for their market. As a result, distributed management solutions are easier to deploy. Third, we gain some flexibility and can change management platforms fairly easily. This is particularly useful when two companies merge and unify the supervision of their IP networks and systems.

It should be stressed that moving from current, monolithic, SNMP-based platforms to solutions based on component software is likely to significantly shake the management-platform market and cause new problems. First, new means buggy. Many years of debugging and real-life testing have gone into HP OpenView, Cabletron Spectrum, and all the major management platforms of the market. It will take years for component-based management platforms to reach the same level of reliability. Second, debugging becomes tricky. What if two components from different vendors do not interact as they are supposed to? Whose fault is it? Who should fix it? This is the usual "It's not me, it's him" situation, well-known to the administrators of heterogeneous networks. To ease their task, customers

---

1. Note that inter-component communication is not specified by WIMA.

can resort to software integrators, whose role is precisely to shield customers from the headaches caused by interferences between multiple vendors. But integrators also reduce the cost savings of going from monolithic to component software: they have to make a profit! They can also (but do not necessarily) reduce the choice of technologies available to customers; this is a pitfall that customers should be wary about when they select a software integrator.

7.2.4 Management-data transfers across firewalls

Our fourth design decision was to take firewalls into account from the outset. In WIMA, we can have zero, one, or several firewalls between the manager and the agent (or between the mid- and top-level managers in distributed hierarchical management). Three scenarios demonstrate why this assumption makes sense:

- An on-call administrator may want to use a PC as a management station from outside the enterprise (e.g., from home) to investigate a problem that occurs in the middle of the night. To access the company's network, he/she would typically go across a firewall.
- In large, geographically dispersed enterprises, manager-manager interactions often go across two firewalls: one at the boundary of the management domain of the top-level manager (headquarters), and another at the boundary of the management domain of each mid-level manager (branch offices or subsidiaries).
- If an enterprise has a small, remote office, it can make economic sense not to buy a manager for this office, but to manage critical remote equipment across the WAN link. In this case, agent-manager interactions go across at least one firewall (the headquarters') and possibly a second (the branch's).

The possible presence of one or several firewall(s) sets new constraints on our communication model, which will be detailed in Chapter 8. By taking these constraints into account in WIMA, we made it possible to use a single management architecture, whether we have a firewall or not in practice. We also addressed a shortcoming in the SNMP management architecture, which did not take firewalls into account from the outset[1].

Note that the three-tier architecture proposed in Section 7.2.2 fits nicely with firewalls, as streamlining accesses to/from agents through a single management server simplifies access control and authentication.

7.2.5 Data repository independent of the management platform

Our fifth design decision was to make the data repository independent of the management platform, thereby allowing the administrator to use the repository of his/her choice to store management data. This was one of our motivations behind the adoption of a three-tier

---

1. To be fair with the designers of SNMP, firewalls were very rare in the late 1980s, when the SNMPv1 management architecture and communication protocol were devised.

architecture (see Section 7.2.2). To be effective, this independence must be achieved at three levels:

- the type of data repository; e.g., a relational database, an object-oriented database, an LDAP directory, an XML repository, or a plain-text NFS file system;
- the implementation of this type of data repository; e.g., an Oracle, Sybase, or mSQL relational database;
- the API used by the management application to access the data repository; e.g., Open DataBase Connectivity (ODBC) or Java DataBase Connectivity (JDBC).

To achieve this loose coupling between the data repository and the management application, we assume that the data repository is logically located on a different machine called the data server (see Fig. 13). This machine may be physically different from, or identical to, the management server; but conceptually, we assume that the two machines are separate.

Because the data repository must be independent of the management platform, the management application can no longer embed special hooks that are specific to a given data-repository technology (e.g., vendor-specific extensions to SQL). Instead, the management application must rely on open APIs to communicate with the data repository. Examples of such APIs include ODBC/JDBC for accessing relational databases via SQL, WBEM's CIM Operations over HTTP (together with the CIM-to-XML Mapping) for CIM schemas, XML Schemas and the Simple Object Access Protocol (SOAP) for XML repositories, and LDAP for LDAP directories.

By imposing the use of open APIs, we fill a void in the SNMP management architecture. The latter did not specify that proprietary APIs should be banned when accessing the data repository. This allowed major management-platform vendors to "close" this market with proprietary solutions (as opposed to keeping it open by using non-proprietary APIs). Note that the openness of these APIs is required by WIMA, but the APIs themselves are not imposed by our management architecture.

The independence of the management application *vis-à-vis* the data repository is consistent with our proposed use of component software and object-oriented frameworks (see Section 7.2.3). Some components give the management application a high-level and technology-independent API to communicate with the data repository. Other components (typically, an object-oriented framework) are specific to a type of data repository. Other components could even be specific to the data repository (e.g., if we want to use the SQL extensions that are implemented by most vendors, but in different ways). Other components are specific to the API used by the management application to access the data repository.

Making the data repository independent of the management platform frees administrators from the shackles of peer-to-peer agreements between database and management-platform vendors—a serious interoperability problem in SNMP-based management that we described in Section 3.3.3.2. Customers can now choose any type of data repository, any implementation of it, and any API. Another advantage is that the management application no longer has to be ported to Oracle, Sybase, mSQL, etc. Instead, it can use a generic API (e.g., string-based SQL) for all RDBMSes, ODBC for RDBMSes running on Windows platforms, XML for all types of data repositories and all operating systems, etc. This decreases the cost of the management platform for vendors, and consequently also for customers (especially with the increased competition caused by the use of component software).

7.2.6 Bulk transfers of regular management data

Our sixth design decision was to facilitate bulk transfers of regular management data. It is based on the assumption that, by going from network management to enterprise management, we will face a steady increase in the amount of management data to move about (see Section 3.4). In order to decrease network latency, network overhead, and CPU overhead at the manager and the agent, we want to reduce the number of messages that are exchanged between the manager and the agent in both directions [243]. We also want to prevent the manager from having to guess the size of the agent's response message when it puts together a request message (see Section 3.3.1.2 and Section 3.3.1.3). In WIMA, we meet these goals by allowing the agent to send an infinitely large reply to the manager's request. The engineering details of our solution will be presented in Chapter 8.

7.2.7 Dealing with legacy systems

Our seventh design decision was to take into account legacy systems in WIMA, instead of assuming that we can start all over again with a clean slate (an error initially made by Microsoft *et al.* when they issued their first WBEM proposal in 1996 [28], and later corrected by the DMTF). In this chapter, we show that we can replace the SNMP management architecture with WIMA. But to be realistic, we must be able to work with the numerous SNMP MIBs that are already deployed worldwide, especially in network equipment. We must also assume that some agents do not have an embedded HTTP server, and that other agents have an HTTP server but do not have the software components that we will later propose to include in agents. Legacy systems will be dealt with in Section 7.3.6 and Section 7.4.4, when we describe migration paths from SNMP- to WIMA-based management.

7.2.8 Richer semantics

Our eighth design decision was to facilitate the use of richer semantics for management data. This will be presented in Chapter 8, when we detail the communication model of WIMA, and in Chapter 9, when we describe the advantages of using XML in integrated management. In short, the main implications are twofold. First, because of the *my-middleware-is-better-than-yours* syndrome, we saw that we cannot base manager-agent interactions on distributed object-oriented middleware. But this does not prevent us from using objects at all. In WIMA, we simply confine the use of Java, C++, or other objects at the edges—especially in the managers, but possibly also in the agents. This design decision proved to be useful when we developed our research prototype JAMAP (see Chapter 10). Second, with XML, we can define elaborate composite data structures that are richer, more expressive, and, in the end, more useful than SNMP varbind lists. We can also define many protocol operations and not simply the few defined in SNMP.

7.2.9 Easy to deploy

Last but not least, our ninth design decision was to make it easy to deploy WIMA-compliant agents and servers. The deployment simplicity was one of the keys to the success experienced by SNMPv1. With SNMP, the NSM community learned that integrating and dealing with deployment concerns is of paramount importance to gain acceptance from the industry. WIMA is not simply a good-looking proposal on paper, it is meant to be used in real-life IP networks and systems.

This translates into many details. First, we integrate in this book many deployment constraints that are due to the way the SNMP market historically developed, and not simply to SNMP technical constraints. We also propose a migration path to deal with legacy systems, as mentioned in Section 7.2.7. And very importantly, the amount of extra code and processing that we require the agents and managers to store and perform is reasonable. Last, we use the same communication and organizational models for agent-manager and manager-manager interactions (see Section 7.1.4.4).

Now that we have described our main architectural and design decisions, let us study in more detail the models that underlie regular management, *ad hoc* management, and notification delivery in WIMA.

7.3 Regular Management and Notification Delivery: The Push Model

In the late 1990s, the push model was put in the spotlight by the large success encountered by push systems (e.g., Pointcast, BackWeb, and Tibco Rendezvous) on the Internet [116][1]. Even though this model is well-known in software engineering, it has always been confined to notification delivery in SNMP-based management. To the best of our knowledge, no SNMP-based management platform uses it for monitoring or data collection today. Yet, as we explained in Section 7.1.4, its very design makes it better suited to regular management than the pull model that underpins SNMP-based management.

In WIMA, the push model underlies both regular management (monitoring and data collection) and notification delivery. Although we commonly say that the push model is based on publish-subscribe, it actually involves four phases. Supposing that the agent

---

1. Note that a number of push systems found today on the market actually follow the pull model at the implementation level.

supports SNMP MIBs (but the rationale remains the same with other information models), these phases are:

- *Publication phase*: Each agent maintains a list of Web pages that advertise the MIBs that it supports and the notifications that it may send to a manager.
- *Discovery phase*: The administrator learns the URLs of these Web pages. Some of them are well known, others are vendor specific.
- *Subscription phase*: Agent by agent, the administrator (the person) subscribes the manager (the program) to different MIB variables and notifications via subscription applets. The push frequency is specified for each MIB variable.
- *Distribution phase*: At each push cycle, the push scheduler of each agent triggers the transfer of MIB data from the agent to the manager.

In this section, we present the details of our push-based architecture. We first study successively the four phases of the push model, then discuss some issues related to the distribution of management, and finally present a migration path from SNMP- to WIMA-based management.

7.3.1 Publication phase

In the first phase, each agent (or mid-level manager in distributed management) publishes:

- What information model(s) it supports (e.g., SNMP or CIM).
- For each supported information model, what virtual management-data repositories it supports. In the case of SNMP, these are the generic MIBs (e.g., MIB-II, ATM MIB, or RMON MIB) and the vendor-specific MIBs. In the case of CIM, these are the core, common, and extension schemas.
- What notifications it can send to the manager (e.g., "interface down").

To publish this data, the agent embeds several management applets, typically stored in EPROM. These applets are available at URLs that remain constant over time for a given agent. In the next section, we explain why we do not use LDAP directories.

7.3.2 Discovery phase

In the next phase, the administrator discovers the following information for each agent:

- The information model(s) supported by the agent: SNMP, CIM, etc.
- The virtual management-data repositories supported by the agent: SNMP MIBs, CIM schemas, etc.
- The URLs of the agent's subscription applets.

The simplest way to discover all of this information would be to have all equipment vendors follow the same URL naming scheme for all their embedded HTML pages and Java applets. Experience has shown that this is unrealistic, because vendors have a natural tendency to do things their own way. A similar problem shows up in a different but related area: vendor-specific MIBs. A comparison between the proprietary MIBs of the main equipment vendors highlights a remarkable heterogeneity: They all have different structures and follow different naming schemes. In other words, the discovery phase cannot be fully automated.

Conversely, if we have no automation whatsoever—that is, if the URLs where the agent publishes its subscription applets are totally random and unpredictable—we have to manually configure the manager, agent by agent. In practice, this means that an operator must type in a multitude of URLs for all the subscription applets of all the agents. Clearly, this is not an option either because it does not scale and is error prone. In short, the discovery phase must be partially automated.

In this section, we propose a scheme whereby some URLs are well-known because they follow a convention adopted by all vendors, and other URLs are discovered via interactive browsing. Browsing requires a starting point, which we call the agent's management home page. Let us describe how the administrator accesses it.

7.3.2.1 A well-known URL for the agent's management home page

In order for the administrator to access the agent's management home page, the manager must know what URL to download. We have five options:

- The manager is manually configured by an operator, for all the agents in its management domain.
- There is an automated way for the agent to tell the manager what the URL of its management home page is.
- There is an automated way for the manager to retrieve this URL from the agent.
- There is an automated way for the manager to retrieve this URL from an external data repository.
- The manager can build this URL automatically because it follows a convention adopted by all vendors.

The first option is tedious, error prone, and does not scale. We rule it out.

The second option is based on notifications. Whenever the URL of its management home page changes, the agent sends the new URL to the manager via a notification. This scheme is not robust if implemented with SNMPv2 notifications, because they are not acknowledged. If we decide to use SNMPv3 informs (i.e., acknowledged notifications), we still face a major problem: deployment. They must be defined in a MIB and supported by deployed agents, which requires extending an existing MIB (usually, such notifications are defined in vendor-specific MIBs) or defining a new MIB. But deploying a new MIB takes a lot of time; so does the upgrade of an already deployed MIB. And even worse, new MIBs are not necessarily adopted by the market, sometimes for non-technical reasons. This solution is thus too risky: we have to exclude it.

The third option cannot rely on Web technologies[1]. It requires that the URL of the agent's management home page be stored in a virtual management-data repository on the agent. This repository can be an SNMP MIB, a CIM schema, etc. In the case of SNMP, the URL of the agent's management home page can be encoded in a string and stored in a MIB. This solution requires either extending an existing SNMP MIB supported by most existing agents (e.g., MIB-II), or defining a new MIB and convincing all vendors to support it (e.g., see Hewlett Packard's approach with the HTTP Manageable MIB [114]). This poses three problems. First, and justifiably so, the IETF has always been reluctant to change existing and widely deployed MIBs for obvious compatibility issues. Second, deploying or upgrading a MIB is time consuming and hazardous (see previous option). Third and worst, this approach would tightly tie Web-based management to a given information model (SNMP in our example, but it could be CIM as well). We do not want this, as one of the requirements for WIMA is that it should not rely on a specific information model (see Section 7.1.3). We therefore eliminate this option.

The fourth option combines the previous two. It requires that the URL of the agent's management home page be stored in an external data repository, that is, a machine that is neither the manager nor the agent. The agent stores (and possibly updates) this URL in the repository, and the manager accesses this information in read-only mode. This is the approach adopted by Sun Microsystems with its Java-based plug-and-play technology: Jini [258]. The data repository can be of different types (see Section 7.2.5); presently, such configuration data is typically stored in LDAP directories. Although this solution works and may appear more suitable than ours to automate discovery, we did not retain it for WIMA for several reasons. First, there is no consensus as yet as to how LDAP directories should be designed, structured, etc. Different vendors support different schemes, large vendors try to impose their own schemes as *de facto* standards, and it is unclear how the situation will evolve. Another problem is that LDAP directories are renowned to be slow. They do not scale well and can constitute bottlenecks when the number of network devices and systems to be managed grows large. A third, serious problem with the use of an external data repository, which is not limited to LDAP directories, is that it poses security problems. We need some external, untrusted agents to access and store data into an internal, trusted data repository without using strong security (see Section 3.4, "Security and firewalls"). This is a security officer's nightmare! We will address security issues in more detail in Chapter 8.

In WIMA, we selected the fifth option: The manager builds this URL automatically because it follows a convention adopted by all vendors. To do so, the agent's management home page must be published at a well-known URL. Let us describe our URL naming scheme.

---

1. Otherwise, it would lead to an infinite loop. To publish the URL of its management home page, the agent would have to publish where it publishes it. By recurrence, it would have to publish where it publishes where it publishes it, etc.

7.3.2.2 URL naming scheme

The agent's management home page is not the only URL that must be well known. In Section 7.3.3 and Chapter 8, we will see that several other URLs should, too. In this section, we define a general URL naming scheme that specifies (i) a number of well-known URLs supported by all vendors, and (ii) a convention for finding out proprietary URLs via interactive browsing.

To define a well-known URL, we can impose a certain pathname, a certain port number, or both. We need both. If we simply impose a pathname, we can for instance reserve the keyword mgmt for "management". The well-known URL for the agent's management home page is then:

```
<http://agent.domain/mgmt/>
```

where agent.domain is either the fully qualified domain name or the IP address of the agent. The problem here is that there are already many Web servers running all over the planet, some in embedded equipment (hence difficult to upgrade), and the odds are that some of them already use the reserved pathname mgmt for other purposes. In fact, it is impossible to find a pathname that we know for sure is not used yet. Consequently, imposing a certain pathname is not sufficient.

Alternatively, we can impose a port number. This approach was proposed by Harrison *et al.* [114] in 1996. They recommend the use of the reserved TCP port 280 (http-mgmt) for Web-based management:

```
<http://agent.domain:280/>
```

By not using the default port 80, and by using instead a port that is dedicated to Web-based management, we significantly reduce the risks of URL clashes. Even though port 280 is rarely used today, it is feasible to make all vendors agree to use it. However, this is not enough. Selecting a well-known port is sufficient for retrieving a single URL, e.g. the agent's management home page. But what about the other well-known URLs?

We really need to impose both the port number and the pathname. By doing so, we get the best of both worlds: We avoid URL clashes by not using the default port 80, and we keep the flexibility offered by fixed pathnames to automate management. As port 280 is dedicated to Web-based management, it is now possible to make all vendors agree on a few basic path-naming conventions.

Note that in practice, an agent may run its embedded HTTP server on any port, as long as the configuration file of its HTTP server is able to map all incoming requests destined for port 280 to the actual port that its embedded HTTP server is listening on (e.g., port 80). In fact, this trick allows a vendor to support the two ports (80 and 280) simultaneously, e.g. for backward compatibility.

The naming convention that we propose in WIMA for the well-known URLs is the following. The management home page of an agent is served by its embedded HTTP server at the following URL:

`<http://agent.domain:280/mgmt/>`

where `agent.domain` is the fully qualified domain name or the IP address of the agent. We keep the pathname prefix `mgmt` (although it is redundant, since port 280 is dedicated to management) so as to avoid clashes with the few existing uses of port 280.

On its management home page, the agent publishes the URLs of different pages that describe the different management architectures and information models that it supports. The format of these pages is free. Examples of pages for multiple management architectures include:

`<http://agent.domain:280/mgmt/arch/wima/>`

`<http://agent.domain:280/mgmt/arch/wbem/>`

`<http://agent.domain:280/mgmt/arch/jmx/>`

Examples of URLs for multiple information models include:

`<http://agent.domain:280/mgmt/infomodel/snmpv1/>`

`<http://agent.domain:280/mgmt/infomodel/snmpv2c/>`

`<http://agent.domain:280/mgmt/infomodel/snmpv3/>`

`<http://agent.domain:280/mgmt/infomodel/cim-spec-2.0/>`

`<http://agent.domain:280/mgmt/infomodel/cim-spec-2.2/>`

`<http://agent.domain:280/mgmt/infomodel/osi/>`

where `cim-spec` refers to the DMTF expression *CIM Specification*. In general, we are not very interested in general information about the information models supported by an agent, but rather in getting a list of all the virtual management-data repositories (SNMP MIBs, CIM schemas, etc.) supported by this agent. These are published at the following URLs:

`<http://agent.domain:280/mgmt/infomodel/smiv1/>`

`<http://agent.domain:280/mgmt/infomodel/smiv2/>`

`<http://agent.domain:280/mgmt/infomodel/cim-schema-2.0/>`

`<http://agent.domain:280/mgmt/infomodel/cim-schema-2.2/>`

`<http://agent.domain:280/mgmt/infomodel/cim-schema-2.3/>`

`<http://agent.domain:280/mgmt/infomodel/cim-schema-2.4/>`

`<http://agent.domain:280/mgmt/infomodel/cim-schema-2.5/>`

`<http://agent.domain:280/mgmt/infomodel/cim-schema-2.6/>`

where `cim-schema` refers to the DMTF expression *CIM Schema*, and versions 2.0 through to 2.6 are the six versions currently supported by the DMTF (previous versions have been rendered obsolete). Note that in the case of SNMP, the semantics of the MIBs depends on the metamodel (SMIv1 or SMIv2) rather than the SNMP management architecture (SNMPv1, SNMPv2c, or SNMPv3) for historical reasons. So, for instance, the following URL lists all the SNMP MIBs expressed in SMIv2 that are supported by the agent (or mid-level manager):

```
<http://agent.domain:280/mgmt/infomodel/smiv2/>
```

When a manager wants to discover the preferred version of SNMP or CIM supported by an agent, it requests a generic URL such as:

```
<http://agent.domain:280/mgmt/infomodel/snmp/default.html>
```
```
<http://agent.domain:280/mgmt/infomodel/smi/default.html>
```
```
<http://agent.domain:280/mgmt/infomodel/cim-spec/default.html>
```
```
<http://agent.domain:280/mgmt/infomodel/cim-schema/default.html>
```

Whenever the agent receives a request for a generic URL, its HTTP server replies with a `Redirection` status code of 301 (Moved Permanently) and a `Location` field indicating its preference, e.g.:

```
<http://agent.domain:280/mgmt/infomodel/snmpv3/>
```
```
<http://agent.domain:280/mgmt/infomodel/smiv2/>
```
```
<http://agent.domain:280/mgmt/infomodel/cim-spec-2.2/>
```
```
<http://agent.domain:280/mgmt/infomodel/cim-schema-2.6/>
```

Similarly, a manager can discover the preferred information model of an agent by requesting the following URL:

```
<http://agent.domain:280/mgmt/infomodel/default.html>
```

This is useful in transition phases, for instance in case CIM gradually takes over SNMP in the years to come. The agent then redirects the manager (with an HTTP status code of 301) to the home page of its preferred information model. If it has no preference, it returns the home page of any supported information model.

The same rationale applies to the management architecture. A manager can discover the preferred management architecture of an agent by accessing the following URL:

```
<http://agent.domain:280/mgmt/arch/default.html>
```

7.3.2.3 From the network map to the agent's management home page

Now that the manager knows the URLs of the management home pages of all the agents in its management domain, it still has to present this information to the administrator for the subscription phase to take place. We propose that direct access to the agent's management home page be available directly from the network map. This can be achieved in different ways, depending on whether the network map is implemented in the form of a plain HTML page, a sensitive map, or a Java applet.

With a plain HTML page, we simply display a textual list of agents in the management domain. Each line corresponds to an agent and contains a hyperlink to this agent's management home page. This approach is minimalist and not user friendly, but it works and can be sufficient to manage small networks.

When the network map is a sensitive map, e.g. a Graphics Interchange Format (GIF) image, the operator clicks on the icon representing the agent. The (x,y) coordinates are mapped to the corresponding agent by a CGI program running on the management server. The output of this CGI program is an HTTP response message with a `Redirection` status code of 301 (Moved Permanently) and a `Location` field containing the URL of the corresponding agent's management home page. Upon receipt of this redirection, the browser automatically contacts the agent and retrieves its management home page. The mapping table used by the CGI program can be generated automatically: From the agent's IP address, it is possible to generate the URL of its management home page.

When the network map is coded as a Java applet, we can have an even more user-friendly GUI. For instance, by clicking on the agent on the network map, an operator can pop up a menu and select the entry called "home page" to retrieve the agent's management home page. One problem however is the applet security model, which by default forbids an applet loaded from the management server to open a connection to another machine, in our case the agent. To work around this limitation, we can use signed applets. Although this solution is simple and neat, it is not always applicable because it requires the Web browser to access a configuration file specifying its access-control policies, and this clashes with our decision to enable the administrator to use a Web browser on *any* machine. There are means to share a configuration file across many machines, e.g. NFS in the Unix world; but there are cases when we need to duplicate the configuration file (e.g., when an on-call administrator troubleshoots an urgent problem from outside the enterprise). In short, a network-map GUI applet is very user-friendly, but there are cases when we need to revert to sensitive maps.

7.3.3 Subscription phase

In the third phase, the administrator downloads the agent's subscription applets into the management station (see Fig. 14) and explicitly subscribes the manager to the regular management data (e.g., SNMP MIB variables or CIM objects) and notifications (e.g., `SNMPv2-trap`'s or CIM events) that he/she is interested in. For the sake of readability, let us assume that the agent supports an SNMP information model (v1, v2, or v3), although everything we say here for SNMP applies equally to other information models. We distinguish two cases: the interactive mode, where the administrator interacts via a Web browser, and the automated mode, where everything is done automatically by programs without human intervention.

7.3.3.1 Interactive, human-oriented mode

In interactive mode, the administrator selects the management applet he/she is interested in from the agent's management home page. For the subscription phase, two entries are of interest to us: the data subscription applet and the notification subscription applet.

The *data subscription applet* allows the administrator to interactively select MIB variables and push frequencies via a user-friendly GUI. This is commonly achieved through some kind of MIB browser. The push frequency can be different for each individual MIB variable, or it can be the same for an entire MIB or even all the MIBs supported by a device. In the case of SNMP, this applet is called the *MIB data subscription applet*. We will come back to this applet in more detail in Chapter 10, when we describe our prototype.

The *notification subscription applet* allows the administrator to interactively select the notifications that he/she wants the manager to receive. In essence, it defines an event filter on the agent. If we have only a few notifications to filter, the full-blown applet can be replaced with a simple HTML form. Notifications for which the administrator showed no interest are discarded by the agent. Unlike its counterpart, the notification subscription applet does not prompt for a push frequency because notifications are inherently asynchronous.

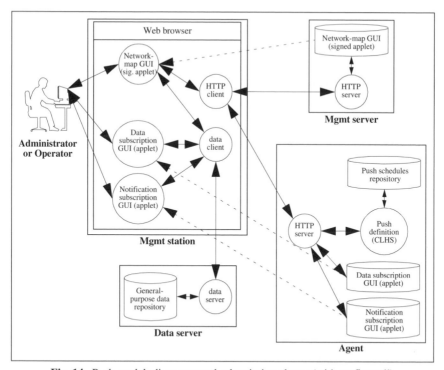

Fig. 14. Push model: discovery and subscription phases (without firewall)

The retrieval of these two subscription applets is illustrated by Fig. 14. The dotted arrows are visual aids that show that the corresponding applet is transferred from one machine to another. The plain arrows indicate that two components communicate directly with each other.

We can have one subscription applet for all information models (but this may not be practical), one per information model (e.g., SNMP or CIM), or one per virtual management-data repository (e.g., one per SNMP MIB or CIM schema). The same rationale applies to notifications. The granularity of the two subscription applets is vendor specific and not mandated by WIMA. Regardless of the granularity, the MIB variables subscribed to through the same GUI and their associated frequencies form what we call a *push schedule*. Push schedules are created by the *push definition* component. This component can be implemented as a Java servlet, a CGI binary, a CGI script, etc. To remain generic, we will call it a *Component Launched by an HTTP Server* (CLHS). This naming convention will be used throughout this book for similar components. If possible, the push schedules are stored persistently by the agent (e.g., in EPROM). Otherwise, they are kept in volatile memory and must be retrieved from the data server (via the management server) upon reboot; we will see how in Section 7.3.3.3.

For the SNMPv1, v2c, and v3 information models, the URL of the data subscription applet is one of the following:

```
<http://agent.domain:280/mgmt/subscribe/smiv1/mibs.html>
<http://agent.domain:280/mgmt/subscribe/smiv2/mibs.html>
```

In the case of CIM, the URL of the data subscription applet simply depends on the version of the CIM schemas supported by the agent. Examples of valid URLs include:

```
<http://agent.domain:280/mgmt/subscribe/cim-schema-2.3/schemas.html>
<http://agent.domain:280/mgmt/subscribe/cim-schema-2.6/schemas.html>
```

For each version of the CIM schema, it is possible to distinguish between the three sets of schemas defined by the DMTF: core, common and extension. In the case of CIM Schema 2.6, this yields:

```
<http://agent.domain:280/mgmt/subscribe/cim-schema-2.6/core.html>
<http://agent.domain:280/mgmt/subscribe/cim-schema-2.6/common.html>
<http://agent.domain:280/mgmt/subscribe/cim-schema-2.6/extension.html>
```

The URLs of the notification subscription applets look like this:

```
<http://agent.domain:280/mgmt/subscribe/snmpv1/traps.html>
<http://agent.domain:280/mgmt/subscribe/snmpv2/notifications.html>
<http://agent.domain:280/mgmt/subscribe/cim-schema-2.6/events.html>
```

Note that this time, SNMP traps and notifications depend on the version of SNMP rather than SMI, because SNMPv2 rendered SNMPv1 traps (`trap` PDUs) obsolete and replaced them with SNMPv2 notifications (`SNMPv2-trap` PDUs), which remained unchanged in SNMPv3. This inconsistency in our URL naming conventions is unfortunate, but alas reflects the history of SNMP.

In interactive mode, we only require that an agent support a well-known URL for its management home page. From there, the administrator can navigate to find the SNMP MIB or the notifications he/she is interested in, select some MIB variables or notifications, and submit the subscription to the agent. But in real networks, the number of devices and systems to manage can be large. In this case, manual configuration is not only tedious and error prone, but also totally unrealistic. As a consequence, our management architecture must not necessarily rely on interactive configuration. We want to have the option to automate this subscription phase, by cloning the push schedules of similar agents and sending them automatically from the management server to the agents.

7.3.3.2 Automated, machine-oriented mode

In automated mode, the situation is not as simple because a manager is not as smart as an administrator. Its semantic analyzer is very weak compared to the administrator's brain, so we cannot expect it to navigate from the agent's management home page to find the pages to subscribe to MIB variables or notifications. If we want to automate this process, the two interactive subscription applets must have two machine-oriented counterparts (the *subscription* CLHS) at well-known URLs. The manager can then use these subscription CLHSes to send a predefined set of push schedules and notification filters to each agent.

The URLs of the data subscription CLHSes supported by the agent look like this:

```
<http://agent.domain:280/mgmt/subscribe/auto/smiv2/mibs>
```

```
<http://agent.domain:280/mgmt/subscribe/auto/cim-schema-2.6/schemas>
```

Note the term `auto` in the pathname. Likewise, examples of URLs for the notification subscription CLHS include:

```
<http://agent.domain:280/mgmt/subscribe/auto/snmpv1/traps>
```

```
<http://agent.domain:280/mgmt/subscribe/auto/snmpv2/notifications>
```

```
<http://agent.domain:280/mgmt/subscribe/auto/cim-schema-2.6/events>
```

For automated subscriptions, the absence of an extension at the end of the pathname allows for any type of subscription CLHS: CGI script, CGI binary, Java servlet, etc. This gives us a lot of flexibility.

7.3.3.3 Data repository

If an agent is not able to store its subscription data (push schedules and notification filters) in EPROM, it loses its configuration upon reboot. In interactive mode, it would be very tedious for the administrator to re-enter all the subscription data of an agent whenever this agent reboots. Therefore, it is important to store this data in persistent storage. Similarly, in automated mode, we need a persistent data repository to retrieve the push schedules and notification filters, clone them from a similar device, and send them to the agent (for the first time or if it has lost its subscription data).

As shown by Fig. 14 and Fig. 15, we use the data repository for storing subscription data. For the sake of readability, the details of the different repositories are not shown on this figure. All repositories are virtually merged into a single *general-purpose data repository* that includes:

- the push schedules for the management data subscribed to by the manager
- the definitions of the notifications subscribed to by the manager
- the network topology used by the network-map applet to construct its GUI

In practice, these three logical data repositories may be physically stored into one or several relational databases (RDBMSes), object-oriented databases (OODBMSes), NFS servers (flat files), LDAP directories, etc.

If an agent loses its subscription data, the restoration procedure that intuitively comes to mind is the following:

- the agent asks the manager for its subscription data
- the manager retrieves the agent's push schedules and notification filters from the data server
- the manager sends the push schedules and notification filters to the agent

We will see in Chapter 8 that, for security reasons, the agent cannot inform the manager that it has just rebooted: the manager must detect it. The procedure to follow must therefore be slightly changed:

- the manager detects that the agent has just rebooted
- the manager retrieves the agent's push schedules and notification filters from the data server
- the manager sends the push schedules and notification filters to the agent

7.3.3.4 Subscription with firewall

In Section 7.3.3.1, we considered a simplified case without a firewall between the agent and the manager (see Fig. 14). The manager can then directly interact with the agent (two-tier architecture); this poses no security threat. This scenario is typically encountered in the management of small intranets, where the internal network is trusted. But in Section 7.2.4, we explained that we want to allow for the presence of a firewall between the agent and the manager. So let us now study the complete scenario with a firewall (see Fig. 15). This scenario applies equally to the interactive and automated modes, with one exception: In automated mode, there is no communication with the management station.

The firewall system commonly allows external agents to interact only with one internal machine (the management server), as opposed to many internal machines (all the potential management stations, that is, all internal PCs and workstations). So, in the firewall case, the communication between the management station and the agent must follow a three-tier architecture and be streamlined via the management server. This is achieved by the *secure relay* CLHS, which forwards unchanged all the HTTP traffic from the internal management station(s) to the external agent(s), and *vice versa*. The role of the management server is then fairly similar to that of an HTTP proxy in the World-Wide Web. The internals of the secure relay are not specified by our management architecture. This CLHS uses access-control lists stored in a data repository that can be physically separate from, or integrated with, the management server.

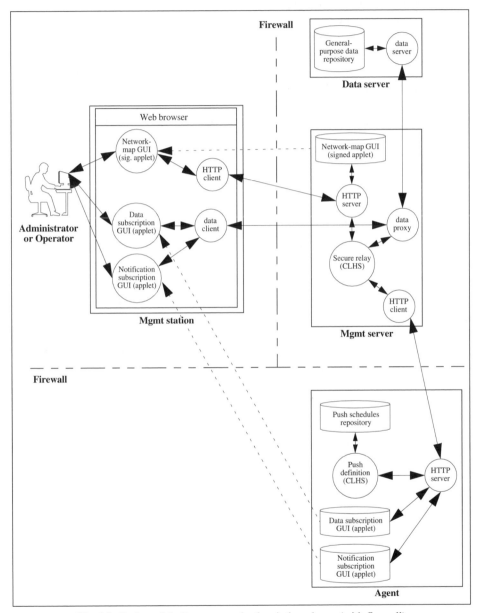

Fig. 15. Push model: discovery and subscription phases (with firewall)

One advantage of this setting is that it allows the administrator to monitor the network or take corrective actions from outside the enterprise (see Section 7.2.4). In this case, the communication goes across a firewall, which can be similar to, or different from, the firewall located between the manager and the agent. The identification and authentication (not represented here) are performed similarly by the secure relay, whether the adminis-trator works from an internal or an external machine. Obviously, direct access to the agents from external management stations must be forbidden for security reasons.

7.3.4 Distribution phase

In the last phase, the case of data collection and monitoring is only marginally different from that of notification delivery in WIMA. The organization and communication models are the same. Only the CLHSes and object-oriented components running on the agent and management server (or on the mid-level and top-level managers) differ. Let us begin with notification delivery, which is slightly simpler.

7.3.4.1 Notification delivery

Notification delivery from the agent to the management server is depicted in Fig. 16, together with event handling within the management server. Event handling will be studied in Section 7.3.4.3.

The agent runs a *health monitor* that checks the agent's own health. This component receives input from a number of *sensors* that can be implemented in hardware or software. For instance, the health monitor checks whether the agent's Ethernet interfaces all sense a carrier, or whether the ventilation of the power supply is still working. (Note that in the IP world, agents are usually not able to monitor many things, unlike the agents typically found in the telecommunications world.) When a problem occurs and is detected, the health monitor sends an alarm to the *notification generator*. Based on the event filter set during the notification subscription, the notification generator decides whether this alarm should be discarded or forwarded to the management server. In the latter case, it sends it to the *notification formatter*. Depending on the information model(s) supported by the agent and the type of notifications subscribed to by the administrator, the notification generator can choose one of many formatters: an SNMPv1 trap formatter, an SNMPv2 notification formatter, a CIM event formatter, etc. The notification formatter receives the alarm in the form of a vendor-specific data structure, and translates it into a standard SNMP notifi-cation, CIM event, and so on. The *network dispatcher* then marshals the data into a communication-protocol message and sends it to the management server. For the time being, we skip the communication path between the agent and the management server (i.e., between the HTTP client and server on Fig. 16); we will describe it in Chapter 8.

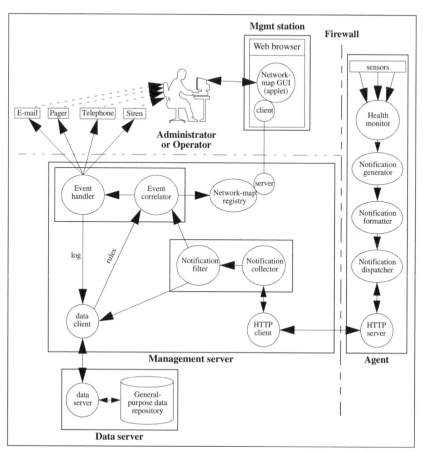

Fig. 16. Push model: distribution phase for notification delivery and event handling

When it arrives on the management server, the notification is handled by the *notification collector*, which unmarshals it. The notification collector passes this notification on to the *notification filter*, whose role is to protect the management application from misconfigured, misbehaving, or malicious agents. If the manager is bombarded with notifications by an agent, this filter silently drops them, tells the notification collector to close the connection to the agent (this connection will be defined in Chapter 8), logs a single entry in the data server, and sends a single event to the event correlator. If the administrator previously set up an event handler for that type of event, he/she can be informed immediately that something is wrong with this agent. Once the notification filter has checked an incoming notification, it sends it to the *event correlator*. As in SNMP-based management platforms, the event correlator is the focal point of monitoring in WIMA. We will come back to it in Section 7.3.4.3, once we have described another important source of events.

7.3.4.2 Data collection and monitoring

Let us now consider data collection and monitoring. As depicted in Fig. 17, the organizational model remains the same, and the building blocks look alike. The two main differences between this case and the previous one lie in the components and CLHSes running on both sides and in what triggers a management-data transfer.

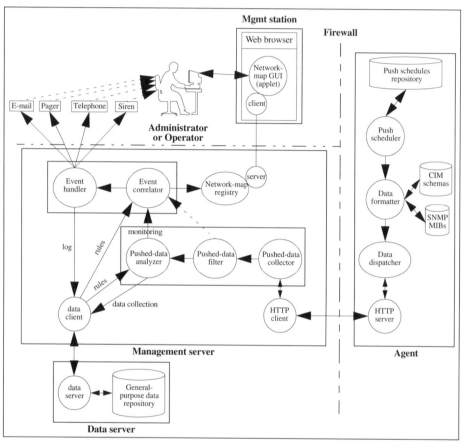

Fig. 17. Push model: distribution phase for data collection and monitoring

When the push scheduler determines that it is now time for the next push cycle, it contacts the *data formatter* and tells it what SNMP MIB variables, CIM objects, etc. to send to the manager. The data formatter retrieves the requested data from the virtual management-data repositories (SNMP MIBs, CIM schemas, etc.), formats these vendor-specific data structures into standard SMIv2 entities, CIM objects, etc. and sends them to the *data dispatcher*. The latter marshals this data and sends it to the management server. Again, we postpone the description of the communication path between the agent and the manager until Chapter 8. This time, on the management server, the data is received by the *pushed-*

data collector, which acts as the notification collector (we will see in Chapter 8 why we preserve two separate processing units, instead of merging them). The data is then unmarshaled and sent to the *pushed-data filter*, which increases the robustness of the management application (same function as the notification filter). If this filter is happy with the rate at which data is coming in from this agent, it passes on the data to an entity that has no equivalent in notification delivery: the *pushed-data analyzer*. At this level, the data forks off, depending on whether it is related to monitoring or data collection.

For data collection, incoming data is not analyzed directly. It is stored into the data repository so as to be analyzed offline, at a later stage. The pushed-data analyzer sends incoming data to the data repository via some kind of technology orthogonal to WIMA (e.g., JDBC, ODBC, or NFS). The client-server nature of this storage operation is simply denoted in Fig. 17 with the *data client* component on the management server and the *data server* component on the data server machine.

For monitoring, the data must be analyzed immediately, as it comes in. To achieve this, the pushed-data analyzer executes a set of *rules* not represented on Fig. 17. Together with the event correlator, the pushed-data analyzer constitutes the smartest part of the management application. In the IP world, the pushed-data analyzer makes up for the lack of self-management functionality in agents (unlike the agents typically found in the telecommunications world). The rules are persistently stored in the data server, and dynamically cached by the management server. They allow the pushed-data analyzer to check that everything is "normal". When the pushed-data analyzer detects a problem, it sends an event to the event correlator—for instance, when a network device no longer sends a heartbeat. The pushed-data analyzer typically interacts with the finite state machines that represent each agent in the management application, and determines whether a problem is transient or semi-permanent. Transient problems are usually ignored, whereas semi-permanent problems are dealt with by event handlers, operators, or both (see next section).

If a piece of data (be it related to monitoring or data collection) does not come in on schedule, the pushed-data analyzer generates an event and sends it to the event correlator. This requires the management server to run a scheduler component that is not depicted in Fig. 17.

7.3.4.3 Event handling

In the previous two sections, we have seen two sources of events: the agents, which send notifications when they are able to detect problems by themselves, and the pushed-data analyzer, which detects problems on behalf of the agents. The event correlator is situated at the intersection of these two flows of events, that is, between regular management and notification handling. It is the "clever" part of the management application. Most notably, it is able to find out the root cause when an avalanche of problems is reported for one or several machine(s). For instance, if a router is hung, the hosts behind that router will appear to be down, but no corrective action should be taken for the hosts: Only the router should be rebooted. Working this out is the role of the event correlator.

Among all the events that are processed by the event correlator, some are masked (e.g., those related to the hosts in the previous example) and silently discarded; others do not require any action (e.g., informative events); yet others trigger some action (e.g., the root-cause event in the previous example). So far, event handling is similar in WIMA- and SNMP-based management platforms. The difference is the way actions are invoked. We distinguish two types of actions (informative and corrective) and three types of mode (interactive, fully automated, and semi-automated).

Informative actions simply aim at informing operators or the administrator that a problem occurred. Whether something should be done in response to this problem is left for a human to decide. Conversely, corrective actions attempt to automatically solve a problem. Apart from rare exceptions, low-severity events always trigger informative actions (nothing to do immediately), whereas medium- and high-severity problems sometimes trigger corrective actions and sometimes trigger informative actions (not all problems can be solved automatically).

In interactive mode, at least one administrator or operator must register a network-map GUI with the *network-map registry* to be told about informative actions. In this case, the event correlator forces an update of all the registered GUIs when the finite state machine of an agent changes its state. Typically, the icon depicting that agent turns red, green, or yellow to reflect the new state of that agent (respectively `problem`, `OK`, or `unknown`). If the network-map GUIs display the network topology in a hierarchical manner, the icons representing the topological hierarchy of this agent will also change their color accordingly.

In fully automated mode, no network map is registered with the network-map registry. NSM is then entirely dependent on *event handlers* defined by the administrator, which are implemented as components in WIMA. The severity level of an event determines the event handler that is invoked by the event correlator. For informative actions, it also determines the emergency mode used to inform the administrator. An event handler can passively log the problem in the data repository, actively send an e-mail message to the administrator, or even take more drastic actions such as paging the administrator or starting off a siren. The way event handlers are configured by the administrator is intrinsically site specific and thus totally independent of WIMA.

In real life, management platforms are often configured to operate in semi-automated mode. This means that some problems are solved automatically by the management application (corrective actions) while others are not (the operators monitoring the network are simply notified about informative actions). For instance, if a central IP router crashes in an intranet, an icon will turn red on the network-map GUI to prompt the operators to take some action (e.g., reboot it, or replace a faulty board). But as other routers take over the failed one, all hosts with preexistent connections are temporarily hung because they have obsolete entries in their Address Resolution Protocol (ARP) cache. One way to alleviate this problem is to automatically clear the ARP cache of all the IP routers of the intranet, as soon as an IP router is deemed to have crashed. In this scenario, the management application clearly takes both informative and corrective actions at the same time.

When an event handler is invoked, it makes sense to log an entry in the data repository. But we must be careful not to run into scalability problems. For instance, when the IP networks and systems being managed are not very stable, the event correlator would have to process a continuous flow of incoming events, and might as a result continuously invoke event handlers. Administrators should therefore be careful not to flood the data repository with too much information. Most of the time, only *some* events should be logged in the data repository. It is often more useful to log event statistics rather than the actual events. The computation of event statistics may be achieved by components running on the management server, and invoked by the event handlers (which then no longer invoke directly the *data client* component). Similarly, icons should not turn red or green too often on the network-map GUI, otherwise operators would not know what to do. Such oscillations can be reduced by adding some dampening (i.e., damping effect) in the finite state machines—e.g., it might take at least a minute to go from green to yellow, and another minute to go from yellow to red.

7.3.4.4 Data repository

Compared with Section 7.3.3.3, we have added a number of repositories for the distribution phase. The general-purpose data repository now includes nine repositories:

- the push schedules for the management data subscribed to by the manager
- the definitions of the notifications subscribed to by the manager
- the network topology used by the network-map applet to construct its GUI
- the event-handler definitions
- the event-handler invocation log
- the pushed data
- a log of the pushed notifications
- a log of the events generated by the pushed-data analyzer
- statistical summaries of events

As we mentioned in the subscription phase, all these logically different data repositories may physically reside in one or more databases, NFS servers, LDAP directories, etc.

7.3.5 Distribution

In NSM, scalability issues are typically addressed by distributing management over several machines. In Chapter 4, we identified three ways of delegating tasks in distributed NSM: by domain, by microtask, and by macrotask. Delegation by microtask is useful in manager-agent delegation, when the "delegatee" is only moderately smart (e.g., an SNMP agent); but it is not very interesting for manager-manager delegation, as managers are supposedly smart and can do much more than mere microtasks. In WIMA-OM-push, we are therefore only interested in delegation by domain and delegation by macrotask. Let us describe these two approaches and how to combine them.

Management server viewed as a distributed system: delegation by macrotask

In the first scenario, the management server is viewed as a distributed system. The components described in Fig. 16 and Fig. 17 are now grouped into management *subsystems* and spread over different machines. We keep a centralized management paradigm, as we keep a single management domain for all the agents, but the management application is now distributed over several machines, each fulfilling a particular management task. In the case depicted in Fig. 18, mandatory management tasks are split into two subsystems: the event subsystem and the pushed-data subsystem. This way of distributing management tasks makes even more sense if we add the optional tasks sometimes found in management platforms (see Section 3.1); e.g., in Fig. 18, we show the billing subsystem; we could also add an accounting subsystem, a security subsystem, etc.

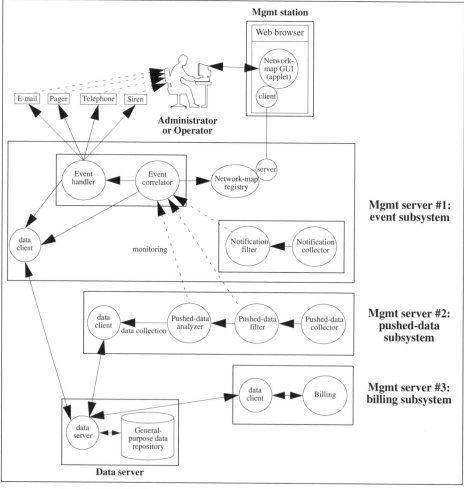

Fig. 18. Distribution: management server viewed as a distributed system

By balancing the load of the management server between several machines, we remain scalable up to a certain degree. But as the load caused by the management-application processing gradually increases, there comes a time when a single management task can no longer be executed on a single machine for all managed networks and systems (e.g., the rule-based event correlator of the event subsystem saturates and cannot keep up with all the events to process and the rules to execute). At this stage, we need to go from one manager running on several machines (centralized management paradigm) to several managers running concurrently and in charge of separate management domains (weakly distributed hierarchical management paradigm).

Distributed hierarchical management: delegation by domain

In the second scenario, we split one large management domain into several smaller management domains and assign one management server per domain. This solution presents several advantages. First, it enables administrators to decrease the amount of management data processed by each machine. This solution scales considerably better than the previous, because management domains can be further split as many times as necessary. Second, it is very well suited to geographically dispersed enterprises. By placing one management server per geographical location, the administrator saves a lot of bandwidth on WAN links, hence a lot of money. Also, for security reasons, it may be impossible for an agent to send data directly to a management server over a WAN link: The firewall protecting the management-server site may demand that this data be streamlined via a remote management server. Third, delegation by domain is an easy way to implement distributed hierarchical management (see our architectural decision in Section 7.1.4.4).

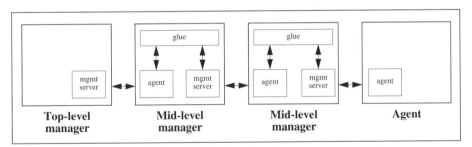

Fig. 19. Mid-level manager = management server + agent + glue

In the case illustrated by Fig. 20, we have one top-level manager, two management domains, and two mid-level managers. To keep this figure readable, we depicted only two agents, one in each management domain; in real life, we would have many more. A top-level manager looks very much like a management server in the manager-agent scenario studied in the previous sections. But a mid-level manager is somewhat more complex, as depicted by Fig. 19, because it glues together a management server (in charge of the agents located in its management domain) and an agent (which sends the data subscribed to by the top-level manager, as well as notifications).

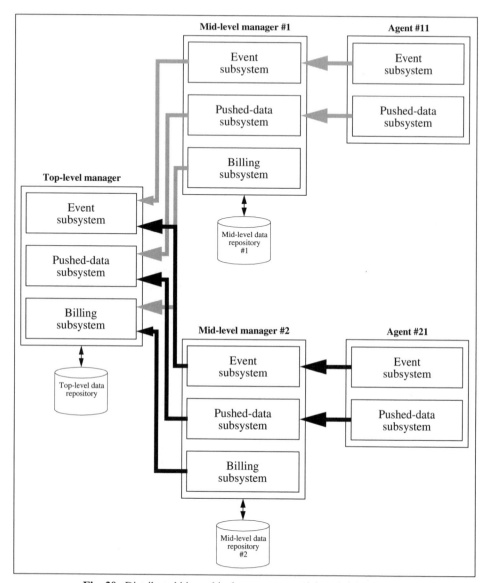

Fig. 20. Distributed hierarchical management: delegation by domain

Fig. 20 shows that the event subsystem of a mid-level manager glues together the event subsystem of an agent and the event subsystem of a management server. Similarly, the pushed-data subsystem of a mid-level manager aggregates the pushed-data subsystem of an agent and that of a management server. Within a mid-level manager, some glue components allow the data received by the management server to be processed and some results of this processing to be sent to the top-level manager. Inversely, other glue components allow high-level policies received from the top-level manager to be translated by a mid-level manager into low-level network and systems configuration data for the agents. The specification of these glue components is outside the scope of this book. It is complex and requires a well thought-out model to link policy-based management and NSM in both directions.

As we mentioned earlier, the organizational and communication models are identical between a top-level manager and a mid-level manager, between two layers of mid-level managers, or between a mid-level manager and an agent (see Fig. 19).

Distributed hierarchical management: delegation by domain and by macrotask

The third scenario is a compound version of the previous two, whereby we integrate delegation by domain and delegation by macrotask. This scenario can be broken down into three variants.

In the first variant, we have strict delegation by domain and partial delegation by macrotask. For each management domain, the different subsystems depicted in Fig. 20 actually run on several machines (possibly one machine per subsystem). A typical example is when offline processing is very resource demanding over extended periods of time. As administrators, we are interested in automating the generation of usage-statistics reports or per-department network-usage bills; but we do not want to slow down significantly the machine where the event correlator is running if offline processing is demanding in terms of CPU, memory, disk, and network bandwidth resources. By running the offline-processing subsystem on one machine and the event subsystem on another, we temporarily (or permanently) solve this problem, and we postpone (or avoid) the split of a management domain and the installation of a new manager, which saves work and money.

The second variant is the mirror image of the previous: We have partial delegation by domain and strict delegation by macrotask. Within a management domain, all subsystems run on different machines. But some subsystems are delegated (e.g., the pushed-data subsystem) while others are not. In other words, only some management tasks are delegated by domain. For instance, billing can be entirely managed by the top-level manager, which directly accesses the data repositories of all the mid-level managers. Another example is event correlation. Distributed event correlation is complex to model and understand. To avoid it, one can simply filter events at each mid-level manager, and correlate the remaining events at the top-level manager.

In the third variant, we have partial delegation by domain and partial delegation by macrotask. This is more complex to achieve and debug than the previous variants. But it can be useful under certain circumstances, e.g. to cope with constraints imposed by legacy management applications. Although allowed in WIMA, this variant is not expected to be used in many cases.

We will come back to distribution in Chapter 9, when we explain how the use of XML can nicely unify and simplify the communication between managers.

7.3.6 Migration path: four-tier architecture

An important deployment issue is to define how to deal with legacy systems. How can we manage an agent that does not embed an HTTP server, or does not support the components described in Fig. 17 (push scheduler, data formatter, and data dispatcher)? In WIMA, we adopted a very simple solution inspired by the way SNMP agents were gradually deployed in the early 1990s: We add a management gateway between the management server and the agent. In other words, we go from a three-tier architecture to a four-tier architecture (see Fig. 21). The management gateway supports both push and pull. On the left side, it allows the management server to subscribe to management data, and it pushes regular data and notifications to the management server as if it were a full-blown WIMA agent. On the right side, it acts as a standard SNMP (or CIM) manager and polls the SNMP (or CIM) agent.

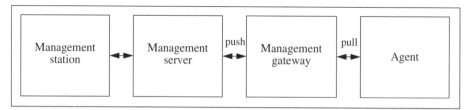

Fig. 21. Migration path: four-tier architecture

This simple migration scheme allows the agent vendor to integrate the management gateway inside the agent at any point in time (as we saw with SNMP in the early 1990s): the migration is then completed.

Note that having a single management gateway for several agents is feasible, but not very practical. We need to run multiple schedulers in parallel on the same machine, which is prone to interferences between the different emulated agents. But it is feasible and allowed by WIMA.

After having presented in detail the push model that underlies regular management and notification delivery in WIMA, let us now turn to the pull model.

7.4 *Ad Hoc* Management: The Pull Model

In this section, we present the details of our pull-based architecture, which is used for *ad hoc* management. To begin with, we describe manager-agent interactions in two steps. In Section 7.4.1, we describe the simple case when we have no firewall and can access the agent directly from the management station (two-tier architecture); in Section 7.4.2, we explain how to deal with a firewall (three-tier architecture). Then, in Section 7.4.3, we describe manager-manager interactions and show how to distribute management. Finally, in Section 7.4.4, we present a migration path to deal with legacy systems.

7.4.1 Two-tier architecture (no firewall)

Ad hoc management is typically used in interactive mode for troubleshooting or short-term monitoring (see Section 2.11). The management data retrieved from the agent is not stored or correlated on the manager side: it is immediately displayed (e.g., graphically as a time series, or textually as a text field) and discarded[1]. In WIMA, *ad hoc* management relies on the pull model for the reasons exposed in Section 7.1.4.3. Before we detail our general-purpose architecture that allows for firewalls between the agent and the management station, let us first study the simpler case when we have no firewall. Our three-tier architecture then becomes a two-tier architecture.

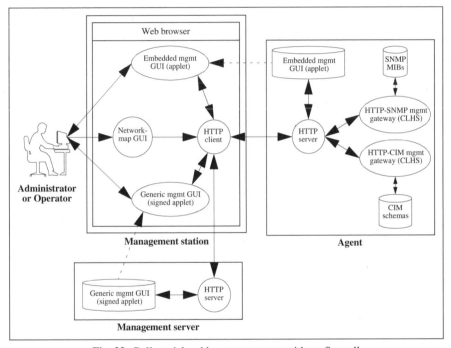

Fig. 22. Pull model: *ad hoc* management without firewall

The direct interactions between the management station and the agent are depicted in Fig. 22. Similarly to the publication and subscription phases in the case of push, the starting point in the case of pull is the network-map GUI, a signed Java applet stored on the management server. From this GUI, we retrieve the agent's management home page by requesting the following URL (see Section 7.3.3.2):

```
<http://agent.domain:280/mgmt/>
```

---

1. An entire time series may occasionally be saved in the general-purpose data repository, as a snapshot. Still, the main purpose of *ad hoc* management data is not to be stored and analyzed afterward, but rather to be analyzed immediately by a human.

From this home page, the administrator selects the URL of the embedded management GUI he/she is interested in (one agent may publish several embedded management GUIs on its home page). The management GUI, which is coded as a Java applet, is then loaded into the administrator's Web browser. Via an SNMP MIB browser or some kind of graphical tool, the administrator selects the SNMP MIB variables, CIM objects, etc. that he/she is interested in receiving. It is possible to tell the applet to retrieve the same entity every N seconds and to abort the retrieval at any time. The details of the communication protocol will be described in Chapter 8.

When a MIB variable is requested by the applet, the request is made to the HTTP server run by the agent. This HTTP server then launches a CLHS (Component Launched by an HTTP Server) that acts as a management gateway between HTTP and the virtual management-data repositories supported by the agent. In Fig. 22, we represented an HTTP-SNMP management gateway accessing SNMP MIBs and an HTTP-CIM management gateway accessing CIM schemas, but these examples are not limiting. Depending on the degree of optimization of the code run by the agent, the HTTP-SNMP management gateway can either directly access the in-memory data structures of the SNMP MIB (e.g., via shared memory) or do an explicit SNMP get. The same is true with other information models. This offers a useful migration path to equipment vendors.

Note that the agent need not necessarily embed all the management GUIs that may be used by the administrator. It is also possible to retrieve a generic management GUI applet from the management server (this applet must be signed, for the security reasons given in Section 7.3.2.3 in the case of the network-map GUI). Unlike embedded management GUIs, which are specific to a given agent, generic management GUIs are shared by many agents, possibly all of them. The main problem with generic management GUIs lies in the details of the communication protocol. In Chapter 8, we will propose conventions to exchange data between a management GUI (be it embedded or generic) and an agent. But the very nature of an embedded management GUI means that its vendor could adopt a proprietary communication protocol instead of ours to request an SNMP MIB variable, CIM object, etc. since the vendor codes both the embedded management applet *and* the components that underlie the management gateways running on the agent. If this is the case, the HTTP requests sent by a generic management GUI following our recommendations in Chapter 8 might not be understood by the proprietary management gateways embedded in the agent. There is a trade-off to be made: Either the agent has the capacity to embed all the necessary management GUIs, in which case the vendor could be inclined to use a proprietary communication protocol; or the agent is very resource constrained and the vendor should implement management gateways that support an open communication protocol.

Now that we have described a simple two-tier, pull-based architecture that is only possible when we have no firewall between the agent and the management server, and is therefore not recommended in WIMA, let us present our complete, general-purpose, three-tier architecture that deals with (but does not require) firewalls for *ad hoc* management.

7.4.2 Three-tier architecture (with firewall)

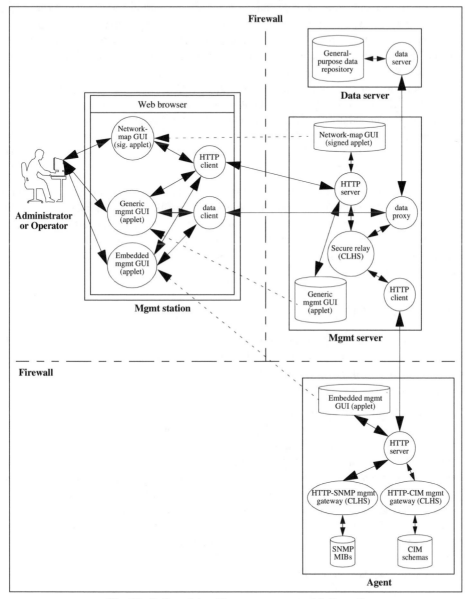

Fig. 23. Pull model: *ad hoc* management with firewall

As we explained in Section 7.2.2 (three-tier architecture) and Section 7.2.4 (firewalls), the management station should always access the agent via the management server. One of the reasons is that it facilitates access control and authentication. In Fig. 23, we added a third tier between the management station and the agent: the management server. This new tier basically proxies all requests back and forth between the management station and the agent (e.g., for *ad hoc* monitoring), or between the management station and the data server (e.g., to save a time series for an SNMP MIB variable). This operation is performed by a component called the *secure relay*. Upon start-up, this secure relay retrieves the access-control lists and policies from the general-purpose data repository (usually, this sensitive data is not stored in the same database as the rest of the management data) and caches them locally. Once an administrator or operator has identified and authenticated himself/herself through a mechanism orthogonal to WIMA, this secure relay controls the access for that person on the agent and decides whether access to the agent should be granted to that person or to one of his/her requests. The access-control granularity, and more generally the security policy, is not specified by WIMA. It can be done on a per-agent basis, per-MIB basis, per-managed-object basis, etc.

Note that the component that implements this secure relay can be sub-divided into several components, and one of them can translate the communication protocol understood by the management gateways running in the agent into another protocol. This is particularly useful in the case of generic management gateways (see the problem exposed in the previous section). We will come back to this in Chapter 9, when we address the issue of translating between two information models.

7.4.3 Distribution

In general, the distribution of management is relevant only if management is automated. It allows for the reduction of the number of events processed per management server and mainly addresses scalability issues. *Ad hoc* management, on the other hand, is always interactive, so it usually does not have to be distributed.

There is a noticeable exception to this: geographically dispersed enterprises protected by firewalls. For security reasons, the firewall of the headquarters (or the firewall of a branch office) may require that all the data coming in from a remote site (respectively coming out of this site) be streamlined via a single machine. In this case, an administrator located at the headquarters can temporarily monitor the error rate of a remote router at the branch office by going from his/her management station to the agent through the top-level manager (located at the headquarters) and a mid-level manager (located at the branch office). Both of these managers can perform some identification, authentication, and access control. In this case, even mere *ad hoc* management requires a full-blown distributed solution. In the case of pull, as in the case of push, we use distributed hierarchical management in WIMA for the reasons exposed in Section 7.1.4.4.

7.4.4 Migration path

The migration path is trivial in the case of pull. The embedded HTTP server, the embedded *management gateway* components, and the embedded management GUIs described in Section 7.4.1 are initially externalized to a machine that acts as a standard SNMP (or CIM) manager toward the agent. Then, all of these entities can be integrated, agent by agent, as vendors add support for them. As in the case of push, we then gradually go from a four-tier architecture to a three-tier architecture (see Fig. 21), agent by agent, as the migration progresses.

Note that in the case of pull, a single external management gateway can be used for several agents. We saw this in the early days of SNMP deployment, when management gateways supported SNMP on one side and proprietary management architecture and protocol on the other side. This is simple to do with SNMP because a single agent can support several MIBs, so one management gateway can support all the MIBs of all the agents. Similarly, in WIMA, one agent can manage multiple virtual management-data repositories (SNMP MIBs, CIM schemas, etc.), so it is fairly simple to group them logically and to make them all accessible from a single external management gateway.

7.5 Summary

In this chapter, we have presented one of the main contributions of this book: WIMA, our Web-based Integrated Management Architecture. First, we described our main architectural decisions. We explained why we focused on the definition of new organizational and communication models; we justified our choice not to define yet another information model; we highlighted the advantages of dissociating the communication and information models; and we proved that the push model is more appropriate than the pull model to transfer regular management data. Second, we detailed our main design decisions. We advocated the use of Web technologies, a three-tier architecture, and components; we took firewalls into account from the very beginning; we made the data repository independent of the management platform, and we made it easy to transfer management data in bulk; then, we addressed deployment and explained how to deal with legacy systems. Third, we presented in detail our push model for regular management and notification delivery, and delineated event handling. Fourth, we described our pull model for *ad hoc* management. In both cases (push and pull), we showed how to distribute management across a hierarchy of managers and proposed a migration path from SNMP- to WIMA-based management.

Chapter 8

A NEW COMMUNICATION MODEL: WIMA-CM

In Chapter 7, we gave a broad view of how management data should be exchanged between a manager and an agent, or between two managers, using Web and push technologies. But what technology do the agent and the manager use to communicate? What protocol do they use to exchange management data? How should this data be formatted, represented, and encoded? What constraints must be satisfied when we have a firewall between the manager and the agent? In this chapter, we answer all these questions and define a new communication model called WIMA-CM (Web-based Integrated Management Architecture - Communication Model). This model consists of two parts. The communication model for push-based regular management is called *WIMA-CM-push*; its pull-based counterpart for *ad hoc* management is called *WIMA-CM-pull*. Most of our work went into defining WIMA-CM-push, which is another core contribution of this book.

This chapter is organized as follows. In Section 8.1, we express in simple terms the two communication problems that we came across in Chapter 7. In Section 8.2, we describe our main design decisions to solve these problems. In Section 8.3, we highlight the drawbacks of using the sockets API as the manager-agent communication API. In Section 8.4, we justify our choice for HTTP-based communication and describe WIMA-CM-push. In Section 8.5, we analyze the important issues of timeouts and reconnections. In Section 8.6, we present WIMA-CM-pull. Finally, we summarize this chapter in Section 8.7.

8.1 Two Communication Problems

In Chapter 7, we described a push-based management architecture for transferring regular management data and notifications (see Fig. 16 p. 159 and Fig. 17 p. 160), and a pull-based

175

management architecture for transferring *ad hoc* management data (see Fig. 23 p. 171). In this section, we extract two simple communication problems from these three complex figures: one for push, one for pull. The goal here is to identify the two ends of the communication pipe between the manager and the agent. These two simple models will be used throughout this chapter, when we describe the exact nature of the communication pipe and how to format the management data transferred across it.

8.1.1 Simplified terminology

To make figures easier to read and explanations less verbose, the *management server* will be called the *manager* in this chapter. This is an example of the terminological abuse mentioned in Section 2.3, whereby we confuse the management application with the machine itself. Moreover, each time we refer to manager-agent communication in a centralized scenario, we also implicitly refer to manager-manager communication in the context of distributed hierarchical management. In other words, whenever we use the word *agent*, we could also refer to another manager, one level down the hierarchical tree. The reason for this is that we use exactly the same communication model for manager-agent and manager-manager communication. We will come back to distributed hierarchical management in more detail in Chapter 9.

8.1.2 Communication problem for pushed data

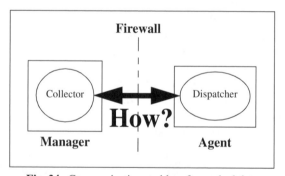

Fig. 24. Communication problem for pushed data

For the push model, whether we deal with monitoring, data collection, or notification delivery, we have a dispatcher on the agent and a collector on the manager, as depicted in Fig. 24. The dispatcher can be a pushed-data dispatcher, a notification dispatcher, or a combination of the two. Similarly, the collector can be a pushed-data collector, a notification collector, or both. As far as the communication between the manager and the agent is concerned, Fig. 16 and Fig. 17 can therefore be abstracted into a single communication problem shown in Fig. 24.

The dispatcher and the collector can be implemented as CLHSes (CGI programs, Java servlets, etc.) invoked via HTTP servers, or standalone programs (Java applications, C++

binaries, C binaries, etc.). They do not even have to be implemented with the same technology. In fact, the exact nature of the two ends of the communication path is transparent to the communication model itself.

8.1.3 Communication problem for pulled data

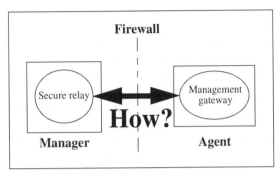

Fig. 25. Communication problem for pulled data

For the pull model, we used HTTP to communicate between the manager and the agent in Fig. 23, but we could have used a domain-specific transfer protocol over TCP or UDP as well. As a result, the HTTP-SNMP gateway depicted in Fig. 23 is replaced in Fig. 25 with a more generic management gateway, which may be internal or external to the agent. As in the previous case, the management gateway and the secure relay may be implemented as any kind of CLHS or standalone program. And once again, the technology used at the two ends of the communication path is transparent to the communication model itself.

8.2 Main Design Decisions

In this section, we present the main design decisions behind our new communication model: (i) the dissociation of the communication and information models; (ii) the use of a reliable transport protocol; (iii) the use of persistent TCP connections; (iv) the creation of the connections by the manager; and (v) the reversed client and server roles. When applicable, we point out the main differences between WIMA-CM and the communication model of the SNMP management architecture.

8.2.1 Dissociation of the communication and information models

As we saw in Section 7.1.3, one of our main architectural decisions was to dissociate completely the information and communication models in WIMA. The main characteristic of WIMA-CM, and in our view its main strength, is that it does not require or rely on the use of any specific information model (SNMP MIBs, CIM schemas, etc.). Instead, each bundle of management data is self-describing. The technology that we propose to use to implement this dissociation is MIME (Multipurpose Internet Mail Extensions). We will describe it in detail in Section 8.4.3, after we have justified a number of other design decisions.

8.2.2 Reliable transport protocol: TCP

In Section 3.3.1.8, we explained the problems induced by SNMP's use of an unreliable transport protocol. The simplest solution to these problems is to go from UDP to TCP to transport management data. This solution presents many advantages. First, it significantly reduces management-data losses. Urgent notifications sent by an agent are no longer lost for silly reasons such as buffer overflows in IP routers. We still have no guarantee of delivery, but at least the TCP part of the kernel tries hard (for 9 minutes in Berkeley-derived kernels) to send the data across. Second, it relieves the management application from managing all the timers and performing all the retries currently necessary to recover from network losses in the case of SNMP polling. Third, it reduces network latency. Fourth, it dramatically improves interoperability. Fifth, it makes it easier to go across firewalls. The first three advantages were already covered in Chapter 3; let us expand on the other two.

8.2.2.1 Interoperability

Application-level acknowledgments (ACKs) are satisfactory in the case of SNMP polling because they are implicit and remain internal to the manager. If the agent does not answer to an SNMP get, the manager issues the same get again once a timer has expired. If the agent answers, it implicitly tells the manager that it has received its request, so the manager gets an implicit ACK from the agent.

The situation is very different in the case of push. The transfers of regular data are triggered by the agent, this time, not by the manager. If we use UDP to transport regular data, we need to define an explicit application-level ACKs policy for the manager to acknowledge receipt of the data. This requires that all agents and managers worldwide agree on the same ACKs policy and implement it in an interoperable way. But would Microsoft, Cisco, IBM, Sun Microsystems, etc. ever agree whether ACKs could be piggy-backed or not, whether management data could be ACK'ed in bulk (i.e., with a single message) or not, whether the format of an ACK could possibly or should necessarily include a Microsoft-specific OLE (Object Linking and Embedding) reference, etc.[1]? How can an ACKs policy be independent of the information model in an interoperable way? By using TCP instead of UDP, we free ourselves from defining such a scheme and we no longer have to convince all vendors to adopt the same ACKs policy. This in itself is a good reason to prefer TCP over UDP for push technologies.

---

1. Note that SNMP-based management avoids this problem by not acknowledging notifications, which leads to some problems as we saw in Section 3.3.1.8.

8.2.2.2 Firewalls

Firewalls are easier to set up for TCP-based applications than for UDP-based applications [58, 59]. When a TCP client communicates with a TCP server, it is easy to learn who created the connection and who initiated a request; with TCP, it is difficult for an external machine to deceive an internal machine by sending a bogus response to a non-existent request[1]. With UDP, the opposite is true: It is comparatively more difficult to learn who initiated a communication, but it is simplistic to send a response without having received a request first. The reason for this is that TCP is stateful whereas UDP is not. With TCP-based applications, TCP sequence numbers allow a firewall to easily match requests/responses coming from an external untrusted machine with the corresponding responses/requests issued by the trusted internal machine. Even better, by blocking incoming TCP segments with the SYN[2] bit set and the ACK bit clear, we prevent external machines from creating TCP connections to internal machines (we will come back to this in Section 8.2.4). Conversely, with UDP, we have no SYN bit and no sequence numbers. For security, UDP-based applications require smart and expensive *application-level gateways* (also called *UDP relays*) to provide for this functionality; such gateways render the two-way communication stateful and make sure that an external machine does not break the normal data flow of a UDP-based application.

So, TCP proves superior to UDP in two respects. First, TCP-based application-level gateways are easier to program than their UDP-based counterparts, because of the availability of sequence numbers in the transport protocol. Second, TCP-based applications can rely on simple *packet-filtering gateways* instead of full-blown, application-level gateways, whereas UDP-based applications cannot; for UDP, application-level gateways are mandatory because packet-filtering gateways are too risky and renowned for being inadequate—the main problem is the impossibility to prevent external machines from sending bogus responses [59]. This second argument is one of the main reasons we selected TCP: Packet-filtering gateways are considerably less expensive and less difficult to configure than application-level gateways. They can be integrated in IP routers, for instance. Although they are less secure (it is easy to make mistakes when defining the access-control lists of a packet-filtering gateway [59]), many enterprises are happy to use them. For small and midsize enterprises, this is a very important argument. By selecting TCP, we do not require application-level gateways in our WIMA architecture whenever we go across a firewall: Enterprises have the choice between inexpensive packet-filtering gateways and expensive application-level gateways. This is a significant improvement over SNMP-based management.

Another argument in favor of using TCP across a firewall is the use of HTTP at the application level. The reason is that most firewalls worldwide are already configured to let

---

1. It is not impossible, however: TCP sequence-number attacks make it possible to "steal" existing TCP connections. But they are only possible with poorly configured firewalls and with old TCP implementations that generate easy-to-predict sequence numbers.
2. SYN stands for *synchronize*. The SYN bit is one of the CODE BITS in the TCP header. It is characteristic of the first segment of a three-way handshake when a TCP connection is established.

HTTP traffic go through, because of the Web. The external Web server of the enterprise is usually not (and should not be, for security reasons such as denial-of-service attacks) the same machine as the manager depicted in Fig. 29. But because chances are that the firewall is already set up to let HTTP traffic go through in both directions, the update of the configuration file of the firewall is trivial: One only has to copy the configuration of the Web server and change the IP address of the machine allowed to go across the firewall. In many companies, especially small and midsize ones, this does not require paying an expensive external consultant. We received very good feedback from the industry about this.

8.2.2.3 Lightweight transport protocol

TCP is not an ideal transport protocol, however. It certainly relieves the application from performing retransmissions, but it also brings in a host of well-known problems [85]:

- TCP automatically comes with flow control, which may not be necessary. Flow control increases network overhead by dynamically adjusting the window size.
- TCP's slow-start mechanism is inefficient over fast network links, especially for LANs operating at 100 Mbit/s and above.
- TCP can be slow to recover from failures, particularly in the case of heavy losses.
- TCP's urgent mode is messy and "leads to much confusion" [253, pp. 292–296]. Apart from that, TCP offers no way to differentiate between high- and low-priority segments within a single connection.
- TCP makes it impossible to time out a segment without timing out the entire connection.

If other lightweight, reliable transport protocols were widely available, they could be viable alternatives to TCP in NSM. Actually, this is not specific to NSM. A BOF (Birds Of a Feather) session chaired by Bradner and Paxson at the 43rd IETF Meeting [85] showed that many people working in different areas would be interested in an intermediary transport protocol halfway between UDP and TCP. This topic was also discussed within the IRTF Network Management Research Group, when we investigated whether administrators should be given the choice to transport SNMP over UDP or TCP. In 2000, the IETF Signaling Transport Working Group specified the Stream Control Transmission Protocol (SCTP) [255]. Initially devised as a means to transport telephone signaling across IP networks, SCTP has become a general-purpose transport protocol. Whether SCTP will be accepted by the market remains to be seen.

There are two well-known problems with defining new transport protocols. First, different applications have different requirements and want to change different things in TCP; this makes it difficult to find, within the IETF, a consensus around a single proposal. But most people agree that the market will be very reluctant to adopt several new transport protocols and will demand a single proposal. Hence, we face a deadlock. Second, there are so many TCP/IP stacks already deployed today that it would take many years and would cost a fortune to upgrade all of them to support the newly specified transport protocol. But no one wants to use a new transport protocol that is not widely deployed, so we have a chicken-

and-egg situation. One example is particularly symptomatic: Even the designers of RTP (Real-time Transport Protocol) decided to layer it on top of existing transport protocols, although everyone agreed that a new transport protocol was needed for delivering real-time data.

In conclusion, if we remain pragmatic, we must acknowledge that today, and in the foreseeable future, we have the choice between only two transport protocols: UDP and TCP. We explained why UDP is inadequate, so we have no other reasonable option than to adopt TCP.

8.2.3 Persistent TCP connections

Once we have selected TCP as the transport protocol, the next natural step is to use persistent TCP connections to exchange management data between the manager and the agents. The reasons are twofold. First, manager-agent associations are more or less permanent, or at least very long-lived: A given agent is managed by a given manager for extended periods of time. Second, persistency avoids the overhead of repeatedly setting up and tearing down TCP connections [242]; this problem is well-known and is the major reason why HTTP/1.1 is gradually superseding HTTP/1.0. So, why do we not already use persistent TCP connections in SNMP-based management today?

8.2.3.1 The Myth of the Collapsing Manager

In the SNMP community, there is a well-established myth that persistent TCP connections between the manager and the agents are not an option because of the memory overhead incurred by the manager when the number of agents grows large. After the *Myth of the Collapsing Backbone* and the *Myth of the Dumb Agent*, both destroyed by Wellens and Auerbach in 1996 [286], another SNMP myth is about to collapse: the *Myth of the Collapsing Manager*, or "Why persistent TCP connections are evil for transferring management data".

As a rule of thumb in production environments, it is often considered that one single manager should not directly manage more than a few hundred not-too-busy agents. Beyond 200–300 agents, we hit well-known problems:

- The LAN segment to which the manager is connected becomes saturated (bottleneck effect).
- A single point of failure for so many machines and network devices becomes unreasonably risky. If one manager dies, too many agents are left on their own.
- The CPU and memory footprints of the management application become too large on the manager side: The event correlator cannot cope with the flow of incoming events, the pushed-data analyzer cannot cope with the number of rules to execute per push cycle, etc.

If the agents are particularly busy (e.g., if they often push data to the manager or if they often report problems), the administrator usually partitions the management domain and installs a new manager in the newly created domain. In such a setting, the maximum number of agents per manager falls well below the range given above, e.g. down to 50 (see Chapter 9 for distribution aspects).

We claim that the memory overhead of several hundred persistent TCP connections is perfectly acceptable on a modern management station. The reason why the *Myth of the Collapsing Manager* was born is that management stations had little memory when SNMPv1 was devised, typically 8–16 Mbytes. Management stations were typically workstations in those days, now they are PCs. Today, a basic desktop has 128 Mbytes of memory, and management stations typically have 512 Mbytes (sometimes more to manage large networks). This is more than enough to cope with hundreds of persistent TCP connections.

The Web gives us a solid argument to substantiate our claim. If we consider the constraints routinely satisfied by the Web servers of famous corporate organizations, it becomes obvious that our solution puts very reasonable requirements on managers. For instance, Kegel [139] reports that some sites routinely cope with thousands of concurrent HTTP or File Transfer Protocol (FTP) connections to a single host (not to a cluster), which is more demanding than our management scenario by an order of magnitude. Both Kegel and the *linux-kernel* mailing list [154] mention work under way to support more than 10,000 concurrent TCP connections, which makes our requirements comparatively minute (lower by two orders of magnitude).

Beyond these mere comparisons, can we put real figures on the memory overhead caused by hundreds of persistent TCP connections on the manager? Let us assume that we have have at most 400 agents managed by a single manager.

8.2.3.2 Assessing the memory overhead of persistent TCP connections is hard

Assessing the memory space required per open socket is a difficult task. First, it depends on the options that were selected when the kernel was built. In Linux, for instance, some C data-structure definitions contain optional fields declared between "#ifdef" and "#endif" block separators (e.g., the support for multiprocessor machines is optional). So, depending on the installation preferences specified by the administrator, the memory overhead caused by the creation of a socket may vary. Second, it depends on kernel caches, and the allocation scheme for new cache entries is operating-system specific. Third, the allocation of some data structures depends on the network topology because the manager caches the IP and Medium Access Control (MAC) addresses of its *neighbors* (see Fig. 26). By definition, a neighbor is adjacent to the manager; it is reached in one hop by a packet going from the manager to the agent (*destination host*). For instance, router1 is the manager's neighbor for the route to agent1 in Fig. 26. Upon the creation of a socket, some data structures are allocated on a per-neighbor basis, others on a per-destination-host basis, yet others on a per-socket basis. Clearly, the number of neighbors depends on the network topology, which is site specific and cannot be modeled *a priori*. Consequently, the memory footprint of the data structures allocated per neighbor cannot be calculated theoretically: We can only compute an upper bound for it.

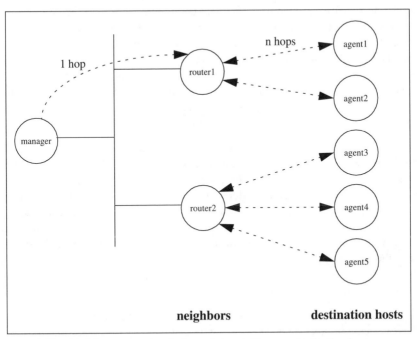

Fig. 26. Memory overhead of a socket: neighbors vs. destination hosts

Assessing the memory overhead of hundreds of active, concurrent TCP connections is even more difficult because of the sheer number of agents and the dependency on the network topology. First, experimentation is ruled out: For all practical purposes, it is not feasible to gather hundreds of PCs in a test network, to use them to send real data to a manager, and to perform actual measurements on the manager. Second, it is not clear that results obtained from simulations would reflect reality, as we will now explain.

8.2.3.3 Simulations: what about side-effects?

We just mentioned that data structures can be allocated per socket, per destination host, or per neighbor. As a result, the manager's memory overhead cannot be evaluated by simply creating hundreds of connections between two machines, one being the manager and the other simulating all the agents: We really have to simulate hundreds of *different* agents. To do so, we have two options.

In the first scenario, we preserve real manager-agent communication over a real network. For instance, we can simulate 100 agents on a single PC, run different copies of the simulator on several PCs sitting behind different neighbors, and have these PCs communicate with the manager over an Ethernet segment. On each PC, we can either impersonate 100 machines from a single kernel (e.g., by using virtual interfaces) or try to run 100 different kernels in user mode (quite a challenge but *a priori* not impossible).

In the second scenario, instead of having real communications over the network, we can instead have a single machine simulate all the agents (400 at most), the manager, and all intermediate network equipment, interconnected according to a certain network topology. We can then simulate 400+ kernels running in user mode as separate processes, separate threads, or a single process. Inter-machine communication is then replaced respectively with interprocess, interthread, or intraprocess communication. We also have to simulate by program the buffering and queuing mechanisms normally implemented by the kernels, as well as the network interfaces and the network links.

The problem with these scenarios is that they are exposed to side-effects that are difficult to assess. In the first scenario, would the simulator be able to deliver data via its single network interface in the same way that real-life agents would? No, because outgoing TCP segments supposedly generated by different machines would be queued in a single queue, outgoing IP packets supposedly coming from different machines would be queued in a single queue, data-link frames supposedly leaving through different network interfaces on different machines would be queued in a single outgoing queue and delivered to the network through a single network interface, etc. How far apart would simulation-based results be from real-life measurements? What would be the effects of this serialization? We do not believe that it is possible to know in advance.

In the second scenario, the connections created within a single machine (AF_LOCAL or AF_UNIX socket family) are different in nature and memory overhead from those created over a network (AF_INET socket family). Some network simulators, e.g. ns [272], do not even use sockets at all. So the measurements from simulations would necessarily be different from those measured in a real network. By which factor? Once again, it is very hard to tell. What about the side-effects of memory management? As we will see in the next section, this is already difficult to assess on a single machine running a single kernel; assessing it on a machine running 400+ kernels in user mode seemed to us to be a daunting task. For instance, if the kernel runs out of memory, allocations fail; but if user space runs out of memory, pages are swapped. Another source of side-effects is when the real kernel (the one running in kernel mode) runs out of free pages or buffers: All 400+ simulated machines are affected, not just one. What impact does this have on the simulation results?

In short, if we had developed a simulator, we would not be able to justify why our results have some credibility[1]. We thus opted for a theoretical study of memory overhead.

8.2.3.4 Theoretical study: *modus operandi*

Having ruled out experimentation and simulation, the only solution left to assess the memory overhead of hundreds of persistent TCP connections on the manager side is to

---

1. In a more general context, see an excellent article by Floyd and Paxson [92] on the difficulty of interpreting simulation results in the IP world.

perform a theoretical analysis. To do so, we studied the kernel code (written in C) of Linux 2.3.99-pre6[1], the latest release of Linux at the time this study was performed. In order to compute this memory overhead, we added up:

- the memory allocated per socket;
- an upper bound for the memory allocated per neighbor;
- an upper bound for the memory allocated per TCP receive buffer; and
- a bit of extra memory to account for memory-management overhead.

Note that to assess the overall memory footprint, we should also account for application-level receive buffers (that is, the management-application variables where we store incoming data on the manager side). But these buffers are needed anyway, regardless of the transport protocol and the persistency of the connections. What we try to assess here is the extra memory overhead induced by the creation of hundreds of persistent TCP connections, not the overall memory footprint of the manager (which also runs the event correlator, the rule analyzer, etc.). Thus, we will ignore the application-level receive buffers in our calculations.

We decided to study not one but two cases. In Section 8.2.3.5, we investigate the worst-case scenario, which gives us an absolute upper bound for the memory footprint on the manager, whatever the network topology encountered, whatever the setup of the agents by the administrator. In Section 8.2.3.6, we present a more realistic scenario that takes into account some common-sense remarks. This allows us to compute a more realistic upper bound of the memory overhead.

In both cases, we assume that we have a maximum of 400 agents managed by a single manager, with two connections per agent: one for pushed data and one for notifications (we will justify these two connections in Section 8.4.2.2). This yields a total of 800 connections for the manager. The default number of file descriptors is large enough (4,096 or 8,192, depending on the options specified when the kernel was built, and dynamically settable via `/proc/sys/fs/file-max`), so we need not increase it on the manager.

8.2.3.5 Worst-case scenario

C data structures in Linux 2.3.99-pre6	bytes
`struct sock`	848
`struct inode`	404
`struct file`	96

Table 3. Memory overhead per socket

The footprint of the C data structures that are allocated whenever a socket is created is the following (see Table 3):

---

1. Linux 2.3.99-preXX were prereleases of Linux 2.4, which came out in January 2001.

848 + 404 + 96 = 1,348 bytes

With 400 agents and two connections per agent, this yields a total of:

1,348 * 400 * 2 = 1,078,400 bytes (data structures allocated on a per-socket basis)

C data structures in Linux 2.3.99-pre6	bytes
struct dst_entry	100

Table 4. Memory overhead per destination host

The footprint of the C data structures that are allocated per destination host (i.e., whenever a connection is created to a new agent) is 100 bytes (see Table 4). We have two sockets but only one `struct dst_entry` per agent. With 400 agents, this yields a total of:

100 * 400 = 40,000 bytes (data structures allocated on a per-destination-host basis)

C data structures in Linux 2.3.99-pre6	bytes
struct neighbour	112
struct hh_cache	44

Table 5. Memory overhead per neighbor

The footprint of the C data structures that are allocated per neighbor (i.e., whenever a connection is created through a new neighbor) is the following (see Table 5):

112 + 44 = 156 bytes

We have already mentioned that the number of neighbors is site specific and cannot therefore be known in advance. Typically, it is very low (between 1 and 3) compared with the number of destination hosts (10s or 100s). In the worst-case scenario, we have one neighbor per destination host (agent). So, let us multiply the memory footprint of the C data structures by the maximum number of agents (400). This yields a total of:

156 * 400 = 62,400 bytes (data structures allocated on a per-neighbor basis)

The total so far is thus:

1,078,400 + 40,000 + 62,400 = 1,180,800 bytes (total except TCP receive buffers)

C data structures in Linux 2.3.99-pre6	bytes
(struct sock *)->rcvbuf	max: 65,535
struct sk_buff	164
(struct sk_buff *)->truesize	MTU + 4

Table 6. Memory overhead of TCP receive buffers

Let us now quantify the memory footprint of the buffers dynamically allocated by the kernel (see Table 6). We have one TCP receive buffer per connection. A TCP receive buffer is a virtual container of metadata and real data. In practice, it is a byte counter. The metadata consists in a doubly linked list of socket buffers (`struct sk_buff`) and a four-byte counter appended at the end of each data block (real data). A reference to this counter is stored in (`struct sk_buff *`)`->end`. The real data and the counter form a data block. A reference to the real data is stored in (`struct sk_buff *`)`->data`.

We have one socket buffer and one data block allocated per incoming packet (layer 3). The application-level data is chunked into a series of data blocks. An IP packet sent by the agent may result in more than one socket buffer allocated by the manager, because the IP routers between the agent and the manager may fragment the IP packets sent by the agent. If MTU discovery is enabled, it allows the agent to set TCP's Maximum Segment Size (MSS) for that connection so as to avoid fragmentation. In this case, the number of IP packets sent by the agent is equal to the number of IP packets received by the manager. We need more than one socket buffer per connection on the manager if:

- the application cannot keep up with the amount of incoming data (CPU-bound);
- IP packets are delivered out of order; or
- IP packets sent by the agent have been fragmented.

Each socket buffer (metadata) has a memory footprint of 164 bytes with typical settings for building Linux 2.3.99-pre6. In the worst case scenario, the memory footprint of a data block is equal to the maximum valid MSS plus four bytes for the counter. The maximum valid MTU has a value of 65,535 [182], which yields a maximum MSS of:

65,535 - 40 = 65,495 bytes

The maximum memory footprint of a data block is therefore:

65,495 + 4 = 65,499 bytes

On the manager, the size of a TCP receive buffer ((`struct sock *`)`->rcvbuf`) is set to `sysctl_rmem_default` by default (in `net/core/sock.c`). The default value of the latter is set to `SK_RMEM_MAX` in `net/core/sock.c`. The constant `SK_RMEM_MAX` is equal to 65,535 (defined in `include/linux/skbuff.h`). Both the maximum and default sizes of a TCP receive buffer can be defined dynamically (that is, without rebooting the machine) by updating the following kernel pseudo-files:

```
/proc/sys/net/core/rmem_max
/proc/sys/net/core/rmem_default
```

The dynamically specified values of `rmem_max` and `rmem_default` cannot exceed SK_RMEM_MAX.

Both `rmem_max` and `rmem_default` apply to all processes running on the machine. But the size of a TCP receive buffer can also be specified by the application on a per-connection basis, by setting the socket option SO_RCVBUF (e.g., when the manager creates the persistent TCP connection). The buffer size specified with SO_RCVBUF cannot exceed SK_RMEM_MAX.

In the worst-case scenario, let us assume that the agents are pushing so much data so quickly that they fill up all the TCP receive buffers on the manager side. Although this worst case is not realistic, it gives us an upper bound for the memory footprint on the manager. The receive window advertised by the manager ensures that the agent will not overflow the manager's TCP receive buffer. According to Stevens [254, pp. 191–192], this value used to be 4,096 bytes in Berkeley-derived kernels, but is now typically somewhere between 8,192 and 61,440 bytes. This guarantees that the TCP receive buffer will not go beyond 65,535 bytes for real data and metadata. In net/core/ sock.c:sock_rmalloc, we see that Linux is even more flexible. The doubly linked list can grow as long as the aggregated size of the metadata and real data does not exceed the maximum allowed (65,535 bytes). One last allocation can exceed this value, but all further requests for new allocations are refused until some data is read in by the application. If N_i is the number of bytes of real data received in the segment that fills up the ith TCP receive buffer, the maximum memory footprint for the ith TCP receive buffer is therefore:

$(65,535 - N_i) + 164 + N_i = 65,699$ bytes (independent of N_i)

The total number of TCP receive buffers needed at one time on the manager depends on the number of agents pushing data at exactly the same time. This is site specific and varies over the time, so it cannot be assessed precisely. Let us be very pessimistic and assume that *all* agents are pushing data at the same time[1]. With 400 agents and one pushed-data connection per agent, this yields:

$65,699 * 400 = 26,279,600$ bytes (TCP receive buffers for pushed data)

Notifications are short and fit into one TCP segment. They are seldom sent by agents. In a pessimistic scenario, let us assume that *all* agents use 1,500 bytes per notification (Ethernet MTU) and have one socket buffer allocated on the manager side per notification connection. This yields:

$(164 + 1,500 + 4) * 400 = 667,200$ bytes (TCP receive buffers for notifications)

The total for TCP buffers is therefore:

$26,279,600 + 667,200 = 26,946,800$ bytes (TCP receive buffers)

This yields a total memory overhead of:

$1,180,800 + 26,946,800 = 28,127,600$ bytes (total without memory-management overhead)

---

1. If this were the case in reality, it would probably mean that the administrator poorly configured the agents. It is simple for the manager to ask different agents to push regular data at slightly different times, either by explicitly requesting different absolute times, or by making sure that the agents use a different initial time t_0 to compute relative times. Agents may unpredictably change the time when they push data if their internal clock drifts, but the synchronization that we recommend in Section 11.4 makes sure that clocks do not drift excessively, which prevents accidental resynchronization of all push times.

Finally, we need to account for Memory-Management Overhead (MMO). For instance, the amount of memory actually allocated in `net/core/skbuff.c` is rounded up to the closest higher multiple of 16 bytes. The worst case is encountered with the allocation of *slabs* (the memory-allocation units used for most dynamic memory allocations in Linux): Whenever we call `kmalloc()`, the amount of memory actually reserved by the kernel is rounded up to the closest higher power of two. So, if we allocate 300 bytes, 512 bytes are actually reserved. In the worst-case scenario, all dynamic memory allocations are of the form $2^N + 1$ bytes, where N is an integer, and result in actual reservations of 2^{N+1} bytes of memory. The worst MMO is therefore:

$$\frac{2^{N+1} - (2^N + 1)}{2^N}$$

This value tends asymptotically toward 100% when N grows. An upper bound for the MMO is therefore 100%. This yields a total memory overhead of:

28,127,600 * 2 = 56,255,200 bytes < 57 Mbytes

In conclusion, the total amount of memory used by all the persistent TCP connections between the manager and the agents is always less than 57 Mbytes. Compared with the 512 Mbytes we expect the manager to have, this memory footprint is perfectly acceptable (11%). Even with only 256 Mbytes of memory, the manager would still cope with 400 persistent connections.

8.2.3.6 Realistic upper bound

In the previous section, we made several crude hypotheses that unduly increased the footprint of TCP receive buffers and, consequently, vastly exaggerated the memory requirements on the manager. Let us try to define a more realistic upper bound of the manager's memory overhead by taking into account a few common-sense and practical remarks.

First, it is unrealistic to assume that the agents will fill up *all* of the manager's TCP receive buffers. In practice, a manager can be temporarily unable to cope with the amount of incoming data (that is, it is CPU-bound rather than I/O-bound). During a short period of time, some TCP receive buffers can indeed fill up, but only a fraction of them. If we choose a high upper bound, we can assume that up to 10% of the agents can fill up the manager's TCP receive buffers. Note that a manager should not remain CPU-bound over extended periods of time, say five or ten minutes in a row. If it does, it has a problem. Either its CPU is not powerful enough, in which case a CPU upgrade is needed, or its management domain is too large, in which case the domain should be split into two subdomains, with one manager per subdomain. There are cases, however, where none of these cures are possible—e.g., in the case of budget restrictions. In this case, the administrator can prevent TCP receive buffers from clogging up the manager's memory by forcing its kernel to reduce the receive window of all the TCP persistent connections (SO_RCVBUF generic socket option). By doing so, we reduce the amount of data that the agents can push per connection, and we force the agents to buffer data in their TCP send buffers. The persistent connections are then said to be *receive-window-limited* [230].

Regarding the remaining 90% of the agents, let us assume that the network is recent enough to support path MTU discovery [182] so as to avoid fragmentation (that is, IP routers support the *do not fragment* bit in the FLAGS field of the IP header), and that the receive window is small enough that we do not need many socket buffers to reorder the IP packets. In that case, we can suppose that the remaining 90% of the agents require on average a maximum of three socket buffers per pushed-data connection at the manager (the value of three comes from Stevens [254, p. 192]), with an MTU equal on average to 1,500 bytes (Ethernet MTU).

A second reason to reduce the memory requirements put on the manager is that notifications are rare events in the IP world. As a result, we should never receive continuous streams of notifications from all the agents at the same time, even in the case of serious network conditions. We can therefore reasonably assume that only 1% of the agents have delivered notifications that could not be processed immediately. Notifications are short by nature and require only one socket buffer and one data block at the manager.

Third, based on typical LAN configurations, we might be tempted to assume that the number of neighbors rarely exceeds three, because a LAN segment is rarely interconnected by more than three IP routers. But with an intelligent hub, all the machines directly attached to the hub (respectively, all the hosts belonging to the same virtual LAN) are (respectively, appear to be) accessed in one hop. So, if the manager and the agents under its control are all connected to an intelligent hub (respectively, belong to the same virtual LAN), all the agents will be both destination hosts and neighbors as far as the manager is concerned. The same is true if we replace the intelligent hub with switching equipment. In view of the generalized use of intelligent hubs in modern LANs, and in view of the current migration toward switching equipment, let us assume that all destination hosts are also neighbors—that is, we have 400 neighbors (worst case).

Finally, the MMO was grossly overestimated in the previous section. If we consider the C data structures involved, we see that `struct sock` requires 1,024 bytes instead of 848, which yields an MMO of 21%, not 100%. Similarly, `struct file` has an MMO of 33%, `struct inode` has an MMO of 27%, etc. All of these values are significantly lower than the MMO of 100% that we considered in the previous section. By looking at the different MMOs, we see that we can very safely assume that the MMO is 40%, as this value is still overestimated.

Under these new hypotheses, the overall memory footprint of the persistent TCP connections becomes:

1,348 * 400 * 2 = 1,078,400 bytes (data structures allocated on a per-socket basis)
100 * 400 = 40,000 bytes (data structures allocated on a per-destination-host basis)
156 * 400 = 62,400 bytes (data structures allocated on a per-neighbor basis)
(65,699 * 400 * 10%) + ((164+1,500+4) * 3 * 400 * 90%) = 4,429,400 bytes (TCP buffers for pushed data)
(164 + 1,500 + 4) * 400 * 1% = 6,672 bytes (TCP buffers for notifications)
1,078,400 + 40,000 + 62,400 + 4,429,400 + 6,672 = 5,616,872 bytes (total without memory-management overhead)
5,616,872 * 1.4 = 7,863,621 bytes < 8 Mbytes (total)

In conclusion, by making more realistic hypotheses, we have proved that in the worst case, we need less than 8 Mbytes of memory to cope with 400 agents. Compared with the 512 Mbytes we expect the manager to have in order to process the rules for so many agents, the amount of memory used up by all the persistent TCP connections between the manager and the agents is negligible (less than 2%). Even 128 Mbytes of memory would be sufficient. The management application itself, and most notably the rules used by the event correlator and pushed-data analyzer in large networks, require considerably more memory and render the issue of persistent TCP connections a non-issue in NSM. Hundreds of persistent TCP connections cause no significant scalability issue for modern managers. The *Myth of the Collapsing Manager* is dead.

8.2.4 Firewalls: persistent connections must be created by the manager

There is a principle of robustness in Internet security that says that TCP connections should preferably be created from a trusted host to an untrusted host, rather than the other way round [59, p. 56]. In our context, this means that the persistent TCP connections should be created by the manager (always trusted), not by the agent (possibly remote and therefore untrusted). By abiding to this rule, we protect ourselves against a number of well-known attacks.

The simplest example of such attacks is *intrusion* [58, p. 7]. If we allow certain external machines to connect via TCP to a reduced set of internal machines, e.g., with filtering rules on the access routers, the odds are that an attacker will find a hole in the filters and will manage to connect to an internal machine which was not properly protected against intrusions. One of the worst kinds of intrusion is `telnet`, which gives the attacker full access to a machine. There are ways to prevent such attacks, and most organizations are reasonably safe against intrusions. But the only way to be completely immune to this type of attack is to prevent external machines (e.g., agents) from connecting to internal machines (e.g., managers).

Another example of attack is *masquerade*, also known as *address spoofing* or *IP spoofing*. It is easy for an attacker to change its IP address to impersonate a remote agent and send management data on its behalf. The answers sent by the manager (e.g., the TCP ACKs) may not reach the attacker's machine, especially if the attacker operates in blind mode[1], but this does not prevent an attack from being conducted. For instance, an attacker can send bogus information to the manager, make it believe that the impersonated agent is experiencing problems, and entice a 24*7 operator to take drastic actions to try and recover from the bogus problem—thereby really breaking the network. By snowball effect, if many agents are impersonated and many actions are taken by the operators, the entire network of a large corporate organization or a large Internet Service Provider (ISP) can be brought to its knees. As we mentioned in Section 4.2.2.3, operators can make very weird decisions when they panic—a human aspect often exploited by *social-engineering* attacks.

A third example is a class of attacks known as *Denial-of-Service (DoS) attacks*. First, an attacker probes all the TCP ports of the manager by trying to access all ports successively (there are ways to hide this kind of probing from simplistic pattern-matching firewalls). The purpose here is to learn what ports are active. Then, he/she connects to some or all active ports and swamps the manager with requests or data coming from many different machines (or even from a single machine if he/she is able to tamper with the IP address of outgoing packets). This is known as *flooding* [58, p. 8]. This can easily make the manager grind to a halt, thereby preventing 24*7 operators from doing their job and exposing the network to potentially serious problems. Instead of swamping the manager, the attacker can alternatively perform an attack known as *TCP SYN flooding*. By creating 10,000s of so-called *half-open connections* (a TCP connection torn down by its source immediately after the SYN packet of the three-way handshake is sent), the attacker can prevent agents from connecting to the manager by using up all available resources on the manager. Most TCP servers begin sending keepalives (SO_KEEPALIVE socket option) after two hours to clean up idle connections; so a manager may remain inactive for two hours after such an attack, a situation which may have a significant impact on a production environment. In case the TCP server is not configured to send keepalives (which is sometimes the case with old software), the manager remains inactive until it is rebooted!

By forcing the connection to be created by the manager, we do not prevent attacks altogether, but we make it harder for an attacker to succeed, especially if he/she operates in blind mode. By not being able to actively create new connections to the target of his/her attack, an attacker is forced to steal existing TCP connections. There are known ways of doing this (e.g., *sequence-number* attacks allow attackers to steal existing TCP connections in blind mode [59, p. 24]), but they are much more sophisticated than the attacks we just described and require much smarter attackers.

Note that creating TCP persistent connections from the manager does not buy us total security. Some attacks are still possible, for instance sequence-number attacks, replay, some DoS attacks, and attacks that require the attacker to read the packets sent by the manager to the agent. In environments that must be protected against such attacks, it is mandatory to use stronger security measures, e.g., Secure Sockets Layer (SSL [247]), IP Security (IPSec [251]), or data-link encryption [238]. The latter is the most expensive

---

1. That is, the attacker does not control any WAN router along the path from the manager to the agent. He cannot eavesdrop traffic along this path and he has no control over the agent. He can only keep the agent mute, e.g., by bombarding it with ICMP packets to prevent it from communicating with its WAN access router [59, p. 166].

but can, under certain conditions [238], provide a very high level of security. But many sites do not want or cannot afford military- or bank-grade security, and are happy with the sole protection offered by filtering gateways—which are typically set up to prevent the creation of TCP connections from the outside. Consequently, we need not (and do not) mandate strong security in WIMA, and particularly in WIMA-CM.

8.2.5 Reversed client and server roles

We just saw that, for security reasons, the persistent TCP connection must be initiated by the manager, not by the agent. Hence, when we go from the pull model that underlies SNMP-based management to the push model that we advocated in Chapter 7, the client and server roles are swapped. The transfer of management data is now initiated by the agent, instead of the manager; but the client side of the persistent connection (that is, the creator of the connection) remains on the manager, and the server side on the agent. Compared to the usual mapping between the manager-agent paradigm and the client-server architecture, the client and the server are on the wrong sides! Somehow, we want the server to initiate the communication, whereas the communication must be initiated by the client in a client-server architecture (see Fig. 27).

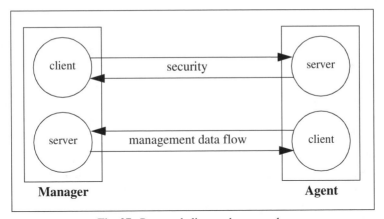

Fig. 27. Reversed client and server roles

To address this issue, we currently have four non-proprietary ways of communicating between the manager and the agent, that is, four APIs for writing the management application: the sockets API, HTTP, Java RMI, and CORBA [244]. We explained in Section 5.4 why Java RMI and CORBA are inadequate in the IP world (see the *my-middleware-is-better-than-yours* syndrome). So we have the choice between using HTTP as a high-level API, or plain sockets as a low-level API. The two solutions are not very different, because both solutions use a TCP connection for the communication pipe. But a few important discrepancies justify our preference for HTTP. We study sockets in Section 8.3 and HTTP in the remainder of this chapter.

8.3 The Sockets API as a Manager-Agent Communication API

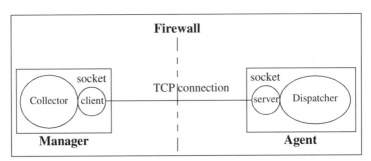

Fig. 28. The sockets API as a manager-agent communication API

Sockets are bidirectional. When a TCP connection is created, the TCP client contacts the TCP server, as usual in the client-server architecture. Once the connection is established, the client can send data to the server, but the server can also independently send data to the client via the same TCP connection. This property is very useful in our management scenario because it solves our problem of server-initiated communication. First, the manager creates a socket for each agent—that is, it creates virtual pipes to all the agents in its management domain. Later, the agents use these pipes to send management data across (regular data or notifications).

To ensure that the TCP connection remains persistent, the collector must not set a receive timeout on the socket when it creates it (SO_RCVTIMEO). If the underlying TCP connection is dropped for whatever reason (e.g., due to a network outage while the agent was pushing data), it is the responsibility of the manager to reconnect to the agent.

This solution offers a major advantage: simplicity. Socket programming is very easy in C, C++, Java, etc. But it also presents serious drawbacks. The main problem is the necessity to define a new, domain-specific transfer protocol *à la* SNMP. HTTP, built on top of TCP, is today's *de facto* standard in transfer protocols. Why should we use a domain-specific protocol rather than this standard? The second problem is deployment. As we saw in Section 6.5, vendors now routinely embed HTTP servers in their network equipment, except sometimes in bottom-of-the-range equipment, and a large proportion of the deployed devices and systems already support HTTP. As a result, management solutions based on HTTP can be easily deployed and adopted by the market. Conversely, deploying a new domain-specific transfer protocol built on top of the sockets API would take years, supposing that vendors all agree to adopt the same protocol (which would be quite a challenge!). The third problem is related to firewalls. We face a potential problem if we need to traverse a firewall between the manager and the agent. Most firewalls let only a few TCP ports go through [58]. So by default, firewalls will generally filter out the TCP connections that we intend to use between the manager and external agents. Thus, in order for this solution to work, all firewall systems must be modified. This may not be a problem for large organizations, because they generally have in-house expertise to set up UDP relays or update TCP filtering rules, or they can afford consultants to do the job. But it is often a problem for small and midsize companies, who generally lack such expertise, and for whom expensive external consultants are only a last resort option. As we said in Section 8.2.2.2, this concern is not theoretical and was confirmed to us by people from the industry. The fourth problem is security. If we use the sockets API, we must use *ad hoc* solutions to secure the persistent TCP connection. Whereas by adopting HTTP, we automatically get several security mechanisms such as HTTP authentication [96] and SSL [247]. Although these mechanisms do not offer strong security, they are better than the simplistic community string offered by SNMPv1 and SNMPv2c, and often meet the needs of customers who cannot afford expensive technologies such as data-link encryption.

For these four reasons, we prefer to base manager-agent communication (as well as manager-manager communication in a distributed scenario) on HTTP rather than on the plain sockets API with a proprietary transfer protocol and proprietary security mechanisms. But we stress that both solutions work.

8.4 HTTP-Based Communication for Pushed Data: WIMA-CM-push

HTTP does not exhibit the property of bidirectionality that we exploited previously. HTTP connections are oriented: It is not possible to create a persistent connection in one direction, from the client to the server, and later send data in the opposite direction. All HTTP methods rely on a strict request-response protocol; for an HTTP server to send a response to an HTTP client, it must have received a request from this client beforehand. It cannot send unsolicited messages.

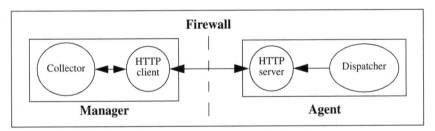

Fig. 29. Distribution via HTTP with a firewall

In this respect, SNMP and HTTP behave differently. SNMP follows a generalized client-server paradigm, whereby the response from the server can be either explicit (pull model of the get, set, and inform operations) or implicit (push model of the snmpv2-trap operation). HTTP, conversely, follows a strict client-server paradigm for all of its methods (GET, POST, HEAD, etc.). With HTTP, the response from the server cannot be implicit. As a result, the implementation of push technologies with HTTP is not natural. How can we solve this problem?

8.4.1 MIME multipart

The first step toward a solution is to rephrase the problem as follows: How can we have an HTTP server send an infinitely large number of replies to a single request from an HTTP client? The second step is to make the agent send one infinite reply instead of an infinite number of finite replies. More specifically, we make the client send a single HTTP GET request to the following well-known URL:

`<http://agent.domain:280/mgmt/connect/all_data>`

where `all_data` can be any kind of CLHS (Component Launched by an HTTP Server). In return, the server sends an endless reply that embeds separators in the payload of the HTTP message (see Fig. 30). To achieve this, Netscape proposed a few years ago to use the multipart type of MIME [98, 187] in a different context (to update an applet GUI in a Web browser). We propose to use the same idea in NSM. At each push cycle, we send a MIME part that includes the description and value of all the MIB variables sent by the push scheduler. Once all the management data has been pushed, we send a MIME boundary; this metadata means *end of push cycle*. As for notifications, they are sent asynchronously, one at a time, through the same connection. In this case, the MIME boundary is interpreted as metadata meaning *end of notification*.

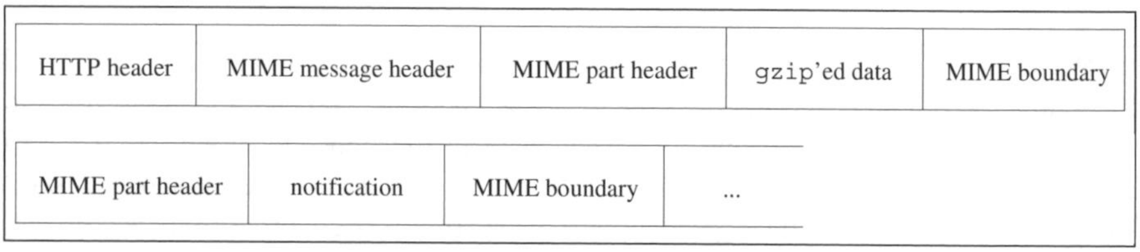

Fig. 30. TCP payload of the infinite HTTP response

HTTP/1.0 and HTTP/1.1 are not fully MIME-compliant protocols [88, Section 19.4.1]. But the use of the MIME multipart type is valid in both HTTP/1.0 [23, Section 3.6.2] and HTTP/1.1 [88, Section 3.7.2], so we have no problem here.

We stress that we do not mandate the use of persistent HTTP/1.1 connections. WIMA-CM-push works with both HTTP/1.0 and HTTP/1.1. We do not want to rely on HTTP/1.1's persistence because the embedded HTTP servers that we find in network equipment today are often trimmed down versions of free HTTP/1.0 servers, with a low footprint and a proven track record in terms of robustness.

Our solution presents two advantages. First, it is simple to implement. We will come back to this in Chapter 10, when we describe our prototype. Second, it makes it easy to traverse firewalls, as we saw in Section 8.2.2.2. It is also exposed to two problems. One is the possibility to have an urgent notification significantly delayed by a large transfer of management data; this is addressed in Section 8.4.2, and leads us to slightly change this scheme. Another is the necessity for the manager to detect when a connection is torn down and to reconnect to the agent automatically; several solutions are described and discussed in Section 8.5.

8.4.2 Some notifications are more equal than others

In a LAN, we do not want to experience large transmission delays for urgent notifications. For instance, a high upper bound for push cycles (i.e., the maximum amount of management data pushed by an agent in a single cycle) is 50 Mbytes. This is transferred in less than 5 seconds over a 100 Mbit/s Ethernet segment, supposing that we have a large memory on the manager and a fast disk on the data repository. But we can experience long delays if we go across a WAN link. For instance, 1 Mbyte of management data takes 3 minutes to be transferred over a 56 kbit/s connection.

In most environments, urgent notifications should be processed within a few seconds (i.e., in pseudo real-time), so the situation will be fine with most LANs but not acceptable with most WANs. The situation becomes worse in environments where urgent notifications ought to be processed within less than a second, typically when we have strong QoS requirements (e.g., network equipment sustaining IP telephony); in such cases, we have problems even with LANs. In other words, as our communication model should cope with all sorts of environments, we cannot wait for an entire push cycle to be completed before we send an urgent notification.

We have two solutions to this problem. Either we interrupt the push cycle and send the notification immediately, via the same TCP connection, or we transmit the notification in parallel, via another TCP connection.

8.4.2.1 One TCP connection per agent: temporary interruption of the push cycle

The first solution assumes that we have only one persistent TCP connection per agent. In this case, we must interrupt the push cycle, send the urgent notification, and either resume the push cycle (send the remainder of the management data) or restart it (send all data again). We will face all sorts of problems if we adopt this solution.

First, how does the manager know that the push cycle was not cleanly completed but was aborted abruptly? As we do not have a separate control connection, we must embed a special *interruption string* in the payload of the HTTP message, e.g., the string "`<INTERRUPTED!!!>`", and make sure that this string never appears in the original data. This can be achieved by (i) using some kind of domain-specific escape sequence, or (ii) using HTTP/1.1 chunked encoding, sending the interruption string as one chunk, and making sure that regular chunks do not consist solely of the interruption string. The former is not elegant in terms of design. The latter requires HTTP/1.1, which is incompatible with our desire to support both HTTP/1.0 and HTTP/1.1. In theory, an alternative to the interruption string is TCP's urgent mode, which is used for instance to send the interrupt key in a `telnet` session. But Stevens recommends against using it because of the poor interoperability among different implementations [253, pp. 292–296], so we rule it out. In short, none of these solutions is really satisfactory.

Second, should the manager process on-the-fly the management data that it reads in, until a MIME boundary or the interruption string is encountered? Or should it buffer all incoming data until a MIME boundary is read in, and discard it without any processing if the interruption string is parsed? Clearly, parsing all the management data and buffering it before giving it to the pushed-data analyzer does not scale, so this solution should be avoided. Alternatively, we can buffer the events sent by the pushed-data analyzer to the event correlator. Once a MIME boundary is parsed, all buffered events are delivered to the event correlator; if the interruption string is encountered instead, the event buffer is emptied. The problem is that this scenario requires one event buffer per agent at the pushed-data analyzer, which does not scale. In short, buffer-based solutions are not adequate: The manager must process the data as it comes in.

Third, if the push cycle is interrupted to leave way to an urgent notification, the push cycle can either be resumed or restarted all over again. If we send the same data again with the same timestamp as before, the manager reads in the same data twice, up to the character where the previous interruption occurred. The manager therefore believes that the agent is bogus and is sending the same data twice: It drops the connection to the agent and notifies the administrator that there is a problem with that agent (via the event correlator and an event handler). To allow the agent to resume the transfer, i.e. not to transfer again the data already received by the manager, we need application-level ACKs of management data. The problem with this approach is that it induces a significant network overhead, which is precisely what we are trying to avoid (and one of the reasons why we decided to depart from the SNMP protocol in the first place).

In summary, none of these solutions is appropriate in the general case. Interrupting a push cycle to leave way for an urgent notification is not adequate.

8.4.2.2 Two TCP connections per agent

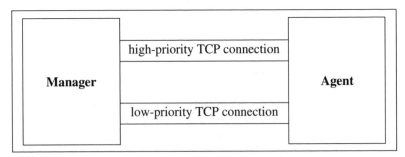

Fig. 31. Two connections per agent

The second solution is to transmit the notification in a separate TCP connection. This allows us to distinguish between high- and low-priority traffic (see Fig. 31). For each agent, one connection is dedicated to the delivery of urgent notifications, and another is used to transfer the rest of the management data (i.e., regular data and non-urgent notifications). The manager connects to the agent by requesting the following URLs:

```
<http://agent.domain:280/mgmt/connect/high_priority>
<http://agent.domain:280/mgmt/connect/low_priority>
```

where `high_priority` and `low_priority` can be any kind of CLHSes. On both sides, the priority-based multiplexing between sockets can rely on multithreading or priority-tagged message queues.

Note that when we refer to *urgent* notifications, we do not have hard real-time constraints in mind, because they would require real-time operating systems on all the agents and the manager—which we usually do not have. The goal here is simply to avoid having to queue an urgent notification while Mbytes of non-urgent regular data are pushed by the agent. But it is no problem at all if a 64-kbyte TCP segment (the maximum for a single low-priority write) is entirely pushed by the agent via the low-priority connection before the priority-based multiplexing system switches to the high-priority write. Similarly, a low-priority notification can be entirely pushed via the low-priority connection before an urgent notification is pushed via the high-priority connection. The same is true for the manager, with low-priority reads and high-priority reads.

8.4.2.3 Generalization to multiple TCP connections per agent

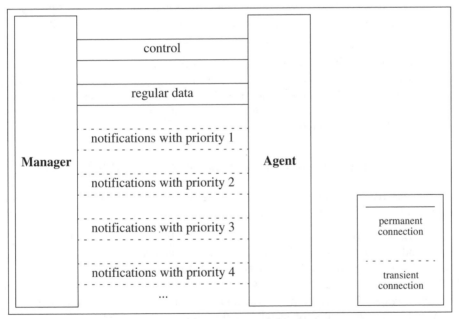

Fig. 32. Multiple connections per agent

In environments with complex QoS constraints, it may be necessary to distinguish more than two levels of priority[1]. For instance, in RFC 1470, there are four predefined levels of

---

1. The author thanks Thimios Panagos for bringing this issue to his attention.

priority (called *levels of severity*): CRITICAL, ERROR, WARNING, and INFO. It would be a waste of resources to create one persistent TCP connection per priority level per agent. And in case the number of priority levels is not known in advance, it would not even be possible.

In such cases, we recommend having one persistent control connection, one persistent connection for regular management data, and transient connections for notifications of different priority levels:

`<http://agent.domain:280/mgmt/connect/control>`

`<http://agent.domain:280/mgmt/connect/regular>`

`<http://agent.domain:280/mgmt/connect/transient?priority=string>`

Once again, `control`, `regular`, and `transient` can be any kind of CLHSes. The control connection allows the agent to request new connections from the manager (*connections on demand*). When the control connection is created, and each time the manager creates a new transient connection to the agent, the manager sends a new HTTP `GET` request to the agent via the control connection, issues a blocking read on the corresponding socket, and waits for a response from the agent; upon receipt of a response, the manager creates a new transient connection with the priority level specified by the agent, issues a new HTTP `GET` request, and enters the same loop. Per-socket timers on the manager make sure that idle transient connections are timed out after a while, e.g., 10 seconds, by using the `SO_RCVTIMEO` generic socket option.

How does a manager find out whether an agent supports two or several levels of priority? The simplest solution for the manager is to request the two types of URLs, and depending on the errors that it gets from the agent, to opt for one solution or the other. Obviously, if an agent supports both schemes, the manager should select the most fine-grained scheme, that is, it should allow for multiple levels of priority.

8.4.3 Specifying the information model in the MIME header

Now that we have chosen to use MIME to separate different push cycles or different notifications, let us specify how we make management data self describing (see Section 8.2.1).

To indicate the type of management data transferred in MIME parts, we use the *content type* header field of each MIME part. This description must include two things: the information model (SNMPv1, SNMPv2c, SNMPv3, CIM, OSI, etc.) and the encoding[1] (XML, string, BER, PER, serialized Java object, binary format, etc.). We have three levels of granularity for specifying the MIME type: the information model, the specification, and the mapping. The mapping is a set of rules for encoding a given information model.

---

1. This is also called *representation*. Strictly speaking, *representation* specifies whether the value of an SNMP OID, a remote method invocation in CIM, etc. is expressed in XML, as a string, etc. *Encoding* indicates whether the data, once represented in a specific format, is further compressed, encrypted, or simply transmitted "as is". In the IP world, there is much confusion between these terms, and many people use them interchangeably. So do we in this book.

Let us begin with examples of MIME types defined with an information-model granularity. If we assume that we encode management data in XML, we can define many MIME types for different information models, e.g.:

- SNMPv1-to-XML
- SNMPv2c-to-XML
- SNMPv3-to-XML
- CIM2.2-to-XML
- CIM2.3-to-XML
- OSI-to-XML

The problem with this approach is that it is too coarse grained. For instance, a certain SNMP protocol can be specified in several RFCs, with slight modifications due to the normal life cycle for an RFC to become a standard at the IETF. SNMPv3, for instance, has already been through three releases: RFCs 2261, 2271, and 2571. This can cause conformance and interoperability problems. A manager might claim to support a given information model, but slight differences between different versions of the specification could cause misunderstandings between agents and managers (see what happened with SNMPv2 in the mid-1990s). Thus, the exact version of the information model must appear in the MIME type. The same rationale is true for the encoding, although encodings normally change very little over time. We therefore need to go down to the specification version of both the information model and the encoding. In case the information model is SNMPv3 and the encoding is BER, we have three possible MIME types to date:

- RFC2261-to-BER
- RFC2271-to-BER
- RFC2571-to-BER

Unfortunately, MIME types are still ambiguous with this level of granularity. For given specifications of the information model and the encoding, we might have different versions of the mapping. For example, the DMTF released several versions of the CIM-to-XML mapping (or *xmlCIM* for short [76]); some even bear the same name but contain slight variations (e.g., xmlCIM 2.0 went through three releases in June 2, July 6, and July 20, 1999). The resulting ambiguity can lead to interoperability problems when an agent and a manager implement two different releases of the mapping. To avoid any compliance problem between two entities claiming to support the same information model and the same encoding, we need to specify the mapping version as well, as shown in the following examples:

- CIM2.2-to-XML-v1.0
- CIM2.2-to-XML-v1.1

At this stage, we have a very accurate way of specifying the information model, the encoding, and the mapping used by the agent. The problem is now the combinatory explosion of MIME types that must be created and registered with the Internet Assigned Numbers Authority (IANA [123]), each time a new version of an information model, an encoding, or a mapping is released. The poor scalability of this scheme makes it very impractical.

In order to reduce the number of MIME types required and the number of interactions with the IANA, we propose to define a single new MIME type (*application/mgmt*) and two MIME parameters, mapping and version, as shown in the following examples:

```
Content-Type="application/mgmt"; mapping:"CIM2.2-to-XML"; version="1.0"
Content-Type="application/mgmt"; mapping:"RFC2571-to-BER"; version="2"
Content-Type="application/mgmt"; mapping:"CIM2.6-to-string"; version="3.0beta1"
```

This is the format that we mandate in WIMA-CM-push. We now have only one MIME type registered with the IANA. As far as the IANA is concerned, the names of the parameters are fixed, and their values are free-style strings. New valid values for the parameters can be defined over time, on an *ad hoc* basis, without contacting the IANA. Tomorrow, a new information model could appear, say XYZ, which could be supported immediately with the following MIME-type parameters:

```
Content-Type="application/mgmt"; mapping:"XYZ-to-XML"; version="1.0beta1"
```

If we use the augmented Backus-Naur Form (BNF) defined in HTTP/1.1 [88, Section 2.1], the content type can be formally defined as shown in Fig. 33.

ContentType = "Content-Type=" NewMimeType Sep " " Mapping Sep " " Version
NewMimeType = <"> "application/mgmt" <">
Sep = ";"
Mapping = "mapping=" <"> InformationModel "-to-" Encoding <">
InformationModel = (*ALPHA Release)
Encoding = (*ALPHA Release)
Version = "version=" <"> Release <">
Release = *(DIGIT | ALPHA | ".")

Fig. 33. Formal definition of the content type

8.4.4 Optional compression of management data

Unlike SNMP, MIME supports a powerful feature: It distinguishes between *content type* and *content transfer encoding*. This allows for transparent compression of data in transit. Compression is optional in the case of MIME: Some parts may be compressed, while others are not. This feature is useful in our NSM scenario in two respects.

First, agents that can compress data dynamically should preferably compress it so as to save network bandwidth, especially when regular management data is transferred in large bulks. But WIMA-CM-push does not mandate that all agents support compression. A direct consequence of this is that the manager should not necessarily expect MIME parts to be compressed. Within the same management domain, some agents may support compression and others may not.

Second, an agent may decide to compress some MIME parts but not all of them. For instance, notifications are inherently short; most of the time, they should not be compressed because the gain would be negligible, or could even be negative (e.g., `gzip` makes very small files bigger because it adds a header to the compressed data). Another example would be agents that compress data when their CPU load is low, but send data uncompressed when faced with a transient burst of activity.

Because of the expected heterogeneity of the agents, even within a single management domain, the manager should be able to process MIME parts that are compressed with different compression schemes (e.g., `gzip`, `bzip2`, `compress`, or `zip`), just like mailers do today. WIMA-CM-push does not impose any specific compression scheme.

As we mentioned already, HTTP/1.0 and HTTP/1.1 are not fully MIME-compliant [88, p. 167], in spite of the requests by the author to the IETF HTTP Working Group, in 1995, when the specification of HTTP/1.0 was written. As a result, there is no Content-Transfer-Encoding header field in HTTP. Fortunately, two HTTP header fields offer similar functionality: Content-Encoding and Transfer-Encoding. A Transfer-Encoding applies to an entire HTTP message, whereas a Content-Encoding applies to a single MIME part (*body part* in HTTP parlance). Clearly, we are interested in specifying the Content-Encoding header field in WIMA-CM-push. The valid values for the Content-Encoding (i.e., the valid compression schemes) are those allowed by the IANA [88, p. 23].

8.4.5 Example of HTTP and MIME-part headers

```
HTTP/1.1 200 OK
Date: Wed, 10 May 2000 02:42:57 GMT
Server: Apache/1.2.4
Last-Modified: Thu, 23 Mar 2000 08:58:33 GMT
Mime-Version: 1.0
Content-Type: multipart/mixed;boundary="RandomBoundaryString"

This is a multipart MIME message.

--RandomBoundaryString
Content-Type="application/mgmt"; mapping="CIM2.2-to-XML"; version="1.0"
Content-Encoding: gzip

Data for Part1

--RandomBoundaryString
Content-Type: "application/mgmt"; mapping="SNMPv2-Trap-to-BER"; version="2"

Data for Part2

--RandomBoundaryString--
```

Fig. 34. Push: HTTP and MIME-part headers of the agent's reply

In Fig. 34, we give an example of HTTP and MIME-part headers for the infinite response sent by the agent.

8.4.6 Simplifications in case we do not have a firewall

So far, we assumed that we could have one or several firewall(s) between the manager and the agent. But what happens if we know for sure that we have none? This case is of particular interest to ISPs, who control their entire network and usually do not need to access equipment via a firewall because their NOC is located at the heart of their network. Let us first study what can be simplified in WIMA-CM-push under this new assumption, and then see if we can integrate the firewall and non-firewall cases into a single communication model.

If we do not go across a firewall, we need no longer create the persistent HTTP connection from the manager. Instead, we can create it from the agent. This allows us to re-establish a normal client-server communication, and to put the HTTP client on the agent and the HTTP server on the manager. This new scenario is depicted in Fig. 35.

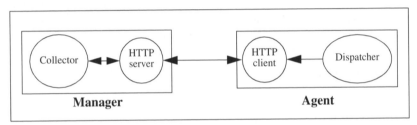

Fig. 35. Distribution via HTTP without firewall

This solution presents several advantages. First, it does not rely on non-intuitive designs that stretch the client-server architecture to its limits: The client is on the agent side and the server on the manager side. Second, the agent can reconnect immediately in case the persistent connection is broken: It does not have to rely on the manager to do that. This improves the robustness by avoiding time windows when the agent wants to send data to the manager but the manager has not yet reconnected to the agent. It also considerably simplifies the management of timeouts and reconnections (see Section 8.5), and suppresses the need for the manager to send keepalives. Finally, as in the firewall case, we do not need a specific version of HTTP: Both HTTP/1.0 and HTTP/1.1 are appropriate.

The main drawback of this solution is that it breaks the nice unity of our management architecture. Firewalls, undeniably, bring in new constraints. But the advantage of using a single solution, whether we have a firewall or not, is homogeneity. An organization that has no requirement for a firewall today may have a very good reason tomorrow to put a firewall in place, e.g. if it changes its operation. An engineer working in a firewall-based organization may be transferred tomorrow to a firewall-free environment. An administrator, coming from a small organization that could not afford a full-blown firewall based on application gateways, could move tomorrow to an organization that can afford to buy a new firewall platform just to benefit from one single new feature. If we use the same management architecture everywhere, things become a lot easier to all these people. Of course, we could give the administrator the choice of creating the connections on the manager or agent side. But, by doing so, would we gain more than we would lose?

8.5 Timeouts and Reconnections

The issue of connection timeouts and reconnections is particularly important for two reasons. First, because of the reversed client and server roles (see Section 8.2.5), we must be careful that the manager detects a problem with the persistent TCP connection and reconnects to the agent in a timely manner. Otherwise, there will be time windows when the agent cannot send management data to the manager due to the absence of a persistent connection. This can cause robustness problems in the case of notifications, or buffering problems on the agent in the case of large push cycles. Second, the robustness of operating systems and Web-based applications relies partly on the automatic cleanup of broken TCP connections. If we do not clean up old broken connections, we could clog up certain resources on the manager and prevent new persistent connections from being created.

Persistent TCP connections can be timed out either by the operating system (transport layer) or the Web application (application layer). How do the timers in charge of this cleanup work? Are they compatible with our use of persistent TCP connections in WIMA-CM-push? What are the best strategies with respect to timeouts and reconnections? In Section 8.5.1, we investigate the timeouts performed by the agent's and manager's operating systems. In Section 8.5.2, we study the timeouts by the application, again on both sides of the communication pipe.

8.5.1 Timeouts by the operating systems

By default, idle TCP connections are not timed out by operating systems. This feature of TCP, often surprising at first, has some advantages (e.g., the network is not overloaded by heartbeat or polling overhead) and disadvantages (e.g., machines are exposed to DoS attacks such as *TCP SYN flooding*). By default, an operating system only cleans up a connection when it reboots or when an outgoing data transfer fails—typically in the case of network outage, when one end sends data and the other end is unreachable. A direct consequence of this is that the sending end can time out a TCP connection but, by default, the receiving end does not.

In WIMA-CM-push, the management data always flows from the agent to the manager. The sending end is always the agent, and the receiving end is always the manager. So, by default, the agent can time out a connection but the manager cannot. This poses a problem, as it is much easier to control the behavior of one entity (the manager) than 10s or 100s of entities (the agents). In this section, we will see different ways of altering this default behavior of TCP.

An operating system can support two types of timeouts. Some apply to all the sockets managed by this operating system (per-kernel granularity), others to a single socket (per-socket granularity). Let us study these two types successively for the agent's and manager's operating systems (four cases in total).

8.5.1.1 Timeouts by the agent's operating system: per-kernel granularity

By default, the agent's operating system times out a persistent TCP connection by limiting the maximum number of retransmissions performed automatically by the TCP layer. The timer in charge of this is called the Agent's TCP Retransmission Timer (A-TRT) in WIMA-CM-push. This timer goes off after a certain amount of time: the Agent's TCP Retransmission Time-Out (A-TRTO). A-TRTO can be expressed in seconds (it then takes continuous values on the time axis) or as a maximum number of retries (it then takes discrete values on the time axis). Let us assume that it is expressed in seconds.

In our management scenario, if the agent's operating system sends data across a persistent TCP connection and its TCP layer does not receive an ACK from the manager within a certain time (A-TRTO), then the agent's operating system drops the connection.

The behavior of A-TRT and the value of A-TRTO depend on the operating system. According to Stevens [253, p. 299], A-TRTO is hard-coded in the kernel of most Unix systems and cannot be modified. In Berkeley-derived implementations, for instance in 4.4BSD (Berkeley Software Distribution), it is equal to about nine minutes [253, p. 299]. This timeout value is the result of an exponential backoff with an upper limit of 64 seconds, which leads to the following series of backoff times between the 13 successive retransmissions:

$$A\text{-}TRTO_{def} = \sim 1.5^1 + 3 + 6 + 12 + 24 + 48 + 64 + 64 + 64 + 64 + 64 + 64 + 64 \text{ seconds}$$
$$= \sim 542.5 \text{ seconds}$$
$$= \sim 9 \text{ minutes } 2.5 \text{ seconds}$$

The behavior of A-TRT is different in Linux 2.3.99-pre6. First, its backoff time does not have an upper limit of 64 seconds, but 120 seconds (the function `net/ipv4/tcp_timer.c:tcp_retransmit_timer` uses `TCP_RTO_MAX` which is defined in `include/net/tcp.h`). Second, the maximum number of retransmissions can be modified dynamically on a system-wide basis with the kernel pseudo-files `/proc/sys/net/ipv4/tcp_retries1` and `/proc/sys/net/ipv4/tcp_retries2`. Third, the successive backoff times are not statically computed as in 4.4BSD; instead, they are computed dynamically as a function of the Retransmission Time-Out (RTO), which itself is dynamically estimated with Karn's and Jacobson's algorithms [32]. As a result, on Linux systems, A-TRTO can be larger or smaller than nine minutes. With the default values of `tcp_retries1` and `tcp_retries2`, it can be anywhere between 13 minutes and 38 minutes, depending on the estimated RTO (see `include/net/tcp.h`).

---

1. The first retransmission occurs after *about* 1.5 seconds, as explained by Stevens [253, pp. 236 and 299].

For the sake of simplicity, let us assume that A-TRTO is equal to nine minutes. This value is very reasonable in our management scenario, and it does not cause any problems in most environments. Let us also assume that the manager is not down for extended periods of time (that is, for more than A-TRTO seconds). The agent's operating system will time out the persistent TCP connection to the manager if, and only if, we experience a long network outage (longer than A-TRTO) when the agent tries to push data. For instance, a network link may be broken, or an IP router along the path may be down. In this case, after nine minutes, the connection is closed by the agent but the manager does not know about it; we have a *half-open connection* clogging up the manager's memory. Worse, the agent knows that there is a problem, but cannot repair it for security reasons (see Section 8.2.4); the manager could repair it, but it does not know that there is a problem. We have a deadlock! To break it, we must find a way for the manager to detect that the TCP connection was broken, so as to reconnect to the agent and restore the persistent communication pipe. (Remember that the agent relies on this pipe when it sends data to the manager.)

8.5.1.2 Timeouts by the manager's operating system: per-kernel granularity

TCP offers a simple way of making the receiving end detect that a connection was broken by the sending end: *keepalive probes*, or *keepalives* for short. Although usually not enabled by default, this feature is widely supported by current TCP/IP stacks. In this section, we study keepalives managed with a kernel-based granularity.

Keepalive probes: default settings

For the manager's operating system to become aware that the connection has been closed by the agent, the simplest is to send *keepalives probes* [253, pp. 331–337], a form of out-of-band data handled by the kernel and transparent to the application using the connection. To do so in our management scenario, the manager's collector must set the SO_KEEPALIVE generic socket option whenever it creates a persistent TCP connection to an agent [254, p. 185]. This socket option has been around for many years and is widely supported. On the manager, all the sockets that have this option set behave in the same manner. For kernels including a Berkeley-derived implementation of TCP (that is, most kernels available to date), this behavior is controlled by the following algorithm:

- As soon as the manager stops receiving data from the agent, it restarts its M-TKT (Manager's TCP Keepalive Timer).
- If a TCP connection remains idle for two hours, M-TKT goes off and the manager's kernel begins sending keepalive probes to the agent.
- As soon as the agent receives a keepalive probe, it must send an ACK to the manager.
- The manager's kernel waits 75 seconds between sending two consecutive keepalive probes.
- If the manager receives anything from the agent (ACK, data, etc.), it stops sending keepalive probes and restarts M-TKT.
- After nine successive keepalive probes are unsuccessfully sent by the manager to the agent, the connection is closed by the manager.

If the network outage ends while the manager is still sending keepalive probes to the agent, but after the agent has dropped the connection, the manager receives a reset (RST) from the agent. As a result, it drops the persistent TCP connection and reconnects to the agent. The chances for this reconnection to succeed are high, as the manager has just received some out-of-band data from the agent.

If the manager has not received any answer from the agent at the end of the keepalive-based probing, it drops the existing persistent TCP connection and attempts to create a new one to the agent. This time, the chances of success are slimmer, as the network outage could still be ongoing, or the agent might still be down.

The advantage of using keepalives is that it allows the manager to clean up sockets for broken connections, especially when an agent reboots. This prevents broken connections from clogging up the manager's memory until the machine is rebooted. A minor disadvantage is that it requires exchanging a bit of extra out-of-band data between the manager and the agent, which slightly increases the network overhead; apart from bandwidth-starved WAN links, we can live with it happily in view of the offered functionality. A second drawback is that all sockets are treated alike; we will solve this problem in Section 8.5.1.4. A third issue is that the manager takes a very long time to reconnect to the agent (e.g., after the agent accidentally rebooted). The Manager's TCP Keepalive Time-Out (M-TKTO) is equal to:

$$\text{M-TKTO}_{def} = 7{,}200 + (9 * 75) = 7{,}875 \text{ seconds} = 2 \text{ hours } 11 \text{ minutes } 15 \text{ seconds}$$

In other words, in the case of prolonged network outage, it takes the manager more than two hours to discover that the persistent TCP connection was broken by the agent:

$$\text{M-TKTO}_{def} - \text{A-TRTO}_{def} = 7{,}875 - {\sim}542.5 = {\sim} 7{,}332.5 \text{ seconds} ={\sim} 2 \text{ hours } 2 \text{ minutes}$$
$$12.5 \text{ seconds}$$

Somehow, this seems grossly inefficient! In most production networks, a management downtime of over two hours for all the agents in a given management domain is simply not acceptable.

Most modern operating systems solve or alleviate this problem by parameterizing some or all of the three values specified in the previous algorithm. These parameters, which we call the *keepalive-control kernel variables*, allow the administrator to customize the handling of keepalives for all the sockets of the machine that have SO_KEEPALIVE set. In Linux 2.3.99-pre6, not only are these values parameterized, but they can also be updated dynamically (without rebooting the machine) via three kernel pseudo-files:

- /proc/sys/net/ipv4/tcp_keepalive_time controls the idle time after which the kernel begins sending keepalive probes.
- /proc/sys/net/ipv4/tcp_keepalive_intvl controls the time elapsed between two successive keepalive probes.
- /proc/sys/net/ipv4/tcp_keepalive_probes controls the number of keepalive probes that are sent before the kernel gives up and declares the other end unreachable.

The default values of these three keepalive-control kernel variables appear in Table 8. This applies to Linux. In perhaps the most famous textbook to date on the internals of TCP [294], Wright and Stevens describe the source code of another famous operating system, 4.4BSD-Lite, where the kernel variables have different names and slightly different semantics and default values. As this is confusing (and it confused the author for some time!), the mapping between the two operating systems is given in Table 7.

Linux 2.3.99-pre6	4.4BSD-Lite
`tcp_keepalive_time`	`tcp_keepidle`
`tcp_keepalive_intvl`	`tcp_keepintvl`
`tcp_keepalive_probes`	`(tcp_maxidle/tcp_keepintvl) + 1`

Table 7. Mapping between Linux and 4.4BSD keepalive-control kernel variables

The main difference in the semantics is that in Linux, we count the first keepalive probe in `tcp_keepalive_probes`, whereas we do not in 4.4BSD-Lite's `TCPTV_KEEPCNT` (equal to the ratio `tcp_maxidle/tcp_keepintvl`). The default value of Linux's `tcp_keepalive_probes` is 9, while in 4.4BSD, `tcp_maxidle` is equal to 10 minutes, `tcp_keepintvl` is equal to 75 seconds, and `TCPTV_KEEPCNT` is equal to 8 [294, pp. 822–831]). Note that Stevens erred in [253, p. 332]: In 4.4BSD, a maximum of 9 probes (not 10 as stated) is sent, as explained by Wright and Stevens [294, pp. 830–831, Figs. 25.17 and 25.18].

In a companion book, Stevens also lists the keepalive-control kernel variables in Solaris, AIX, BSD/386, etc. [253, Appendix E]. They all follow 4.4BSD's naming convention, but some of these operating systems only allow one or two of these variables to be set. In our management scenario, the administrator should therefore be careful to select a modern operating system for the manager, in order to have good control over keepalives.

Keepalive probes: recommended settings

Now that we know how to modify these keepalive-control kernel variables, what values should we give them in NSM? How fast do we want to start sending keepalive probes? Should M-TKTO be larger or smaller than A-TRTO? The answers to these questions depend on the reactivity that the administrator expects from the manager, and this reactivity is highly site specific. If we assume that all agents take about nine minutes to time out a connection in the case of network outage, we recommend that the keepalive-control kernel variables be assigned the values listed in Table 8. They yield the following M-TKTO:

$$\text{M-TKTO}_{rec} = 540 + (6 * 10) = 600 \text{ seconds} = 10 \text{ minutes}$$

As we can see, M-TKTO_{rec} is much more reasonable than M-TKTO_{def} in NSM. With our recommended settings, the manager can detect reasonably quickly that an agent has closed its side of the connection. A timeout of 10 minutes also corresponds to one of the typical polling periods[1] for a LAN in standard SNMP-based management, and a typical push

period in Web-based management. Obviously, it makes sense to have an M-TKTO close to
the push period. Moreover, by not being too close to nine minutes (that is, by selecting 600
seconds instead of 541), we make it possible for the clocks of the manager and the agent to
slightly drift apart, and we allow for some kernel latency at the manager and the agent (e.g.,
in case several signals are queued). We also account for the imprecision in the value of A-
TRTO_{def} (see footnote 1, p. 206).

Linux 2.3.99-pre6 kernel variable	default value	recommended value in NSM
tcp_keepalive_time	7,200 seconds	540 seconds
tcp_keepalive_intvl	75 seconds	10 seconds
tcp_keepalive_probes	9	6

Table 8. Per-kernel TCP keepalives: default and recommended values

An M-TKTO of 10 minutes may not be appropriate for all sites, however. For instance, it
can be set to a much larger value (e.g., the default value of two hours) in a small LAN if
reactivity is not of paramount importance and we simply want to clean up the manager's
memory from time to time. By making M-TKTO bigger, we reduce the network overhead
caused by out-of-band data.

M-TKTO can also be set to less than A-TRTO, say one minute. At first glance, such a
setting may seem bizarre: We deliberately choose to send keepalive probes when the TCP
connection is healthy, thereby increasing the network overhead. But there are cases where
this behavior is desirable[1]. For instance, it allows the manager to detect a network fault
before the agent; and the role of a manager is precisely to detect faults. It also enables the
manager to detect the crash of critical agents in a timely manner, which may be very
important in some environments. For example, if we want a critically important agent to
send the manager a heartbeat every 30 seconds, M-TKTO should preferably be set to
35 seconds rather than 10 minutes. Because of the increased network overhead caused by
reducing M-TKTO for *all* agents, there is a trade-off between how quickly we want to
detect that an important agent is down, and how much network overhead we are willing to
pay for it.

Per-kernel timeouts: problems with heterogeneous agents

Per-kernel keepalives, and more generally per-kernel timeouts, work fine as long as we
have a very homogeneous set of agents in a management domain. If all the agents have
almost the same A-TRTO, it is fine for the manager to have the same M-TKTO for all its
sockets. But the situation is very different when we have heterogeneous agents. Hetero-

---

1. The typical periods are 5, 10, and 15 minutes.
1. It may also cause problems. What happens if a manager reconnects to an agent before this agent has dropped
   the previous connection? We need a mechanism on the agent to drop the old connection and make the
   management application switch to the new connection.

geneous systems and devices have heterogeneous operating systems, hence possibly different kernel settings. A-TRTO may thus vary from agent to agent—e.g., we already showed that it can vary between Linux and 4.4BSD machines. As equipment vendors do not want to incur the risk that a piece of equipment stops working because an administrator mistakenly set some kernel variables to absurd values, it is generally not possible for administrators to configure A-TRTO in COTS agents. In practice, we must live with the fact that different agents have different A-TRTO's, and the best we can do is to try and address this heterogeneity problem on the manager side.

What value should we then assign to M-TKTO if most agents in a management domain have an A-TRTO of about nine minutes, but a couple of agents have an A-TRTO hard-coded to one hour? What happens if some agents do not support keepalives and therefore appear to be dead to the manager? How should we deal with agents that can unpredictably "freeze" their management layer over extended periods of time because other tasks have a higher priority[1]?

If we favor network overhead over robustness, M-TKTO ought to be equal to the largest A-TRTO of all the agents in the manager's management domain. A major problem with this approach is that modern, top-of-the-range IP routers might be unmanageable for two hours just because one old bottom-of-the-range device has an A-TRTO of two hours—this is simply not an option.

If we favor robustness over network overhead, M-TKTO should be equal to the smallest A-TRTO of all the agents in the manager's management domain. By doing so, we guarantee that problems with the most critical machines are detected as soon as possible. An important drawback of this approach is that the manager keeps reconnecting to agents whose kernel does not support keepalives, or does not answer to keepalives for long periods of time, thinking that these agents have just rebooted. These spurious reconnections generate unnecessary network traffic, increase unnecessarily the CPU overhead of the manager and the agents involved, and cause many time windows during which the agents are not manageable, although in good health. A second problem is that, if one agent has a really small A-TRTO, M-TKTO will also be unreasonably small, which will unduly increase the network overhead.

In short, choosing a system-wide, per-kernel keepalive policy to decide when a manager should reconnect to an agent is not easy in a heterogeneous environment. There is a trade-off between robustness and network overhead, and the best value for M-TKTO is site specific. If we have a large distribution of A-TRTO values across a population of widely heterogeneous agents, there is simply no satisfactory M-TKTO.

---

1. Several years ago, the author experienced such a problem with FDDI concentrators, whose management application was assigned a very low priority by the vendor in order to maximize real-data throughput. Their SNMP agents could remain silent to the manager's requests during several minutes in a row, up to half an hour in the case of very large data transfers. This made the manager waste a lot of CPU cycles performing retries, and sometimes even convinced 24*7 operators that an FDDI concentrator was down and should be rebooted.

Fortunately, all of these problems can be alleviated by controlling the manager's timeouts on a per-socket basis rather than on a per-kernel basis. Per-socket timeouts give us the granularity required in heterogeneous environments, hence in most real-life networks. Let us first study the agent side in Section 8.5.1.3, then the manager side in Section 8.5.1.4.

8.5.1.3 Timeouts by the agent's operating system: per-socket granularity

On the agent side, we have two means of overriding the per-kernel A-TRTO on a per-socket basis: the send timer and the retransmission timer. Both of these timers are managed by the kernel (kernel timers), but their timeout value can be altered by the application.

The *send timer* is controlled by the SO_SNDTIMEO generic socket option (send timeout) [254, pp. 193–194]. It allows the agent's dispatcher to set a per-socket inactivity timer[1] to detect a network outage or a crash of the manager. With SO_SNDTIMEO, the send timeout can be different for different sockets on the same machine (unlike what we saw in Section 8.5.1.1). One advantage of this solution is that it allows the administrator to override A-TRTO when this per-kernel timeout value is not configurable. One problem with this solution is that Posix.1g does not mandate the support for SO_SNDTIMEO, although this socket option appeared years ago with 4.3BSD Reno, back in 1990 [254, pp. 20,194]. As a result, some operating-systems vendors may be inclined not to support it. Linux kernel developers added support for it rather recently: SO_SNDTIMEO was not supported in Linux 2.3.28, released in November 1999, but it is in 2.3.99-pre3, released in March 2000 (see net/core/sock.c:sock_setsockopt). To the best of our knowledge, few commercial Linux vendors already support it, because of the usual time lag between development and commercial versions of Linux. Therefore, COTS agents are likely to not support it yet. We thus cannot rely on this solution in WIMA-CM-push.

The *retransmission timer* is controlled by the TCP_MAXRT TCP socket option (retransmission timeout) [254, p. 202]. It allows the administrator to override A-TRTO on a per-socket basis. TCP_MAXRT allows the agent's dispatcher to set a limit on the number of retransmissions performed by the agent's kernel if no ACK is received from the manager. TCP_MAXRT is specified in seconds by the application, but it can be rounded up by the kernel to the closest highest value accepted by the kernel [254, p. 202] (see the discrete values of the backoff times in Section 8.5.1.1). This rounding up is the main difference between TCP_MAXRT and SO_SNDTIMEO; apart from that, the end result is fairly similar. The main problem with TCP_MAXRT is that it is recent (it appeared with Posix.1g) and still rarely supported [254, p. 202]. At the time we performed this study of the Linux kernel, its latest version, Linux 2.3.99-pre6, did not support it (this can be checked in net/ipv4/tcp.c:tcp_setsockopt), despite the well-known swiftness of the Linux community to implement new features. We therefore do not believe that TCP_MAXRT is a good candidate on the agent side.

---

1. In Berkeley-derived implementations of TCP, the send timer is an inactivity timer, not an absolute send timer [254, p. 194]. It does not go off if a write takes longer than SO_SNDTIMEO seconds: It goes off if one TCP segment sent during a write operation is not ACK'ed by the agent within SO_SNDTIMEO seconds.

The problem of course is whether equipment vendors will give administrators control over the embedded dispatcher. The chances are slim, unless the code of the dispatcher is downloaded into the agent dynamically or the dispatcher is written by a third-party vendor. Although this solution works (e.g., SO_SNDTIMEO with Linux 2.99-pre6), we recommend working at the manager level instead.

8.5.1.4 Timeouts by the manager's operating system: per-socket granularity

On the manager side, we have two means of controlling connection timeouts on a per-socket basis: the receive timer and the keepalive timer. Both of these timers are managed by the kernel (kernel timers), but their timeout value can be altered by the application.

The *receive timer* is controlled by the SO_RCVTIMEO generic socket option (receive timeout) [254, pp. 193–194]. It allows the manager's collector to set a per-socket inactivity timer to detect a network outage or a crash of the agent. With SO_RCVTIMEO, the receive timeout can be different for different sockets on the same machine (unlike what we saw in Section 8.5.1.2). One advantage of this solution is that the collector has to set the SO_RCVTIMEO option only once in the lifetime of the connection (we will see other solutions in Section 8.5.2 where this is not the case). Similar to what we said for SO_SNDTIMEO in the previous section, one problem with SO_RCVTIMEO is that Posix.1g does not mandate its support. But an important difference with the previous case is that we are now on the manager side, so the administrator can choose what operating system to run on this machine (this is not the case with most COTS agents, which generally come with an opaque operating system). The *receive timer* solution is therefore acceptable in WIMA-CM-push.

TCP socket option	Linux 2.3.99-pre6 kernel variable
TCP_KEEPIDLE	tcp_keepalive_time
TCP_KEEPINTVL	tcp_keepalive_intvl
TCP_KEEPCNT	tcp_keepalive_probes

Table 9. Keepalive control: mapping between TCP socket options and kernel variables

The *keepalive timer* is controlled by the TCP_KEEPALIVE TCP socket option [254, p. 201]. It allows the administrator to override M-TKTO on a per-socket basis. TCP_KEEPALIVE allows the manager's collector to set a limit on the time it takes the manager to time out a connection that does not answer to keepalive probes. In practice, this single TCP socket option is often replaced with three: TCP_KEEPIDLE, TCP_KEEPINTVL, and TCP_KEEPCNT, which correspond to the three keepalive-control kernel variables described in Section 8.5.1.2. This is the case in Linux 2.3.99-pre6 (see net/ipv4/tcp.c) and, according to the input we received on the USENET newsgroup *comp.protocols.tcp-ip*, also in 4.4BSD. In Linux, the mapping between these three TCP socket options and the keepalive-control kernel variables is straightforward, as depicted in Table 9. The four TCP socket options are linked by the following equation:

`TCP_KEEPALIVE = TCP_KEEPIDLE + (TCP_KEEPINTVL x TCP_KEEPCNT)`

In 4.4BSD and BSD derivatives, they are linked by the following equation:

`TCP_KEEPALIVE = TCP_KEEPIDLE + (TCP_KEEPINTVL x (TCP_KEEPCNT + 1))`

One problem with `TCP_KEEPALIVE` is that it is recent (it appeared with Posix.1g) and still rarely supported [254, p. 185]. However, `TCP_KEEPIDLE`, `TCP_KEEPINTVL`, and `TCP_KEEPCNT` were already supported in Linux 2.3.28.

The main advantage of the two solutions presented in this section is that they allow the administrator to modulate the reactivity of the manager depending on how critical a piece of equipment is to the robustness of the network. In Table 8, p. 210, we already proposed some reasonable values in NSM for `TCP_KEEPIDLE`, `TCP_KEEPINTVL`, and `TCP_KEEPCNT`. But we saw in Section 8.5.1.2 that there are cases where we would like the timeout value on the manager side to be less than the timeout value on the agent side, and other cases were we would like it to be greater. For example, if we want a critically important agent to send a heartbeat every 30 seconds to the manager, we can set the timer for that socket to go off after 35 seconds, not 10 minutes. Per-socket timeouts on the manager side give us the granularity necessary to manage heterogeneous agents.

A second important advantage of using per-socket timeouts on the manager side is that we can directly tie the receive timeout and the keepalive timeout values with the push period for each agent. This solution is very suitable in the NSM context. During the subscription phase, the manager must then register the smallest push period specified for a given agent, and later set the keepalive or receive timeout value for that socket to just above this smallest push period. This behavior is especially recommended for important management data, e.g. heartbeats.

The advantage of `SO_RCVTIMEO` over {`TCP_KEEPIDLE`, `TCP_KEEPINTVL`, and `TCP_KEEPCNT`} is that it does not cause extra network overhead. It does not require out-of-band data to be exchanged over the network. The disadvantage is that the possibility to manage per-socket keepalives is more widely available than the possibility to manage per-socket receive timers. But unlike what we saw with agents earlier, the administrator can choose what machine to use for the manager, so this last point is not really an issue. In conclusion, the best solution in our view is to select a manager whose operating system supports `SO_RCVTIMEO`, or otherwise to use {`TCP_KEEPIDLE`, `TCP_KEEPINTVL`, and `TCP_KEEPCNT`}.

To conclude Section 8.5.1, per-kernel timeouts work fine but do not provide us with the granularity necessary in most real-life environments, whereas per-socket timeouts are easier to control on the manager side than on the agent side. So we should preferably use per-socket timeouts on the manager side. We have two options: `SO_RCVTIMEO` and the trio {`TCP_KEEPIDLE`, `TCP_KEEPINTVL`, and `TCP_KEEPCNT`}. The former causes less network overhead, but the latter is more widely available. Both are appropriate in WIMA-CM-push.

8.5.2 Timeouts by the applications

In Section 8.5.1, we studied in detail what happens when the persistent TCP connection between the manager and the agent is dropped by the operating system at one of the two ends. Let us now investigate what happens when this connection is torn down at the application level. We distinguish four cases (see Fig. 29, p. 195). On the manager side, the connection can be broken by the HTTP client or the collector; on the agent side, by the HTTP server or the dispatcher.

8.5.2.1 Timeouts by the application on the manager side

Application-level keepalives are ruled out by the design decision made in Section 8.4.1. We send a single query from the manager and an infinite reply from the agent, so there is no possibility for the manager to regularly send application-level keepalives via the same connection. The only thing the manager can do is to restart a timer each time it receives data from the agent, and drop the connection and reconnect immediately when this timer goes off. We have three techniques to achieve this: SIGALRM, select() and poll().

SIGALRM

The first technique relies on the SIGALRM signal. It can be broken down into three steps. First, the collector calls alarm() and passes the timeout value as argument. This makes the kernel start the *alarm-clock timer*. Second, the collector issues a blocking read(). Third, a SIGALRM signal is generated by the kernel when the timer goes off. As a result, the read() system call is interrupted and the signal handler for SIGALRM is called instead. The problem with this solution is well known[1]: Signals are not appropriate to handle traffic coming concurrently from many sources. First, we can have only one signal handler for SIGALRM per process or per thread. As the manager must communicate with many agents, we are forced to run many collectors (potentially up to several hundred) on the manager side, one per thread. Second, signal handling varies from machine to machine when Posix signals are not used, which makes the coding very difficult and error prone (Posix signals are not yet supported by all operating systems). Third, and worst, standard signals such as SIGALRM are not queued by the kernel and can be lost if several signals are generated in burst. This last problem renders this technique inadequate in our context.

select()

The second technique is based on the select() system call in the C library, or its equivalent in other programming languages. The collector issues a blocking select() instead of a blocking read(). With select(), we can tell the kernel that we are interested in reading from several sockets, and how long we are prepared to wait. The

---

1. So much so that it is sometimes ignored. For instance, Stevens mentions this solution only when we read from a single socket [254, pp. 349–352]. And Kegel does not even mention it when he reviews I/O strategies for reading from many sockets [139].

timeout value is passed as an argument to select () and controls the *select timer*. The select () system call returns either when some traffic is coming from a socket or when the select timer goes off. We have two options: We can either run a single select () and a single collector for all the sockets, or one select () and one collector per socket (each collector then runs in a separate thread). With the first option, a single collector is connected to all the agents. This is very bad, because we then have a single timeout value for all the sockets (see the problems mentioned in Section 8.5.1.2). With the second option, we have one select timer per connection (hence per agent). If select () returns due to a timeout, we drop the connection and immediately attempt to reconnect to the agent; otherwise, we read incoming data on the socket and re-enter the select () loop. The advantage of select () is that it is widely supported. Unlike SO_RCVTIMEO and the keepalive-control socket options, which require recent operating systems, a timeout policy based on select () can be implemented with virtually all operating systems. The main problem with select () is that it is limited to FD_SETSIZE sockets; this limit is hard-coded in the kernel. FD_SETSIZE is often equal to 1,024 [254, p. 152], but it can have a different value. With a maximum of 400 agents and two sockets per agent, we need 800 sockets on the manager, which is just below the maximum of 1,024. This solution is therefore fine for WIMA-CM-push, but may cause problems in the future if, for some reason, we want to manage more than 400 agents per management domain. Other, very technical problems with select () are described by Banga *et al.* [18].

poll ()

The third technique uses poll (), a variant of select (). The internals of poll () are different from those of select (), but these two system calls offer similar functionality to the application programmer. They both take a timeout value as argument, they both return a readable socket or an error in the case of timeout, etc. The main difference between these two system calls is that poll () has no hard-coded equivalent to FD_SETSIZE. Based on this difference, some kernel experts claim that poll () is superior to select () for dealing with a large number of sockets [139, 254, p. 171]). Other kernel experts argue with this statement and claim that the implementation of poll () is often inefficient, e.g. in Linux (see the *linux-kernel* mailing-list archive [154]); Banga *et al.* claim that poll () is less efficient than select () when the proportion of interesting file descriptors exceeds 3/64, because select () only copies 3 bits per file descriptor while poll () copies 64 [18]. When experts disagree, it usually means that there is no clear-cut winner. Another difference is that poll () is less widely available than select () [254, p. 172]. Note that a small variant of poll () is to work directly with /dev/poll [139], which is faster than poll () when the number of sockets is very large. As far as WIMA-CM-push is concerned, select (), poll (), and /dev/poll are all fairly similar. They all work fine in our context as long as we have only one connection per thread.

Signal-driven I/O and real-time signals

For the sake of completeness, we should also mention two other techniques: signal-driven I/O (Input/Output) and real-time signals. In the case of signal-driven I/O, we tell the kernel to send a SIGIO signal to the application when something happens on a socket. Unfortunately, this technique is useless in the case of TCP sockets, as described in detail by Stevens [254, pp. 590–591]. In short, the problem is that SIGIO is generated too often by the kernel, and we do not precisely know what happened just before its signal handler was called.

As for real-time signals, the problem is that they are rarely supported by current operating systems [139]. Unlike standard signals such as SIGALRM and SIGIO, real-time signals are queued and priority-based. As a result, we should never lose real-time signals unless the manager crashes (we can lose SIGALRM signals). Moreover, some sockets (hence some agents) can be assigned a higher priority than others, so management data coming from critical backbone routers can have precedence over data coming from mere hosts. These two properties are very useful in our management scenario. Unfortunately, real-time signals are still too rarely supported to be considered in WIMA-CM-push. Note that this may change in the future.

Collector vs. HTTP client

Now that we have investigated the different possibilities to time out the persistent TCP connection, let us see how to use them at the application level. On the manager, the TCP connection can be timed out either by the collector or the HTTP client. Presumably, the components used to implement the management application on the manager let the collector create the persistent TCP connection, and the HTTP client is just a library that offers a high-level API to perform an HTTP GET, POST, etc. If this is the case, all the system calls and signals studied previously apply to the collector. If, on the other hand, the HTTP client provides the collector with an opaque interface to the network and transparently handles all the reconnections and timeouts, then all the system calls and signals studied before apply to the HTTP client. The important point here is that it is transparent to WIMA-CM-push whether timeouts and reconnections are implemented by the collector or the HTTP client.

8.5.2.2 Timeouts by the application on the agent

On the agent side, there are two possible strategies to manage timeouts at the application level. One is to do this in the configuration file of the HTTP server; another is to configure the dispatcher. Both methods can be used concurrently, although only one is necessary.

Timeouts by the agent's HTTP server

For several years, developers of standard HTTP servers such as Apache [11] have protected their software against memory exhaustion caused by half-open connections. This problem, which used to plague busy HTTP servers on the Web, is often due to the impatience of users when heavy network congestion occurs. It can also be due to attacks, e.g. TCP SYN flooding, as mentioned in Section 8.2.4. Some people find it hard to wait more than a few seconds to download a Web page, and often reload the same page several times before it eventually gets completely transferred. By doing so, they create half-open connections on the machine hosting the HTTP server if the HTTP client does not cleanly close the TCP connection, or if the close does not reach the HTTP server due to heavy network congestion. For busy HTTP servers, half-open connections can very quickly use up all the memory available on the machine, thereby preventing the HTTP server from accepting new connections.

Two strategies have been often used in the past to free the memory resources clogged up by idle connections. One is to assign a maximum lifetime to all HTTP/TCP connections and to time them out systematically after a certain time, regardless of whether they are idle or active. The other strategy is to assign a maximum period of inactivity to all HTTP/TCP connections, and to restart the inactivity timer of a connection each time some traffic goes across this connection.

In the days of HTTP/1.0, timeout values were often hard-coded in the HTTP server. With the advent of persistent connections in HTTP/1.1, the management of timeout values was refined. Most HTTP/1.1 servers today allow administrators to configure these timeout values in their configuration file. Some allow them to assign a maximum lifetime to all connections, others a maximum period of inactivity to all connections.

Note that there is a noticeable difference in scale between the Web and WIMA when it comes to timing out persistent TCP connections. On the Web, busy HTTP servers handle hundreds of thousands or millions of requests per day (e.g, for the Olympic Games [106]); in burst periods, this corresponds to tens or hundreds of requests per second. In NSM, supposing that the network is very unstable and that the manager keeps reconnecting to a critically important agent every minute (worst-case scenario), we still have only one new connection per minute. Moreover, persistent connections are short-lived on the Web; they are typically cleaned up after a maximum of 30 seconds, according to Gettys [122]. Conversely, in WIMA-CM-push, persistent connections are long-lived for regular management: We want the TCP connection between the manager and the agent to persist as long as both ends are up and running, hopefully for days or weeks. We want transient connections only in the case of *ad hoc* management (see WIMA-CM-pull in Section 8.6). So we do not want to set a maximum lifetime on incoming connections: The longer a persistent connection lasts, the better. We therefore recommend to clean up the agent's memory every two hours, that is, to assign a maximum inactivity period of 7,200 seconds. We could optimize this value by making the inactivity timeout value slightly greater than the smallest period of all the push cycles registered with the agent, and updating it whenever the manager changes its subscription. But in practice, the extra functionality does not justify the extra code that must be embedded in the agent to achieve this.

One may argue that cleaning up the agent's memory so rarely makes it vulnerable to DoS attacks based on half-open connections. But the best way to shield an agent from DoS attacks is clearly not to ask it to time out idle HTTP connections very often. It is the task of a firewall to protect internal machines from external attackers; agents have other tasks to fulfill. Without firewalls, DoS attacks can fill up the memory of all critical agents in a matter of seconds. This is independent of WIMA, and even independent of Web-based management.

Timeouts by the agent's dispatcher

If we have little or no control over the configuration of the agent's HTTP server (e.g., if we use an HTTP server with a minimum footprint such as Hong's Embedded Web Server [135]), an alternative is to control the timeout in the dispatcher. But we already mentioned that access to the internals of COTS agents is very unlikely in practice. Unless the dispatcher is downloaded by the administrator into the agent (mobile code), it is preferable to control timeouts in the HTTP server's configuration file.

8.5.3 Synthesis

To conclude with timeouts and reconnections, let us summarize our recommendations and explain what to do when a manager fails to reconnect to an agent. We will also address a special case that we purposefully skipped thus far to simplify the organization of this long section.

Recommended solutions

Per-kernel timeouts are easier to set up than per-socket timeouts, but they do not offer the granularity that we seek (in real-life networks, some agents are more critical than others), and they are inappropriate in the case of heterogeneous environments. So we recommend to use per-socket timeouts.

On the agent side, we should rely on the default settings of the kernel and application because most COTS agents do not let the administrator control their internals (retransmission timer, send timer, etc.). The control of timeouts and reconnections should therefore be achieved by the manager. In most environments (especially those with no hard real-time constraints), we do not need to control timeouts on both sides of the communication pipe simultaneously.

On the manager side, timeouts can be managed at the kernel or application level. Four solutions are appropriate in our context: SO_RCVTIMEO, the trio {TCP_KEEPIDLE, TCP_KEEPINTVL, and TCP_KEEPCNT}, select(), and poll() (with its variant /dev/poll). The first two are slightly better because they need to be installed only once (select() and poll() need to be restarted each time we have processed an incoming read). One issue is that three out of the four solutions require a modern operating system on the manager. In some environments, this is not a problem because the administrator can control what machine to use for the manager; in this case, we recommend using SO_RCVTIMEO or /dev/poll. In other environments, this may cause some problems;

we then recommend using `select()` as long as the expected number of agents within a single management domain does not exceed 400.

Note that different solutions can be combined. For instance, if we do not have a multithreaded operating system on the manager, we can use `SO_RCVTIMEO` to specify per-socket timeouts, and we can block in read on all sockets simultaneously with `select()`, `poll()`, or `/dev/poll`.

Last, there is no need to impose a specific way of timing out idle connections in WIMA-CM-push. This is specific to a given manager and independent of the agents. Within a hierarchy of managers, some managers may use one scheme while others use another. Our recommendations here are destined for developers of component-based management applications. The main goal of this section was to prove the feasibility of our solution (our design decisions do not lead to a dead end), identify the issues, and assess the trade-offs.

Informing operators

Regardless of the technique actually used by the manager to reconnect to the agent, it is important to note that machines (agents) sometimes remain down for long periods of time in real-life environments, possibly several days. It would therefore be very inefficient for the manager to retry indefinitely to reconnect to an agent until this agent eventually comes back to life. A better scenario is to make the collector send an informative alarm to the event correlator as soon as a persistent TCP connection is timed out, then to retry to reconnect twice (which yields a total of three attempts[1]), and in the case of failure, to give up and send a critical alarm to the event correlator. The corresponding event handlers could make the corresponding icon on the network-map GUI turn yellow and red, respectively, for instance. It should be possible for operators to resume the management of an agent from the network-map GUI, e.g., through a context-sensitive pop-up menu. Resuming the management of this agent would involve creating a new persistent TCP connection from the manager to the agent, which would trigger the push scheduler on the agent side.

The collector should also inform the pushed-data analyzer that the agent is considered to be permanently down and is therefore no longer managed. By doing so, the collector informs the pushed-data collector that rules related to that agent should not be executed until further notice.

Write timeouts by the manager

There is one rare case that we have not investigated thus far: write timeouts by the manager (we only studied write timeouts by the agent). The only time the HTTP client can time out a connection while performing a write is immediately after the creation of the TCP connection, when the HTTP client sends its single HTTP `GET` request. If the agent crashes or the network breaks down precisely then, between the creation of the TCP connection and

---

1. This value is indicative. The components making up the management application should allow the number of retries to be configured by the administrator.

the acknowledgment of the HTTP GET request, the write system call issued by the HTTP client times out when the manager's retransmission timer goes off (we already investigated how this timer works in Section 8.5.1.1 and Section 8.5.1.3). The TCP connection is then automatically broken by the kernel. In this case, the HTTP client does nothing else than report a failure to the collector. The reconnection strategy that we recommend to follow is the same as that recommended when an already established TCP connection is timed out by the manager: three retries and two types of alarm.

8.6 HTTP-Based Communication for Pulled Data: WIMA-CM-pull

Now that we have covered in detail the complex case of push-based regular management, let us present the much simpler case of pull-based *ad hoc* management.

In the case of pull, the manager creates a new TCP connection and issues one HTTP GET per retrieved management data (e.g., per SNMP MIB variable or per CIM object). Once the data is retrieved, the TCP connection is torn down by the manager. Everything is initiated from the manager side (creation of the connection and client-server request), so we have no problems with firewalls (no reversed client and server roles). The connection is not persistent, so we need not perform timeouts and reconnections. If a transmission fails, no retry is performed automatically. We let the interactive user (administrator or operator) decide whether a new attempt should be made.

Several data retrieved in a row require the creation of several connections. In the case of SNMP, we cannot retrieve a varbind list (i.e., a vector of MIB variables) with a single HTTP GET, but only one MIB variable. The priority here is to keep the communication model simple, not to make it efficient, because by definition *ad hoc* management occurs rarely (it is normally used for troubleshooting). This design is similar to the way the Web operates today with HTTP/1.0 servers.

The MIME headers that we use in WIMA-CM-pull are the same as those defined in WIMA-CM-push, as depicted in Fig. 36. We use the same content type *application/mgmt*, with the same parameters: *mapping* and *version*. As a result, WIMA-CM-pull is also independent of the information model: We can transfer SNMP data, CIM data, etc.

The syntax of the URLs accessed by the manager follows a very simple rule. On the agent, we have a program called get; it can be implemented as any kind of CLHS (Component Launched by an HTTP Server). This program takes a single argument in input: the identifier of the data that we want to retrieve. In the case of SNMP, this identifier is called oid and corresponds to the OID of the MIB variable. For instance, if the manager wants to retrieve an SNMP MIB variable from MIB-II [173], it issues an HTTP GET request for a URL structured as follows:

```
<http://agent.domain:280/mgmt/subscribe/snmpv1/mib-2/get?oid=A.B.C.D>
```

where `agent.domain` is the fully qualified domain name of the agent (as defined in Section 7.3.2.2), and `A.B.C.D` is the OID of the SNMP MIB variable that the manager wants to retrieve. The header of the agent's reply looks like this:

```
HTTP/1.1 200 OK
Date: Wed, 10 May 2000 02:42:57 GMT
Server: Apache/1.2.4
Last-Modified: Thu, 23 Mar 2000 08:58:33 GMT
Mime-Version: 1.0
Content-Type: "application/mgmt"; mapping="SNMPv2-Trap-to-BER"; version="2"


Data
```

Fig. 36. Pull: HTTP header of the agent's reply

The sole difference with WIMA-CM-push is that we do not use MIME multipart to structure the agent's reply in WIMA-CM-pull.

8.7 Summary

In this chapter, we have presented the second core contribution of this book: WIMA-CM, the communication model of our Web-based integrated management architecture. To begin with, we detailed our main design decisions for push-based regular management: the dissociation between the information and communication models, which allows us to transfer SNMP, CIM, or other management data; the use of persistent TCP connections between the manager and all the agents in its management domain; and the implications of the possible presence of firewalls (reversed client and server roles, and creation of the connections by the manager). Then, we explained why we use HTTP to communicate between the manager and the agent, and how we structure the infinite reply of the agent with MIME multipart. We addressed the issue of urgent notifications and detailed the headers of the different MIME parts. We concluded the push-part of WIMA-CM by studying the tricky and multifaceted problem of timeouts and reconnections, and by making several recommendations. Finally, we presented a much simpler communication model for pull-based *ad hoc* management, where the priority was simplicity rather than efficiency.

Chapter 9

XML in Integrated Management

In the previous chapter, we did not require that the communication model rely on a specific scheme for representing management data. All representation and encoding schemes are allowed in WIMA-CM, including BER-encoded SMI, strings, serialized Java objects, HTML, and XML. In this chapter, we explain why one of them, XML, is better suited than the others for managing IP networks and systems and, more generally, for integrating enterprise management. The main advantages of using XML to represent management data in persistent HTTP/TCP connections lie in its flexibility, its simplicity, and its property of being a standard, ubiquitous technology (as are HTTP and MIME). We show that XML is especially convenient for distributing management, for dealing with multiple information models, and for supporting high-level semantics.

This chapter is organized as follows. In Section 9.1, we analyze why XML is useful in NSM. In Section 9.2, we explain how to use XML for representing management data. In Section 9.3, we describe how to deal with multiple information models with XML. In Section 9.4, we give examples of the higher-level semantics allowed by XML in agent-to-manager and manager-to-manager communication. In Section 9.5, we describe how XML unifies management-data transfers for all enterprise-management types. Finally, we summarize this chapter in Section 9.6.

9.1 Why Use XML in NSM?

The eXtensible Markup Language (XML) has been all over the press since late 1998. Beyond the hype, what is so special about it? And more specifically, what advantages does it bring to NSM?

9.1.1 Overview of XML

XML is a standard developed under the supervision of the World-Wide Web Consortium (W3C). Its building blocks are currently the XML 1.0 specification [35], issued in February 1998, and the Namespaces specification [34], issued in January 1999. XML was initially devised as a document-interchange format for Web publishing. It primarily corrected several flaws in HTML [104, pp. 14–17] and was meant to gradually replace HTML on the Web. But developers of Web browsers have proved to be slow to add support for XML, and the replacement of HTML is not expected to happen anytime soon. In Web publishing, XML complements HTML more than it replaces it, e.g. to represent complex biomolecules or mathematical equations (see CML and MathML in Section 9.1.2).

The main success of XML was not encountered in Web publishing, however. It soon turned out that XML was also good for structuring and unambiguously identifying complex data structures that may never be viewed or printed, but simply exchanged between applications running on distant machines [33]. This explains why XML is successful in software engineering at large, and not simply in the niche market of Web publishing. XML is fast becoming the *lingua franca* between distant applications that do not speak the same languages, are not developed by the same vendors, and do not necessarily run on top of the same middleware, or the same virtual machine, or the same operating system. More and more, the HTTP/XML combination is becoming the standard way to implement a three-tier architecture in the software industry.

Stricto sensu, XML is a metalanguage, that is, a language used to describe other languages. By extension, we call an *XML document* any document expressed in a markup language defined in XML. XML documents have a logical structure (elements) and a physical structure (entities) [104, 33]. Entities can be named, stored separately, and reused to form elements. There are currently two ways of specifying the elements allowed in a particular type of XML document: DTDs (Document Type Definitions [104, 33]) and XML Schemas [86]. The latter are gradually replacing the former. XML documents are normally transferred via HTTP. Information held in XML format is self-describing and allows different viewers to render it differently (as sound, graphics, text, etc.), or different users to customize its rendering by the same viewer.

Readers who are interested in knowing more about XML can find many books on this topic in the literature, including Goldfarb and Prescod [104] for introductory material and Megginson [175] for advanced material. Note that only recent books describe XML Schemas.

9.1.2 Who uses XML?

Although XML is a fairly recent technology, it is already used in many areas. For instance, all major relational databases already support an XML API. The press also regularly reports that the Electronic Data Interchange (EDI) industry is gradually being taken over by XML, which allows for dramatic cost cuts.

XML-based markup languages have already been proposed in many sectors of the industry [284, 30], including the following:

- MathML (Mathematical Markup Language), one of the first markup languages written in XML, already supported by most mathematical software tools
- SMIL (Synchronized Multimedia Integration Language)
- SyncML for data synchronization in mobile communications
- XML-QL (XML Query Language), an SQL-like query language for accessing data repositories
- XML/EDI (XML for Electronic Data Interchange)
- DrawML, VML (Vector Markup Language), SVG (Scalable Vector Graphics), and PGML (Precision Graphics Markup Language) for 2D graphics
- HGML (HyperGraphics Markup Language) for wireless access to graphical data
- SDML (Signed Document Markup Language)
- DSML (Directory Services Markup Language)
- cXML (commerce XML) for business-to-business electronic commerce
- CML (Chemical Markup Language) and BIOML (Biopolymer Markup Language) in the chemical industry
- VoxML (Voice Markup Language) for voice applications
- MusicML (Music Markup Language), a set of labels for notes, beats, and rests that allows compositions to be stored as text but displayed as sheet music by Web browsers
- AML (Astronomical Markup Language) and AIML (Astronomical Instrument Markup Language) in astronomy
- OFX (Open Financial Exchange) and tpaML (Trading Partner Agreement Markup Language) in the finance industry

9.1.3 Advantages of using XML in general

How could XML become so pervasive in so many different areas and in such a short time? The main advantages of using it in the software industry at large (that is, not specifically in NSM) are fivefold.

First, XML is easy to learn. Familiarity with CORBA, J2EE, or DCOM platforms and technologies requires about half a year of training and practice, whereas XML requires only a few weeks. The reason is that XML is considerably less elaborate and sophisticated, hence easier to understand and become familiar with.

Second, XML is very inexpensive because many XML parsers and editors are already available for free [276]. Middleware platforms, conversely, are generally fairly expensive, especially those supporting CORBA and J2EE. The few existing CORBA platforms that are both feature rich and free are rarely used in industry for maintenance reasons.

Third, XML allows software developers to use the same technology everywhere, whatever the application domain. This results in significant cost savings for software-development project managers. In this respect, XML is as successful as HTTP, Web browsers, and Java applets before it.

Fourth, XML documents are human readable, and not simply machine readable (unlike BER-encoded documents, for instance). This simplifies debugging significantly.

Fifth, because it is so easy to learn, simple to use, and inexpensive, the industry has adopted it as *the* way to interface with legacy systems. This feature is particularly useful when two companies A and B merge: There has to be an old application somewhere (e.g., a proprietary database) in company A that cannot be ported to a modern system at a reasonable cost, or within a reasonable time, but still has to communicate with its counterpart in company B. XML is suitable for that.

9.1.4 Advantages of using XML in NSM

As XML is becoming ubiquitous, the number of people who are familiar with it is growing fast. It therefore makes sense to capitalize on this know-how in NSM as well. But beyond this sole reusability of technical expertise, and beyond the general-purpose advantages of XML listed above, XML also exhibits several advantages that are specific to NSM. We identified five that could soon make XML become the *lingua franca* in NSM.

A truce in the middleware war

The first and foremost strength of XML in NSM is that it brings a truce to the middleware war. Object-oriented DPEs such as CORBA, Java, or DCOM cause a number of problems that we summarized in a catchphrase introduced in Section 5.4: *my-middleware-is-better-than-yours*. Compared to these DPEs, XML keeps a low profile. It does not offer a full-blown, object-oriented DPE. Instead, when combined with HTTP, it offers a lightweight, inexpensive way of exchanging structured data between distant applications. Both XML and HTTP/1.0 are lightweight, ubiquitous, and inexpensive[1], and combining the two offers a very appealing solution to transfer management data in the IP world.

In short, the HTTP/XML combination is an efficient cure against the *my-middleware-is-better-than-yours* syndrome.

Right kind of semantics for NSM

Before the days of Web-based management, NSM was struggling between two extremes: the poor semantics of SNMP MIBs, which is partly due to the poor expressiveness of SMI, and the torments of the *my-middleware-is-better-than-yours* syndrome. HTTP/XML-based distribution allows for the right kind of semantics in NSM: low enough compared to full-blown, object-oriented DPEs, and high enough compared to mere strings or BER-encoded SMI data.

When the edges (agent and manager) are object oriented, HTTP/XML, viewed as middleware for distribution, is more general-purpose than Java, CORBA, or DCOM. In particular, we will see in Section 9.4.4 that XML makes it possible to mimic object-oriented

---

1. HTTP/1.1 is also ubiquitous and inexpensive, but it does not qualify as "lightweight".

distribution by transferring state as XML data and by allowing the manager to invoke methods on remote objects running on the agent, provided that the manager knows the object naming scheme used by the agent.

Low footprint on agents

The third advantage of using XML in NSM is that it has a reasonably low footprint on agents. This is of paramount importance in the IP world, as we saw in Section 5.4. CORBA has a large footprint, so has DCOM, which makes them inadequate for managing certain devices and systems. As for Java, J2ME (Java 2 Micro Edition) has a small footprint, J2SE (Java 2 Standard Edition) has a medium footprint, and J2EE (Java 2 Enterprise Edition) has a large footprint on agents. This advantage in NSM is a direct consequence of HTTP/XML being low-profile middleware.

Mobile code

Fourth, XML supports simple forms of mobile code such as remote evaluation and code on demand (defined in Section 4.1.3.1). For instance, a script can be transferred from a manager to an agent (or from a top-level manager to a mid-level manager in distributed hierarchical management) between `<script>` and `</script>` tags, and attributes can convey metadata such as the name and version of the scripting language. This enables administrators to smoothly integrate weakly and strongly distributed hierarchical management paradigms over time, as agents get smarter and can bear an increasing proportion of the management-application processing. This advantage is very important for the next management cycle: It leaves a door open for the future, once the security issues inherent to mobile code are better understood and addressed. XML's support for simple forms of mobile code is also part of the "right kind of semantics" mentioned earlier.

Dealing with the heterogeneity of information models

Last, XML copes with the heterogeneity of the information models: SNMP, CIM, OSI, etc. We mentioned this in Chapter 8 and will devote Section 9.3 entirely to this issue.

9.1.5 Advantages of using XML in integrated management

XML has the potential to become the *lingua franca* not only in NSM, but also in integrated management at large. Indeed, XML can be used for all enterprise-management types: network management, systems management, application management, service management, policy-based management, etc. The HTTP/XML combination is a true enabler of the so-called "global enterprise management" vision that marketing people have been trumpeting for years. XML is not a representation scheme dedicated to a specific management function: It is a general-purpose means of representing self-describing data. In the IP world, we have never been so close to integrating management. We will come back to this in Section 9.5.

Note that WIMA is not the sole management architecture leveraging HTTP/XML: So does the DMTF's WBEM architecture, since the proprietary HMMP protocol initially envisioned was dropped in favor of the standard HTTP and XML technologies.

9.1.6 Disadvantages of using XML in general

Before ending this section, it is important to balance the advantages of XML listed so far with its well-known disadvantages, and to investigate the impact of the latter on NSM.

First, XML is verbose. XML documents are undoubtedly longer than their SNMP counterparts consisting of BER-encoded MIB data. This verbosity calls for compression, as we advocate in WIMA. In our experience, compressed XML documents cause a reasonable network overhead.

Second, XML elements and entities are so simple to create that vendors lack incentive to comply with standards (i.e., with DTDs and XML Schemas defined by the IETF, DMTF, etc.). It is possible that, in the future, standardization efforts in information modeling will eventually fall apart, and that vendors of management platforms will prefer to write gateways translating vendor-specific ontologies into their own ontology. This important issue, currently considered (among others) by the IRTF Network Management Research Group, goes far beyond the scope of this book. Like many others, the author hopes that customers will demand that vendors comply with standards.

Third, validating an XML document takes time and consumes both CPU and memory resources. This is acceptable in NSM, provided that validation is not imposed by management platforms, and that administrators can choose when and where they want managers (or even agents) to validate incoming XML documents.

9.2 XML for Representing Management Data: Model- and Metamodel-Level Mappings

Once an NSM information modeler has decided to use XML to represent management data, the very first problem he/she is faced with is the way SNMP MIB variables or CIM objects[1] should be mapped to XML. There are basically two ways of representing management data in XML: at the model and metamodel levels. In DMTF parlance, these are respectively called the schema and metaschema mappings. So far, this important issue has been only briefly touched upon by the DMTF in a slightly cryptic style [76 p. 6, 73 pp. 9–10] and has been eluded by the IETF. In this section, we strive to clarify the strengths and weaknesses of these two different approaches, which are both allowed in WIMA and present different advantages.

---

1. As we have pointed out several times already, WIMA is independent of the information model. For the sake of readability, we only mention SNMP MIBs and CIM schemas in this chapter.

9.2.1 Model-level mapping

A model-level mapping is one in which the DTD or XML Schema is specific to a particular SNMP MIB (set of MIB variables), CIM schema (set of CIM classes), or what we generically call a virtual management-data repository. The XML elements and attributes defined in the DTD or XML Schema bear the same names as the SNMP MIB variables (OIDs) or the CIM classes, properties, etc. A simple example of model-level mapping is the following:

```
<interface>
<bandwidth type="string">100 Mbit/s</bandwidth>
</interface>
```

9.2.1.1 Strengths of model-level mapping

The main advantage of a model-level mapping is that the DTDs, the XML Schemas, and the XML documents complying with them are all easy for people to read. They resemble the examples typically found in beginner's guides to XML, with a nice and intuitive containment hierarchy. They are also simple to parse and render graphically (e.g., with a Web browser).

Another important advantage is what the DMTF calls the *validation power*: Validating XML parsers can perform in-depth checks (e.g., type checking) on XML documents. This is particularly relevant to organizations who demand robust management applications.

9.2.1.2 Weaknesses of model-level mapping

The main disadvantage of a model-level mapping is that we need many DTDs or XML Schemas: one per SNMP MIB or CIM schema. This can be a problem for agents that are resource constrained but support many SNMP MIBs and CIM schemas. This is not a problem on the manager side, however, as we can easily increase the amount of memory of the management server if need be.

Another weakness is that the translation from SMI definitions for SNMP MIBs, or from Managed Object Format (MOF) definitions for CIM schemas, to XML is not easy to automate, because the logics of hierarchical containment of XML elements does not always directly map onto the logics of containment of SMI, MOF, etc.

A third problem, specific to CIM (which is object oriented), is the possible explosion of the namespace on the agent side if we define too many classes. Dealing with a large namespace on the manager side, on the other hand, is acceptable.

Last, whenever an SNMP MIB or a CIM schema is updated, a new DTD or XML Schema needs to be released and deployed. Updating all deployed managers and agents with these new releases causes some overhead.

9.2.1.3 Example: SNMP-MIB-to-XML mapping

Let us illustrate the concept of model-level mapping by considering a simple example in the SNMP realm: the mapping of MIB-II to XML. MIB-II [173] is *the* standard SNMP MIB, and is supported by almost all SNMP-aware network devices and systems. For the sake of conciseness, let us consider only the Interfaces Group in MIB-II (given in Appendix A). Fig. 37 shows a DTD for this Interfaces Group[1]. Fig. 38 gives an example of XML document that complies with this DTD. To keep these figures reasonably small, we do not represent metadata related to access control, description, etc.

```
<!-- Parameter entities -->
<!ENTITY % statusValues "(up | down | testing)">
<!ENTITY % octetsTable "(unicastPackets?, nonUnicastPackets?, discards?, errors?)">
<!-- We only consider the Interfaces Group here -->
<!ELEMENT mib-2 (interfacesGroup?)>
<!ELEMENT interfacesGroup (numberOfInterfaces?, interfacesTable?)>
<!ELEMENT numberOfInterfaces (#PCDATA)>
<!ELEMENT interfacesTable (interface+)>
<!ELEMENT interface (description?, type?, mtu?, speed?, physicalAddress, status?, lastChange?,
inOctets?, outOctets?, specific?)>
<!ATTLIST interface index (#PCDATA) #REQUIRED>
<!ELEMENT description (#PCDATA)>
<!-- Valid types are specified by RFC1213. To keep this example simple, accept any string of characters-->
<!ELEMENT type (#PCDATA)>
<!ELEMENT mtu (#PCDATA)>
<!ELEMENT speed (#PCDATA)>
<!ELEMENT physicalAddress (#PCDATA)>
<!ELEMENT status EMPTY>
<!ATTLIST status administrative %statusValues; operational %statusValues;>
<!ELEMENT lastChange (#PCDATA)>
<!-- Use a parameter entity for inOctets and outOctets -->
<!ELEMENT - - inOctets (%octetsTable;?, unknownProtocols?)>
<!ELEMENT unicastPackets (#PCDATA)>
<!ELEMENT nonUnicastPackets (#PCDATA)>
<!ELEMENT discards (#PCDATA)>
<!ELEMENT errors (#PCDATA)>
<!ELEMENT unknownProtocols (#PCDATA)>
<!ELEMENT - - outOctets (%octetsTable;?, queueLength?)>
<!ELEMENT queueLength (#PCDATA)>
<!ELEMENT specific (#PCDATA)>
```

Fig. 37. Model-level XML mapping of the Interfaces Group in SNMP MIB-II: DTD

The definition of the MIB-II Interfaces Group is written in SMIv1. If we translate these SMI definitions into XML, several transformations are natural because we do not want XML documents to be tweaked by SMI idiosyncrasies, such as the impossibility of having

---

1. We do not claim that this DTD is the best for this example. As usual with XML, there is often a thin line between an element and an attribute, so several DTDs would make sense for the MIB-II Interfaces Group.

nested tables. For instance, four MIB variables are identical for inbound and outbound octets: the number of unicast packets, the number of non-unicast packets, the number of discards, and the number of errors. Rather than duplicating them as in MIB-II, it makes sense to group them in the DTD into a single parameter entity (octetsTable). Another example is the similarity between the administrative status and the operational status. These two MIB variables are closely related, have identical semantics, and can take only three valid values. It therefore makes sense to create a single element (status) with two optional attributes (administrative and operational) and a single set of attributes stored in a parameter entity (statusValues). By making such transformations, we get a DTD that is easy to read for a human (see Fig. 37), and XML documents complying with this DTD are also easy to read (see Fig. 38).

```
<?xml version="1.0" encoding="UTF-8"?>
<!DOCTYPE SNMP-MIB-II-INTERFACES-GROUP SYSTEM "snmp-rfc1213-excerpt.dtd">
<push cycle="4567" localTime="Fri, 7 Jul 2000 10:55:05 +0200" frequency="600">
 <mib-2 oid="1.3.6.1.2.1">
  <interfacesGroup>
   <interfacesTable>
    <interface index="1">
     <status administrative="up" operational="up"/>
     <inOctets>
      <unicastPackets>
       80000
      </unicastPackets>
      <errors>
       12
      </errors>
     </inOctets>
    </interface>
   </interfacesTable>
  </interfacesGroup>
 </mib-2>
</push>
```

Fig. 38. Model-level XML mapping of the Interfaces Group in SNMP MIB-II:
example of XML document

Note that all the XML elements in Fig. 37 are optional (this is denoted by the question marks in the DTD), except interface and index, which are obviously mandatory. This allows a manager or an agent to transfer any number of MIB variables within a single XML document.

In Fig. 38, we consider the example of data pushed by an agent. This XML document complies with the DTD specified in Fig. 37. In this example, the administrator subscribed the manager for the administrative and operational statuses of the agent's interface #1, as well as the number of inbound unicast packets and the number of inbound errors (for more details about the semantics, see Appendix A).

9.2.1.4 Example: CIM-schema-to-XML mapping

In the WBEM/CIM realm, let us consider a simple schema consisting of a single CIM class. This class is defined in Appendix C and comes from a DMTF white paper [73]. We will use the same class in Section 9.2.2.4 when we consider metamodel-level mappings. An example of model-level mapping of this CIM class is given in Fig. 39.

We see that the class name and property names explicitly appear in the DTD and XML document. We also notice that the XML document is fairly concise and its structure is very simple to understand.

```
<!ELEMENT class (caption, description, installDate, name)>
<!ATTLIST class className (#PCDATA) #REQUIRED status (OK | Error | Degraded | Unknown)>
<!ELEMENT caption (#PCDATA)>
<!ATTLIST caption type="string" #FIXED maxlen="64" #FIXED>
<!ELEMENT description (#PCDATA)>
<!ATTLIST description type="string" #FIXED>
<!ELEMENT installDate (#PCDATA)>
<!ATTLIST installDate type="datetime" #FIXED>
<!ELEMENT name (#PCDATA)>
<!ATTLIST name type="string" #FIXED>
```

(a) DTD

```
<?xml version="1.0" encoding="UTF-8"?>
<!DOCTYPE  SIMPLE-CIM-CLASS  SYSTEM  "simple-cim-class.dtd">
<cimclass  classname="CIM_ManagedSystemElement"  status="OK">
  <caption maxlen="64">
    This is my caption
  </caption>
  <description>
    This is my description
  </description>
  <installDate>
    "Fri, 7 Jul 2000 10:55:05 +0200"
  </installDate>
  <name>
    This is my name
  </name>
</cimclass>
```

(b) Example of XML document

Fig. 39. Model-level XML mapping of a simple CIM class

9.2.2 Metamodel-level mapping

A metamodel-level mapping is one in which the DTD is generic and identical for all SNMP MIBs, all CIM schemas, or more generically all the virtual management-data repositories specified with the same metamodel. In other words, there is only one DTD per metamodel (SMIv1, SMIv2, CIM metaschema, etc.). The XML elements and attributes in the DTD bear generic names such as *class*, *property*, *operation*, and more generally all the keywords defined by the metamodel. With a metamodel-level mapping, the simple example presented at the beginning of Section 9.2.1 becomes:

```
<class name="interface"
<property name="bandwidth" type="string">
<value>100 Mbit/s</value>
</property>
</class>
```

9.2.2.1 Strengths of a metamodel-level mapping

The main advantage of a metamodel-level mapping is simplicity. A single DTD or a single XML Schema allows us to deal with all SNMP MIBs or CIM schemas, and all the past and future releases of a given SNMP MIB or CIM schema.

Another strength is that the translation of SMI definitions for SNMP MIBs, or MOF definitions for CIM schemas, to XML is straightforward to automate. This makes it easy to write external or internal management gateways for legacy systems. This is an important factor during the migration phase from SNMP- to CIM-based management (or from SNMP- to WIMA-based management, see Section 7.3.6 and Section 7.4.4).

A third advantage is that by having a single DTD (or a single XML Schema) for all SNMP MIBs (or all CIM schemas), we reduce the overhead for the agent[1]. In particular, for CIM, the memory footprint of the namespace is guaranteed to remain reasonably small because the number of metamodels supported by an agent is always limited (usually one or two).

Last, a metamodel-level mapping guarantees forward and backward compatibility for generic XML tools. Forward compatibility is a rare feature, which is precious to both vendors and customers.

9.2.2.2 Weaknesses of a metamodel-level mapping

The main disadvantage of a metamodel-level mapping is that the DTDs are difficult (sometimes *very* difficult) for humans to read and can only reasonably be interpreted by machines. This makes debugging cumbersome. Graphical rendering is also more complex and less user-friendly.

Another important problem is validation. With metamodel-level mappings, XML parsers can only do very basic validation because they operate at a level of abstraction where they see classes, properties, method names, and all sorts of very generic elements. This makes it easy for a manager or an agent to send a valid but nonsensical XML document.

---

1. We also reduce it for the manager, but this issue is less important for the manager, as we mentioned already in Section 9.2.1.2.

Another weakness of a metamodel-level mapping is that XML documents are significantly more verbose than with a model-level mapping. We will illustrate this in the next two examples. A metamodel-level mapping increases network overhead (XML documents are significantly longer) and slightly increases latency (especially parsing, marshaling, and unmarshaling time).

9.2.2.3 Example: SMI-to-XML mapping

In the case of SNMP, two examples of SMI-to-XML mappings can be found in the literature. The first was published by John *et al.* in 1999 [132]. The DTD that they propose for SMIv2 is very basic and consists only of ELEMENT definitions (no entities, no attributes, not even for constant strings). To be fair to the authors, this DTD was not the central part of their work, which focused on the specification of an XML-based management architecture that supports dynamically modifiable MIBs.

The second example is a comprehensive SMI-to-XML mapping issued in 2000 by Schönwälder and Strauss [226]. In their Internet-Draft, they propose a way to use XML to exchange SMIv1, SMIv2, and SMIng module definitions (that is, descriptions of SNMP MIB variables) between XML-enabled applications. The DTD specified in their Internet-Draft was integrated into the SimpleWeb IETF MIB converter [234] maintained by the University of Twente, The Netherlands. The resulting representation of the MIB-II Interfaces Group in XML is available in Appendix B. The Interfaces Group alone takes 10 pages, which gives a clear indication of the verbosity of this type of mapping. We can also see that a lot of information is duplicated, just as in MIB-II, e.g. the values that the administrative and operational statuses can take, or the managed objects that are similar for inbound and outbound traffic. This XML document was generated automatically and almost instantaneously by the SimpleWeb converter, which demonstrates how easy it is for a machine to translate SMI into XML.

9.2.2.4 Example: CIM-metaschema-to-XML mapping

In the case of CIM, many examples of metaschema mappings are available from the DMTF. In Appendix C, we reproduce an example of CIM-to-XML mapping done at the metamodel level. This example comes from a DMTF white paper. We notice immediately that the readability of this XML document is quite poor for a human. It takes some time to get accustomed to the extra level of indirection caused by the metamodel-level mapping, which makes debugging rather difficult. We also see how limited validation is with this type of mapping. Finally, it is obvious that this XML document can be generated automatically by a CIM-aware agent.

9.2.3 Comparison between model- and metamodel-level mappings

First, if we compare Appendix B with Fig. 38 (MIB-II Interfaces Group) and Appendix C with Fig. 39 (simple CIM class), we see immediately that XML documents complying with a metamodel-level mapping are less readable and more verbose than XML documents complying with a model-level mapping. This is not simply due to the fact that the two mappings in Appendix B and Appendix C are more detailed and comprehensive, but rather to the very nature of these two types of mapping.

Second, if we analyze Schönwälder and Strauss's DTD [226] and compare it with our partial DTD listed in Fig. 37, we also clearly see that the former is hampered by SMI idiosyncrasies; e.g., columnar objects are mapped to column XML elements. Although this makes automated translation very easy, it significantly hinders human understanding and generates a non-intuitive containment hierarchy of XML elements. In our view, the containment hierarchy proposed in Fig. 37 is more natural and easier to understand.

Third, model- and metamodel-level mappings both allow for the dynamic discovery of properties and methods through a mechanism known as introspection in object-oriented programming. As we will see in Section 9.4.4, CIM offers native support for introspection. This feature is very useful because, in real life, virtual management-data repositories (CIM schemas) change over time, or are subclassed by management-application developers.

In short, model- and metamodel-level mappings both have their advantages and disadvantages. We cannot conclude that one is always superior to the other, so both are allowed in WIMA. The choice between these two types of mapping is necessarily a trade-off, and depends on the criteria that are of most importance to the management-application designer. These criteria are often site specific. In this chapter, we identified eight:

- readability of the XML document for a human (vs. a machine)
- verbosity vs. conciseness of the XML document
- automated translation to XML by a management gateway
- validation power
- footprint of one DTD vs. numerous DTDs on agents
- deployment of one DTD vs. numerous DTDs
- memory footprint of the namespace on agents
- forward compatibility of generic XML tools.

9.3 XML for Dealing with Multiple Information Models

In Section 8.4.3, we explained that management data in transfer (that is, when it is not stored as in-memory data structures by the agent or the manager) can be represented in many ways in WIMA: not only XML, but also HTML, plain strings, BER-encoded SMI, serialized Java objects, etc. Because management data encoded in XML documents is self-describing, XML is particularly suitable for coping with multiple information models.

In the example depicted in Fig. 40, we have two management domains. In the left domain, `mid-level manager #1` and all the agents support the SNMP information model; in the right domain, `mid-level manager #2` and all the agents support the CIM information model. (For the sake of readability, the agents are not represented on Fig. 40.) The administrator needs to integrate management data coming from these two domains (e.g., to work out the root cause of problems occurring at the boundary of these domains, or to perform global statistics on the collected data). Let us denote by XYZ the information model that the administrator has decided to adopt to integrate management data. By definition, XYZ is site specific.

Translator components are in charge of converting specific information models (SNMP and CIM in our example) into XYZ. These components can be integrated into the management server of each mid-level manager, or can run on a separate machine. The communication between the event translators (respectively, the pushed-data translators) and the notification/event filters (respectively, the pushed-data analyzers) can rely on HTTP/XML, especially if the translators run on a separate machine; they can also use another, more efficient interprocess mechanism (e.g., shared memory) for scalability reasons, provided that the components run on the same machine. These two alternatives are depicted by the string "??XML??" on Fig. 40. As for the communication between the event translators (respectively the pushed-data translators) and the XYZ event correlator (respectively the XYZ data repository), it relies on HTTP/XML.

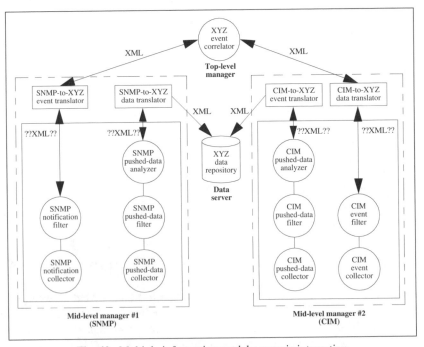

Fig. 40. Multiple information models: generic integration

The issue of translating from one information model into another for the purpose of integration is complex and has been dealt with by other authors, especially Mazumdar [165, 166, 167] and Rivière [213, 214].

The approach we just described is called *generic integration*. Whatever XYZ, whatever the information model used within a management domain, we always go via translators for both events and data. The main advantage of this solution is that the support for a new information model simply requires that new translators be written, which is elegant in terms of design. The main problem is that, because XYZ is likely to be one of the information models already used by one of the mid-level managers (SNMP or CIM in our example), we are unnecessarily inefficient for this information model: Going through a level of indirection unnecessarily adds some latency.

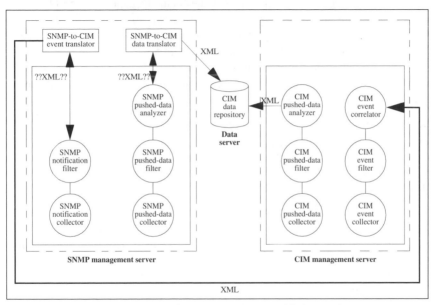

Fig. 41. Multiple information models: specific integration

This problem can be solved by resorting to *specific integration* (see example depicted in Fig. 41)[1]. This time, we no longer have translators on all mid-level managers, nor an external event correlator. Instead, the administrator chooses his/her preferred information model (in our example, CIM) and runs translators only on the mid-level managers that support another information model (in our example, the SNMP management server). The main advantage of this solution is that it is globally more efficient than the previous. The chief disadvantage is that it is less generic. If the administrator decides to change his/her preferred information model (e.g., after the merger of his/her company with another),

---

1. There are many other variants not described here. One of them consists in translating all events and pushed data and storing them in an enterprise-specific format that is independent of SNMP and CIM (e.g., as table entries in a relational database).

specific integration requires significantly more work than generic integration. As usual in the software industry, there is a trade-off between modularity and efficiency. As this decision is inherently site specific, one could expect that component-software developers implement both solutions and let the administrator decide whether efficiency should prevail over design modularity, or *vice versa*.

9.4 XML for High-Level Semantics

In NSM, the level of semantics and the expressiveness of management data are closely related. The level of semantics depends on the abstractions modeled in the virtual management-data repository (SNMP MIB or CIM schema). It is a characteristic of the model. Conversely, the level of expressiveness lies in the metamodel. A highly expressive metamodel gives the information modeler ample latitude to define abstractions that are useful to the administrator. A poorly expressive metamodel would, for instance, only allow for integers and strings, thereby seriously constraining the definition of appropriate abstractions. A high-level semantics in the model demands a high expressiveness of the metamodel. Of course, a highly expressive metamodel does not necessarily lead to a semantically rich model: It depends on the information modelers' skills.

By extension, the semantic richness often designates both of these characteristics. To simplify things, we will therefore say that high-level semantics allow an information modeler to "think" and manipulate abstractions as a human typically does, whereas low-level semantics force him/her to go down to an abstraction level that is more cumbersome to a human: the nuts and bolts of IT and networking, so to speak.

WIMA/XML supports much richer semantics than that offered by SNMP and SMI. It renders easy many tasks that are not so simple in SNMP-based management. We will give three examples in this section: the transfer of an entire MIB table in one bulk, the suppression of "holes" in sparse tables, and the transfer of an entire time series in one bulk. Beyond SNMP, WIMA/XML is also well suited to object-oriented agents and managers. In our last example, we will describe the remote invocation of a method encapsulated by a remote object.

9.4.1 Transfer of an entire SNMP MIB table

In Section 3.3.1.2 and Section 3.3.1.3, we studied the problems caused by the small maximum size of an SNMP message and the difficulty to transfer MIB tables efficiently via the SNMP protocol (when building a request message, the manager must guess the size of the agent's response). In WIMA in general, and in XML in particular, we have no limit on the maximum size of an HTTP message: An XML document can be *a priori* infinitely large. This allows the agent to push an entire MIB table (or even an entire MIB) in one bulk. In Section 9.2.1.3, we already gave an example of XML document showing how to transfer a part of, or the whole of, MIB-II.

9.4.2 Suppression of "holes" in sparse SNMP tables

In Section 3.3.1.3, we also described the problems caused by the possible presence of "holes" in sparse SNMP tables. With XML, it is very simple to remove these "holes" altogether, thereby relieving the management server from doing the extra computations required to check for the presence of these "holes" and to get rid of them. To do so, we propose to use a new attribute (`errorCode`) and replace the "hole" with an error code, typically `noSuchInstance` in the case of sparse SNMP tables:

```
<value errorCode="noSuchInstance">
</value>
```

The possible values of `errorCode` are specific to a given information model (SNMPv1, v2c, or v3 in the above example). A validating XML parser can check the value assigned to `errorCode` against the information model specified in the header of the XML document.

9.4.3 Time series of a MIB variable

In SMI, there is no provision for time series. As a result, there is no simple means in SNMP to store and retrieve an entire time series for a single managed object, such as the inbound error rate of interface #1 sampled every 10 minutes over a period of 24 hours. This is a problem for offline statistical analysis of SNMP data, which typically works on time series. Today, this type of analysis requires administrators to reconstruct time series from the collected data, e.g. in the form of temporal MIBs [12]. Another problem is that some SNMP data can be lost, e.g. due to buffer overflows. This leads to "holes" in the reconstructed time series, and these "holes" are sometimes awkward to deal with. For instance, if we build a time series for per-interface inbound traffic, what do linear or quadratic interpolations lead to in the case of bursty traffic? And does it make sense to interpolate the missing value of an error rate?

This problem is easy to solve in WIMA: Time series can be stored at the agent and transferred in one bulk via HTTP/XML. Storing time series at the agent is easy because they usually take up little space when stored as in-memory data structures. For instance, a gauge and a timestamp stored as 32-bit integers each require four bytes of memory. Sampled every 10 minutes over a period of 24 hours, such a MIB variable would generate a time series with the following memory footprint on the agent:

$$(4 + 4) * (60 / 10) * 24 = 1,152 \text{ bytes}$$

For many agents, such a small overhead is negligible, and dozens (sometimes hundreds) of such time series could easily be stored locally. The advantage of storing a time series at the agent is that the agent can then push an entire time series once a day, in bulk. This is useful because during this operation, the agent can carefully retransmit data if need be, and can even retry an hour later. This makes data transfers very resilient. Another case when this can be particularly useful is when the agent is disconnected from the manager for extended periods of time, because it is switched off for several hours in a row (e.g., a desktop PC or a mobile phone[1]), because it is in a mountainous area not covered by any antenna (e.g., a mobile phone or a roaming PC), etc. Clearly, there is a trade-off between keeping time series in volatile memory, where they take few resources but may be lost in case the agent crashes, and keeping them in persistent storage (e.g., EPROM) where they use up more resources but survive a crash.

When the data is stored at the agent, it can be transferred via XML in a simple way, as depicted in Fig. 42. For the sake of readability, we assume here that the first timestamp occurs at time t_0 and we only represent the first four values and the last; intermediate values are replaced with the string " [. . .] ".

Note that the usefulness of time series is not limited to agent-manager interactions. They can also be beneficial in distributed hierarchical management, when mid-level managers are required to push daily statistics to the top-level manager. For instance, the top-level manager might want to be informed by each mid-level manager of the number of serious events handled by its event correlator every 15 minutes, over a period of 24 hours. QoS management is another typical example: It is interesting for the top-level manager to get time series of the number of bandwidth reservations that could not be honored by the boundary routers of each management domain.

```
<?xml version="1.0" encoding="UTF-8"?>
<!DOCTYPE  SNMP-MIB-II-INTERFACES-GROUP  SYSTEM  "snmp-rfc1213-excerpt.dtd">
<push cycle="4567" localTime="Fri, 7 Jul 2000 10:55:05 +0200" frequency="86400">
 <mib-2 oid="1.3.6.1.2.1">
  <interfacesGroup>
   <interfacesTable>
    <interface index="1">
     <inOctets>
      <unicastPackets>
       <value "timestamp"0">81000</value>
       <value "timestamp"600">65000</value>
       <value "timestamp"1200">73000</value>
       <value "timestamp"1800">70000</value>

       [...]

       <value "timestamp"85800">100000</value>
      </unicastPackets>
     </inOctets>
    </interface>
   </interfacesTable>
  </interfacesGroup>
 </mib-2>
</push>
```

Fig. 42. Time series with XML

---

1. Also known as a *cell phone*.

9.4.4 Distributed object-oriented programming with XML

For object-oriented information models (e.g., for CIM), XML elements and entities can be used to implement simple forms of object serialization and remote method invocation, thereby offering an ersatz of distributed object-oriented programming.

Serialization

The serialization of objects running at the edges of the persistent HTTP/TCP connection (that is, the agent or the manager) must deal with both state and behavior. The serialization of an object state is straightforward. The state variables (or *properties* in DMTF parlance) are translated into XML elements and entities, as already described. The serialization of an object behavior (or *methods* in DMTF parlance) can be more complex. It is easy to achieve when the methods are implemented with scripting languages (see the support for mobile code described in Section 9.1.4, with the proposed tags <script> and </script>). Otherwise, the entire object (including both state and behavior) must be serialized, and transferred within an XML document as opaque binary data. This technique enables the transfer of processor-independent Java objects, processor-specific C++ objects, etc. But because the internal structure of the transferred object is then completely invisible, XML parsers cannot validate the data, and humans can neither read nor debug the objects in transit.

Remote method invocation

An example of remote invocation of object methods in XML can be found in the DMTF's specification for CIM operations over HTTP [77]. The DMTF's model is reasonably simple and can be generalized to almost any object-oriented information model. The CIM DTD [75] defines two elements: <METHODCALL> for invoking a method on a remote object, and <METHODRESPONSE> for receiving the response of this method call. These two elements are hierarchically contained in an operation element. A simple operation can contain a single method call or response. Two elements are defined by the CIM DTD for simple operations: <SIMPLEREQ> for the request and <SIMPLERSP> for the response. A multiple operation, on the other hand, allows multiple method invocations to be grouped together, thereby reducing the number of messages exchanged between the manager and the agent. In the CIM DTD, the corresponding elements are <MULTIREQ> and <MULTIRSP>. An example of method invocation including a complete request and a complete response is given in Appendix D.

The DMTF's specification for CIM operations over HTTP also supports some kind of introspection (via *intrinsic methods*) for discovering dynamically the subclasses of a CIM class (EnumerateClasses), the instances of a CIM class (EnumerateInstances), the CIM objects that are associated with a specific CIM object (Associators), etc. Extra metadata is available via *qualifiers*.

This example demonstrates that although XML does not directly support remote method invocation in the way CORBA or Java RMI do, it does provide the means of encoding method invocation and passing parameters, and of checking the type of each parameter at invocation time. Thus, with XML, it is possible to cleanly trigger an action on a distant agent or manager. There is no need to resort to SNMP's ugly programming by side effect (see Section 3.3.2.2).

In summary, XML nicely interfaces with object-oriented information models, which offer high-level semantics to management-applications designers—higher than data-oriented information models such as SNMP's. By using HTTP and XML, we do not incur the problems of object-oriented DPEs, and we have a simple, yet sufficient for all NSM purposes, way of interacting with objects at the edges. In other words, we get the best of both the object-oriented and non-object-oriented worlds.

9.5 XML for Integrated Management: a Unified Communication Model

Although WIMA allows for many data representation schemes, unifying the communication model around a single scheme brings at least three advantages: all management data is in the same format (configuration files, performance statistics, policies, etc.); we no longer have to translate between different representation schemes; and we can directly store XML data in the data server for offline processing or archival.

For all these reasons, other representation schemes should preferably be reserved for interfacing with legacy systems (e.g., it makes a vendor's life easier to encode SNMP data in BER during the transition phase) or for debugging (e.g., clear-text strings), but new WIMA-compliant management servers and agents should preferably support XML natively[1].

In Section 9.1.5, we claimed that we have never been so close to integrating management in the IP world, now that we have the powerful combination of HTTP and XML. Let us illustrate this with an example, and demonstrate the advantages of having a unified communication model for integrating enterprise management.

In the hierarchical tree depicted in Fig. 43, we use the same communication model between all devices and systems: HTTP, MIME multipart, and MIME parts consisting of XML documents. In this example, we have two management domains—a situation typically encountered by geographically dispersed enterprises. Each management domain is supervised by a mid-level 1 manager. For the domain on the left, the mid-level 1 manager is directly in charge of the agents. With agent 1 (e.g., a large file server with multiple interfaces), the mid-level 1 manager performs both network and systems management tasks. With agent 2 (e.g., a mere hub), it only performs network management. For the management domain on the right, the mid-level 1 manager delegates network management

---

1. Still, WIMA does not make it *mandatory* to use XML.

to one mid-level 2 manager and systems management to another mid-level 2 manager. Unlike its counterpart on the left, the right mid-level 1 manager does not directly interact with the agents in its domain: only the mid-level 2 managers do. For all these interactions, we use the same communication model based on HTTP/MIME/XML.

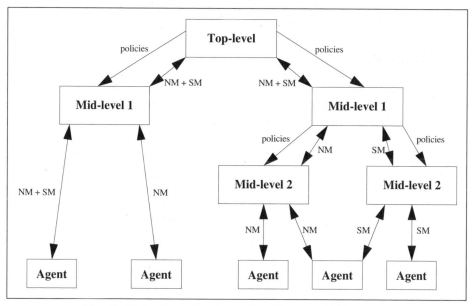

Fig. 43. XML: Hierarchically distributed integrated management

Some agents can be under the supervision of multiple mid-level 2 managers, e.g. agent 4 in the example depicted in Fig. 43. This sharing of an agent by multiple managers with different roles is classic and results from what Sloman and Twidle call a *domain overlap* [235]. Still, whether an agent is supervised by a mid-level 1 manager, a mid-level 2 manager, or multiple managers, the communication model remains the same: HTTP/ MIME/XML.

Between all the managers, we have regular exchanges of network and systems management data, all based on HTTP/MIME/XML. Parallel to that, managers exchange policies, that is, high-level abstractions of management translated by managers into lower-level abstractions that can directly be sent to and understood by agents. Policy exchanges also rely on HTTP/MIME/XML. On top of this, we could add application management and service management: They, too, would be based on the same communication model.

This brief example shows that the combination of HTTP, MIME, and XML provides us with a powerful means of unifying the communication model for integrated management.

Note that this unification would not be so straightforward if another representation scheme were used. BER-encoded SMI is used in the three SNMP management architectures, but its verbosity, together with the fact that it is not readable by humans (and is thus difficult to debug), make it impractical for other information models (see Section 3.3.1.4). Plain strings are good for debugging but are not suitable for elaborate information models such as CIM; nor is HTML with its fixed tags. Serialized Java objects are not general purpose enough; nor are binary CORBA objects, vendor-specific C++ objects, etc. In conclusion, XML's flexibility, simplicity, and small footprint on agents make it, in our view, the best technology to date for integrating the management of IP networks and systems.

9.6 Summary

In this chapter, we have shown the advantages of using a communication model based on HTTP/MIME/XML in WIMA. First, we identified the advantages of using XML in general, in NSM, and in integrated enterprise management. Second, we explained how to use XML for representing management data and identified the strengths and weaknesses of model- and metamodel-level mappings. Third, we justified why the fact that XML documents are self-describing makes XML particularly appropriate for dealing with multiple information models. Fourth, we used four examples to illustrate the high level of semantics offered by XML (which even supports simple forms of distributed object-oriented programming). Fifth, we studied an example demonstrating how XML unifies distributed and integrated management in NSM and beyond. This concludes the third core contribution of this book.

Chapter 10

A WIMA-BASED RESEARCH PROTOTYPE: JAMAP

In order to validate our new management architecture, a research prototype called the JAva MAnagement Platform (JAMAP) was developed with the precious help of two students (see "Acknowledgments" in Preface). The latest release is JAMAP 0.4 [147]. The main goals of this endeavor were the following:

- demonstrate the feasibility and simplicity of our push-based organizational model
- demonstrate the feasibility and simplicity of our communication model
- highlight the usefulness of advanced Web technologies in NSM
- show how to deal with agents supporting native SNMP MIBs
- prove to network-device and system vendors that the support for WIMA is simple

In this chapter, we show that all of these objectives were met. Note that the goal of developing JAMAP was neither to implement a full-blown management platform for use in a production environment, nor to carry out in-depth performance evaluation. Thus we did not benchmark JAMAP against other management platforms.

Parallel to JAMAP, a management platform (POS-EWS) developed at POSTECH, Pohang, Korea was made WIMA-compliant by Hong's research team [133] while this book was being written. In particular, POS-EWS uses a push-based model and a variant of WIMA's communication model. In addition, it uses the Document Object Model (DOM [275]) to discover the XML Schemas supported by the agents, and XPath [63] to identify and select a group of managed objects. An SNMP-to-XML management gateway was also developed to interface with SNMP agents. This implementation led to a a commercial Web-based management platform for Linux servers sold by Netstech in Korea. This, too, demonstrates the feasibility and usefulness of our WIMA management architecture.

This chapter is organized as follows. In Section 10.1, we describe how JAMAP implements WIMA. In Sections 10.2 through to 10.4, we present the detailed design of the three tiers of our management architecture: the management station, the management server, and the agent. In Section 10.5, we show how we made reusability a reality in JAMAP. Finally, we summarize this chapter in Section 10.6.

10.1 Overview of JAMAP

JAMAP is an example of WIMA-based management platform. It implements many of the concepts presented in Chapter 7 and Chapter 8. It supports XML for representing data exchanged between an agent and a manager, but the use of XML for integrating enterprise management was not implemented.

Our main motivation behind the development of this research prototype was to demonstrate the feasibility of WIMA. Another motivation was to prove its simplicity.

JAMAP should not be considered *the* way to implement WIMA. To begin with, we made a number of simplifications for the sole purpose of reducing the development time and having the prototype ready for internal demonstrations. Moreover, some hot software-engineering issues (e.g., "What exactly is a software component?", or "Is Java appropriate for implementing component software?") are still very much open to debate—and outside the scope of this book. JAMAP is just one way of implementing our WIMA management architecture. It does not seek optimality.

10.1.1 Key design decisions at a glance

The main novelty demonstrated by JAMAP is the push-based transfer of regular management data, from the agent to the management server, via a persistent HTTP connection structured with MIME multipart.

JAMAP supports the following features:

- Java-based three-tier architecture: management station, management server, and agent
- publish-subscribe pattern
- push-based distribution for regular management and notification delivery
- pull-based distribution for *ad hoc* management
- rule-based event generation for monitoring
- rule-based event filtering for event correlation
- basic event handlers
- multiple agents
- multiple managers
- physical distribution of the servlets logically running on a single manager
- persistent HTTP/TCP connections with MIME multipart
- transparent compression of MIB data
- management data encoded in XML, serialized Java objects, or plain-text strings

- SNMP MIBs
- protection of the manager against agents bombarding data or events
- bulk transfers of management data (multiple MIB variables per MIME part)

JAMAP supports simplified versions of the following:

- secure relay for traversing firewalls
- event correlator
- data repository

Due to a lack of time, JAMAP does not yet implement three features of WIMA:

- network-map registry
- automated reconnections
- keepalives

JAMAP does not support the following features, which we referred to in the previous chapters but which are not part of WIMA *per se*:

- event masking based on the network topology
- CIM schemas

When we say that JAMAP is not a full-fledged management platform, we mean that there are no management functions taking real actions and that the GUIs are still basic, especially the network map. But the data repository is populated with the right data, the events reach the event correlator and are handled according to their severity, and everything is in place to build a real management platform around this prototype.

10.1.2 More on the design of JAMAP

The core of JAMAP was coded in only two weeks for one agent and one manager. It consisted of:

- a push scheduler on the agent
- a data dispatcher on the agent
- one persistent HTTP connection
- a basic data collector on the manager
- MIME multipart
- dynamic data compression and decompression (`gzip`)

JAMAP 0.1 was demonstrated internally after four months of work. Overall, all the developments that led to JAMAP 0.4 took a bit less than a year.

As expected, most of the coding effort went into implementing the management server, especially the rule-based system that includes a GUI-based rule editor. Based on the experience gathered while building this prototype, we believe that professional-grade WIMA-compliant managers could be developed and tested by vendors in about six months, which is reasonable. WIMA-compliant agents for IP devices and systems would require less than a month of work.

As far as the information model is concerned, JAMAP currently supports only SNMP MIBs. JAMAP does not require that native SNMP MIBs be changed in the agents; it interfaces with these MIBs via Java classes written by AdventNet (see Section 10.5). On the agent side, we tested MIB-II [173] and the Host Resources MIB [281] on a Linux PC, and MIB-II on a Sun Microsystems server. On the manager side, we tested a Linux PC, a Windows PC, a Sun Microsystems server, and a Silicon Graphics server. All of these machines ran exactly the same code, which proves the portability of Java when developers refrain from using proprietary extensions.

The components described in Chapter 7 are implemented as Java classes or servlets on both sides of the persistent communication pipe (management server and agent). Servlets use HTTP/1.0 or HTTP/1.1 to communicate with one another, be they on the same or different machine(s). Consequently, servlet-to-servlet communication within the management server is based on HTTP (as opposed to more efficient mechanisms such as shared memory, for instance). We do not use object-oriented frameworks *per se* in JAMAP, but we use JDK 1.2.2 and JDK 1.3.0, which some people consider frameworks.

Access to the data repository is based on NFS for Unix machines. Java objects are directly stored in serialized format. For convenience, we use one file per SNMP OID or notification.

We can encode one or several management data per MIME part. A push cycle consists of a single MIME part in JAMAP, which demonstrates the power of bulk transfers in WIMA.

For data subscription, we provide the administrator with an SNMP MIB browser. To implement this, we reused the MIB browser and some Java classes that AdventNet makes freely available on the Web (see Section 10.5).

MIME parts carrying SNMP notifications are not compressed because the compression ratio would be poor for so little data, and the increased latency would not be worth the meager savings in network overhead.

Finally, the servlets running on the management server can be distributed over several physical machines. This distribution will be clarified in Section 10.3.

10.1.3 Advanced Java technologies in JAMAP

We use two advanced Java technologies in JAMAP: servlets and serialization. Let us briefly describe them.

Java servlets

JAMAP relies heavily on HTTP-based communication between Java applets and servlets. Servlets [66] appeared at the end of the 1990s on the Web. They are an improvement over CGI programs. Unlike the latter, which are typically written in a scripting language such as

Perl [282] or Tcl/Tk [195], servlets are Java classes loaded in a Java Virtual Machine (JVM) via an HTTP server. The HTTP server must be configured to use servlets and associate a URL with each loaded servlet. At start-up time, one servlet object is instantiated for each configured servlet. When a request is performed on a servlet URL, the HTTP server invokes a method of the servlet depending on the HTTP method used by the request. All servlets implement one method per HTTP method. For instance, the `doGet()` method is invoked when an HTTP GET request comes in for the corresponding URL.

Modern operating systems generally support multithreading. As a result, most HTTP servers now support concurrent accesses. Several HTTP clients may therefore invoke concurrently the same method of the same servlet. This allows the sharing of the same servlet by multiple persistent connections. We used this feature extensively in JAMAP when we tested it with several agents. Like any URLs, Java servlets can also leverage the general-purpose features of HTTP servers (e.g., access control).

During the early developments of JAMAP, servlet environments were in constant evolution. We had problems with the Apache HTTP server version 1.3.4 and the Apache servlet engine Jserv 0.8, because Jserv 0.8 did not support concurrent accesses to servlets and the response stream was buffered [31]. By the time these problems were reportedly corrected, we had switched to Jigsaw, an HTTP server developed by the W3C, which offered good support for servlets. Later, we kept Jigsaw and upgraded several times to the latest version. JAMAP 0.4 was tested against Jigsaw 2.2.0.

Java serialization

Serialization is a feature of Java that allows an arbitrarily complex object to be translated into a byte stream. In JAMAP, we used it for ensuring the persistence of the state of an object and for transferring objects over the network. Objects containing references to other objects are processed recursively until all necessary objects are serialized. The keyword `transient` can be added to the declaration of an attribute (e.g., an object reference) to prevent its serialization.

For network transfers, instead of defining a protocol, one can use serializable classes dedicated to communication. Such classes offer a `writeObject()` method on one side, and a `readObject()` method on the other. Serialization proved to be very useful in JAMAP for persistence, notably to store rules and agents' subscription tables.

10.1.4 Overview of the communication aspects

Fig. 44 and Fig. 45 are synthetic views of the communication between the different Java applets and servlets running on the agent, management server, and management station. Fig. 44 depicts push-based monitoring and data collection, while notification delivery and event handling are represented on Fig. 45. The three-tier architecture described in Section 7.2.2 appears clearly on these two figures.

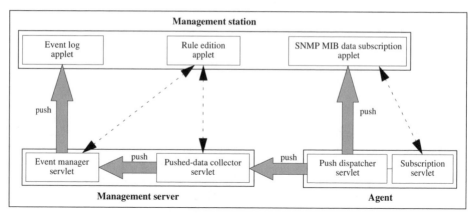

Fig. 44. JAMAP: Communication between Java applets and servlets for
monitoring and data collection

The push arrow between the push dispatcher servlet and the SNMP MIB data subscription
applet represents the path followed by MIB data retrieved interactively (in attended mode,
data can be either pushed or pulled). The other push arrows depict regular management
transferred in unattended mode. The dotted arrows represent the applet-to-servlet dialogs
that take place during the subscription phase.

Note that the same push mechanism is used everywhere: between the agent and the
management server, between the management server and the management station, between
the agent and the management station, or between the servlets within the management
server. Low-level classes also use the same producer-consumer pattern everywhere.

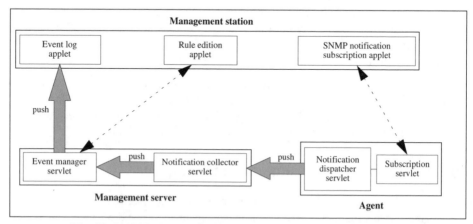

Fig. 45. JAMAP: Communication between Java applets and servlets for
notification delivery and event handling

10.1.5 Distribution phase for monitoring and data collection

The distribution phase for monitoring and data collection is depicted in Fig. 46. If we compare this figure with the generic one presented in Chapter 7 for WIMA (Fig. 17, p. 160), the main difference is the presence of Java servlets in JAMAP. They glue together components that are logically related. As mentioned already, servlets communicate via HTTP. As a result, Java objects living in different servlets (e.g., the pushed-data analyzer and the event correlator) also communicate via HTTP.

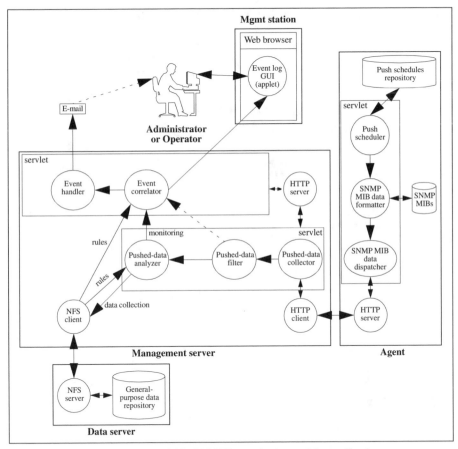

Fig. 46. Push model in JAMAP: monitoring and data collection

Another difference is that we simplified considerably the visualization of events in JAMAP, in order to reduce the development time. Instead of writing a full-blown network-map GUI, aware of the network topology and updating dynamically the colors of the icons representing network devices and systems, we simply implemented a log window called the *event log GUI* applet. In this window, we log one entry per incoming event, line by line. Since we do not use network-map GUIs, we do not have a network-map registry either: The event correlator sends events directly to the log window, which runs permanently in the Web browser of the management station. Consequently, JAMAP currently supports only one management station. But it would be rather simple to send the same event to multiple log windows running in different Web browsers.

The third noticeable difference between Fig. 46 and Fig. 17 is that, in JAMAP, event handlers can only archive events or use e-mail to contact the administrator or an operator. This was deemed acceptable for a prototype.

10.1.6 Distribution phase for notification delivery

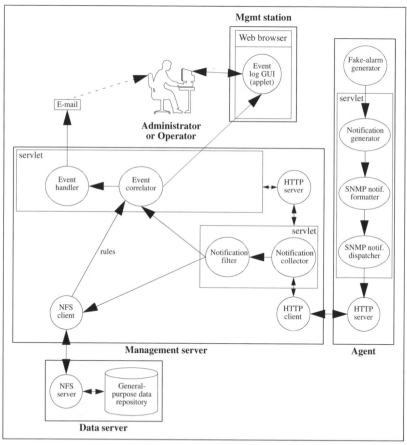

Fig. 47. Push model in JAMAP: notification delivery and event handling

The distribution phase for notification delivery is depicted in Fig. 47, together with event handling within the management server. If we compare this figure with the generic one presented in Chapter 7 for WIMA (Fig. 16, p. 159), the main difference is again the presence of Java servlets in JAMAP. We clearly see the separation between the notification collector servlet, in charge of receiving a specific type of events coming from agents (notifications), and the event manager servlet, in charge of correlating all kinds of events (see Section 10.3).

Another difference between this figure and the generic WIMA figure is the absence of sensors in the agent. In Section 10.4.3, we will explain that, in JAMAP, the health monitor is replaced with a fake-alarm generator for the sake of simplicity.

Finally, as in the previous section, we use an event log GUI instead of a network-map GUI, and event handlers can only archive events or notify the administrator via e-mail.

This concludes our high-level description of how JAMAP implements WIMA. In the next three sections, we will investigate the detailed design of the different applets and servlets running on the three tiers of our management architecture: the management station, the management server, and the agent.

10.2 Management Station

The management station is the desktop of the administrator or operator. It can be any machine (a Linux PC, a Windows PC, a Mac, a Unix workstation, etc.) as long as it runs a Web browser and supports Java. Unlike the management server, the management station is not static: The administrator can work on different machines at different times of the day. During the subscription phase, he/she configures the agent via the SNMP MIB data subscription applet and the SNMP notification subscription applet. The rules used by the pushed-data collector and the event manager servlets can be modified at any time via the rule edition applet. Events are displayed by the event log applet.

10.2.1 SNMP MIB data subscription applet

The SNMP MIB data subscription applet communicates directly with the agent (see Fig. 46). It provides the subscription system for regular management. It is also used to retrieve and view SNMP MIB data interactively, either once (pull based) or over a longer period of time (push based). Its main tasks are the following:

- browse SNMP MIBs graphically
- select SNMP OIDs or SNMP tables and retrieve their values once (pull model)
- select SNMP OIDs or SNMP tables and monitor them for a while (they are displayed as text fields, time graphs, or tables)
- monitor some computed values (e.g. interface utilization)
- subscribe to SNMP OIDs or SNMP tables and specify a push frequency (per OID or per table)

Computed values are typically the results of equations parameterized by multiple SNMP OIDs. We implemented a sort of multiplexer to support them. This kind of simple prepro- cessing could be delegated to the agent in the future (e.g., with mobile code).

10.2.2 SNMP notification subscription applet

Like the SNMP MIB data subscription applet, the SNMP notification subscription applet also communicates directly with the agent (see Fig. 47). It enables the administrator to set up an agent-side notification filter. SNMP notifications that have not been subscribed to by the manager are silently discarded by the agent.

10.2.3 Rule edition applet and rule mapping applet

The rule edition applet depicted in Fig. 44 and Fig. 45 is in fact implemented as two separate applets, the rule edition applet and the rule mapping applet, which control the behavior of two objects:

- the pushed-data analyzer object (which lives in the pushed-data collector servlet)
- the event correlator object (which lives in the event manager servlet)

The administrator writes rules in Java via the rule edition applet. These rules can be derived from a collection of templates or written from scratch. (Java is used here as a portable scripting language.) When the rules are saved, they are compiled dynamically to check for syntax errors.

Next, the rule mapping applet allows the administrator to map an OID retrieved at a certain frequency, and from a certain agent, onto a given rule. This mechanism allows a single rule to be used for multiple agents, multiple frequencies, and multiple OIDs. It also allows the administrator to temporarily activate and deactivate a rule without deleting it.

Rule-base event correlators usually support four types of rule. For an *instantaneous rule*, we have one value of an OID for a given agent at a certain time. This is the simplest type of rule: {condition, action}. For instance, an event can be generated by the pushed-data analyzer if the value of an SNMP OID exceeds a given threshold. A typical instantaneous rule for the event correlator would be that if a system is believed to be down, then all applications running on it should also be down, so events reporting that a database is not working on this system should be discarded.

For a *temporal rule*, we have a time series for a given agent and OID. For instance, the pushed-data analyzer can check if the average value of a given SNMP OID increased by 10% or more over the last two hundred push cycles. Unlike instantaneous rules, temporal rules require persistent rule objects. If we consider the {condition, action} allegory again, the condition of the rule applies this time to a vector of values retrieved at different push cycles. The object executing this rule must therefore keep the values of the OID between consecutive push cycles. A *spatial rule* deals with many OIDs, at the same time, for one or several agents. Multiple conditions must be fulfilled for the action to be taken, but there is no need for persistent rule objects. Last, a *spatiotemporal rule* deals with many OIDs, at different times, for one or several agents. This is the most complex type of rule: We have multiple conditions, and each of them requires a vector of values gathered over a period of time. Not all event correlators support spatiotemporal rules.

All of these rules can be arbitrarily complex, as there is no clear-cut distinction between what is in the realm of offline data mining and what should be performed immediately, in pseudo real-time. The trade-off is that the pushed-data analyzer should not be slowed down too much by an excessive amount of rules, otherwise it would not be able to apply all the relevant rules to incoming data between two consecutive push cycles.

JAMAP currently supports instantaneous and temporal rules, for which the rule edition applet provides templates. Spatial rules have been designed but not implemented yet. *A priori*, spatiotemporal rules would require another type of event correlator, because they require a significant amount of processing time and the interpretation of Java bytecode is too slow for that purpose.

10.2.4 Event log applet

The event log applet (see Fig. 46 and Fig. 47) is connected to the management server to receive events. We use it as a debugger, as we do not manage a production network with JAMAP. This applet displays a simple list of events and manages a blinking light and sound system to catch the operator's attention in the case of incoming events. It is intended to remain permanently in a corner of the administrator's and operator's desktop screens. Eventually, it should be complemented by (or replaced with) the network map GUI applet.

10.3 Management Server

The management server runs three core servlets: the pushed-data collector servlet, the notification collector servlet, and the event manager servlet. These servlets are not specific to SNMP, and we can easily support other information models through subtyping. The management server can be distributed over multiple machines if need be (e.g., for scalability reasons), as the communication between servlets relies on HTTP and the data server is already a separate machine. For instance, we managed to run the three servlets on three different machines. We could also run data mining on a fourth. This simple case of distribution, which preserves a centralized management paradigm, was described in Section 7.3.5 (see Fig. 18).

10.3.1 Pushed-data collector servlet

The pushed-data collector servlet consists of three core objects, plus many instrumentation objects not represented on Fig. 46. The pushed-data collector object connects to the agent upon start-up and enters an infinite loop where it listens to the socket for incoming data. When it receives data, it passes it unchanged to the pushed-data filter object and enters the infinite loop again. If the agent gracefully closes the persistent connection, e.g. in the case of a clean reboot, the pushed-data collector should (but does not in JAMAP 0.4) immediately reconnect to it so as to ensure a persistent connection. None of the advanced keepalive schemes described in Section 8.5 are currently implemented in JAMAP.

The pushed-data filter object controls the flow of incoming data. If it detects that too much traffic is coming from a given agent (that is, from a given socket), it tells the pushed-data collector object to close permanently the connection to that agent (that is, the collector should not attempt to reconnect to the agent until the administrator explicitly tells it to do so). The rationale here is that a misbehaving agent is either misconfigured, bogus, or under the control of an intruder pursuing a denial of service attack, and that the good health of the management system should be protected against this misbehaving agent. When this happens, the administrator is informed once via e-mail.

If the pushed-data filter object is happy with the incoming data, it passes it unchanged to the pushed-data analyzer object. The latter unmarshals the data and checks, OID by OID, whether it was subscribed to for monitoring, data collection, or both.

In the case of data collection, the SNMP OID is not processed immediately. Instead, it is stored in a persistent repository (an NFS-mounted file system) via a logger object. We assume that an external process will use it afterward to perform some kind of data mining (e.g., it could look for a trend in the variations of the CPU load of an IP router to be able to anticipate when an upgrade is needed).

In the case of monitoring, the SNMP OID is processed immediately. The pushed-data analyzer object applies the rules relevant to that agent and that OID. If it notices something important (e.g., a heartbeat is received from an IP router that was considered down), the pushed-data analyzer object generates an urgent event and sends it via HTTP to the event correlator object living in the event manager servlet. We took special care for the case when the same SNMP OID is used for both monitoring and data collection.

A nice feature of our rule system is that rules may be dynamically compiled and loaded in by the servlet. Dynamic class loading is a feature of the Java language. The core API provides a method to instantiate objects from a class by giving its name in the form of a string. The class loader of the JVM searches the class file in the file system and loads it into the JVM's memory. This enables the servlet to load a class at runtime without knowing its name in advance. Once a class is loaded, it behaves just as any other class. We are limited only by the fact that a class cannot be modified at runtime. This means that if a rule is already registered under a certain class name and that rule is modified by the administrator, another class name must be used for that new version of the rule.

To solve this problem, we implemented a simple technique that consists in postfixing the class name with a release number and incrementing this release number automatically. As a result, the administrator can create, modify, and debug rules dynamically. The drawback is that the memory used by loaded classes (especially those corresponding to the "old" rules) is freed only when the JVM is restarted. The administrator should therefore be careful not to fill up the memory during the rule debugging phase. Clearly, this feature should be used with special care on a production system; but it was very useful to us for debugging rules.

In JAMAP 0.4, the pushed-data collector servlet is also used for configuration purposes. In a future release, this should be achieved by a separate servlet: the rule handling servlet.

10.3.2 Notification collector servlet

As depicted in Fig. 47, the notification collector servlet consists of two core objects: the notification collector and the notification filter. Contrary to pushed data, no analyzer is needed for notifications because we already know what happened: We do not have to work it out.

The notification collector object works as the pushed-data collector object. The notification filter object also works as the pushed-data filter object. In JAMAP 0.4, we use a single persistent connection between the agent and the manager for transferring all notifications. We would need several if we wanted to manage different priority levels for notifications, as described in Section 8.4.2. The notifications accepted by the notification filter are forwarded unchanged to the event correlator object living in the event manager servlet, without any further processing.

10.3.3 Event manager servlet

The event manager servlet connects to one notification collector servlet and one or several pushed-data collector servlets (only one is depicted in Fig. 44 and Fig. 45), then waits for incoming events. More precisely, incoming events are processed by the event sink object, which is not represented on the figures. This event sink plays a role similar to that of the pushed-data and notification filters: It checks whether too many events were sent by a single source. If so, it disconnects the event manager servlet from the faulty data collector servlet or notification collector servlet. Otherwise, events are forwarded to an event queue based on their severity. The four event queues supported by JAMAP 0.4 correspond to fatal, critical, warning, and informative events. These four event queues run as threads with different priorities. Leveraging multithreading and thread prioritization, the event correlator object issues a blocking read on all threads, and processes the event coming from the event queue corresponding to the highest severity level.

Next, the event correlator object is supposed to correlate this event with the network topology, in order to discard masked events. For instance, if a router is down, all machines accessed across it appear to be down to the pushed-data analyzer. Based on its knowledge of the network topology, the event correlator should keep only those events that cannot be ascribed to the failure of other equipment. In JAMAP 0.4, topology-based event masking is not yet implemented.

When an event is not masked by the event correlator object, it is transmitted to the event handler object corresponding to its severity level (i.e., the level of emergency perceived by the origin sender of the event and encapsulated inside it). Each event handler interfaces with a specific notification system: an e-mail system, a pager, a telephone, a siren, etc. In our prototype, we only support e-mail.

In the future, it would be nice to replace our event correlator object with a full-blown event correlator written in Java by another research team. This would be consistent with the "spirit" of component software.

10.4 Agent

The agent runs two core servlets: the push dispatcher servlet and the notification dispatcher servlet. In JAMAP 0.4, these two servlets are used during both the subscription phase and the distribution phase. In a future release, we intend to isolate the configuration management aspects from the distribution aspects by creating a third servlet: the subscription servlet. To facilitate understanding, we will pretend in this section that this has already been implemented and will thus describe the subscription, the push dispatcher, and the notification dispatcher servlets. Other servlets used for debugging and testing purposes are not detailed here.

10.4.1 Subscription servlet

The agent is configured interactively via two applets run by the management station: the SNMP MIB data subscription applet described in Section 10.2.1, and the SNMP notification subscription applet described in Section 10.2.2. Both of them communicate with the subscription servlet running on the agent (see Fig. 46 and Fig. 47). In JAMAP, there is no support for fully automated configuration.

The SNMP OIDs subscribed to by the administrator are sent to the subscription servlet by the SNMP MIB data subscription applet, in the form of serialized Java objects. They are stored persistently by the agent in its data subscription table. On the agent, the subscription sheet servlet can be accessed to display the contents of the data subscription table.

Similarly, the notifications selected by the administrator (that is, the agent-side event filter) are transmitted by the SNMP notification subscription applet to the subscription servlet as serialized Java objects. They are stored persistently by the agent in the notification subscription table.

Unlike the two subscription applets mentioned above, the subscription servlet is independent of any information model. The agent's data and notification subscription tables contain self-describing data, and can therefore encapsulate SNMP OIDs, CIM objects, etc. In JAMAP, these two tables constitute the agent's configuration files.

In the future, the subscription servlet should be able to retrieve the agent's configuration files from the data server via the management server. Thus, the agent would not necessarily have to store its configuration in non-volatile memory—a desirable feature for bottom-of-the-range equipment.

10.4.2 Push dispatcher servlet

The push dispatcher servlet consists of three core objects (the push scheduler, the MIB data formatter, and the SNMP MIB data dispatcher) plus a number of instrumentation objects not represented on Fig. 46. Its main function is to push data toward the manager's data collector during the distribution phase.

The push scheduler object gets the data subscription table from the subscription servlet, and uses this configuration data to trigger the push cycles. At each push cycle, it contacts the SNMP MIB data formatter object and gives it a list of SNMP OIDs whose values should be retrieved immediately. The SNMP MIB data formatter object accesses the in-memory data structures of the SNMP MIBs via some proprietary, tailor-made mechanism (currently, AdventNet's Java classes), formats the SNMP MIB data as a series of {OID, value} pairs, and sends it to the SNMP MIB data dispatcher object. The latter compresses the data with `gzip`, assembles the data in the form of a MIME part, pushes the MIME part through, and sends a MIME separator afterward to indicate that the push cycle is over. In JAMAP 0.4, we can have one or several {OID, value} pairs per MIME part.

10.4.3 Notification dispatcher servlet

The notification dispatcher servlet consists of three core objects (the notification generator, the SNMP notification formatter, and the SNMP notification dispatcher) plus a number of instrumentation objects not shown on Fig. 47. Its main function is to send asynchronous notifications to the manager's notification collector during the distribution phase.

In theory, during the distribution phase, the health monitor should check continuously the health of the agent based on input from sensors. When a problem is detected, the health monitor should asynchronously fire an alarm to the notification generator object in the notification dispatcher servlet via some proprietary mechanism. In practice, instead of getting real alarms from a health monitor, we generate fake ones by accessing the alarm generator servlet from the management station. Each time this servlet is accessed, a fake alarm is sent to the notification generator object.

Based on the notification subscription table retrieved from the subscription servlet, the notification generator object checks whether this alarm should be discarded. If it was not subscribed to by the manager, the alarm is silently dropped. If it was, the notification generator object sends it to the SNMP notification formatter object. The latter formats it as an `SNMPv2-trap` PDU and sends it to the SNMP notification dispatcher object, which in turn wraps it in the form of a MIME part, pushes it to the management server via HTTP, and sends a MIME separator afterward to indicate that this is the end of the notification.

10.5 Reusability

In order to reduce our development efforts, we reused some third-party classes and components[1]. They are briefly described in this section. This demonstrates, if need be, that reusable component software is not necessarily exposed to the *Field of Dreams* and *Abracadabra* antipatterns [155]!

---

1. We used many in JAMAP 0.1, but stopped using several in JAMAP 0.4 because similar classes had become natively available from JDK in the meantime, or because we changed the design of the management platform.

AdventNet SNMP suite

We used the following classes of the AdventNet SNMP suite [1]:

- the `MibTree` class: a Java bean displaying the SNMP MIB tree as a GUI
- the `MibNode` class: a node of the SNMP MIB tree
- the `SnmpVar` class: a Java bean encapsulating an {OID, value} pair
- the `SnmpTarget` class: a Java bean abstracting an SNMP device
- the `SnmpTable` class: a Java bean encapsulating an SNMP table

AdventNet's classes are the main building blocks of our GUIs. Reusing them allowed us to save a lot of development time.

JDK's Java compiler class

We used the `sun.tools.javac.Main` class of Sun Microsystems's JDK Java compiler [259] to implement dynamic compilation in the rule system—a useful feature described in Section 10.2.3. Note that this class may change between successive versions of the JDK, which hampers the portability of the code of our rule editor.

Clark's XML parser

In order to parse XML messages, we used Clark's XML parser [62] (package `com.jclark.xml.sax`) as per Anderson's advice [7]. These classes also enabled us to reduce development time.

10.6 Summary

The purpose of developing JAMAP, a WIMA-based research prototype, was to demonstrate the feasibility and simplicity of the core contributions of our work, primarily the use of push, persistent HTTP connections, and MIME multipart. JAMAP is written entirely in Java. It implements the push model to perform regular management (permanent monitoring and data collection for offline analysis) and notification delivery, and the push and pull models for *ad hoc* management (temporary monitoring and troubleshooting). The communication between agents and managers relies on HTTP transfers between Java applets and servlets over persistent TCP connections. The SNMP MIB data is encapsulated in serialized Java objects that are transmitted as MIME parts via HTTP. This data is transparently compressed with `gzip`, which saves network bandwidth without increasing latency too significantly. The manager consists of two parts: the management server, a static machine that runs the servlets, and the management station, which can be any desktop running a Web browser. The other actors involved in a three-tier, client-server architecture are the agent, which supports native SNMP MIBs, and the data repository, which consists of binary and text files accessed via NFS by the management server.

Chapter 11

HOW DOES OUR SOLUTION COMPARE WITH OTHERS?

In this chapter, we compare our approach with its main contenders to date for the next management cycle (SNMP, WBEM, and JMX), and highlight the relevance of our architectural and design choices. We also identify some similarities and complementarities between WIMA and these three management architectures.

This chapter is organized as follows. In Section 11.1, we compare WIMA with the SNMP management architecture, whose replacement was an explicit objective of this work, and demonstrate that we succeeded in solving most of the problems identified in Chapter 3, including all the most severe ones. In Section 11.2, we compare WIMA to WBEM, identify some similarities between them, and point out some problems in WBEM. We also show how the DMTF's management architecture could benefit from our work by integrating some of our design decisions. In Section 11.3, we compare WIMA with JMX, which epitomizes the Java-based management architecture promoted by Sun Microsystems. We point out the strengths and weaknesses of JMX, and conclude that it can hardly be integrated with WIMA. In Section 11.4, we analyze some known weaknesses in WIMA and explain how to cope with or avoid them. Finally, we summarize this chapter in Section 11.5.

11.1 Comparison with SNMP-Based Management

In this section, we show that almost all of the problems identified in SNMP are solved in WIMA (27 out of 30, to be precise). We also investigate the complementarity of these two management architectures.

11.1.1 Almost all of the problems in SNMP have been solved

If we review the characteristics of SNMP described in Section 3.1, and the problems identified in SNMP-based management in Section 3.3, we see that WIMA is a better solution for the next management cycle:

- Agents are no longer considered equal and "dumb". Some agents can execute scripts transferred via XML, while others can simply push MIB variables.
- Polling is no longer used for retrieving regular management data. This improves scalability, network overhead, and latency.
- The data repository is no longer tightly coupled with the management platform. This frees customers from the impediments of peer-to-peer agreements between database and management-platform vendors: They can use any third-party database with any management platform. In particular, they can reuse for NSM the database already installed in their intranet, thereby leveraging in-house know-how.
- In WIMA, the goal shifts from network to integrated management. WIMA facilitates the integration of different management areas, notably with XML, and does not concentrate solely on the management of network devices.
- WIMA is scalable. Through distribution across a hierarchy of managers, it can cope with the ever growing amount of management data to move about and process at the managers. It can also transfer some of the management workload to the agents.
- WIMA makes bulk transfers of management data much more efficient than in the SNMP realm.
- WIMA is immune to the `get-bulk` overshoot effect because it does not rely on `get-bulk`.
- WIMA is immune to the problems caused by the maximum size of an SNMP message because it does not use the SNMP communication protocol.
- By transferring tables in XML, WIMA makes it possible for smart agents to suppress the "holes" in sparse tables described in Section 3.3.1.3.
- By allowing the agent to send large amounts of data in one bulk, we significantly improve the consistency of large SNMP tables.
- BER encoding is no longer mandatory, so we are no longer exposed to its weak efficiency and its impact on the network overhead.
- Management data can be compressed transparently, e.g. with `gzip`, which reduces network overhead significantly without affecting latency too much.
- In WIMA, we use a reliable transport protocol: TCP. By doing so, we do not lose important notifications for silly reasons such as buffer overflows in IP routers.

- In WIMA, we can leverage Web security (SSL, HTTP authentication, etc.) to provide different levels of security. In SNMP, we have either no security (SNMPv1 and v2c) or high security (SNMPv3).
- Firewalls are difficult to traverse with SNMP. They were extremely rare when SNMPv1 was devised, and SNMP made no special provisions for crossing them easily, not even SNMPv3. In WIMA, we solved this problem by changing the communication model to accommodate firewall constraints.
- In SNMP, we have no high-level semantics, only instrumentation MIBs. By making it possible to work with other information models, especially CIM, WIMA allows management-application designers to work with high-level semantics. The flexibility of XML is particularly useful for this. The DMTF, for instance, is currently working on schemas offering high-level semantics that can be leveraged in WIMA.
- The scarcity of protocol primitives in SNMP is addressed in WIMA by abandoning the SNMP communication protocol, by using HTTP and XML instead, and by allowing for feature-rich information models (most notably CIM, which supports an infinitely large number of operations).
- The SNMP information model is not object oriented, whereas object orientation is now ubiquitous in software engineering. By allowing for the use of CIM, WIMA gives access to an object-oriented information model.
- SNMP's distasteful programming by side effect can be avoided in WIMA. With CIM, clean method invocations are possible.
- The confusion between the SNMP management architecture and the SNMP protocol is not possible in WIMA because we use two different terms.
- In WIMA, component- and object-oriented management platforms are more modular than SNMP-based management platforms, and increased competition should hopefully make them less expensive.
- To vendors, the possibility to have a single device- or vendor-specific management GUI for all management platforms is an immense source of savings. This should contribute to making the cost of embedded management software remain low, and therefore decrease the software bill for customers.
- Once vendor-specific management GUIs are developed, their time-to-market is brought down to zero in WIMA—a remarkable improvement over SNMP, where it typically takes several months, and sometimes infinitely longer.
- Start-ups are on a par with large equipment vendors regarding management. They are no longer left aside because of the high entrance cost in the management-platform market.
- MIB versioning is solved in WIMA by embedding the vendor-specific management GUI(s) in the agent.
- Domain-specific expertise is no longer needed: WIMA relies on standard Web technologies that pervade software engineering today.
- Finally, we mentioned that SNMP evolves too slowly. By allowing WIMA to cope with any information model, we make it possible for new entrants (e.g., the DMTF, TMF, OMG, etc.) to offer quicker solutions to open problems. If the definition of new SNMP MIBs takes too much time, we can use CIM schemas instead.

Among all the problems identified in Chapter 3, only three of them are not solved in WIMA:

- Because we decided to make it possible to work with legacy SNMP MIBs, the verbosity of the OID naming scheme in SNMP is not solved. This is partially addressed by the possibility to compress management data in transit.
- For the sake of robustness, the management server still has to be a dedicated machine. Arguably, one could use a highly available server, in which case other applications unrelated to management could run on the same machine. But the cost effectiveness of such a solution is questionable, and not many enterprises can justify the expense of a fault-tolerant system for running their management platform.
- The possibility to easily move the software of the management server from one machine to another, which is not guaranteed by WIMA. It can be achieved, e.g. by coding the components in Java. But there is a trade-off between portability and efficiency. Note that this property is desirable but not necessary.

11.1.2 Complementarities between WIMA and SNMP

The complementarity between WIMA and SNMP is primarily guaranteed by the fact that WIMA can cope with any information model, and in particular SNMP MIBs. It is also possible to use BER encoding inside HTTP messages to interface easily with existing SNMP-based management platforms.

11.2 Comparison with WBEM

In this section, we compare WIMA with WBEM. We first show some similarities in these two approaches. Then, we unveil two problems in WBEM. Finally, we investigate the complementarity between these two management architectures.

11.2.1 Similarities: HTTP and XML

Although they do not share the same communication model, WIMA and WBEM both use HTTP for manager-agent and manager-manager communications, and XML for representing management data inside HTTP messages. In WBEM, the use of XML is mandatory; in WIMA, it is simply recommended.

It should be noted that when the author made his design decision to use HTTP and XML in WIMA, shortly after the W3C had released XML, he was not aware that the WBEM Consortium had already abandoned HMMP in favor of HTTP and XML. This similarity is thus the result of sheer coincidence, as opposed to cross pollination.

11.2.2 Problems with WBEM

We identified two problems in WBEM: the lack of an organizational model and the use of HTTP extension headers.

11.2.2.1 WBEM lacks an organizational model

WBEM has evolved significantly over the past years. However, to date, there is still one important deficiency in it: it lacks an organizational model. WBEM specifies information and communication models[1], but there are no written recommendations as to what management paradigm managers and agents should follow (centralized management, weakly distributed hierarchical management, strongly distributed hierarchical management, or distributed cooperative management), how managers and agents should be organized (Should managers pull data off the agents? Should agents push data to the managers?), how they should interact (client-server, peer-to-peer, multicast, etc.), and how they should share the management-application workload (e.g., should agents be "dumb" or should they perform management tasks?). Whether manager-agent and manager-manager interactions should rely on the pull model, the push model, mobile code, and so on is entirely left to the designers of CIM agents and managers.

As a result, when people build CIM-based management applications, they will progress by trial and error if they have enough time, or they will simply map onto WBEM/CIM what they are already familiar with in the IP world. They will thus probably build most management applications around the pull model, which has been used for over a decade despite all the problems unveiled in this book.

In WIMA, conversely, we clearly specify when the push model should be used and when the pull model is preferred. We advocate the use of weakly distributed hierarchical management, and demand that manager-manager and manager-agent interactions be based on the same protocol.

11.2.2.2 HTTP extension headers

The reliance of WBEM on HTTP extension headers (see Section 6.6.1) causes three problems: the reliance on a controversial extension scheme for HTTP/1.1, the pseudo support for HTTP/1.0, and the compliance deadlock for embedded HTTP servers.

Controversial extension scheme for HTTP/1.1

HTTP/1.0 and HTTP/1.1 both define a large set of HTTP header fields, often called *HTTP headers* for short. None of them allows for domain-specific HTTP headers. In other words, to claim compliance with HTTP/1.0 or HTTP/1.1, an application must not define and use its own HTTP headers.

---

1. At the time this book goes to print, manager-manager communications are already specified, but manager-agent communications are not yet (they should be shortly).

Over time, this has caused some dissatisfaction in the HTTP community, because many Working Groups build protocols on top of HTTP, and many of them want to add domain-specific HTTP headers to the standard HTTP headers. A solution to this problem was proposed in RFC 2774 [189]: HTTP extension headers. This RFC is a proposed extension to HTTP/1.1. It specifies a set of conventions that allow applications to define and use domain-specific headers with HTTP/1.1.

The problem with this approach is that it has caused a lot of controversy at the W3C and IETF. This is testified by the unusual beginning of RFC 2774 [189, p. 1]:

"IESG Note

This document was originally requested for Proposed Standard status. However, due to mixed reviews during Last Call and within the HTTP Working Group, it is being published as an Experimental document. This is not necessarily an indication of technical flaws in the document; rather, there is a more general concern about whether this document actually represents community consensus regarding the evolution of HTTP. Additional study and discussion are needed before this can be determined."

CIM operations over HTTP depend on HTTP extension headers to work (see [77, Sections 3.1, 3.3.4, 3.3.5, 3.3.6, 3.3.7, and 3.3.8]). In our view, it seems unwise to base an important building block of the WBEM management architecture on a technology whose future is so uncertain.

HTTP extension headers break HTTP/1.0

RFC 2774 makes it clear that the use of HTTP extension headers demands HTTP/1.1:

"The proposal uses features in HTTP/1.1 but is compatible with HTTP/1.0 applications in such a way that extended applications can coexist with existing HTTP applications. Applications implementing this proposal MUST be based on HTTP/1.1 (or later versions of HTTP)" [189, p. 3].

As a result, CIM operations over HTTP do not work with HTTP/1.0:

- If we abide by the HTTP/1.0 specification, we cannot use domain-specific HTTP headers, so we cannot define CIM extension headers, thus CIM operations cannot be encapsulated in HTTP.
- If we do use CIM extension headers, we use domain-specific HTTP headers, hence we break HTTP/1.0.

This is in contradiction with the claimed support for HTTP/1.0 in the specification for CIM operations over HTTP:

"In recognition of the large installed base of HTTP/1.0 systems, the encapsulation is designed to support both HTTP/1.0 and HTTP/1.1" [77, p. 5].

"It is RECOMMENDED that CIM clients and CIM servers support HTTP/1.1. CIM clients and servers MAY support HTTP/1.0 instead" [77, p. 44].

This issue was brought before the DMTF WBEM Interoperability Working Group by the author. It is serious because the vast majority of the embedded HTTP servers deployed to date are based on HTTP/1.0. As a result, CIM operations over HTTP do not work with most deployed equipment, unless applications deliberately break the HTTP/1.0 specification...

Compliance deadlock

Another problem is the compliance deadlock. When customers purchase a new piece of equipment, their request for bids can require the support for an embedded HTTP server. Arguably, they can even require an HTTP/1.1 server, although few vendors, according to our sources, give customers the choice between HTTP/1.0 and HTTP/1.1. But how can they possibly require an HTTP/1.1 server modified with WBEM's HTTP extension headers, when HTTP extensions are simply an experimental RFC? This is unrealistic. Moreover, if other Working Groups define other HTTP extension headers for other purposes (e.g., for dynamic service provisioning), who will ensure that all these extensions are not mutually exclusive? And how will equipment vendors keep up with the definition of new extension schemes? As it is currently specified, WBEM's reliance on HTTP extension headers is a time bomb, in our view.

11.2.3 Complementarities between WIMA and WBEM

There is some scope for the integration of WIMA and WBEM. To begin with, WIMA's organizational model could be adopted by WBEM, especially the push model for transferring regular management data. The use of MIME multipart and the encapsulation of XML documents in MIME parts could also be adopted by WBEM. Note that this integration would require the modification of the DMTF's specification for encapsulating CIM operations in HTTP messages, as the use of HTTP extension headers is incompatible with WIMA. One possibility would be to replace HTTP extension headers with XML metadata inside the MIME parts.

11.3 Comparison with JMX

In this section, we compare WIMA with JMX and investigate complementarities between these two management architectures.

Similarities: components

The main similarity between WIMA and JMX is the reliance on component software on the manager side. Because of their complexity, management servers are by nature good candidates for component software. Agents can also be implemented with components, but most of the time, their complexity does not require it, and efficiency often demands the faster execution of C or C++ binaries.

The my-middleware-is-better-than-yours syndrome: a killer

JMX fundamentally relies on Java middleware to be supported by all agents and managers worldwide. In Section 5.4, we explained that this approach is flawed in our view, because it is an instance of the *my-middleware-is-better-than-yours* syndrome. Because it seems highly unlikely that one middleware will eventually win the middleware war, we believe that it would be unwise to base the management architecture of the next management cycle on middleware that may be rejected by the market in a couple of years. In comparison, WIMA is far less risky.

Note that since Java was split into three frameworks—J2EE (EJBs for managers), J2SE (JavaBeans for top- and middle-of-the-range agents), and J2ME (components for consumer electronics and embedded devices)—it is not clear how a single management architecture can live with heterogeneous components. What happens if a J2EE-based manager uses Java RMI to manage a J2ME-based agent? What is called *Java RMI* in these two worlds is quite different. This problem is not yet addressed in JMX, to the best of our knowledge.

JMX and FMA

As mentioned in Section 6.7, JMX focused so far on the agent side, while FMA (Federated Management Architecture) concentrated on the manager side. JMX uses MBeans. FMA has migrated from domain-specific FederatedBeans to standard JavaBeans and EJBs. Consequently, these two architectures are currently incompatible. We still need, from Sun Microsystems and the Java community, an integrated management architecture that will cover both the agent and the manager sides in distributed Java-based management. This, too, is an argument for not selecting JMX for the next management cycle.

Complementarities between WIMA and JMX

The main complementarity that we see between WIMA and JMX is the component-oriented management server, once JMX has specified the manager side. Whether the management server is implemented in Java is transparent to WIMA, and the component-software approach adopted in JMX is consistent with our design decisions in WIMA. The agent side could also be implemented in Java, although the need for component software is less obvious on an agent. Apart from that, WIMA and JMX offer little scope for integration.

11.4 Known Problems with WIMA

WIMA is not immune to problems. We identified three: the reliability of new software, the need for management software integrators, and the need for clock synchronization. We describe them in this section and show that none is fatal in the long term.

Reliability of new software

The main problem in WIMA is the reliability of new management platforms based on COTS components and object-oriented frameworks. To put it simply, new means "buggy". Years of debugging and real-life testing have already gone into all the major SNMP-based management platforms, which gives a lot of confidence to potential buyers. Component-oriented software is comparatively new, so the solution that we propose in WIMA is more prone to errors. On the other hand, component software is all about reuse, so component-based management platforms should presumably take less time to be reasonably debugged if the same component is reused in many different contexts.

Note that all possible solutions for the next management cycle are exposed to this problem, except one: SNMP-based management. If we do not change anything, we take no risks, but we have to live with the same problems for many years!

Need for management software integrators

The second source of concern in WIMA is the need for management-software integrators. As we mentioned in Section 7.2.3, components are frequently developed by different vendors in the component-software market. In order to be shielded from liability issues when two components from different vendors do not interact as they are supposed to, many customers should prefer to buy component software from software integrators. These integrators test that the components work well together, they take care of all legal aspects in the case of litigation, and they can also transparently replace a family of components with another if a component is no longer supported (e.g., due to repeated interoperability problems, legal issues, or bankruptcy).

The concerns with software integrators are twofold. First, they have to make some profit, so they reduce the cost savings compared with SNMP-based management platforms. Second, true competition only exists when a customer is ready to visit many vendor booths at a trade show. By going through a software integrator, high are the risks of seeing a reincarnation of the dreaded concept of a "preferred partner"... and of going back to equally dreaded peer-to-peer agreements between vendors. The good news is, because the business of software integration is not overly complex, we can expect many companies to come into this market, thereby increasing competition and the chances for a customer to find a good integrator. The other good news is that, at any point in time, a customer can decide that he/she now knows enough of the component-software market to free him/herself from any integrator.

Synchronization of the clocks

The last issue in WIMA is clock synchronization. If all the managers and agents do not regularly synchronize their internal clocks, some of these clocks will significantly drift apart over time. This is not a problem for monitoring, because it does not matter, when an agent is configured to send a heartbeat to its manager every 5 minutes, whether the manager receives it every 299 seconds or every 301. But it can be a problem for data collection, because the data repository often stores the values for a given MIB variable in the form of a time series. Without synchronization, the manager could receive too many or too few push cycles per day. In this case, to build consistent time series for all MIB variables, some data would have to be discarded arbitrarily and others would have to be interpolated at a random cycle number. Clearly, this is undesirable. And there is a simple solution to this problem: loose synchronization, typically once per day or once per hour.

In WIMA-based management, it is therefore recommended to synchronize the clocks of all the managers and agents on a regular basis. There are many, well-known ways of achieving loose synchronization. Agents and managers can receive clock updates via radio waves, or they can use a protocol such as NTP (Network Time Protocol). These two solutions can also be combined: The management server can update its clock with an absolute time received via radio waves, and it can in turn update the clocks of the agents with NTP. Alternatively, the manager can exchange a few synchronization packets with all the agents in its domain, with an *ad hoc* protocol. Another solution is to make it mandatory for an agent to include a timestamp in each MIME part: We simply have to specify the format of this timestamp in WIMA. In all these cases, the synchronization overhead is negligible compared to the network and CPU savings induced by going from pull to push.

Note that this synchronization problem is caused by the use of the push model: The agent's clock decides when it is time for the next push cycle, and the manager's clock may disagree with it. With the pull model, the manager's clock decides when it is time for the next pull cycle, so time series always get the right number of entries (unless some data does not come in, e.g. in the case of network congestion, in which case it is possible to store an error code such as `notAvailable` for a specific entry, as opposed to a random entry).

11.5 Summary

In this chapter, we showed that WIMA compares well with the other approaches suggested thus far for the next management cycle. In Section 11.1, we compared WIMA to SNMP-based management and concluded that the vast majority of the problems identified in SNMP have been solved in WIMA. In Section 11.2 and Section 11.3, we compared WIMA with WBEM and JMX, two standardization efforts run by industrial consortia. We identified some problems in these two approaches, but also some complementarities with WIMA, notably for WBEM. Finally, in Section 11.4, we described some known problems in WIMA and suggested ways to solve them.

Chapter 12

CONCLUSION

In this last chapter, we summarize the main contributions of our monograph and give some directions for future work.

12.1 Summary

In this book, we have proposed a new architecture for network and systems management in the IP world: WIMA (Web-based Integrated Management Architecture). WIMA is destined to replace SNMP in the next management cycle. Its primary achievement is that it solves almost all of the problems that we identified in SNMP-based management (that is, in the solution currently adopted by the IP world). WIMA is also simple to implement, and does not rely on unrealistic assumptions such as "All IP network devices and systems worldwide must support the same object-oriented middleware". In this section, we summarize our technical contributions, the relevance of our work, and what is needed to migrate from SNMP to WIMA.

Technical contributions

The core contributions of this book are threefold. First, we advocate that regular management data should be pushed by agents, not pulled by managers. This leads us to adopt a push-based organizational model for regular management in WIMA. Second, we argue that (i) standard Web technologies should be used instead of the domain-specific SNMP, and (ii) management data should be reliably transmitted across persistent TCP connections to avoid the loss of important data. WIMA's communication model is based on persistent HTTP connections between the manager and the agent (or between the top- and mid-level managers in distributed management). Within these connections, HTTP messages are structured with MIME multipart. Each MIME part can be an XML document, a binary file with BER-encoded data, a textual file with data encoded in plain strings, etc. MIME parts can be transparently compressed, which reduces network overhead significantly. By creating connections from the manager side, we facilitate crossing firewalls. Our communication model is totally independent of the information model, which allows us to transfer SNMP data, CIM data, etc. Third, we recommend the use of XML for (i) distributing management across a hierarchy of managers (weakly distributed hierarchical management), (ii) integrating management, (iii) dealing with multiple information models (especially SNMP MIBs and CIM schemas), and (iv) supporting high-level semantics.

This book also includes four secondary contributions. First, two taxonomies classify all the management paradigms that have been proposed to date, and help administrators select a paradigm or technology well suited to their needs. Our simple taxonomy is based on a single criterion (the organizational model of the management architecture), while our enhanced taxonomy is based on four criteria (the delegation granularity, the semantic richness of the information model, the degree of automation of management, and the degree of specification of a task). Second, our detailed analysis of the problems with SNMP-based management substantiates a claim often made but rarely substantiated: SNMP-based management is too simple, it will not suffice in the near future. Many assumptions made in the late 1980s, when SNMPv1 was devised, are no longer valid today. So many things should be changed, in the management architecture and the communication protocol, that it is easier to start afresh with a brand-new management architecture and to take legacy systems into account. Third, our design innovations are validated by a research prototype, the JAva MAnagement Platform (JAMAP), which demonstrates their simplicity and feasibility. Finally, our analysis of the state of the art gives a useful overview of the vast and expanding area now known as Web-based management.

Relevance of this work

The problem that we solved with WIMA is not purely academic: It is a real concern to the enterprise-management industry. As we saw in Chapter 4, many proposals have been made since the mid-1990s to address the problems experienced by SNMP-based management, and most notably scalability. Since the late 1990s, two industrial consortia, the Distributed Management Task Force (DMTF) and the Java Community (centered on Sun Microsystems), have dedicated considerable manpower to solving this problem. So far, WBEM/CIM and Java-based management are their main deliverables.

The results exhibited by WIMA are significant, too. If we compare it with SNMP-based management (see Section 11.1), we see that almost all of the problems identified in SNMP-based management are solved in WIMA (27 out of 30), including the most severe ones. These are not purists' conundrums, but real-life problems: firewalls, distribution, network overhead, cost, etc. If we compare WIMA with WBEM, we see that it complements the information modeling work already performed by the DMTF and addresses some issues related to the use of HTTP extensions for traversing firewalls. Finally, if we compare WIMA with Java-based management, we see that its more flexible design protects it from the *my-middleware-is-better-than-yours* syndrome.

The third reason that leads us to believe that our approach is relevant is the excellent feedback that we received from large and small vendors in the networking industry. The service industry also showed notable interest in our activities.

What does it take to migrate from SNMP- to WIMA-based management?

When a new management architecture comes out, the market always faces a chicken-and-egg situation: Equipment vendors are willing to support it if management-platform vendors already do, and *vice versa*. Because writing a new manager is a lot more work than writing a new agent, we believe that the way out of this deadlock is to convince equipment vendors to support WIMA in their network devices and systems. As soon as a number of agents have been shipped with embedded support for WIMA, some start-ups will develop WIMA-compliant management platforms to enter the lucrative management market.

What do equipment vendors need to do to support WIMA? They must embed four software components in their network devices and systems: an HTTP server (we saw that this is often already the case), a push system, a scheduler, and one or several vendor-specific management GUIs. Typically, this software would be embedded in EPROM. Writing the push and scheduling systems is simple and inexpensive. Reprogramming existing management GUIs as Java applets is probably the most costly part, but the potential gains are enormous (write portable code once, run it anywhere).

Once WIMA-compliant agents are available on the market, the second step of the migration process is for management-platform vendors to develop professional-grade component software for management servers. When different components are developed by different vendors, we need software integrators to shield the customers from inter-vendor liability mazes ("It does not work, whose fault is it?"). The current explosion of the Web-based management market, with start-ups flocking in, leads us to believe that we could soon have a mature market of WIMA-compliant management servers. Note that the risk factor for these vendors is lower with WIMA than with most alternatives: object-oriented middleware, mobile code, multi-agent systems, etc.

The third step toward WIMA-based management is for administrators to loosely synchronize the clocks of the managers and agents. There are simple solutions to achieve this, e.g. the Network Time Protocol (NTP). This type of synchronization is already routinely performed in many networks worldwide.

12.2 Directions for Future Work

Many areas could be investigated as a follow-up to this work. We propose six directions for future work: wireless networks, IP telephony, integrated management, SNMP-to-XML mapping, integration of SNMP MIBs and CIM schemas, and Web services.

WIMA for wireless networks

The work presented herein focuses on fixed IP networks and systems. Preliminary work suggests that WIMA can also cope with IP wireless networks and systems. For instance, push technologies are promising to manage cell phones and Web-enabled handheld devices, because these devices can remain inaccessible by the manager for extended periods of time under normal circumstances. By using push instead of pull technologies, we prevent the manager from performing many retries when, for instance, the agent is voluntarily switched off, or when it is in an area that is not covered by any antennae.

WIMA for IP telephony

Another worthwhile research area is the suitability of WIMA in QoS-driven networks, and especially in IP telephony. The challenges are great because the telecommunications world is used to notification-driven management, with smart agents, whereas WIMA is particularly efficient for transferring bulks of management data from the agent to the manager, to let the manager do most of the management application. Still, WIMA can also deal with smart agents, and it would be interesting to compare its efficiency with that of other management architectures. Signaling, for instance, has not yet been investigated in the context of WIMA.

WIMA for integrated management

Although we mentioned several times the advantages of WIMA in integrated management at large, only network and systems management were studied here. We already saw that application management is very similar to systems management, so we expect the integration of application management to be straightforward. Early work also suggests that WIMA can be extended to policy-based management, especially when we use XML to represent management data. To an XML document, it is transparent whether the semantics of the management data is high (for policy-based management) or low (for network and systems management). Service management still remains to be investigated, but the possibility in WIMA to transfer mobile code within XML documents should prove to be useful for dynamic service provisioning.

SNMP-to-XML mapping: model or metamodel level?

In Section 9.2, we explained the difference between model- and metamodel-level mappings. An important research area for integrating SNMP-compliant agents and managers with their CIM counterparts is whether the SNMP-to-XML mapping should be performed at the model level (that is, one XML Schema per SNMP MIB), or at the metamodel level (that is, a single XML Schema for all SNMP MIBs).

Integration of SNMP MIBs and CIM schemas

A fifth interesting research area is the coexistence and integration of the SNMP and CIM information models. What are the issues when we have to deal with multiple information models? What semantics do we lose when we translate CIM schemas into SNMP MIBs, and *vice versa*? A few years ago, IIMC and JIDM studied information-model integration for SNMP, OSI, and CORBA (see Section 4.1.3.2). It would be very useful to extend this work to CIM, which is backed by many vendors and seems likely to gradually complement, or perhaps even replace, the SNMP information model in the next management cycle.

Web Services, UDDI, and SOAP

Last, Web Services [277] have received much attention recently, and the World-Wide Web Consortium (W3C) seems to be very serious about this standardization effort. These APIs and languages are meant to facilitate and standardize application-to-application communication via HTTP/XML messages. The Simple Object Access Protocol (SOAP), particularly SOAP 1.2 [110, 111], looks promising for standardizing XML message envelopes and Remote Procedure Calls (RPCs). It would be interesting to slightly change the communication model of WIMA (and possibly also WBEM's) to leverage these technologies and assess the gains they bring about.

Universal Description, Discovery and Integration (UDDI [21]) is another promising technology. It can be viewed as a metaservice for locating Web Services. Although not yet formally endorsed by the W3C, it is backed by a large industrial consortium and may encounter a certain success in the market. Adding support for UDDI in WIMA should be straightforward, as it requires rather simple changes in the publish-subscribe mechanisms described in Section 7.3.

If Web technologies continue to pervade the software industry, Web Services, UDDI, and SOAP could soon *de facto* become some of the building blocks of Web-based management.

ACRONYMS

ACK	ACKnowledgment
API	Application Programming Interface
ARP	Address Resolution Protocol
ASN.1	Abstract Syntax Notation 1
ASP	Active Server Page
ATM	Asynchronous Transfer Mode
A-TRT	Agent's TCP Retransmission Timer
A-TRTO	Agent's TCP Retransmission Time-Out
AWT	Abstract Window Toolkit
BDI	Belief Desire Intention
BER	Basic Encoding Rules
BNF	Backus-Naur Form
BOF	Birds Of a Feather
BSD	Berkeley Software Distribution
CD	Compact Disk
CD-ROM	Compact Disk - Read-Only Memory
CER	Canonical Encoding Rules
CGI	Common Gateway Interface
CIM	Common Information Model
CIMOM	Common Information Model Object Manager
CLHS	Component Launched by an HTTP Server
CLI	Command-Line Interface
CLNS	ConnectionLess Network Service
CMIP	Common Management Information Protocol
CMIS	Common Management Information Service
COD	Code On Demand
CONS	Connection-Oriented Network Service
CORBA	Common Object Request Broker Architecture
COTS	Commercial Off-The-Shelf

CPU	Central Processing Unit
DAI	Distributed Artificial Intelligence
DAP	Distributed Application Performance
DCE	Distributed Computing Environment
DCOM	Distributed Component Object Model
DER	Distinguished Encoding Rules
DISMAN	DIStributed MANagement
DMI	Desktop Management Interface
DMTF	Distributed Management Task Force
DoS	Denial of Service
DPE	Distributed Processing Environment
EDI	Electronic Data Interchange
EJB	Enterprise JavaBean
EPROM	Erasable Programmable Read-Only Memory
FCAPS	Fault, Configuration, Accounting, Performance, and Security
FDDI	Fiber Distributed Data Interface
FIPA	Foundation for Intelligent Physical Agents
FMA	Federated Management Architecture
FPGA	Field-Programmable Gate Array
FSM	Finite State Machine
FTP	File Transfer Protocol
GDMO	Guidelines for the Definition of Managed Objects
GIF	Graphics Interchange Format
GRM	General Relationship Model
GUI	Graphical User Interface
HMMP	HyperMedia Management Protocol
HMMS	HyperMedia Management Schema
HMOM	HyperMedia Object Manager
HTML	HyperText Markup Language
HTTP	HyperText Transfer Protocol
IANA	Internet Assigned Numbers Authority
ICMP	Internet Control Message Protocol
IDL	Interface Definition Language
IESG	Internet Engineering Steering Group
IETF	Internet Engineering Task Force
IIMC	ISO-Internet Management Coexistence
IIOP	Internet Inter-ORB Protocol
I/O	Input/Output
IRTF	Internet Research Task Force
IP	Internet Protocol
IPSec	IP Security
ISO	International Organization for Standardization
ISP	Internet Service Provider
IT	Information Technology

ITU-T	International Telecommunication Union - Telecommunication standardization sector
J2EE	Java 2 Enterprise Edition
J2ME	Java 2 Micro Edition
J2SE	Java 2 Standard Edition
JAMAP	JAva MAnagement Platform
JDBC	Java DataBase Connectivity
JDK	Java Development Kit
JIDM	Joint Inter-Domain Management
JMAPI	Java Management Application Programming Interface
JMX	Java Management eXtensions
JNI	Java Native Interface
JVM	Java Virtual Machine
KQML	Knowledge Query and Manipulation Language
LAN	Local-Area Network
LDAP	Lightweight Directory Access Protocol
LWER	LightWeight Encoding Rules
M2M	Manager to Manager
MAC	Medium Access Control
MAS	Multi-Agent System
MbD	Management by Delegation
MBean	Management Bean
MIB	Management Information Base
MIME	Multipurpose Internet Mail Extensions
MMO	Memory-Management Overhead
MOF	Managed Object Format
MRTG	Multi-Router Traffic Grapher
MSS	Maximum Segment Size
M-TKT	Manager's TCP Keepalive Timer
M-TKTO	Manager's TCP Keepalive Time-Out
MTU	Maximum Transmission Unit
NFS	Network File System
NIM	Network Information Model
NIS	Network Information Service
NMF	Network Management Forum
NOC	Network Operations Center
NSM	Network and Systems Management
NTP	Network Time Protocol
ODBC	Open DataBase Connectivity
ODMA	Open Distributed Management Architecture
OID	Object IDentifier
ODP	Open Distributed Processing
OLE	Object Linking and Embedding
OMG	Object Management Group
OODBMS	Object-Oriented DataBase Management System

ORB	Object Request Broker
OSI	Open Systems Interconnection
PC	Personal Computer
PDP	Policy Decision Point
PDU	Packet Data Unit
PEP	Policy Enforcement Point
PER	Packed Encoding Rules
PNG	Portable Network Graphics
POS-EWS	POSTECH Embedded Web Server
QoS	Quality of Service
R&D	Research and Development
RDBMS	Relational DataBase Management System
REV	Remote EValuation
RFC	Request For Comments
RMI	Remote Method Invocation
RM-ODP	Reference Model - Open Distributed Processing
RMON	Remote MONitoring
ROI	Return On Investment
RPC	Remote Procedure Call
RST	Reset
RTO	Retransmission Time-Out
RTP	Real-time Transport Protocol
SCTP	Stream Control Transmission Protocol
SLA	Service-Level Agreement
SMI	Structure of Management Information
SNMP	Simple Network Management Protocol
SOAP	Simple Object Access Protocol
SQL	Structured Query Language
SS7	Signaling System No. 7
SSL	Secure Sockets Layer
SYN	SYNchronize
TCO	Total Cost of Ownership
TCP	Transmission Control Protocol
TFTP	Trivial File Transfer Protocol
TINA	Telecommunications Information Networking Architecture
TMF	TeleManagement Forum
TMN	Telecommunications Management Network
TOS	Type Of Service
UDDI	Universal Description, Discovery and Integration
UDP	User Datagram Protocol
UML	Unified Modeling Language
URI	Uniform Resource Identifier
URL	Uniform Resource Locator
VACM	View-based Access Control Model

VP	Virtual Path
VPN	Virtual Private Network
WAIS	Wide-Area Information Servers
WAN	Wide-Area Network
WbASM	Web-based ATM-Switch Management
WBEM	Web-Based Enterprise Management
WIMA	Web-based Integrated Management Architecture
WIMA-CM	Web-based Integrated Management Architecture - Communication Model
WIMA-OM	Web-based Integrated Management Architecture - Organizational Model
XMI	XML Metadata Interchange
XML	eXtensible Markup Language
xmlCIM	CIM-to-XML mapping

REFERENCES

1. AdventNet. *SNMP Package*. Available at <http://www.adventnet.com/products.html>.
2. Agent Society. *Home Page*. Available at <http://www.agent.org/>.
3. S. Aidarous and T. Plevyak (Eds.), *Telecommunications Network Management: Technologies and Implementations*. IEEE Press, New York, NY, USA, 1998.
4. D.S. Alexander, W.A. Arbaugh, M.W. Hicks, P. Kakkar, A.D. Keromytis, J.T. Moore, C.A. Gunter, S.M. Nettles, and J.M. Smith. "The SwitchWare active network architecture". *IEEE Network*, 12(3):29–36, 1998.
5. B. Alpers and H. Plansky. "Concepts and Application of Policy-Based Management". In A.S. Sethi, Y. Raynaud, and F. Faure-Vincent (Eds.), *Integrated Network Management IV. Proc. 4th IFIP/IEEE International Symposium on Integrated Network Management (ISINM'95), Santa Barbara, CA, USA, May 1995*, pp. 57–68. Chapman & Hall, London, UK, 1995.
6. S.W. Ambler. *Building Object Applications That Work*. Cambridge University Press, Cambridge, UK, 1998.
7. R. Anderson, M. Birbeck, *et al. Professional XML*. Wrox Press, 2000.
8. N. Anerousis. "Scalable Management Services Using Java and the World Wide Web". In A.S. Sethi (Ed.), *Proc. 9th IFIP/IEEE International Workshop on Distributed Systems: Operations & Management (DSOM'98), Newark, DE, USA, October 1998*, pp. 79–90.
9. N. Anerousis. "An Information Model for Generating Computed Views of Management Information". In A.S. Sethi (Ed.), *Proc. 9th IFIP/IEEE International Workshop on Distributed Systems: Operations & Management (DSOM'98), Newark, DE, USA, October 1998*, pp. 169–180.
10. N. Anerousis. "A Distributed Computing Environment for Building Scalable Management Services". In M. Sloman, S. Mazumdar, and E. Lupu (Eds.), *Integrated Network Management VI. Proc. 6th IFIP/IEEE International Symposium on Integrated Network Management (IM'99), Boston, MA, USA, May 1999*, pp. 547–562. IEEE, Piscataway, NJ, USA, 1999.
11. Apache Software Foundation. *The Apache Project*. Available at <http://www.apache.org/httpd.html>.
12. T.K. Apostolopoulos and V.C. Daskalou. "Temporal Network Management Information Model and Services". *Journal of Network and Systems Management*, 6(3):245–265, 1998.
13. M. Armstrong. *A Handbook of Personnel Management Practice*. 4th edition. Kogan Page, London, UK, 1991.

14. C. Atkinson. "Meta-Modeling for Distributed Object Environments". In *Proc. 1st International Enterprise Distributed Object Computing Conference (EDOC '97), Gold Coast, Australia, October, 1997*. IEEE Computer Society Press, Los Alamitos, CA, USA, 1997.

15. ATM Forum. *SNMP M4 Network Element View MIB*. Revision AF-NM-0095.001. July 1998.

16. M. Baldi, S. Gai, and G.P. Picco. "Exploiting Code Mobility in Decentralized and Flexible Network Management". In K. Rothermel and R. Popescu-Zeletin (Eds.), *Proc. 1st International Workshop on Mobile Agents (MA'97), Berlin, Germany, April 1997*. LNCS 1219:13–26, Springer, Berlin, Germany, 1997.

17. M. Baldi and G.P. Picco. "Evaluating the Tradeoffs of Mobile Code Design Paradigms in Network Management Applications". In R. Kemmerer and K. Futatsugi (Eds.), *Proc. 20th International Conference on Software Engineering (ICSE'98), Kyoto, Japan, April 1998*, pp. 146–155. IEEE, Piscataway, NJ, USA, 1998.

18. G Banga, J.C. Mogul, and P. Druschel. "A Scalable and Explicit Event Delivery Mechanism for UNIX". In *Proc. 1999 USENIX Annual Technical Conference (Usenix'99)*, Monterey, CA, USA, June 1999.

19. F. Barillaud, L. Deri, and M. Feridun. "Network Management using Internet Technologies". In A. Lazar, R. Saracco, and R. Stadler (Eds.), *Integrated Network Management V. Proc. 5th IFIP/ IEEE International Symposium on Integrated Network Management (IM'97), San Diego, CA, USA, May 1997*, pp. 61–70. Chapman & Hall, London, UK, 1997.

20. W.J. Barr, T. Boyd, and Y. Inoue. "The TINA Initiative". *IEEE Communications Magazine*, 31(3):70–76, 1993.

21. T. Bellwood, L. Clément, D. Ehnebuske, A. Hately, M. Hondo, Y.L. Husband, K. Januszewski, S. Lee, B. McKee, J. Munter, and C. von Riegen (Eds.). *UDDI Version 3.0*. Published Specification, UDDI.org, 19 July 2002. Available at
<http://uddi.org/uddi-v3.00-published-20020719.htm>.

22. H. Berndt, T. Hamada, and P. Graubmann. "TINA: Its Achievements and Its Future Directions". *IEEE Communications Surveys & Tutorials*, 3(1):2–16, 2000.

23. T. Berners-Lee, R. Fielding, and H. Frystyk (Eds.). *RFC 1945. Hypertext Transfer Protocol -- HTTP/1.0*. IETF, May 1996.

24. T. Berners-Lee, R. Fielding, and L. Masinter (Eds.). *RFC 2396. Uniform Resource Identifiers (URI): Generic Syntax*. IETF, August 1998.

25. L. Bernstein and C.M. Yuhas. "Truce in Protocol Wars". *Journal of Network and Systems Management*, 1(2):103–105, 1993.

26. A. Bieszczad and B. Pagurek. "Towards Plug-and-Play Networks with Mobile Code". In *Proc. International Conference for Computer Communications (ICCC'97), November 1997, Cannes, France*.

27. A. Bieszczad, T. White, and B. Pagurek. "Mobile Agents for Network Management". *IEEE Communications Surveys*, 1(1):2–9, 1998.

28. BMC Software, Cisco, Compaq, Intel, and Microsoft. *Industry Leaders Propose Web-Based Enterprise Management Standards Effort*. Press Release, July 1996.

29. R. Booth. *XML As a Representation for Management Information—A White Paper*. Draft. Microsoft, May 1998.

30. J. Bosak and T. Bray. "XML and the Second-Generation Web". *Scientific American*, May 1999.

31. L. Bovet. *The Push Model in a Java-Based Network Management Application*. M.S. thesis, Computer Science Dept., EPFL, Lausanne, Switzerland, March 1999.

32. R. Braden (Ed.). *RFC 1122. Requirements for Internet Hosts—Communication Layers*. IETF, October 1989.

33. N. Bradley. *The XML Companion*. Addison-Wesley, Harlow, UK, 1998.

34. T. Bray, D. Hollander, and A. Layman (Eds.). *Namespaces in XML. W3C Recommendation REC-xml-names-19990114*. W3C, January 1999. Available at <http://www.w3.org/TR/1999/REC-xml-names-19990114>.

35. T. Bray, J. Paoli, and C.M. Sperberg-McQueen (Eds.). *Extensible Markup Language (XML) 1.0. W3C Recommendation REC-xml-19980210*. W3C, February 1998. Available at <http://www.w3.org/TR/1998/REC-xml-19980210>.

36. M. Breugst and T. Magedanz. "Mobile Agents—Enabling Technology for Active Intelligent Network Implementation". *IEEE Network*, 12(3):53–60, 1998.

37. W.H. Brown, R.C. Malveau, H.W. McCormick III, and T.J. Mowbray. *AntiPatterns: Refactoring Software, Architectures, and Projects in Crisis*. Wiley, New York, NY, USA, 1998.

38. B. Bruins. "Some Experiences with Emerging Management Technologies". *The Simple Times*, 4(3):6–8, 1996.

39. M. Brunner and R. Stadler. "Service Management in Multiparty Active Networks". *IEEE Communications Magazine*, 38(3):144–151, 2000.

40. W. Bumpus. "DMTF Expands Its Role in Developing Information Model Standards". *Journal of Network and Systems Management*, 6(3):357–360, 1998.

41. W. Bumpus, J.W. Sweitzer, P. Thompson, A.R. Westerinen, and R.C. Williams. *Common Information Model : Implementing the Object Model for Enterprise Management*. Wiley, New York, NY, USA, 2000.

42. R. Burns and M. Quinn. "The Cyber-Agent Framework". *The Simple Times*, 4(3):12–15, 1996.

43. F. Buschmann, R. Meunier, H. Rohnert, P. Sommerlad, and M. Stal. *Pattern-Oriented Software Architecture—A System of Patterns*. Wiley, Chichester, UK, 1996.

44. B. Callaghan, B. Pawlowski, and P. Staubach (Eds.). *RFC 1813. NFS Version 3 Protocol Specification*. IETF, June 1995.

45. A.T. Campbell, H.G. De Meer, M.E. Kounavis, K. Miki, J.B. Vicente, and D. Villela. "A Survey of Programmable Networks". *ACM Computer Communication Review*, 29(2):7–23, 1999.

46. J. Case, M. Fedor, M. Schoffstall, and J. Davin (Eds.). *RFC 1157. A Simple Network Management Protocol (SNMP)*. IETF, May 1990.

47. J. Case, K. McCloghrie, M. Rose, and S. Waldbusser (Eds.). *RFC 1451. Manager-to-Manager Management Information Base*. IETF, April 1993.

48. J. Case, K. McCloghrie, M. Rose, and S. Waldbusser (Eds.). *RFC 1902. Structure of Management Information for Version 2 of the Simple Network Management Protocol (SNMPv2)*. IETF, January 1996.

49. J. Case, K. McCloghrie, M. Rose, and S. Waldbusser (Eds.). *RFC 1905. Protocol Operations for Version 2 of the Simple Network Management Protocol (SNMPv2)*. IETF, January 1996.

50. J. Case, K. McCloghrie, M. Rose, and S. Waldbusser (Eds.). *RFC 1906. Transport Mappings for Version 2 of the Simple Network Management Protocol (SNMPv2)*. IETF, January 1996.

51. J. Case, K. McCloghrie, M. Rose, and S. Waldbusser (Eds.). *RFC 1907. Management Information Base for Version 2 of the Simple Network Management Protocol (SNMPv2)*. IETF, January 1996.

52. CCITT (now ITU-T). *Recommendation M.3400. TMN management functions*. ITU, Geneva, Switzerland, October 1992.

53. CCITT (now ITU-T). *Recommendation X.700. Data Communication Networks—Management Framework for Open Systems Interconnection (OSI) for CCITT Applications*. ITU, Geneva, Switzerland, September 1992.

54. CCITT (now ITU-T). *Recommendation X.701. Data Communication Networks—Information Technology—Open Systems Interconnection—Systems Management Overview*. ITU, Geneva, Switzerland, January 1992.

55. CCITT (now ITU-T). *Recommendation X.710. Data Communication Networks: Open Systems Interconnection (OSI); Management. Common Management Information Service Definition for CCITT Applications*. ITU, Geneva, Switzerland, March 1991.

56. CCITT (now ITU-T). *Recommendation X.711. Data Communication Networks—Open Systems Interconnection (OSI); Management. Common Management Information Protocol Specification for CCITT Applications*. ITU, Geneva, Switzerland, March 1991.

57. CCITT (now ITU-T). *Recommendation X.722. Data Communication Networks—Information Technology—Open Systems Interconnection—Structure of Information Management: Guidelines for the Definition of Managed Objects*. ITU, Geneva, Switzerland, January 1992.

58. D.B. Chapman and E.D. Zwicky. *Building Internet Firewalls*. O'Reilly & Associates, Sebastopol, CA, USA, 1995.

59. W.R. Cheswick and S.M. Bellovin. *Firewalls and Internet Security—Repelling the Wily Hacker*. Addison-Wesley, Reading, MA, USA, 1994.

60. M.J. Choi, H.T. Ju, H.J. Cha, S.H. Kim, and J.W.K. Hong. "An Efficient and Lightweight Embedded Web Server for Web-based Network Element Management". In *Proc. IEEE/IFIP Network Operations and Management Symposium (NOMS 2000), Hawaii, USA, April 2000*, pp. 187–200. IEEE Press, New York, NY, USA, 2000.

61. Cisco. *Release Notes for Cisco IOS Release 12.1*. March 20, 2000. Available at <http://www.cisco.com/univercd/cc/td/doc/product/software/ios121/121relnt/xprn121/121reqs.htm>.

62. J. Clark. *XML parser*. Available at <http://www.jclark.com/xml/>.

63. J. Clark and S. DeRose (Eds.). *XML Path Language (XPath) Version 1.0. W3C Recommendation REC-xpath-19991116*. W3C, November 1999. Available at <http://www.w3.org/TR/1999/REC-xpath-19991116>.

64. CMU. *CMU SNMP library*. Available at <http://www.net.cmu.edu/groups/netdev/software.html>.

65. G. Coulouris, J. Dollimore, and T. Kindberg. *Distributed Systems: Concepts and Design*. 2nd edition. Addison-Wesley, Wokingham, UK, 1994.

66. J.D. Davidson and S. Ahmed. *Java Servlet API Specification. Version 2.1a*. Sun Microsystems, November 1998.

67. L. Deri. "Surfin' Network Resources Across the Web". In *Proc. IEEE 2nd International Workshop on Systems Management, Toronto, ON, Canada, June 1996*, pp. 158–167. IEEE Computer Society Press, Los Alamitos, CA, USA, 1996.

68. L. Deri. *HTTP-based SNMP and CMIP Network Management*. Internet-Draft <draft-deri-http-mgmt-00.txt> (now expired). IETF, November 1996.

69. L. Deri. "JLocator: A Web-Based Asset Location System". In A.S. Sethi (Ed.), *Proc. 9th IFIP/IEEE International Workshop on Distributed Systems: Operations & Management (DSOM'98), Newark, DE, USA, October 1998*, pp. 3–13.

70. L. Deri. *ntop - network top*. Available at <http://www.ntop.org/>.

71. P. Deutsch (Ed.). *RFC 1951. DEFLATE Compressed Data Format Specification version 1.3*. IETF, May 1996.

72. DMTF. *Desktop Management Interface Specification*. Version 2.00. March 1996.

73. DMTF. *XML As a Representation for Management Information - A White Paper*. Version 1.0. September 1998. Available at <http://www.dmtf.org/standards/xmlw.php>.

74. DMTF. *Common Information Model (CIM) Specification*. Version 2.2. June 1999. Available at <http://www.dmtf.org/standards/cim_spec_v22/>.

75. DMTF. *CIM DTD*. July 1999. Available at
    <http://www.dmtf.org/download/spec/xmls/CIM_DTD_V20.txt>.
76. DMTF. *Specification for the Representation of CIM in XML*. Version 2.0. July 1999. Available
    at <http://www.dmtf.org/download/spec/xmls/CIM_XML_Mapping20.php>.
77. DMTF. *Specification for CIM Operations over HTTP*. Version 1.0. August 1999. Available at
    <http://www.dmtf.org/download/spec/xmls/CIM_HTTP_Mapping10.htm>.
78. DMTF. *WBEM Initiative*. Available at <http://www.dmtf.org/standards/standard_wbem.php/>.
79. DMTF. *Common Information Model (CIM) Core Model Whitepaper*. Version 2.4. August 2000.
    Available at <http://www.dmtf.org/var/release/Whitepapers/DSP0111.pdf>.
80. DMTF. CIM Schema Version 2.6. Available at
    <http://www.dmtf.org/standards/cim_schema_v26.php>.
81. D.F. D'Souza and A.C. Wills. *Objects, Components, and Frameworks with UML: The Catalysis
    Approach*. Addison-Wesley, Reading, MA, USA, 1999.
82. T. Elrad, R.E. Filman, and A. Bader (Eds.). Special Issue on Aspect-Oriented Programming.
    Communications of the ACM, 44(10):28–97, 2001.
83. D. Evans. *Supervisory Management: Principles and Practice*. 2nd edition. Cassell Educational
    Ltd, London, UK, 1986.
84. T. Faber. "ACC: Using Active Networking to Enhance Feedback Congestion Control
    Mechanisms". *IEEE Network*, 12(3):61–65, 1998.
85. A. Falk and V. Paxson. "Requirements for Unicast Transport/Sessions (RUTS) BOF". In *Proc.
    43rd IETF Meeting*, Orlando, FL, USA, December 1998. Available at
    <http://www.ietf.org/proceedings/98dec/43rd-ietf-98dec-142.html>.
86. D.C. Fallside (Ed.). *XML Schema Part 0: Primer. W3C Recommendation REC-xmlschema-0-
    20010502*. W3C, May 2001. Available at
    <http://www.w3.org/TR/2001/REC-xmlschema-0-20010502/>.
87. D. Fensel. *Ontologies: A Silver Bullet for Knowledge Management and Electronic Commerce*.
    Springer, Berlin, Germany, 2001.
88. R. Fielding, J. Gettys, J. Mogul, H. Frystyk, L. Masinter, P. Leach, and T. Berners-Lee (Eds.).
    RFC 2616. Hypertext Transfer Protocol -- HTTP/1.1. IETF, June 1999.
89. T. Finin, R. Fritzson, D. McKay, and R. McEntire. "KQML as an Agent Communication
    Language". In N.R. Adam, B.K. Bhargava, and Y. Yesha (Eds.), *Proc. 3rd International
    Conference on Information and Knowledge Management (CIKM'94), Gaithersburg, MD, USA,
    November 1994*, pp. 456–463. ACM Press, New York, NY, USA, 1994.
90. FIPA. *Home Page*. Available at <http://www.fipa.org/>.
91. FIPA. *FIPA ACL Message Structure Specification*. Revision XC00061D. August 2000.
92. S. Floyd and V. Paxson. "Difficulties in Simulating the Internet". *IEEE/ACM Transactions on
    Networking*, 9(4):392–403, 2001.
93. M. Fowler. *Analysis Patterns: Reusable Object Models*. Addison-Wesley, Menlo Park, CA,
    USA, 1997.
94. M. Fowler and K. Scott. *UML Distilled*. 2nd edition. Addison-Wesley, Reading, MA, USA,
    2000.
95. S. Franklin and A. Graesser. "Is it an agent, or just a program?: a taxonomy for autonomous
    agents". In J.P. Müller, M.J. Wooldridge, and N.R. Jennings (Eds.), *Intelligent Agents III. Proc.
    ECAI'96 Workshop (ATAL), Budapest, Hungary, August 1996*. LNAI 1193:21–35, Springer,
    Berlin, Germany, 1997.
96. J. Franks, P. Hallam-Baker, J. Hostetler, S. Lawrence, P. Leach, A. Luotonen, and L. Stewart
    (Eds.). *RFC 2617. HTTP Authentication: Basic and Digest Access Authentication*. IETF, June
    1999.

97. Free Software Foundation. *GNU General Public License*. Available at
     <http://www.gnu.org/copyleft/gpl.html>.
98. N. Freed and N. Borenstein (Eds.). *RFC 2046. Multipurpose Internet Mail Extensions (MIME).
     Part Two: Media Types*. IETF, November 1996.
99. A. Fuggetta, G.P. Picco, and G. Vigna. "Understanding Code Mobility". *IEEE Transactions on
     Software Engineering*, 24(5):342–361, 1998.
100. J. Galvin and K. McCloghrie (Eds.). *RFC 1445. Administrative Model for version 2 of the
     Simple Network Management Protocol (SNMPv2)*. IETF, April 1993.
101. E. Gamma, R. Helm, R. Johnson, and J. Vlissides. *Design Patterns: Elements of Reusable
     Object-Oriented Software*. Addison-Wesley, Menlo Park, CA, USA, 1994.
102. M.R. Genesereth. *Knowledge Interchange Format*. Draft proposed American National Standard
     (dpANS) NCITS.T2/98-004. 1998. Available at <http://logic.stanford.edu/kif/dpans.html>.
103. R.H. Glitho. "Contrasting OSI Systems Management to SNMP and TMN". *Journal of Network
     and Systems Management*, 6(2):113–133, 1998.
104. C.F. Goldfarb and P. Prescod. *The XML Handbook*. Prentice Hall, Upper Saddle River, NJ,
     USA, 1998.
105. G. Goldszmidt. *Distributed Management by Delegation*. Ph.D. dissertation, Columbia
     University, New York, NY, USA, December 1995.
106. G. Goldszmidt and A. Stanford-Clark. "Load Distribution for Scalable Web Servers: Summer
     Olympics 1996—A Case Study". In A. Seneviratne, V. Varadarajan, and P. Ray (Eds.), *Proc.
     8th IFIP/IEEE International Workshop on Distributed Systems: Operations & Management
     (DSOM'97), Sydney, Australia, October 1997*, pp. 53–64.
107. J. Gosling and H. McGilton. *The Java Language Environment: a White Paper*. Sun
     Microsystems, October 1995.
108. L.E. Greiner. "Evolution and Revolution as Organizations Grow". *Harvard Business Review*,
     50(4):37–46, 1972.
109. T.R. Gruber. "A Translation Approach to Portable Ontology Specifications". *Knowledge
     Acquisition*, 5:199–220, 1993.
110. M. Gudgin, M. Hadley, J.J. Moreau, H. Frystyk Nielsen. *SOAP Version 1.2 Part 1: Messaging
     Framework. W3C Working Draft WD-soap12-part1-20011217*. W3C, December 2001.
     Available at <http://www.w3.org/TR/2001/WD-soap12-part1-20011217/>.
111. M. Gudgin, M. Hadley, J.J. Moreau, H. Frystyk Nielsen. *SOAP Version 1.2 Part 2: Adjuncts.
     W3C Working Draft WD-soap12-part2-20011217*. W3C, December 2001. Available at
     <http://www.w3.org/TR/2001/WD-soap12-part2-20011217/>.
112. C. Harler. *Web-Based Network Management: Beyond the Browser*. Wiley, New York, NY,
     USA, 1999.
113. D. Harrington, R. Presuhn, and B. Wijnen (Eds.). *RFC 2571. An Architecture for Describing
     SNMP Management Frameworks*. IETF, May 1999.
114. B. Harrison, P.E. Mellquist, and A. Pell. *Web Based System and Network Management*.
     Internet-Draft <draft-mellquist-web-sys-01.txt> (now expired). IETF, November 1996.
115. M.J. Hatch. *Organization Theory: Modern, Symbolic, and Postmodern Perspectives*. Oxford
     University Press, Oxford, UK, 1997.
116. M. Hauswirth and M. Jazayeri. "A Component and Communication Model for Push Systems".
     In O. Nierstrasz and M. Lemoine (Eds.), *Software Engineering. Proc. 7th European Software
     Engineering Conference held jointly with the 7th ACM SIGSOFT Symposium on the
     Foundations of Software Engineering (ESEC/FSE'99)*, Toulouse, France, September 1999.
     LNCS 1687:20–38, Springer, Berlin, Germany, 1999.

117. H.G. Hegering and S. Abeck. *Integrated Network and System Management*. Addison-Wesley, Wokingham, UK, 1994.

118. H.G. Hegering, S. Abeck, and B. Neumair. *Integrated Management of Networked Systems: Concepts, Architectures, and Their Operational Application*. Morgan Kaufmann, San Francisco, CA, USA, 1999.

119. J.R. Hess, D.C. Lee, S.J. Harper, M.T. Jones, and P.M. Athanas. "Implementation and Evaluation of a Prototype Reconfigurable Router". In *Proc. 7th Annual IEEE Symposium on Field-Programmable Custom Computing Machines (FCCM'99), Napa, CA, USA, April 1999*, pp. 44–50.

120. J.W.K. Hong, J.Y. Kong, T.H. Yun, J.S. Kim, J.T. Park, and J.W. Baek. "Web-Based Intranet Services and Network Management". *IEEE Communications Magazine*, 35(10):100–110, 1997.

121. J.W.K. Hong, S.S. Kwon, and J.Y. Kim. WebTrafMon: Web-based Internet/Intranet network traffic monitoring and analysis system. *Computer Communications*, 22(14):1333–1342, 1999.

122. HTTP-WG mailing list. Thread entitled *"Drawbacks of persistent connections"*. June 1998. Available at <http://www.ics.uci.edu/pub/ietf/http/hypermail/1998q2/0191.html>.

123. IANA. *Protocol Numbers and Assignment Services*. Available at <http://www.iana.org/numbers.html>. (Note that the IANA Web site supersedes RFC 1700, which is obsolete.)

124. ISO/IEC JTC1/SC21 N6131. *ISO/IEC Working Draft 8824-3. Information Technology—ASN.1 Encoding Rules—LightWeight Encoding Rules (LWER)*. ISO, Geneva, Switzerland, 1994. *(Cited in [180].)*

125. ISO WG4 N1851. *Open Distributed Management Architecture*. Working Draft 3. ISO, July 1995.

126. V. Issarny, L. Bellissard, M. Riveill, and A. Zarras. "Component-Based Programming of Distributed Applications". In S. Krakowiak and S. Shrivastava (Eds.), *Advances in Distributed Systems—Advanced Distributed Computing: From Algorithms to Systems*. LNCS 1752:327–353, Springer, Berlin, Germany, 2000.

127. ITU-T. *Recommendation M.3010. Principles for a Telecommunications management network*. ITU, Geneva, Switzerland, May 1996.

128. ITU-T. *Recommendation X.690. Information Technology—ASN.1 Encoding Rules: Specification of Basic Encoding Rules (BER), Canonical Encoding Rules (CER) and Distinguished Encoding Rules (DER)*. ITU, Geneva, Switzerland, July 1994.

129. ITU-T. *Recommendation X.691. Information Technology—ASN.1 Encoding Rules: Specification of Packed Encoding Rules (PER)*. ITU, Geneva, Switzerland, April 1995.

130. ITU-T. *Recommendation X.725. Data Networks and Open System Communications—OSI Management—Information Technology—Open Systems Interconnection—Structure of Information Management: General Relationship Model*. ITU, Geneva, Switzerland, November 1995.

131. ITU-T. *Recommendation X.753. Information technology—Open Systems Interconnection—Systems management: Command sequencer for systems management*. ITU, Geneva, Switzerland, October 1997.

132. A. John, K. Vanderveen, and B. Sugla. "An XML-Based Framework for Dynamic SNMP MIB Extension". In R. Stadler and B. Stiller (Eds.), *Active Technologies for Network and Service Management. Proc. 10th IFIP/IEEE International Workshop on Distributed Systems: Operations & Management (DSOM'99), Zurich, Switzerland, October 1999*. LNCS 1700:107–120, Springer, Berlin, Germany, 1999.

133. H.T. Ju, M.J. Choi, S. Han, Y. Oh, J.H. Yoon, H. Lee, and J.W.K. Hong. "An Embedded Web Server Architecture for XML-Based Network Management". In R. Stadler and M. Ulema

(Eds.), *Proc. 8th IEEE/IFIP Network Operations and Management Symposium (NOMS 2002)*, Florence, Italy, April 2002, pp. 5–18.

134. H.T. Ju, M.J. Choi, and J.W.K. Hong. "EWS-Based Management Application Interface and Integration Mechanisms for Web-Based Element Management". *Journal of Network and Systems Management*, 9(1):31–50, 2001.

135. H.T. Ju, M.J. Choi, S.H. Kim, H.J. Cha, and J.W.K. Hong. "Embedded Web Server Technology for Web-based Network Element Management". In *Proc. Asia-Pacific Network Operations and Management Symposium (APNOMS'99)*, Kyongju, Korea, September 1999, pp. 317–332.

136. G. Karjoth, N. Asokan, and C. Gülcü. "Protecting the Computation Results of Free-Roaming Agents". In K. Rothermel and F. Hohl (Eds.). *Proc. 2nd International Workshop on Mobile Agents (MA'98)*, Stuttgart, Germany, September 1998. LNCS 1477:195–207, Springer, Berlin, Germany, 1998.

137. W. Kasteleijn. *Web-Based Management*. M.S. thesis, University of Twente, Enschede, The Netherlands, April 1997.

138. R. Kawamura and R. Stadler. "Active Distributed Management for IP Networks". *IEEE Communications Magazine*, 38(4):114–120, 2000.

139. D. Kegel. *The C10K Problem*. April 2000. Available at <http://www.kegel.com/c10k.html>.

140. B.W. Kernighan and D.M. Ritchie. *The C Programming Language*. 2nd edition. Prentice Hall, Englewood Cliffs, NJ, USA, 1988.

141. M. Knapik and J. Johnson. *Developing Intelligent Agents for Distributed Systems*. McGraw Hill, New York, NY, USA, 1998.

142. D. Kosiur. *Understanding Policy-Based Networking*. Wiley, New York, NY, USA, 2001.

143. J. Kramer. "Chapter 3. Distributed Systems". In M. Sloman (Ed.). *Network and Distributed Systems Management*, pp. 47–66. Addison-Wesley, Wokingham, UK, 1994.

144. B. Krishnamurthy and J. Rexford. Web Protocols and Practice. Addison-Wesley, 2001.

145. G.P. Kumar and P. Venkataram. "Artificial intelligence approaches to network management: recent advances and a survey". *Computer Communications*, 20(15):1313–1322, 1997.

146. C. Larman. *Applying UML and Patterns: an Introduction to Object-Oriented Analysis and Design*. Prentice Hall, Upper Saddle River, NJ, USA, 1998.

147. C. Ledrich. *XML and the Push Model in Web-Based Management*. M.S. thesis, Institut Eurécom, France, August 2001.

148. A. Leinwand and K. Fang Conroy. *Network Management: a Practical Perspective*. 2nd edition. Addison-Wesley, Reading, MA, USA, 1996.

149. D. Levi, P. Meyer, and B. Stewart (Eds.). *RFC 2573. SNMPv3 Applications*. IETF, April 1999.

150. D. Levi and J. Schönwälder (Eds.). *RFC 2592. Definitions of Managed Objects for the Delegation of Management Scripts*. IETF, May 1999.

151. L. Lewis. *Managing Business and Service Networks*. Kluwer Academic/Plenum Publishers, New York, NY, USA, 2001.

152. D. Libes. *Exploring Expect: A Tcl-based Toolkit for Automating Interactive Programs*. O'Reilly & Associates, Sebastopol, CA, USA, 1994.

153. J. Lindsay. *The Web Based Management Page*. Available at <http://joe.lindsay.net/webbased.html>.

154. Linux-kernel mailing list. Thread entitled "> *15,000 Simultaneous Connections*". September 1999. Available at <http://www.uwsg.indiana.edu/hypermail/linux/kernel/9909.0/0798.html>.

155. J. Long. "Software Reuse Antipatterns". *ACM Software Engineering Notes*, 26(4):68–76, 2001.

156. Lynx. Available at <http://lynx.browser.org/>.

157. J.P. Martin-Flatin and S. Znaty. "Annotated Typology of Distributed Network Management Paradigms". Technical Report SSC/1997/008, SSC, EPFL, Lausanne, Switzerland, March 1997.

158. J.P. Martin-Flatin and S. Znaty. "A Simple Typology of Distributed Network Management Paradigms". In A. Seneviratne, V. Varadarajan, and P. Ray (Eds.), *Proc. 8th IFIP/IEEE International Workshop on Distributed Systems: Operations & Management (DSOM'97), Sydney, Australia, October 1997*, pp. 13–24.

159. J.P. Martin-Flatin. *IP Network Management Platforms Before the Web*. Technical Report SSC/1998/021, version 2, SSC, EPFL, Lausanne, Switzerland, December 1998.

160. J.P. Martin-Flatin, S. Znaty, and J.P. Hubaux. "A Survey of Distributed Enterprise Network and Systems Management". *Journal of Network and Systems Management*, 7(1):9–26, 1999.

161. J.P. Martin-Flatin. "Push vs. Pull in Web-Based Network Management". In M. Sloman, S. Mazumdar, and E. Lupu (Eds.), *Integrated Network Management VI. Proc. 6th IFIP/IEEE International Symposium on Integrated Network Management (IM'99), Boston, MA, USA, May 1999*, pp. 3–18. IEEE, Piscataway, NJ, USA, 1999.

162. J.P. Martin-Flatin, L. Bovet, and J.P. Hubaux. "JAMAP: a Web-Based Management Platform for IP Networks". In R. Stadler and B. Stiller (Eds.), *Active Technologies for Network and Service Management. Proc. 10th IFIP/IEEE International Workshop on Distributed Systems: Operations & Management (DSOM'99), Zurich, Switzerland, October 1999*. LNCS 1700:164–178, Springer, Berlin, Germany, 1999.

163. J.P. Martin-Flatin. *Web-Based Management of IP Networks and Systems*. Ph.D. dissertation no. 2256, Swiss Federal Institute of Technology, Lausanne (EPFL), Switzerland, October 2000.

164. M.C. Maston. "Using the World Wide Web and Java for Network Service Management". In A. Lazar, R. Saracco, and R. Stadler (Eds.), *Integrated Network Management V. Proc. 5th IFIP/IEEE International Symposium on Integrated Network Management (IM'97), San Diego, CA, USA, May 1997*, pp. 71–84. Chapman & Hall, London, UK, 1997.

165. S. Mazumdar. "Inter-Domain Management between CORBA and SNMP". In *Proc. 7th IFIP/IEEE International Workshop on Distributed Systems: Operations & Management (DSOM'96), L'Aquila, Italy, October 1996*.

166. S. Mazumdar and T. Roberts (Eds.). *Translation of GDMO Specification into CORBA-IDL*. Report of the XoJIDM task force, August 1995.

167. S. Mazumdar (Ed.). *Translation of SNMPv2 Specification into CORBA-IDL*. Report of the XoJIDM task force, September 1996.

168. K. McCloghrie. "The SNMP Framework". *The Simple Times*, 4(1):9–10, 1996.

169. K. McCloghrie (Ed.). *RFC 2011. SNMPv2 Management Information Base for the Internet Protocol using SMIv2*. IETF, November 1996.

170. K. McCloghrie (Ed.). *RFC 2012. SNMPv2 Management Information Base for the Transmission Control Protocol using SMIv2*. IETF, November 1996.

171. K. McCloghrie (Ed.). *RFC 2013. SNMPv2 Management Information Base for the User Datagram Protocol using SMIv2*. IETF, November 1996.

172. K. McCloghrie and J. Galvin (Eds.). *RFC 1447. Party MIB for version 2 of the Simple Network Management Protocol (SNMPv2)*. IETF, April 1993.

173. K. McCloghrie and M. Rose (Eds.). *RFC 1213. Management Information Base for Network Management of TCP/IP-based internets: MIB-II*. IETF, March 1991.

174. R.A. Meersman. "The use of lexicons and other computer-linguistic tools in semantics, design and cooperation of database systems". In Y. Zhang (Ed.), *Cooperative Databases and Applications '99. Proc. 2nd International Symposium on Cooperative Database Systems for Advanced Applications (CODAS'99), Wollongong, Australia, March 1999*. Springer, Berlin, Germany, 1999.

175. D. Megginson. *Structuring XML Documents*. Prentice Hall, Upper Saddle River, NJ, USA, 1998.

176. P. Merle, C. Gransart, and J.M. Geib. "CorbaWeb: A Generic Object Navigator". In *Proc. 5th International World Wide Web Conference (WWW5), Paris, France, May 1996*. Elsevier, Amsterdam, The Netherlands, 1996.

177. J. Metzler and L. DeNoia. *Layer 3 Switching*. Prentice Hall, Upper Saddle River, NJ, USA, 1999.

178. B. Meyer. *Object-Oriented Software Construction*. 2nd edition. Prentice Hall, Upper Saddle River, NJ, 1997.

179. K. Meyer, M. Erlinger, J. Betser, C. Sunshine, G. Goldszmidt, and Y. Yemini. "Decentralizing Control and Intelligence in Network Management". In A.S. Sethi, Y. Raynaud, and F. Faure-Vincent (Eds.), *Integrated Network Management IV. Proc. 4th IFIP/IEEE International Symposium on Integrated Network Management (ISINM'95), Santa Barbara, CA, USA, May 1995*, pp. 4–16. Chapman & Hall, London, UK, 1995.

180. N. Mitra. "Efficient Encoding Rules for ASN.1-Based Protocols". *AT&T Technical Journal*, 73(3):80–93, 1994.

181. J.D. Moffett and M.S. Sloman. "Policy Hierarchies for Distributed Systems Management". *IEEE Journal on Selected Areas in Communications*, 11(9):1404–1414, 1993.

182. J. Mogul and S. Deering (Eds.). *RFC 1191. Path MTU Discovery*. IETF, November 1990.

183. M.A. Mountzia. "A distributed management approach based on flexible agents". *Interoperable Communication Networks*, 1:99–120, 1998.

184. P. Mullaney. "Overview of a Web-Based Agent". *The Simple Times*, 4(3):8–12, 1996.

185. N.J. Muller and L.L. Muller. "Using the World Wide Web for Network Support". *International Journal of Network Management*, 5(6):326–341, 1995.

186. L.J. Mullins. *Management and Organisational Behaviour*. 2nd edition. Pitman, London, UK, 1989.

187. Netscape. *An Exploration of Dynamic Documents*. 1995. Available at <http://home.mcom.com/assist/net_sites/pushpull.html>.

188. G. Neufeld and S. Vuong. "An overview of ASN.1". *Computer Networks and ISDN Systems*, 23:393–415, 1992.

189. H. Nielsen, P. Leach, and S. Lawrence (Eds.). *RFC 2774. An HTTP Extension Framework*. IETF, February 2000.

190. T. Oetiker and D. Rand. *MRTG: Multi-Router Traffic Grapher*. Available at <http://www.mrtg.org/>.

191. J.L. Oliveira and J.A. Martins. "A Management Architecture Based on Network Topology Information". Journal of Network andSystems Management, 2(4):401–414, 1994.

192. OMG. *The Common Object Request Broker: Architecture and Specification*. Revision 2.0. OMG Document formal/96-03-04, July 1995. (Superseded by formal/97-02-25.)

193. OMG. *The Common Object Request Broker: Architecture and Specification*. Revision 2.2. OMG Document formal/98-02-01, February 1998.

194. S. Ortiz. "Active Networks: The Programmable Pipeline". *IEEE Computer*, 31(8):19–21, 1998.

195. J.K. Ousterhout. *Tcl and the Tk Toolkit*. Addison-Wesley, Reading, MA, USA, 1994.

196. G. Pavlou. *Telecommunications Management Network: a Novel Approach Towards its Architecture and Realisation Through Object-Oriented Software Platforms*. Ph.D. dissertation, University College London, UK, March 1998.

197. G. Pavlou. "Chapter 2. OSI Systems Management, Internet SNMP, and ODP/OMG CORBA as Technologies for Telecommunications Network Management". In S. Aidarous and T. Plevyak (Eds.), *Telecommunications Network Management: Technologies and Implementations*, pp. 63–110. IEEE Press, New York, NY, USA, 1998.

198. G. Pavlou. "Using Distributed Object Technologies in Telecommunications Network Management". *IEEE Journal on Selected Areas in Communications*, 18(5):644–653, 2000.

199. J. Pavón, J. Tomás, Y. Bardout, and L.H. Hauw. "CORBA for Network and Service Management in the TINA Framework". *IEEE Communications Magazine*, 36(3):72–79, 1998.

200. J. Pavón. "Building Telecommunications Management Applications with CORBA". *IEEE Communications Surveys*, 2(2):2–16, 1999.

201. D.T. Perkins. "SNMP Versions". *The Simple Times*, 5(1):13–14, 1997.

202. D. Perkins and E. McGinnis. *Understanding SNMP MIBs*. Prentice Hall, Upper Saddle River, NJ, USA, 1997.

203. D.T. Perkins. "Questions Answered". *The Simple Times*, 6(1):13–17, 1998.

204. U. Pfeifer and N. Gövert. *freeWAIS-sf*. Available at <http://ls6-www.informatik.uni-dortmund.de/ir/projects/freeWAIS-sf/>.

205. M. Post, C.C. Shen, and J. Wei. "The Manager/Agency Paradigm for Distributed Network Management". In *Proc. 1996 IEEE Network Operations and Management Symposium (NOMS'96), Kyoto, Japan, April 1996*, 1:44–53. IEEE, Piscataway, NJ, USA, 1996.

206. J. Postel. *RFC 768. User Datagram Protocol*. IETF, August 1980.

207. K. Psounis. "Active Networks: Applications, Security, Safety, and Architectures ". *IEEE Communications Surveys*, 2(1):2–16, 1999.

208. I. Pyarali and D.C. Schmidt. "An Overview of the CORBA Portable Object Adapter". Special Issue on CORBA. *ACM StandardView*, March 1999.

209. D. Raggett, A. Le Hors, and I. Jacobs (Eds.). *HTML 4.01 Specification. W3C Recommendation REC-html401-19991224*. W3C, December 1999. Available at <http://www.w3.org/TR/1999/REC-html401-19991224/>.

210. A.S. Rao and M.P. Georgeff. "Modeling rational agents within a BDI-architecture". In R. Fikes and E. Sandewall (Eds.), *Proc. Knowledge Representation and Reasoning (KR&R-91), San Mateo, CA, USA, April 1991*, pp. 473–484. Morgan Kaufmann, 1991.

211. D. Raz and Y. Shavitt. "Active Networks for Efficient Distributed Network Management". *IEEE Communications Magazine*, 38(3):138–143, 2000.

212. A.J. Riel. *Object-Oriented Design Heuristics*. Addison-Wesley, Reading, MA, USA, 1996.

213. A.I. Rivière. *GEMINI: A Generic Environment for Management Information Integration*. Ph.D. dissertation, P. Sabatier University of Toulouse, France, December 1997.

214. A.I. Rivière and M. Sibilla. "Management Information Models Integration: From Existing Approaches to New Unifying Guidelines". *Journal of Network and Systems Management*, 6(3):333–356, 1998.

215. M.T. Rose. *The Simple Book: an Introduction to Networking Management*. Revised 2nd edition. Prentice Hall, Upper Saddle River, NJ, USA, 1996.

216. M.T. Rose and K. McCloghrie (Eds.). *RFC 1155. Structure and Identification of Management Information for TCP/IP-based Internets*. IETF, May 1990.

217. M. Rose and K. McCloghrie (Eds.). *RFC 1212. Concise MIB Definitions*. IETF, March 1991.

218. M.T. Rose and K. McCloghrie. *How to Manage Your Network Using SNMP*. Prentice Hall, Upper Saddle River, NJ, USA, 1995.

219. J. Rumbaugh, I. Jacobson, and G. Booch. *The Unified Modeling Language Reference Manual*. Addison-Wesley, Reading, MA, USA, 1999.

220. T. Sander and C Tschudin. "Protecting Mobile Agents Against Malicious Hosts". In G. Vigna (Ed.). *Mobile Agents and Security*. LNCS 1419:44–60, Springer, Berlin, Germany, 1998.

221. J. Saperia and J. Schönwälder (Eds.). *Policy-Based Enhancements to the SNMP Framework*. Internet-Draft <draft-schoenw-policy-snmp-00.txt> (now expired). IETF, September 1999.

222. J. Schönwälder. "Network management by delegation—From research prototypes towards standards". *Computer Networks and ISDN Systems*, 29(15):1843–1852, 1997.

223. J. Schönwälder. "Emerging Internet Management Standards". Tutorial given at the *6th IFIP/ IEEE International Symposium on Integrated Network Management (IM'99)*, Boston, MA, USA, May 1999. Available at <http://www.ibr.cs.tu-bs.de/~schoenw/slides/im-99.ps.gz>.

224. J. Schönwälder and F. Strauss. "Next Generation Structure of Management Information for the Internet". In R. Stadler and B. Stiller (Eds.), *Active Technologies for Network and Service Management. Proc. 10th IFIP/IEEE International Workshop on Distributed Systems: Operations & Management (DSOM'99), Zurich, Switzerland, October 1999*. LNCS 1700:93–106, Springer, Berlin, Germany, 1999.

225. J. Schönwälder, J. Quittek, and C. Kappler. "Building Distributed Management Applications with the IETF Script MIB". *IEEE Journal on Selected Areas in Communications*, 18(5):702–714, 2000.

226. J. Schönwälder and F. Strauss. *Using XML to Exchange SMI Definitions*. Internet-Draft <draft-irtf-nmrg-smi-xml-00.txt> (work in progress). IETF, June 2000.

227. J. Schönwälder (Ed.). *SNMP over TCP Transport Mapping*. Internet-Draft <draft-irtf-nmrg-snmp-tcp-09.txt> (work in progress). IETF, May 2002.

228. J. Schönwälder. *Scotty—Tcl Extensions for Network Management Applications*. Available at <http://wwwhome.cs.utwente.nl/~schoenw/scotty/>.

229. B. Schwartz, A.W. Jackson, W.T. Strayer, W. Zhou, R.D. Rockwell, and C. Partridge. "Smart Packets: Applying Active Networks to Network Management". *ACM Transactions on Computer Systems*, 18(1):67–88, 2000.

230. J. Semke, J. Mahdavi, and M. Mathis. "Automatic TCP Buffer Tuning". In *Proc. ACM SIGCOMM'98, Vancouver, BC, Canada, September 1998. ACM Computer Communication Review*, 28(4):315–323, 1998.

231. J.K. Shrewsbury. "An Introduction to TMN". *Journal of Network and Systems Management*, 3(1):13–38, 1995.

232. J. Siegel. *CORBA Fundamentals and Programming*. Wiley, New York, NY, USA, 1996.

233. SimpleWeb. *SNMP / Network Management Software*. Available at <http://www.simpleweb.org/software/>.

234. SimpleWeb. *The IETF MIBs*. Available at <http://www.simpleweb.org/ietf/mibs/>.

235. M. Sloman. "Policy Driven Management for Distributed Systems". *Journal of Network and Systems Management*, 2(4):333–360, 1994.

236. M. Sloman (Ed.). *Network and Distributed Systems Management*. Addison-Wesley, Wokingham, UK, 1994.

237. M. Sloman and K. Twidle. "Chapter 16. Domains: A Framework for Structuring Management Policy". In M. Sloman (Ed.). *Network and Distributed Systems Management*, pp. 433–453. Addison-Wesley, Wokingham, UK, 1994.

238. R. Smith. *Internet Cryptography*. Addison-Wesley, Reading, MA, USA, 1997.

239. J.M. Smith, K.L. Calvert, S.L. Murphy, H.K. Orman, and L.L. Peterson. "Activating Networks: A Progress Report". *IEEE Computer*, 32(4):32–41, 1999.

240. K. Sollins (Ed.). *RFC 1350. The TFTP Protocol (Revision 2)*. IETF, July 1992.

241. F. Somers. "HYBRID: Unifying Centralised and Distributed Network Management using Intelligent Agents". In *Proc. 1996 IEEE Network Operations and Management Symposium (NOMS'96), Kyoto, Japan, April 1996*. 1:34–43. IEEE, Piscataway, NJ, USA, 1996.

242. S.E. Spero. *Analysis of HTTP Performance Problems*. June 1995. Available at <http://www.w3.org/Protocols/HTTP-NG/http-prob.html>.

243. R. Sprenkels and J.P. Martin-Flatin. "Bulk Transfers of MIB Data". *The Simple Times*, 7(1):1–7, March 1999.

244. P. Sridharan. *Advanced Java networking*. Prentice Hall, Upper Saddle River, NJ, USA, 1997.

245. M. St. Pierre, J. Fullton, K. Gamiel, J. Goldman, B. Kahle, J. Kunze, H. Morris, and F. Schiettecatte (Eds.). *RFC 1625. WAIS over Z39.50-1983*. IETF, June 1994.

246. W. Stallings. *SNMP, SNMPv2, and CMIP: the Practical Guide to Network Management Standards*. Addison-Wesley, Reading, MA, USA, 1993. *(Obsoleted by [249], except for CMIP)*.

247. W. Stallings. "SSL: Foundation for Web Security". *The Internet Protocol Journal*, 1(1):20–29, 1998.

248. W. Stallings. "SNMPv3: A Security Enhancement to SNMP". *IEEE Communications Surveys*, 1(1):2–17, 1998.

249. W. Stallings. *SNMP, SNMPv2, SNMPv3, and RMON 1 and 2*. Third edition. Addison-Wesley, Reading, MA, USA, 1999.

250. W. Stallings. *Network Security Essentials: Applications and Standards*. Prentice Hall, Upper Saddle River, NJ, USA, 2000.

251. W. Stallings. "IP Security". *The Internet Protocol Journal*, 3(1):11–26, 2000.

252. J.W. Stamos and D.K. Gifford. "Remote Evaluation". *ACM Transactions on Programming Languages and Systems*, 12(4):537–565, 1990.

253. W.R. Stevens. *TCP/IP Illustrated, Volume 1*. Addison-Wesley, Reading, MA, USA, 1994.

254. W.R. Stevens. *Unix Network Programming, Volume 1*. 2nd edition. Prentice Hall, Upper Saddle River, NJ, USA, 1998.

255. R. Stewart, Q. Xie, K. Morneault, C. Sharp, H. Schwarzbauer, T. Taylor, I. Rytina, M. Kalla, L. Zhang, and V. Paxson (Eds.). *RFC 2960. Stream Control Transmission Protocol*. IETF, October 2000.

256. B. Stroustrup. *The C++ Programming Language*. Addison-Wesley, 1987.

257. Sun Microsystems. *RFC 1094. NFS: Network File System Protocol Specification*. IETF, March 1989.

258. Sun Microsystems. *Jini Technology Executive Overview*. Revision 1.0. January 1999.

259. Sun Microsystems. *Java Development Kit 1.1*. March 1999. Available at <http://java.sun.com/products/jdk/1.1/>.

260. Sun Microsystems. *Java Management Extensions White Paper*. Revision 01. June 1999.

261. Sun Microsystems. *Java Management Extensions Instrumentation and Agent Specification, v1.0*. December 1999.

262. Sun Microsystems. *Federated Management Architecture (FMA) Specification Version 1.0*. Revision 0.4. January 2000

263. Sunsoft. *Java Management API Architecture*. Revision A. September 1996.

264. C. Szyperski. *Component Software : Beyond Object-Oriented Programming*. Addison-Wesley, Harlow, UK, 1998.

265. D.L. Tennenhouse, J.M. Smith, W.D. Sincoskie, D.J. Wetherall, and G.J. Minden. "A Survey of Active Network Research". *IEEE Communications Magazine*, 35(1):80–86, 1997.

266. D.L. Tennenhouse and D. Wetherall. "Towards an Active Network Architecture". *ACM Computer Communication Review*, 26(2):5–18, 1996.

267. K. Terplan. *Web-Based Systems & Network Management*. CRC Press, Boca Raton, Florida, USA, 1999.

268. The Open Group. *DCE 1.1: Remote Procedure Call*. Document Number C706. August 1997.

269. The Open Group. *The WBEMsource Initiative*. Available at <http://www.opengroup.org/wbemsource/>.

270. J.P. Thompson. "Web-Based Enterprise Management Architecture". *IEEE Communications Magazine*, 36(3):80–86, 1998.

271. K.P. Twidle. *Domain Services for Distributed Systems Management*. Ph.D. dissertation. Imperial College, London, UK, 1993.

272. UCB. *UCB/LBNL/VINT Network Simulator - ns (version 2)*. Available at <http://www.isi.edu/nsnam/ns/>.

273. D.C. Verma. *Policy-Based Networking: Architecture and Algorithms*. New Riders, Indianapolis, IN, USA, 2000.

274. G. Vigna (Ed.). *Mobile Agents and Security*. LNCS 1419, Springer, Berlin, Germany, 1998.

275. W3C. *Document Object Model (DOM)*. Available at <http://www.w3.org/DOM/>.

276. W3C. *Extensible Markup Language (XML)*. Available at <http://www.w3.org/XML/>.

277. W3C. *Web Services Activity*. Available at <http://www.w3.org/2002/ws/>.

278. S. Waldbusser (Ed.). *RFC 1271. Remote Network Monitoring Management Information Base*. IETF, November 1991.

279. S. Waldbusser (Ed.). *RFC 1757. Remote Network Monitoring Management Information Base*. IETF, February 1995.

280. S. Waldbusser (Ed.). *RFC 2021. Remote Network Monitoring Management Information Base Version 2 using SMIv2*. IETF, January 1997.

281. S. Waldbusser and P. Grillo (Eds.). *RFC 2790. Host Resources MIB*. IETF, March 2000.

282. L. Wall, T. Christiansen, and R.L. Schwartz. *Programming Perl*. 2nd edition. O'Reilly & Associates, Sebastopol, CA, USA, 1996.

283. G. Waters (Ed.). *RFC 1910. User-based Security Model for SNMPv2*. IETF, February 1996.

284. Web Developer's Virtual Library. *XML Specifications, Proposals and Vocabularies*. Available at <http://wdvl.com/Authoring/Languages/XML/Specifications.html>.

285. T.D. Weinshall and Y.A. Raveh. *Managing Growing Organizations: A New Approach*. Wiley, Chichester, UK, 1983.

286. C. Wellens and K. Auerbach. "Towards Useful Management". *The Simple Times*, 4(3):1–6, 1996.

287. M. Welsh, S.D. Gribble, E.A. Brewer, and D. Culler. *A Design Framework for Highly Concurrent Systems*. Technical Report UCB/CSD-00-1108, Computer Science Division, U.C. Berkeley, April 2000.

288. A. Westerinen, J. Schnizlein, J. Strassner, M. Scherling, B. Quinn, S. Herzog, A. Huynh, M. Carlson, J. Perry, and S. Waldbusser (Eds.). *RFC 3198. Terminology for Policy-Based Management*. IETF, November 2001.

289. R. Wies. "Policies in Network and Systems Management—Formal Definition and Architecture". *Journal of Network and Systems Management*, 2(1):63–83, 1994.

290. I. Wijegunaratne and G. Fernandez. *Distributed Applications Engineering: Building New Applications and Managing Legacy Applications with Distributed Technologies*. Springer, London, UK, 1998.

291. B. Wijnen, R. Presuhn, and K. McCloghrie (Eds.). *RFC 2575. View-Based Access Control Model (VACM) for the Simple Network Management Protocol (SNMP)*. IETF, April 1999.

292. E. Wilde. *Wilde's WWW. Technical Foundations of the World Wide Web*. Springer, Berlin, Germany, 1999.

293. M. Wooldridge and N.R. Jennings. "Agent Theories, Architectures and Languages: a Survey". In M. Wooldridge and N.R. Jennings (Eds.). *Intelligent Agents. Proc. ECAI-94, Workshop on Agent Theories, Architectures and Languages, Amsterdam, The Netherlands, August 1994*. LNAI 890:1–39. Springer, Berlin, Germany, 1995.

294. G.R. Wright and W.R. Stevens. *TCP/IP Illustrated, Volume 2*. Addison-Wesley, Reading, MA, USA, 1995.

295. R. Yavatkar, D. Pendarakis, and R. Guerin (Eds.). *RFC 2753. A Framework for Policy-based Admission Control*. IETF, January 2000.

296. Y. Yemini. "The OSI Network Management Model". *IEEE Communications Magazine*, 31(5):20–29, 1993.

297. Y. Yemini, G. Goldszmidt, and S. Yemini. "Network Management by Delegation". In I. Krishnan and W. Zimmer (Eds.), *Proc. IFIP 2nd International Symposium on Integrated Network Management (ISINM'91), Washington, DC, USA, April 1991*, pp. 95–107. Elsevier/North-Holland, Amsterdam, The Netherlands, 1991.

298. T. Yemini and S. da Silva. "Towards Programmable Networks". In *Proc. 7th IFIP/IEEE International Workshop on Distributed Systems: Operations & Management (DSOM'96), L'Aquila, Italy, October 1996*.

299. T. Zhang, S. Covaci, and R. Popescu-Zeletin. "Intelligent Agents in Network and Service Management". In *Proc. IEEE Global Telecommunications Conference (GLOBECOM'96), London, UK, November 1996*. 3:1855–1861. IEEE, Piscataway, NJ, USA, 1996.

300. S. Znaty and O. Cherkaoui. "IDEAL: An Integrated Resource Management Language". In *Proc. IEEE Global Telecommunications Conference (GLOBECOM'97), Phoenix, AZ, USA, November 1997*. 1:202–206. IEEE, Piscataway, NJ, USA, 1997.

Appendix A

THE INTERFACES GROUP IN SNMP MIB-II

In this appendix, we give the IETF's definition of the Interfaces Group in RFC 1213 [173, pp. 16–23], which is used in Chapter 9. This material is reproduced here for the reader's convenience with the permission of the Internet Society, which the author acknowledges with appreciation.

```
-- the Interfaces group

-- Implementation of the Interfaces group is mandatory for
-- all systems.

ifNumber OBJECT-TYPE
    SYNTAX  INTEGER
    ACCESS  read-only
    STATUS  mandatory
    DESCRIPTION
            "The number of network interfaces (regardless of
            their current state) present on this system."
    ::= { interfaces 1 }


-- the Interfaces table

-- The Interfaces table contains information on the entity's
```

-- interfaces. Each interface is thought of as being
-- attached to a 'subnetwork'. Note that this term should
-- not be confused with 'subnet' which refers to an
-- addressing partitioning scheme used in the Internet suite
-- of protocols.

ifTable OBJECT-TYPE
    SYNTAX SEQUENCE OF IfEntry
    ACCESS not-accessible
    STATUS mandatory
    DESCRIPTION
        "A list of interface entries. The number of
        entries is given by the value of ifNumber."
    ::= { interfaces 2 }

ifEntry OBJECT-TYPE
    SYNTAX IfEntry
    ACCESS not-accessible
    STATUS mandatory
    DESCRIPTION
        "An interface entry containing objects at the
        subnetwork layer and below for a particular
        interface."
    INDEX { ifIndex }
    ::= { ifTable 1 }

IfEntry ::=
    SEQUENCE {
        ifIndex
            INTEGER,
        ifDescr
            DisplayString,
        ifType
            INTEGER,
        ifMtu
            INTEGER,
        ifSpeed
            Gauge,
        ifPhysAddress
            PhysAddress,
        ifAdminStatus
            INTEGER,
        ifOperStatus
            INTEGER,

```
        ifLastChange
            TimeTicks,
        ifInOctets
            Counter,
        ifInUcastPkts
            Counter,
        ifInNUcastPkts
            Counter,
        ifInDiscards
            Counter,
        ifInErrors
            Counter,
        ifInUnknownProtos
            Counter,
        ifOutOctets
            Counter,
        ifOutUcastPkts
            Counter,
        ifOutNUcastPkts
            Counter,
        ifOutDiscards
            Counter,
        ifOutErrors
            Counter,
        ifOutQLen
            Gauge,
        ifSpecific
            OBJECT IDENTIFIER
    }


ifIndex OBJECT-TYPE
    SYNTAX  INTEGER
    ACCESS  read-only
    STATUS  mandatory

    DESCRIPTION
        "A unique value for each interface.  Its value
        ranges between 1 and the value of ifNumber.  The
        value for each interface must remain constant at
        least from one re-initialization of the entity's
        network management system to the next re-
        initialization."
    ::= { ifEntry 1 }
```

ifDescr OBJECT-TYPE
  SYNTAX DisplayString (SIZE (0..255))
  ACCESS read-only
  STATUS mandatory
  DESCRIPTION
        "A textual string containing information about the
        interface. This string should include the name of
        the manufacturer, the product name and the version
        of the hardware interface."
  ::= { ifEntry 2 }

ifType OBJECT-TYPE
  SYNTAX INTEGER {
          other(1),   -- none of the following
          regular1822(2),
          hdh1822(3),
          ddn-x25(4),
          rfc877-x25(5),
          ethernet-csmacd(6),
          iso88023-csmacd(7),
          iso88024-tokenBus(8),
          iso88025-tokenRing(9),
          iso88026-man(10),
          starLan(11),
          proteon-10Mbit(12),
          proteon-80Mbit(13),
          hyperchannel(14),
          fddi(15),
          lapb(16),
          sdlc(17),
          ds1(18),   -- T-1
          e1(19),   -- european equiv. of T-1
          basicISDN(20),
          primaryISDN(21),   -- proprietary serial
          propPointToPointSerial(22),
          ppp(23),
          softwareLoopback(24),
          eon(25),   -- CLNP over IP [11]
          ethernet-3Mbit(26),
          nsip(27),   -- XNS over IP
          slip(28),   -- generic SLIP
          ultra(29),   -- ULTRA technologies
          ds3(30),   -- T-3
          sip(31),   -- SMDS

```
            frame-relay(32)
          }
   ACCESS  read-only
   STATUS  mandatory
   DESCRIPTION
          "The type of interface, distinguished according to
          the physical/link protocol(s) immediately 'below'
          the network layer in the protocol stack."
   ::= { ifEntry 3 }

ifMtu OBJECT-TYPE
   SYNTAX  INTEGER
   ACCESS  read-only
   STATUS  mandatory
   DESCRIPTION
          "The size of the largest datagram which can be
          sent/received on the interface, specified in
          octets.  For interfaces that are used for
          transmitting network datagrams, this is the size
          of the largest network datagram that can be sent
          on the interface."
   ::= { ifEntry 4 }

ifSpeed OBJECT-TYPE
   SYNTAX  Gauge
   ACCESS  read-only
   STATUS  mandatory
   DESCRIPTION
          "An estimate of the interface's current bandwidth
          in bits per second.  For interfaces which do not
          vary in bandwidth or for those where no accurate
          estimation can be made, this object should contain
          the nominal bandwidth."
   ::= { ifEntry 5 }

ifPhysAddress OBJECT-TYPE
   SYNTAX  PhysAddress
   ACCESS  read-only
   STATUS  mandatory
   DESCRIPTION
          "The interface's address at the protocol layer
          immediately 'below' the network layer in the
          protocol stack.  For interfaces which do not have
          such an address (e.g., a serial line), this object
```

should contain an octet string of zero length."
    ::= { ifEntry 6 }
ifAdminStatus OBJECT-TYPE
    SYNTAX INTEGER {
            up(1),   -- ready to pass packets
            down(2),
            testing(3)   -- in some test mode
            }
    ACCESS read-write
    STATUS mandatory
    DESCRIPTION
            "The desired state of the interface. The
            testing(3) state indicates that no operational
            packets can be passed."
    ::= { ifEntry 7 }

ifOperStatus OBJECT-TYPE
    SYNTAX INTEGER {
            up(1),   -- ready to pass packets
            down(2),
            testing(3)   -- in some test mode
            }
    ACCESS read-only
    STATUS mandatory
    DESCRIPTION
            "The current operational state of the interface.
            The testing(3) state indicates that no operational
            packets can be passed."
    ::= { ifEntry 8 }

ifLastChange OBJECT-TYPE
    SYNTAX TimeTicks
    ACCESS read-only
    STATUS mandatory
    DESCRIPTION
            "The value of sysUpTime at the time the interface
            entered its current operational state. If the
            current state was entered prior to the last re-
            initialization of the local network management
            subsystem, then this object contains a zero
            value."
    ::= { ifEntry 9 }

ifInOctets OBJECT-TYPE

SYNTAX Counter
ACCESS read-only
STATUS mandatory
DESCRIPTION
        "The total number of octets received on the
        interface, including framing characters."
    ::= { ifEntry 10 }

ifInUcastPkts OBJECT-TYPE
    SYNTAX Counter
    ACCESS read-only
    STATUS mandatory
    DESCRIPTION
        "The number of subnetwork-unicast packets
        delivered to a higher-layer protocol."
    ::= { ifEntry 11 }

ifInNUcastPkts OBJECT-TYPE
    SYNTAX Counter
    ACCESS read-only
    STATUS mandatory
    DESCRIPTION
        "The number of non-unicast (i.e., subnetwork-
        broadcast or subnetwork-multicast) packets
        delivered to a higher-layer protocol."
    ::= { ifEntry 12 }

ifInDiscards OBJECT-TYPE
    SYNTAX Counter
    ACCESS read-only
    STATUS mandatory
    DESCRIPTION
        "The number of inbound packets which were chosen
        to be discarded even though no errors had been
        detected to prevent their being deliverable to a
        higher-layer protocol. One possible reason for
        discarding such a packet could be to free up
        buffer space."
    ::= { ifEntry 13 }

ifInErrors OBJECT-TYPE
    SYNTAX Counter
    ACCESS read-only
    STATUS mandatory

DESCRIPTION
  "The number of inbound packets that contained
  errors preventing them from being deliverable to a
  higher-layer protocol."
::= { ifEntry 14 }

ifInUnknownProtos OBJECT-TYPE
  SYNTAX Counter
  ACCESS read-only
  STATUS mandatory
  DESCRIPTION
  "The number of packets received via the interface
  which were discarded because of an unknown or
  unsupported protocol."
::= { ifEntry 15 }

ifOutOctets OBJECT-TYPE
  SYNTAX Counter
  ACCESS read-only
  STATUS mandatory
  DESCRIPTION
  "The total number of octets transmitted out of the
  interface, including framing characters."
::= { ifEntry 16 }

ifOutUcastPkts OBJECT-TYPE
  SYNTAX Counter
  ACCESS read-only
  STATUS mandatory
  DESCRIPTION
  "The total number of packets that higher-level
  protocols requested be transmitted to a
  subnetwork-unicast address, including those that
  were discarded or not sent."
::= { ifEntry 17 }

ifOutNUcastPkts OBJECT-TYPE
  SYNTAX Counter
  ACCESS read-only
  STATUS mandatory
  DESCRIPTION
  "The total number of packets that higher-level
  protocols requested be transmitted to a non-
  unicast (i.e., a subnetwork-broadcast or

subnetwork-multicast) address, including those
that were discarded or not sent."
::= { ifEntry 18 }

ifOutDiscards OBJECT-TYPE
    SYNTAX Counter
    ACCESS read-only
    STATUS mandatory
    DESCRIPTION
        "The number of outbound packets which were chosen
        to be discarded even though no errors had been
        detected to prevent their being transmitted. One
        possible reason for discarding such a packet could
        be to free up buffer space."
    ::= { ifEntry 19 }

ifOutErrors OBJECT-TYPE
    SYNTAX Counter
    ACCESS read-only
    STATUS mandatory
    DESCRIPTION
        "The number of outbound packets that could not be
        transmitted because of errors."
    ::= { ifEntry 20 }
ifOutQLen OBJECT-TYPE
    SYNTAX Gauge
    ACCESS read-only
    STATUS mandatory
    DESCRIPTION
        "The length of the output packet queue (in
        packets)."
    ::= { ifEntry 21 }

ifSpecific OBJECT-TYPE
    SYNTAX OBJECT IDENTIFIER
    ACCESS read-only
    STATUS mandatory
    DESCRIPTION
        "A reference to MIB definitions specific to the
        particular media being used to realize the
        interface. For example, if the interface is
        realized by an ethernet, then the value of this
        object refers to a document defining objects
        specific to ethernet. If this information is not

present, its value should be set to the OBJECT
IDENTIFIER { 0 0 }, which is a syntatically valid
object identifier, and any conformant
implementation of ASN.1 and BER must be able to
generate and recognize this value."
::= { ifEntry 22 }

Appendix B

METAMODEL-LEVEL XML MAPPING OF THE INTERFACES GROUP IN SNMP MIB-II

In this appendix, we include the metamodel-level XML mapping of the Interfaces Group in SNMP MIB-II. This document is an excerpt of the representation of MIB-II module definitions in XML. It was generated by using the SimpleWeb IETF MIB converter [234] maintained by the University of Twente, The Netherlands. This mapping is used in Chapter 9.

```
<?xml version="1.0"?>
<!DOCTYPE smi:smi SYSTEM "/ietf/mibs/modules/xml/smi.dtd">

<!-- This module has been generated by smidump 0.2.4.
   then manually edited by J.P. Martin-Flatin -->

<smi xmlns:smi="http://www.irtf.org/nmrg/">
 <module name="RFC1213-MIB" language="SMIv1">
 </module>

 <imports>
  <import module="RFC1155-SMI" name="mgmt"/>
  <import module="RFC1155-SMI" name="NetworkAddress"/>
  <import module="RFC1155-SMI" name="IpAddress"/>
```

```
<import module="RFC1155-SMI" name="Counter"/>
<import module="RFC1155-SMI" name="Gauge"/>
<import module="RFC1155-SMI" name="TimeTicks"/>
<import module="RFC1212-MIB" name="OBJECT-TYPE"/>
</imports>

<typedefs>
<typedef name="DisplayString" basetype="OctetString">
</typedef>
<typedef name="PhysAddress" basetype="OctetString">
</typedef>
</typedefs>

<nodes>
<node name="mib-2" oid="1.3.6.1.2.1">
</node>

<!-- Deleted all groups except the Interfaces Group -->

<node name="interfaces" oid="1.3.6.1.2.1.2">
</node>
<scalar name="ifNumber" oid="1.3.6.1.2.1.2.1" status="current">
  <syntax>
   <type module="" name="Integer32"/>
  </syntax>
  <access>readonly</access>
  <description>
    The number of network interfaces (regardless of
    their current state) present on this system.
  </description>
</scalar>
<table name="ifTable" oid="1.3.6.1.2.1.2.2" status="current">
  <description>
    A list of interface entries.  The number of
    entries is given by the value of ifNumber.
  </description>
  <row name="ifEntry" oid="1.3.6.1.2.1.2.2.1" status="current">
   <linkage>
    <index module="RFC1213-MIB" name="ifIndex"/>
   </linkage>
   <description>
     An interface entry containing objects at the
     subnetwork layer and below for a particular
     interface.
```

```
    </description>
<column name="ifIndex" oid="1.3.6.1.2.1.2.2.1.1" status="current">
  <syntax>
    <type module="" name="Integer32"/>
  </syntax>
  <access>readonly</access>
  <description>
      A unique value for each interface.  Its value
      ranges between 1 and the value of ifNumber.  The
      value for each interface must remain constant at
      least from one re-initialization of the entity's
      network management system to the next re-
      initialization.
  </description>
</column>
<column name="ifDescr" oid="1.3.6.1.2.1.2.2.1.2" status="current">
  <syntax>
    <typedef basetype="OctetString">
    <parent module="RFC1213-MIB" name="DisplayString"/>
    <range min="0" max="255"/>
    </typedef>
  </syntax>
  <access>readonly</access>
  <description>
      A textual string containing information about the
      interface.  This string should include the name of
      the manufacturer, the product name and the version
      of the hardware interface.
  </description>
</column>
<column name="ifType" oid="1.3.6.1.2.1.2.2.1.3" status="current">
  <syntax>
    <typedef basetype="Enumeration">
    <namednumber name="other" number="1"/>
    <namednumber name="regular1822" number="2"/>
    <namednumber name="hdh1822" number="3"/>
    <namednumber name="ddn-x25" number="4"/>
    <namednumber name="rfc877-x25" number="5"/>
    <namednumber name="ethernet-csmacd" number="6"/>
    <namednumber name="iso88023-csmacd" number="7"/>
    <namednumber name="iso88024-tokenBus" number="8"/>
    <namednumber name="iso88025-tokenRing" number="9"/>
    <namednumber name="iso88026-man" number="10"/>
    <namednumber name="starLan" number="11"/>
```

```
        <namednumber name="proteon-10Mbit" number="12"/>
        <namednumber name="proteon-80Mbit" number="13"/>
        <namednumber name="hyperchannel" number="14"/>
        <namednumber name="fddi" number="15"/>
        <namednumber name="lapb" number="16"/>
        <namednumber name="sdlc" number="17"/>
        <namednumber name="ds1" number="18"/>
        <namednumber name="e1" number="19"/>
        <namednumber name="basicISDN" number="20"/>
        <namednumber name="primaryISDN" number="21"/>
        <namednumber name="propPointToPointSerial" number="22"/>
        <namednumber name="ppp" number="23"/>
        <namednumber name="softwareLoopback" number="24"/>
        <namednumber name="eon" number="25"/>
        <namednumber name="ethernet-3Mbit" number="26"/>
        <namednumber name="nsip" number="27"/>
        <namednumber name="slip" number="28"/>
        <namednumber name="ultra" number="29"/>
        <namednumber name="ds3" number="30"/>
        <namednumber name="sip" number="31"/>
        <namednumber name="frame-relay" number="32"/>
      </typedef>
    </syntax>
    <access>readonly</access>
    <description>
        The type of interface, distinguished according to
        the physical/link protocol(s) immediately `below'
        the network layer in the protocol stack.
    </description>
  </column>
  <column name="ifMtu" oid="1.3.6.1.2.1.2.2.1.4" status="current">
    <syntax>
      <type module="" name="Integer32"/>
    </syntax>
    <access>readonly</access>
    <description>
        The size of the largest datagram which can be
        sent/received on the interface, specified in
        octets.  For interfaces that are used for
        transmitting network datagrams, this is the size
        of the largest network datagram that can be sent
        on the interface.
    </description>
  </column>
```

```
<column name="ifSpeed" oid="1.3.6.1.2.1.2.2.1.5" status="current">
 <syntax>
  <type module="RFC1155-SMI" name="Gauge"/>
 </syntax>
 <access>readonly</access>
 <description>
    An estimate of the interface's current bandwidth
    in bits per second. For interfaces which do not
    vary in bandwidth or for those where no accurate
    estimation can be made, this object should contain
    the nominal bandwidth.
 </description>
</column>
<column name="ifPhysAddress" oid="1.3.6.1.2.1.2.2.1.6" status="current">
 <syntax>
  <type module="RFC1213-MIB" name="PhysAddress"/>
 </syntax>
 <access>readonly</access>
 <description>
    The interface's address at the protocol layer
    immediately `below' the network layer in the
    protocol stack. For interfaces which do not have

    such an address (e.g., a serial line), this object
    should contain an octet string of zero length.
 </description>
</column>
<column name="ifAdminStatus" oid="1.3.6.1.2.1.2.2.1.7" status="current">
 <syntax>
  <typedef basetype="Enumeration">
   <namednumber name="up" number="1"/>
   <namednumber name="down" number="2"/>
   <namednumber name="testing" number="3"/>
  </typedef>
 </syntax>
 <access>readwrite</access>
 <description>
    The desired state of the interface. The
    testing(3) state indicates that no operational
    packets can be passed.
 </description>
</column>
<column name="ifOperStatus" oid="1.3.6.1.2.1.2.2.1.8" status="current">
 <syntax>
```

```
   <typedef basetype="Enumeration">
    <namednumber name="up" number="1"/>
    <namednumber name="down" number="2"/>
    <namednumber name="testing" number="3"/>
   </typedef>
  </syntax>
  <access>readonly</access>
  <description>
     The current operational state of the interface.
     The testing(3) state indicates that no operational
     packets can be passed.
  </description>
 </column>
 <column name="ifLastChange" oid="1.3.6.1.2.1.2.2.1.9" status="current">
  <syntax>
   <type module="RFC1155-SMI" name="TimeTicks"/>
  </syntax>
  <access>readonly</access>
  <description>
     The value of sysUpTime at the time the interface
     entered its current operational state.  If the
     current state was entered prior to the last re-
     initialization of the local network management
     subsystem, then this object contains a zero
     value.
  </description>
 </column>
 <column name="ifInOctets" oid="1.3.6.1.2.1.2.2.1.10" status="current">
  <syntax>
   <type module="RFC1155-SMI" name="Counter"/>
  </syntax>
  <access>readonly</access>
  <description>
     The total number of octets received on the
     interface, including framing characters.
  </description>
 </column>
 <column name="ifInUcastPkts" oid="1.3.6.1.2.1.2.2.1.11" status="current">
  <syntax>
   <type module="RFC1155-SMI" name="Counter"/>
  </syntax>
  <access>readonly</access>
  <description>
     The number of subnetwork-unicast packets
```

```
      delivered to a higher-layer protocol.
    </description>
  </column>
  <column name="ifInNUcastPkts" oid="1.3.6.1.2.1.2.2.1.12" status="current">
    <syntax>
      <type module="RFC1155-SMI" name="Counter"/>
    </syntax>
    <access>readonly</access>
    <description>
      The number of non-unicast (i.e., subnetwork-
      broadcast or subnetwork-multicast) packets
      delivered to a higher-layer protocol.
    </description>
  </column>
  <column name="ifInDiscards" oid="1.3.6.1.2.1.2.2.1.13" status="current">
    <syntax>
      <type module="RFC1155-SMI" name="Counter"/>
    </syntax>
    <access>readonly</access>
    <description>
      The number of inbound packets which were chosen
      to be discarded even though no errors had been
      detected to prevent their being deliverable to a
      higher-layer protocol.  One possible reason for
      discarding such a packet could be to free up
      buffer space.
    </description>
  </column>
  <column name="ifInErrors" oid="1.3.6.1.2.1.2.2.1.14" status="current">
    <syntax>
      <type module="RFC1155-SMI" name="Counter"/>
    </syntax>
    <access>readonly</access>
    <description>
      The number of inbound packets that contained
      errors preventing them from being deliverable to a
      higher-layer protocol.
    </description>
  </column>
  <column name="ifInUnknownProtos" oid="1.3.6.1.2.1.2.2.1.15" status="current">
    <syntax>
      <type module="RFC1155-SMI" name="Counter"/>
    </syntax>
    <access>readonly</access>
```

```
<description>
    The number of packets received via the interface
    which were discarded because of an unknown or
    unsupported protocol.
</description>
</column>
<column name="ifOutOctets" oid="1.3.6.1.2.1.2.2.1.16" status="current">
  <syntax>
    <type module="RFC1155-SMI" name="Counter"/>
  </syntax>
  <access>readonly</access>
  <description>
    The total number of octets transmitted out of the
    interface, including framing characters.
  </description>
</column>
<column name="ifOutUcastPkts" oid="1.3.6.1.2.1.2.2.1.17" status="current">
  <syntax>
    <type module="RFC1155-SMI" name="Counter"/>
  </syntax>
  <access>readonly</access>
  <description>
    The total number of packets that higher-level
    protocols requested be transmitted to a
    subnetwork-unicast address, including those that
    were discarded or not sent.
  </description>
</column>
<column name="ifOutNUcastPkts" oid="1.3.6.1.2.1.2.2.1.18" status="current">
  <syntax>
    <type module="RFC1155-SMI" name="Counter"/>
  </syntax>
  <access>readonly</access>
  <description>
    The total number of packets that higher-level
    protocols requested be transmitted to a non-
    unicast (i.e., a subnetwork-broadcast or
    subnetwork-multicast) address, including those
    that were discarded or not sent.
  </description>
</column>
<column name="ifOutDiscards" oid="1.3.6.1.2.1.2.2.1.19" status="current">
  <syntax>
    <type module="RFC1155-SMI" name="Counter"/>
```

```
    </syntax>
    <access>readonly</access>
    <description>
       The number of outbound packets which were chosen

       to be discarded even though no errors had been
       detected to prevent their being transmitted.  One
       possible reason for discarding such a packet could
       be to free up buffer space.
    </description>
  </column>
  <column name="ifOutErrors" oid="1.3.6.1.2.1.2.2.1.20" status="current">
    <syntax>
      <type module="RFC1155-SMI" name="Counter"/>
    </syntax>
    <access>readonly</access>
    <description>
       The number of outbound packets that could not be
       transmitted because of errors.
    </description>
  </column>
  <column name="ifOutQLen" oid="1.3.6.1.2.1.2.2.1.21" status="current">
    <syntax>
      <type module="RFC1155-SMI" name="Gauge"/>
    </syntax>
    <access>readonly</access>
    <description>
       The length of the output packet queue (in
       packets).
    </description>
  </column>
  <column name="ifSpecific" oid="1.3.6.1.2.1.2.2.1.22" status="current">
    <syntax>
      <type module="" name="ObjectIdentifier"/>
    </syntax>
    <access>readonly</access>
    <description>
       A reference to MIB definitions specific to the
       particular media being used to realize the
       interface.  For example, if the interface is
       realized by an ethernet, then the value of this
       object refers to a document defining objects
       specific to ethernet. If this information is not
       present, its value should be set to the OBJECT
```

```
      IDENTIFIER { 0 0 }, which is a syntatically valid
      object identifier, and any conformant
      implementation of ASN.1 and BER must be able to
      generate and recognize this value.
    </description>
   </column>
  </row>
 </table>

 <!-- Deleted all groups except the Interfaces Group -->

</nodes>

</smi>
```

Appendix C

METAMODEL-LEVEL XML MAPPING OF A SIMPLE CIM CLASS

In this appendix, we include an example of CIM-to-XML metamodel-level mapping given by the DMTF [73]. The purpose of this example is not to show *the* way to map the CIM class below in XML, but rather to illustrate the metamodel-level mapping philosophy of the DMTF. This mapping is used in Chapter 9. This material is reproduced here for the reader's convenience with the express consent of the DMTF, which the author acknowledges with appreciation.

The MOF syntax for the class is shown below:

```
[Abstract] class CIM_ManagedSystemElement
{
[MaxLen(64)] string Caption;
string Description;
[MappingStrings{"MIF.DMTF|ComponentID|001.5"}] datetime InstallDate;
string Name;
[Values{"OK","Error","Degraded","Unknown"}] string Status;
};
```

The corresponding XML mapping for this class is shown below:

```
<?xml version="1.0" ?>

<!DOCTYPE CIM SYSTEM
"http://WBEM_TECRA_2/wbem/cim.dtd">
<CIM CIMVERSION="2.0"
DTDVERSION="1.0" >
<CLASS>
<CLASSPATH>
<NAMESPACEPATH>
<HOST>WBEM_TECRA_2</HOST>
<NAMESPACE>
<NAMESPACENODE>ROOT</NAMESPACENODE>
<NAMESPACE>
<NAMESPACENODE>CIMV2</NAMESPACENODE>
</NAMESPACE>
</NAMESPACE>
</NAMESPACEPATH>
<CLASSNAME>CIM_ManagedSystemElement</CLASSNAME>
</CLASSPATH>
<QUALIFIER NAME="Abstract"
LOCAL="true" TYPE="boolean"
OVERRIDABLE="EnableOverride"
TOSUBCLASS="Restricted"
TRANSLATABLE="false">
<VALUE>TRUE</VALUE>
</QUALIFIER>
<PROPERTY NAME="Caption" CLASSORIGIN=
"CIM_ManagedSystemElement"
LOCAL="true"TYPE="string">
<QUALIFIER NAME="CIMTYPE"
LOCAL="true" TYPE="string"
OVERRIDABLE="EnableOverride"
TOSUBCLASS="ToSubclass"
TRANSLATABLE="false">
<VALUE>string</VALUE>
</QUALIFIER>
<QUALIFIER NAME="MaxLen" LOCAL="true"
TYPE="sint32"
OVERRIDABLE="EnableOverride"
TOSUBCLASS="Restricted"
TRANSLATABLE="false">
<VALUE>64</VALUE>
```

```
</QUALIFIER>
<QUALIFIER NAME="read" LOCAL="true"
TYPE="boolean"
OVERRIDABLE="EnableOverride"
TOSUBCLASS="Restricted"
TRANSLATABLE="false">
<VALUE>TRUE</VALUE>
</QUALIFIER>
</PROPERTY>
<PROPERTY NAME="Description"
CLASSORIGIN="CIM_ManagedSystemElement"
LOCAL="true" TYPE="string">
<QUALIFIER NAME="CIMTYPE"
LOCAL="true" TYPE="string"
OVERRIDABLE="EnableOverride"
TOSUBCLASS="ToSubclass"
TRANSLATABLE="false">
<VALUE>string</VALUE>
</QUALIFIER>
<QUALIFIER NAME="read" LOCAL="true"
TYPE="boolean"
OVERRIDABLE="EnableOverride"
TOSUBCLASS="Restricted"
TRANSLATABLE="false">
<VALUE>TRUE</VALUE>
</QUALIFIER>
</PROPERTY>
<PROPERTY NAME="InstallDate"
CLASSORIGIN="CIM_ManagedSystemElement"
LOCAL="true" TYPE="datetime">
<QUALIFIER NAME="CIMTYPE"
LOCAL="true" TYPE="string"
OVERRIDABLE="EnableOverride"
TOSUBCLASS="ToSubclass"
TRANSLATABLE="false">
<VALUE>datetime</VALUE>
</QUALIFIER>
<QUALIFIER NAME="MappingStrings"
LOCAL="true" TYPE="string"
OVERRIDABLE="EnableOverride"
TOSUBCLASS="Restricted"
TRANSLATABLE="false">
<VALUE.INDEXED INDEX
="0">MIF.DMTF|ComponentID|001.5</VALUE.INDEXED>
```

```
</QUALIFIER>
<QUALIFIER NAME="read" LOCAL="true"
TYPE="boolean"
OVERRIDABLE="EnableOverride"
TOSUBCLASS="Restricted"
TRANSLATABLE="false">
<VALUE>TRUE</VALUE>
</QUALIFIER>
</PROPERTY>
<PROPERTY NAME="Name"
CLASSORIGIN="CIM_ManagedSystemElement"
LOCAL="true" TYPE="string">
<QUALIFIER NAME="CIMTYPÉ"
LOCAL="true" TYPE="string"
OVERRIDABLE="EnableOverride"
TOSUBCLASS="ToSubclass"
TRANSLATABLE="false">
<VALUE>string</VALUE>
</QUALIFIER>
<QUALIFIER NAME="read" LOCAL="true"
TYPE="boolean"
OVERRIDABLE="EnableOverride"
TOSUBCLASS="Restricted"
TRANSLATABLE="false">
<VALUE>TRUE</VALUE>
</QUALIFIER>
</PROPERTY>
<PROPERTY NAME="Status"
CLASSORIGIN="CIM_ManagedSystemElement"
LOCAL="true" TYPE="string">
<QUALIFIER NAME="CIMTYPE"
LOCAL="true" TYPE="string"
OVERRIDABLE="EnableOverride"
TOSUBCLASS="ToSubclass"
TRANSLATABLE="false">
<VALUE>string</VALUE>
</QUALIFIER>
<QUALIFIER NAME="read" LOCAL="true"
TYPE="boolean"
OVERRIDABLE="EnableOverride"
TOSUBCLASS="Restricted"
TRANSLATABLE="false">
<VALUE>TRUE</VALUE>
</QUALIFIER>
```

```
<QUALIFIER NAME="Values" LOCAL="true"
TYPE="string"
OVERRIDABLE="EnableOverride"
TOSUBCLASS="Restricted"
TRANSLATABLE="false">
<VALUE.INDEXED INDEX
="0">OK</VALUE.INDEXED>
<VALUE.INDEXED INDEX
="1">Error</VALUE.INDEXED>
<VALUE.INDEXED INDEX
="2">Degraded</VALUE.INDEXED>
<VALUE.INDEXED INDEX
="3">Unknown</VALUE.INDEXED>
</QUALIFIER>
</PROPERTY>
</CLASS>
</CIM>
```

Appendix D

REMOTE METHOD INVOCATION OF A CIM OBJECT

In this appendix, we include an example of remote method invocation of a CIM object given by the DMTF [77, Section A.10]. Compared to the original document, we simply removed the HTTP header of the two messages. The purpose of this example is to illustrate the containment hierarchy of operations and method invocations as well as the use of the namespace. This XML document is used in Chapter 9. This material is reproduced here for the reader's convenience with the express consent of the DMTF, which the author acknowledges with appreciation.

Request message:

```xml
<?xml version="1.0" encoding="utf-8" ?>
<CIM CIMVERSION="2.0" DTDVERSION="2.0">
 <MESSAGE ID="87872" PROTOCOLVERSION="1.0">
  <SIMPLEREQ>
   <METHODCALL NAME="SetPowerState">
    <LOCALINSTANCEPATH>
     <LOCALNAMESPACEPATH>
      <NAMESPACE NAME="root"/>
      <NAMESPACE NAME="myNamespace"/>
     </LOCALNAMESPACEPATH>
     <INSTANCENAME CLASSNAME="MyDisk">
      <KEYBINDING NAME="C:"><KEYVALUE>C:</KEYVALUE></KEYBINDING>
     </INSTANCENAME>
    </LOCALINSTANCEPATH>
```

```
    <PARAMVALUE NAME="PowerState"><VALUE>1</VALUE></PARAMVALUE>
    <PARAMVALUE NAME="Time">
     <VALUE>00000001132312.000000:000</VALUE>
    </PARAMVALUE>
   </METHODCALL>
  </SIMPLEREQ>
 </MESSAGE>
</CIM>
```

Response message:

```
<?xml version="1.0" encoding="utf-8" ?>
 <CIM CIMVERSION="2.0" DTDVERSION="2.0">
  <MESSAGE ID="87872" PROTOCOLVERSION="1.0">
   <SIMPLERSP>
    <METHODRESPONSE NAME="SetPowerState">
     <RETURNVALUE>
      <VALUE>0</VALUE>
     </RETURNVALUE>
    </METHODRESPONSE>
   </SIMPLERSP>
  </MESSAGE>
 </CIM>
```

INDEX